Praise for
HOTEL LUX

'I loved this sweeping, thrilling Romance of Irish Communism – and American, English, German, Polish, Russian, Ukrainian Communism. *Hotel Lux* takes the old history of the left and makes it fresh, new and moving.'

OWEN HATHERLEY

'*Hotel Lux* illuminates the intertwined lives of a group of self-described 'restless souls with impossible desires', moving between a legendary Moscow hotel, Weimar Berlin, 1920s Manhattan, London's East End and the west of Ireland. Maurice Casey writes with vivid empathy and his impressive research skills uncover complex networks of politics, ideology and love. A remarkably accomplished reconstruction of a forgotten world, its ideals, disappointments and delusions.'

ROY FOSTER

'Tells the story of early 20th century communism through the eyes of those who lived it and felt and believed in it – while also living their entirely normal, rackety, emotional lives.'

HALLIE RUBENHOLD

'An extraordinary trip through twentieth century history, grounded in the singular characters occupying a single hotel in 1920s Moscow. This is a fascinating tale of exiles and emigres, zealots and dreamers, brought to thrumming life by an extraordinary cache of private letters, and Casey's superb and propulsive portraiture. A historical, and humane, tour de force.'

SÉAMAS O'REILLY

'*Hotel Lux* is an enthralling debut, from a brilliant young scholar, that finds the messy, honest humanity at the heart of an epic ideological tsunami. Through his many years of dogged research, Dr Maurice Casey has carefully and generously revived a doomed generation of extraordinary friends, lovers, neighbours, comrades and family-members whose fizzing revolutionary idealism was slowly crushed between the jaws of Stalinism and Nazism. Not only is it a compelling narrative, Casey thrills us by revealing the secrets of the historian's craft; suddenly we're with him in the Moscow archives, or rummaging through boxes in unexpected attics, or bulk-emailing strangers who share a surname, or tweeting random Spaniards in the hunt for living descendants of forgotten radicals. *Hotel Lux* is clearly a labour of love, and finds room for unexpected hope amongst the eventual tragedy.'

GREG JENNER

'Casey is a dazzling new voice in Irish writing. *Hotel Lux* is an extraordinary debut, one that weaves together years of research to create a rich tapestry of the ordinary lives of forgotten revolutionaries. There's real beauty here, as stories of Moscow's Hotel Lux burst from the page to begin their afterlives in reader's imagination. It's astoundingly brilliant, propulsive, compulsive, and deeply moving. I couldn't put it down once I checked into the Hotel Lux.'

AIMÉE WALSH

'Beautifully written and researched. Full of the fire of curiosity and the magic of discovery, *Hotel Lux* is a book that uncovers the radical in the everyday, the everyday in the radical.'

SEÁN HEWITT

'Maurice Casey's *Hotel Lux* is a rich and bracing work that brings to fresh light a fascinating new contour in the history of transcontinental communism.'

ADRIAN DUNCAN

'Casey takes us inside the fabled Hotel Lux, a place where revolutionaries, dreamers and agitators shared food, beds and doctrine, and reveals in exquisite detail how this Moscow building became a crucible in which ideals were tested, and lives forever entwined.'

SIMON PARKIN

'I loved this book. I love these women. Casey deftly interweaves their stories with the struggles across Europe of the day (many of which still echo today). A story of ordinary people attempting the extraordinary: to follow their dream of building a more just world. Casey brings the voices of these women bang up front and allows us to know them in a real and rounded way. There's also great humour and lightness of touch not always found in such an impeccably researched historical account.'

TARA FLYNN

HOTEL LUX

MAURICE J. CASEY

HOTEL LUX

AN INTIMATE HISTORY OF COMMUNISM'S FORGOTTEN RADICALS

FOOTNOTE

First published in 2024 by
Footnote Press

www.footnotepress.com

Footnote Press Limited
4th Floor, Victoria House, Bloomsbury Square, London WC1B 4DA

Distributed by Bonnier Books UK, a division of Bonnier Books
Sveavägen 56, Stockholm, Sweden

First printing
1 3 5 7 9 10 8 6 4 2

A CIP catalogue record for this book is available from the British Library.

ISBN (hardback): 978 1 804 44099 5
ISBN (ebook): 978 1 804 44100 8
ISBN (trade paperback): 978 1 804 44118 3

Printed and bound in Great Britain
by Clays Ltd, Elcograf S.p.A.

MIX
Paper | Supporting
responsible forestry
FSC
www.fsc.org FSC® C018072

1. The site of the Hotel Lux on Tverskaya Street, c. 1910s. *Wikimedia*

For Ciara

'And if I speak of my people,
It's only of you that I think.'
– Elisa de Jager

Contents

Part III: The Found Generation 1929–1945

Part IV: The Living Commune 1940s–1970s

Introduction

Prologue: Restless Souls

1

30 May 1925. A taxi steers through the streets of Moscow towards a hospital beyond the walls of the Kremlin complex. Its passenger, Emmy, is a heavily pregnant German revolutionary. A surviving photograph of Emmy from this year captures her with dark hair tied up, a soft gaze directed into the camera. In the image, she is wearing a white shirt with a black tie loosely pulled around her collar: unconventional dress for an unconventional woman. Soon, Emmy will hold her first daughter in her arms. Emmy will choose a family name for her: Elisa.

Edo, the father, is not present as his daughter is born beyond the Kremlin walls. He is outside Soviet Russia. His role as leader of one of Europe's most important trade unions will afford him little time for a 'normal' domestic life. It will be more than a decade before Edo and Emmy will finally spend an extended period together, following years of separation compelled by their commitments to revolutionary politics and anti-fascist resistance. But all this still lies on the horizon as the hospital staff working close to the former palace of the Tsars help bring baby Elisa into the world.

Initially, Emmy did not have a cab arranged nor the funds to cover her medical care in Moscow. Her friend May, an Irishwoman residing in the same hotel as Emmy, provided both as a favour. All that follows moves through and from this single moment. This is a story of international communism, refracted through a single kind gesture one woman performed for another at Moscow's Hotel Lux. It is a story that travels through the transit stations of Europe's twentieth century: Moscow, Dublin, London, Paris, New York and Berlin.

2

In the summer of 1973, almost half a century after she arrived in Moscow, then a revolutionary city, May O'Callaghan, a 92-year-old Irish communist, suffered a fatal blood clot and died in a North London nursing home. Shortly afterwards, Emmy Leonhard, an elderly revolutionary living by the banks of Lake Geneva, received the news of her friend's death. In the last years of her life, Emmy had seen little of the woman she knew by the nickname O.C., yet her friend remained present in her mind as the content and ambitious woman she had first met in 1920s Moscow.

With May's death, the curtain fell on a long period of Emmy's life. Working on her typewriter, Emmy composed a message to another old friend, Nellie Cohen, a retired secretary from an East London Jewish family who now lived in a gated community near London's Hampstead Heath. Emmy knew that Nellie's friendship with May ran even deeper than her own, stretching back to the suffrage struggle during the First World War. Beginning her letter with 'My dear Nellie,' Emmy described how May's death was expected yet deeply impactful. 'It is a happy and great time of my life which ends with her,' Emmy opened, before reciting different moments in their shared journey through the world revolution.

Writing to Nellie in the wake of May's death, Emmy spilled no ink on differences in revolutionary doctrine. Instead, she focused on cherished memories. Emmy could still recall her first lunch with May in the canteen of the Hotel Lux: 'I remember how horrified she was by bortsch – though she became accustomed to it later.' The women had lived loudly and freely in Moscow, a city where their own ideals were reflected in the slogans upon the banners and posters they passed as they walked the streets. In the Hotel

Lux, a boarding house for the international revolutionary elite, they shared bedrooms, bathrooms and breakfasts with the guiding lights of the radical world. In her letter to Nellie, Emmy remembered how another guest at the hotel, the future leader of the British Communist Party, a 'pure and well-behaved soul', was 'shocked' by her and May's mischievous behaviour in the Soviet capital.

So many of the dreams and catastrophes of the twentieth century reverberated through the corridors of the Hotel Lux, where both women lived. Established during the closing act of the Russian Empire, history would soon be witnessed from the windows of the Lux. A photograph depicts the hotel in the revolutionary year of 1917. It must have been a cold winter's day when the image was captured: individuals in wool hats and heavy coats mill about a barricade made of wooden logs and a repurposed cart that stands in front of the hotel's neoclassical colonnades. In this photograph I can spot what I believe to be the windows of the room that would become May's home for several transformative years.

May lived in room 5 in the Hotel Lux and Emmy resided in room 14. Perhaps they shared a corridor; it seems likely that they shared a floor. Whenever Emmy visited May in her room, she would have encountered the room's enviable view overlooking the wide street below. It was here that May would sometimes sit and work as the sounds of parades passing by the front of the hotel came in through the windows. It was also here, in this room, that May would occasionally host an improvised literary salon, introducing Soviet intellectuals to their peers from America, Britain and elsewhere.

On the evenings after their work in the headquarters of the international communist movement, soldiers would sometimes collect Emmy and May and take them to a military encampment outside Moscow. The memory retained a sensory impression. 'I still hear the soldiers at night singing,' Emmy wrote in her 1973 letter. Summoning a memory of one of the extraordinary characters the two women met in Soviet Moscow, Emmy recalled how it was there in the Red Army encampment that May met a 'girl who later became a general in the Red Army'.

Emmy listed the prominent Bolsheviks with whom she was acquainted in those heady days; Nikolai Bukharin (executed, 1938), Karl Radek (executed, 1939) and Leon Trotsky (assassinated, 1940). 'Still the greatest group of men who I have ever met,' she declared. 'Stalin was also among them,' Emmy continued ominously, 'but was so uninteresting and unimportant that nobody ever thought that he was going to destroy all the others.' Emmy knew that Nellie's younger sister Rose was among the hundreds of thousands of people who disappeared during Stalin's purges. Of course, Nellie knew this too. This tragic fact went unmentioned in the letter.

Bringing the letter to a close, Emmy turned to the last memory she wanted to share with Nellie, the story of the day her first daughter was born. 'I suppose you know the story of how O.C. helped Elisa to be born. She found the cab which brought me to the Kremlin hospital and she paid the fee for the doctor and midwife, which I had not got.' This day in the summer of 1925 was a moment of personal significance for Emmy, not only because it marked the birth of her daughter, but because it created a lasting link between her family's future and that of her Irish friend. Why did Emmy choose to remember May's favour at this moment, almost five decades after it occurred? The answer is suggested by the letter's closing line.

Emmy thanked Nellie for providing May with company in her last days. She expressed how happy she was that her own daughter Elisa and Nellie's daughter Joyce, born in New York in 1929, had become 'such good friends'. The two women, Elisa and Joyce, first met in 1949 on the other side of a global conflict that the Leonhard family had survived only through their foresightedness and determination. The close relationship between Elisa and Joyce, the two beloved daughters of Emmy and Nellie, could trace its origin to the support May provided for both women when their daughters were born. Indeed, without May, the grown-up Joyce and Elisa would have almost certainly never met.

Even secular revolutionaries can believe in a version of an afterlife, one where the courageous acts of individuals echo through generations. May's provision of a taxicab and payment of a medical bill was one such act with radical reverberations. In her letter to Nellie, Emmy underlined why, at this moment, Elisa and Joyce's relationship mattered. As the two women mourned a friend and a revolution, Emmy emphasised that the intimate bond between their daughters ensured that 'O.C. will ever be for us, as long as we live, a living presence'. Although a lifelong revolutionary, Emmy belonged to a generation that was unlikely to state frankly what she surely must have known: that her daughter Elisa and Nellie's daughter Joyce were more than just 'good friends'.

In so many ways, the remarkably durable friendship between these three women was not the kind of story I expected to find. The letter seemed even more unexpected due to the setting in which I found it: a plastic storage box lifted down from the attic of a Cotswolds home. Not the kind of place where historians normally find nostalgic memories of revolutionary commitment. In addition to that, my research had shown that Nellie and May ended up on one side of a sharp political divide, Emmy on the other.

Emmy left the German communist party in the late 1920s, joining the revolutionary opposition, whose figurehead was Leon Trotsky. Nellie remained a supporter of the Soviet-aligned British communist party even after Stalin's terror consumed the life of her younger sister. Always more interested in culture than politics, May, on the other hand, was more inclined to drift into memories of her time among the Soviet literary elite than involve herself in its doctrinal debates. While Emmy spent the 1930s on the run across Europe with her two girls, Nellie and May spent the same years raising Nellie's daughter firstly in New York's communist bohemia and later in a London suburb. As I made my way through the archives of their lives, I realised that the remarkable longevity of their friendship resulted from a debt both Nellie and Emmy owed to May. May O'Callaghan, in ways both direct and indirect, helped bring their children into the world. And those respective daughters were fated to one day meet and fall in love.

3

Contained within Emmy Leonhard's letter to Nellie Cohen are the contours of the story told within this book. This narrative is an account of the world revolution and how it was experienced by ordinary people swept up within it. It is a story of how international communism both created families and scarred them across generations. It is also a story about the efforts required to recover the experiences of people normally relegated to the footnotes in someone else's biography.

None of the people central to this story are well known today. Yet Emmy Leonhard, May O'Callaghan and Nellie Cohen, along with those close to them, experienced the world-shaking moments of their era on a personal level: from the revolutionary wave at the end of the Great War to the incredible violence that returned to Europe less than two decades later. Their obscurity provides us with an opportunity to observe familiar historical events from an unconsidered vantage point.

Examining the lives of the regular foot soldiers of insurrectionary change rather than the leaders, martyrs or executioners is also a test in historical empathy. It forces us to contemplate how a single radical life can provide both a story of bravery and a catalogue of comrades betrayed in the service of a grand cause. Uncovering these more ordinary revolutionary lives, we find stories of people who may have been much closer to us in their temperaments and vulnerabilities than the better-studied ideologues.

But this book is not a portrait of people chosen as random exemplars of communist commitment. This is a story of deeply intertwined revolutionary families, whose connections to one another cut across the ideological dividing lines of so much political history. In charting the connections between those who came together both through political ideals and human desire, we can trouble the borders that restrain histories of global lives within national confines. Few activist lives take place within one nation, yet so much political history is confined by the arbitrary frontiers of states.

A history told through ties of kinship rather than shared nationality allows us to chart a radical route through the twentieth-century world. Although it makes its way through many places, this route has a central station through which all these family stories flow: the Hotel Lux in Moscow, once home to the global communist leadership – and, as it turns out, the forgotten figures who supported their revolutionary project.

Beyond the Hotel Lux, this narrative takes place in less considered locus points of revolutionary activity: private soirées, bookstores, bedrooms, transatlantic voyages, prison camps and newspaper offices. To reconstruct and repopulate these unfamiliar locations has required an international source base of love letters, poems, novels, surveillance material, cassette recordings, unpublished memoirs, children's drawings, coded correspondence and the fading memories of a generation.

Alongside a history of world revolution, this book intertwines the story of how I followed this historical trail through attics, storage cupboards and more than twenty-five separate archives in Ireland, the UK, the US, Russia, Spain, the Netherlands and Australia. To fill in the gaps left by archivists and their institutions, I tracked down the families who owed their own existence to this radical world. Repeatedly, I have been struck by the burning relevance of the questions asked by my protagonists almost a century ago: how do we bring an end to war and imperialism? What does real gender equality look like? How can politics transform our understandings of family, friendship and love? Because they asked these questions, we should heed their conclusions. Even if only to suggest solutions of our own.

At each step on my journey, I asked myself: why am I seeking historical justice for a lost world of communists and revolutionaries from the early twentieth century? What are the stakes of this remembrance? Instead of threading this political history to where Marx intended (the realisation of a worldwide commune) or where the Soviet project concluded (in grim stagnation by means of mass oppression) I was searching for different destinations in this history:

stories of the courage, determination and moral crises experienced by minor figures in the great revolutionary drama; stories that might speak to recurring discussions about the sacrifices and rewards entailed by a life of intense devotion to a single, all-consuming cause.

Although revolutionary political biographies are often told as a tale of gradual disillusionment, I do not consider the radical dreams of the early twentieth century to have been an illusion. The idea of enchantment provides a more flexible concept, one that recognises that an individual radical life can contain moments of enchantment, disenchantment and re-enchantment. The intensity with which millions came to believe that a better world was possible in a period that endured two world wars and witnessed both the Stalinist terror and the Nazi Holocaust was not based on illusions but real experiences of hope and solidarity. Of course, the cataclysms of the early twentieth century caused many to lose their faith and zeal. But others managed to reformulate their ideas to account for these disasters without losing sight of a vision of a just society. It is only through tracing the lives of those who lived through those dramatic decades on their own terms and in their own words that their stories of enchantment can make any kind of sense to us today.

The history of international communism in the twentieth century is usually narrated through studies of states, political parties and the people who led them. Such histories help us understand the factors that brought the project about and resulted in its failure. But to truly understand the peculiar intensity with which people came to believe in the idea of a global commune we need to tell this story as an *intimate* history: a story of revolutionary friendship, love and betrayal experienced by ordinary people. We need to recover those personal and deeply human documents like the letter Emmy Leonhard wrote to Nellie Cohen after the loss of their friend May O'Callaghan. Such sources, and the lives of those who created them, reveal how so many radicals of the early twentieth century came to realise they had so much more to lose than their chains.

O'C

2. May O'Callaghan, c. 1925. In the author's possession

1

Close to where I am typing, in my apartment in Belfast, there is a framed photograph of May O'Callaghan. It was taken almost one hundred years ago. In the image, she looks exactly as she was then, in Moscow's Hotel Lux – or so I read in a letter by one of the women who knew her best in the Soviet capital. The photograph is in imperfect condition. It was once held in a different frame and the corners of the image were folded to accommodate its shape.

Historians accept the inevitability of such flaws. We can rescue the people of the past from obscurity, providing a portrait of those who would otherwise disappear. But our depictions are always imprecise. Once time has taken its toll on people, it continues to damage the sources they left behind.

The photograph came into my possession as a gift from someone who did not realise he possessed it nor whom it depicted. In that sense, I am both the recipient of this source and the person who recovered it. May gave this photograph to her friend, an Irish novelist, in 1928. He, in turn, gave it to the Cohens. This family gave it to Emmy Leonhard. I discovered the photograph in a long-neglected box, stored beneath an attic window looking onto waves crashing against the Galician coast. I found this box in the home of Emmy's grandson. He, in turn, gifted the photograph to me in the summer of 2021. This chain of succession implicates me in this story too and makes me a minor part in its flow.

Above all, the photograph reminds me of the trajectory of research: from the initial find that piques our curiosity about a person from history to that moment when our detailed investigation convinces us we can, in our minds, see them moving and hear them speaking. The detective story of how we find the paper trail and piece it together can be the most exhilarating part of the research story.

The woman in the frame first entered my sightlines as a disguised name in a long out-of-print autobiography. In tracing the story of her world, I must also trace how a brief, pseudonymous reference became for me the story of a century, a revolution and a romance.

2

I ordered Joseph Freeman's *An American Testament* from an anti-quarian bookseller the summer before I started my PhD in late 2016, having learned of its existence through a footnote. This footnote made a claim that seemed worth investigating: in the 1920s, an Irishwoman lived and worked in a Moscow revolutionary headquarters. Joseph Freeman's book was cited as the source. The historian said little more about the woman, but identified the pseudonym Freeman used for her, 'O'B', and what the historian believed to be her real name: Kathleen O'Brennan.

But the more I searched, the more convinced I became that this was a misidentification. I ordered Freeman's book to test my theory in more detail and to see if I could uncover the real identity of this Irishwoman in post-revolutionary Moscow.

The book arrived with a red cloth cover with the embossed initials 'LBC': Left Book Club. A cursory trawl through an online catalogue revealed that the book had two print runs, both in the 1930s. The first edition was released in the US in 1936 and then, in 1937, a London-based leftist press issued the book once more. Each publication came with glowing reviews. The book even converted some people to the communist cause, just as its author initially hoped. Then a meeting was held in Moscow, a message was sent to Freeman in New York and his editors were informed: no more reprints. In Moscow myself, nearly eighty years later, I would find an extraordinary transcript, evidence that Freeman's book had been subjected to a trial with a select group of Hotel Lux residents acting as a jury. The book was deemed a threat to the movement for its sympathetic depictions of communists who sided with Stalin's opponent, Leon Trotsky. Reading it for the first time, I was oblivious of *An American Testament*'s many strange afterlives and unaware that, for me, this book would initiate a years-long research adventure.

'This narrative is rooted in the belief that mankind is passing through a major transformation,' wrote Freeman in his tantalising preface. Sitting in my student flat, I was swept into the radical world that Freeman depicted in his writing. The voices in his book resonated out from the pages. Their strident commitment to a revolutionary cause was vividly depicted. The climactic chapters of the book, based largely in Moscow's Hotel Lux in 1926 and 1927, captured an impression of a revolutionary society in transition and froze it in time.

This was not the turgid Marxian deluge that swamped so many other communist memoirs from the thirties nor the needling dissections of political shifts that characterised so much later historical writing on the topic. Both Freeman's genius and his later accusations of 'political unreliability' were rooted in how he structured his story. He traced the faces of individuals swept up in mass politics: the comrades in this work were flawed romantics, bound as much to one another as to their task of building socialism. Long before historians of international communism became interested in such questions, Freeman had described the importance of intimate friendships in shaping political destinies.

The writing, characters and scenarios seemed so vivid that I wondered: why was this book still so obscure? Here was an auto-biography, albeit an avowedly communist one, that provided pen portraits of some of the most remarkable literary and political figures of the early twentieth century. Even the author Joseph Freeman, a radical writer born in Ukraine to Jewish parents and raised in New York, had a life story that spoke to so many experiences that shaped modern history. Although often verbose and with occasional passages that have aged poorly, the book's literary quality was undeniable. Even an anti-communist scholar of the mid-century was moved to describe it as 'one of the few Communist human documents worth preserving'.[1] As I read, I became transfixed by a single suggestive passage about Freeman's Irish employer in Moscow, subtly altered in the British publication of *American Testament* but unedited in the American release, describing 'O. B.', Freeman's boss in Moscow: 'For years she had moved in the radical literary and political circles of Dublin and London. Liam O'Flaherty was one of her friends and her favorite "genius." "Oh, he's a wild one!" O. B. would tell me. "Drunk as a lord and crazy for the women but, mark my word, he'll be the pride of English literature." O. B. had spent a number of years in the suffrage fight under the Pankhursts, then followed them into labour journalism.'[2]

Over several passages, Freeman recounted his employment under this Irishwoman in Moscow who hosted a literary salon in her

Hotel Lux room. These brief accounts left me with a burning curiosity. During the 1920s and 30s, roughly 600 communists worked in the movement's Moscow headquarters at any one time. This translator found herself as an elite within an elite. It seemed extraordinary: during the debates that defined the course of the world revolution, to some degree shaping the twentieth century, the head of English translation at the Comintern was an Irishwoman. As a historian of Irish radicalism interested in marginal figures rather than revolutionary idols, I was intrigued, to say the least. I needed to know who this woman was and what had brought her to 1920s Moscow.

Whatever sense of feverish curiosity I felt about this Irish translator was matched by my wonder at the setting I found her in. The Hotel Lux emerged from the pages like a location that would seem outlandish in a work of fiction. As I read through sources and memoirs, the long-vacant rooms of the hotel began to fill in my historical imagination. Friends gathered in a large room and danced to imported jazz records; an American anarchist sat on his bed and attempted to communicate with his Russian wife; anti-colonial revolutionaries discussed recipes from home in a shared canteen; rumours about political unreliability were whispered in a hallway. The metallic clack of typewriter keys producing polemics, protocols and poetry echoed endlessly.

Arguments played out on every floor. Arguments about massacres of communists in Shanghai, arguments about revolutionary paths not taken, arguments about the duty of white communists towards their comrades in the colonies, arguments about a woman's role within the revolutionary movement and disputes over shower rotas, kitchen space and whether it is 'comradely' to hire a servant. What seemed like towering questions of the international movement could be declared immaterial overnight. Guests passed through the rooms only to end up leading revolutions, facing firing squads or fading into obscurity. Surely, I thought, the whole history of international communism – and, by extension, a major part of modern world history – could be traced through this hotel?

I was not, of course, the first person to stumble upon the extraordinary story of the Hotel Lux and become entranced. I will not be the last. An important account of the hotel was written by a former resident, Ruth von Mayenburg. Her book drew on her memories of the hotel in the 1930s, as Moscow Radio blasted throughout a building that existed under a growing shadow. Margarete Buber-Neumann, yet another German former resident of the Lux, vividly depicted the darkness of the shadow that later descended over the hotel. Her husband, Heinz Neumann, was arrested from their Hotel Lux room during the terror of the late 1930s and soon thereafter executed. Freeman, I later learned, was friendly with Neumann in the Hotel Lux. But Freeman's autobiography, written before his own reassessment of his attachment to communism, looked towards a future political horizon rather than back on a betrayed revolution. Yet his book, though clearly written by someone with strong convictions, avoided the tunnel vision of the fanatic.

The complexity of the hotel, at once a house of sanctuary and horror, has proved difficult to capture for historians. Here, after all, was a place where the distance between the emotional extremes of the communist experience, from delirious optimism to terrified disenchantment, was often the width of a corridor. 'Is the fact that the global communist leadership was quartered in a single building of historical relevance, should it matter to historiographers of world communism?' asks historian Karl Schlögel in an essay on the Lux.[3] Of course, the answer is yes. The life of each guest who entered the hotel provides the historian with a kaleidoscopic impression of the twentieth century. Each Lux guest encountered the hotel as a way station on a much longer revolutionary journey. In some tragic cases, the hotel was their terminus. The people who passed through each of its rooms could provide material for potentially hundreds of differing accounts of modern history.

How did an Irishwoman end up among the radical elite of 1920s Moscow – and then end up entirely forgotten? That was the question that started my search, but I soon realised it was too narrowly conceived and that all the threads of my investigation moved through one place: the Hotel Lux. What started as an investigation into one woman who lived in the Lux became an attempt to disentangle how several people from across the world converged on a single place in the mid-1920s and how their lives and activist careers were impacted by the friendships they made within that hotel.

3

Transfixed by this hotel and its residents, I knew there was a story worth telling, I just needed a clue to get me started. Freeman was poor at disguising identities – something I would soon discover and which investigators in Moscow realised long before. His brief descriptions of 'O'B' left enough research breadcrumbs to follow a path forward. It took me a morning, an email and a photocopier in Oregon to decipher O'B's identity. The identities of friends of 'O'B' mentioned in Freeman's autobiography proved even easier to decipher. Some were even listed under their real names.

Once I found their names, I was able to search archival data-bases for personal papers. Eventually, I developed a hunch about a correspondent listed in the archival catalogue of an American librarian who had lived in Moscow in the 1920s. I wrote to the archive that held the American librarian's private papers and requested scans of the material. A link to download a large file soon appeared in my email inbox. This order, based on little more than a moment of intuition, ultimately altered the direction of my career. It was one of those research moments when fate intervened on my behalf: I was about to be introduced to moments and movements more elaborate and exciting than anything I had previously encountered.

The scanned letters, which extended to almost two hundred pages of material, were my first introduction to the voice and personality of May O'Callaghan. One of the first letters in the folder was a postcard depicting Westminster, sent by May to a friend in room 336 of the Hotel Lux. The card was full of references to friends and comrades and written with liveliness and palpable affection. This, I would learn, was May's standard epistolary style, although she was also fond of well-intentioned jibes and the occasional flood of self-introspection. Name-dropping was one of her vices, but for me it was a virtue, allowing me to trace who knew whom. Many letters suggested May was friends with eminent figures of interwar politics and culture. And yet, aside from a few stray references in books about other people, nobody had ever written about her. What I found just as striking, as a historian of committed revolutionaries, many of whom were not known for their humour, was that May never took herself too seriously. There was always a touch of levity, even when the historical moment she was living through was full of peril.

The survival of personal documents that suggest the rhythm of someone's thoughts, particularly when that person was – historically speaking – a minor player in a greater drama, is a rare occurrence. The private worlds of many, even among the 'great and good', remain *terra incognita* for historians. We make our peace with this fact and attempt, through creative readings and fragmentary references, to add texture to an elusive life. But sometimes historians encounter a tranche of long-neglected documents. Suddenly, an entire lost life becomes fully realised in our imagination.

I immediately realised the file now open on my laptop contained an exceptional find. These letters revealed decades of a forgotten Irishwoman's radical life, from her time in 1920s Moscow until her death, represented in her own reflective and often witty words. Through this initial find, I could identify almost everyone who came into her orbit during an extraordinary moment both in her own life and in revolutionary history. And through the wider stories of these comradeships, I began to imagine that I could reconstruct an entire lost world along a network of intimate bonds. But I could not have anticipated the twists that this story would take.

When I first looked over the scanned letters of May O'Callaghan, I immediately noticed her sign-off, the name by which all her friends knew her: O'C. The genesis of Freeman's pseudonym was suddenly clear. Freeman retreated one letter in the alphabet to lightly disguise O'C as 'O.B.'. Now there was a name, an alias and my first folder of letters. On that day towards the start of my doctoral research, I thought my next destination should be where Freeman suggested May O'Callaghan's political awakening took place: 'in the suffrage fight under the Pankhursts'. Although I could not have foreseen it in that moment, I was about to devote much of my twenties to tracing a single friendship circle, and a queer romance fostered within it, all of which arose from the revolutionary tumult that created the modern world.

PART I

Dashing Young Revolutionaries

The Dreadnought

1

May O'Callaghan's life had a propensity for curious synchronicities. The year of her birth, 1881, was the same year that a young woman stepped onto a snow-covered St Petersburg street, hurled a grenade into the carriage of Tsar Alexander II and set in motion a chain of revolutionary events and counter-revolutionary responses that would ultimately lead May to Moscow. The assassin was a member of the Russian revolutionary movement People's Will, an organisation devoted to the ideals of 'bread and liberty'. 'In court, four of the five condemned to death defended their libertarian demands with dignity and courage,' the revolutionary Victor Serge wrote in his memoirs, 'on the scaffold, they embraced one another and died calmly.'[1] Their embrace of revolutionary politics and of each other as they faced their execution transformed their movement. It is one tributary flowing in the revolutionary tide that would bring the Russian Empire to its knees, propel Lenin's Bolsheviks to power and, ultimately, lead an Irish journalist with bobbed hair to the capital of the world revolution.

Julia Mary 'May' O'Callaghan was born on 14 August 1881 in Wexford, far from those who conspired to upset Russian imperialism with explosive devices. She grew up, however, not so far from those who conspired to upend British imperialism by similar means. Early in May's life, the O'Callaghans moved from Wexford town to Ballinsesker, a tiny village overlooking a dramatic stretch of the Irish coast. Little May was the youngest of four children, three daughters and one son, born to Patrick O'Callaghan, a head constable of the Royal Irish Constabulary (RIC), the police force of pre-independence Ireland and an arm of British power in the country. Patrick and his wife, Julia, were both Roman Catholics, a faith that seems to have only vaguely influenced May's cultural sensibility. In time, the RIC would become acquainted with the fear of assassination that was beginning to stalk their counterparts in the tsarist police, but in the late nineteenth century, this was a relatively peaceful posting for a constable.

When I visited Ballinsesker in 2017, the O'Callaghans still featured in local memory even though none had lived in the village since before the Second World War. The house where May grew up still stands, hidden behind a vine-covered wall and facing out to the Irish sea. Nobody has lived in it for quite some time. On the cloudy winter's day when I visited, I was taken by the beauty of the setting – a view only slightly marred by a long-abandoned car half-swallowed into the ground. I reflected on the border-crossing family journey that had begun at the same spot more than a century before as I took in the view of the wide ocean disappearing into the horizon.

How did May's childhood in this picturesque, if isolated corner of the world shape her into the woman she became? She expressed a few revealing thoughts in a letter to a friend she met in Moscow: mentions of her mother never showing 'her feelings to us kids' and her 'damned complexes' that she considered peculiarly Irish in origin.[2] In an elusive reference to her own sexuality, something she would come to grapple with during her Soviet years, she described 'an absurd shyness where I love' that she believed to be 'an inheritance'. In a similarly personal piece of writing, she told another friend she met in the Hotel Lux that because she was 'basically sentimental – like all Irish' she had tried 'to stifle the finest thing nature had given me: depth of feeling'.[3] 'I have been told since childhood that I am clever,' she recalled in this same letter, which I found in a folder labelled 'unidentified "confession"' in the archives of the University of Oregon. In this confession, May described a recurring frustration to harness what she termed her 'mere brain power' to truly open herself up to the pain that would inevitably come with a determined quest for a more meaningful life. Reading between these revealing fragments, we can discern a young woman beset by a central contradiction: she was raised to realise her own potential and yet prevented from achieving her ambitions both by societal convention and self-abnegation.

Despite the complexes she claimed to inherit from them, May's parents nonetheless gave her something valuable and unusual for young Irishwomen of her era: a third-level education. Patrick and Julia O'Callaghan cultivated the talent of their 'clever' daughter May and her siblings. At least two of the four O'Callaghan children received university educations and lived cosmopolitan lives from an early age. As a young adult, May followed an older sister to Austria, where May studied at the University of Vienna and later tutored in English. At the close of the nineteenth century Viennese society was a cradle of modernity, where Freudian psychoanalysis, social democracy and scientific discovery were discussed and championed in art-nouveau cafés and along the imperious streets. What were the political and cultural influences of May's life in Vienna? Revealing her keen interest in both continental literary currents and the cultural revival of her native Ireland, Austrian papers advertised lectures by 'Frau' May O'Callaghan on the writings of Oscar Wilde and George Bernard Shaw. The young May was evidently keen to immerse herself in the literary world.

May's Viennese life was marked by a cultural sensibility and a talent for languages that would later define her involvement with revolutionary causes. Yet how she became involved in such causes was more an accident than a steady process of radicalisation. Nellie Cohen recalled that May's initial journey to London was never planned as a permanent move. The sister May followed to Vienna had married an Austrian businessman involved in shipping lines. In 1914 he engaged his Irish sister-in-law to promote his business in the United States. On her way to her destination, May stopped in London, unaware that she was travelling on the eve of a world war. In the wake of the assassination of Archduke Franz Ferdinand, the rivalries between European powers erupted violently, eventually defacing the continent with a latticework of trenches as the First World War devolved into a stalled front.

When the conflict first broke out, May's options for leaving Britain were limited. In need of an income, she answered an advertisement placed in a newspaper seeking a sub-editor for a recently launched feminist journal: *The Woman's Dreadnought*. The advertisement was placed by the suffragette Sylvia Pankhurst. In her memoir of the war years, Pankhurst introduced May in affectionate tones, describing her as having a charismatic ability for conversation and sharing the Irish 'gift of humour'.[4]

A series of chance happenings, including the allure of a new job and the bold act of a Serbian nationalist, combined to provide May with her first introduction to the world of radicalism. Soon she would find accommodation with other women working to bring about their employers' revolution. The lines dividing her political, personal and professional lives would be forever blurred.

2

In November 1913, in the year before May O'Callaghan became tied to the British capital, a cross-section of Irish and British revolutionaries had stood together on a platform in London's Royal Albert Hall. They had gathered to express their solidarity with the Dublin Lockout, when thousands of Irish workers participated in a major strike for better conditions and the right to unionise. In late 1913, those with a prescient reading of world events sighted war on the horizon, while a determined minority already looked beyond the emerging conflict towards a world revolution. An early inkling of this insurrectionary spirit was a workers' revolt sparked in Dublin the year before the First World War broke out. Ireland's capital was then a major city within the British Empire, a fact which sat uneasily with a growing number of its residents.

Among those most opposed to Ireland's continuing subjugation to British rule were the radicals gathered on the Royal Albert Hall platform. Speakers included James Connolly, the Irish socialist who would meet his end before a firing squad several years later, and Charlotte Despard, the elderly Anglo-Irish suffragist. The room was packed with supporters. 'Quite a large attendance of the audience were women,' noted one reporter, many of whom 'wore Suffrage badges and sashes'.[5] Another attendee remembered the vivid red colour of the uniforms worn by these young women attendants 'splashing colour on the great assembly'.[6] This conflagration of socialists and militant suffragettes from both Ireland and Britain was the product of links fostered and sustained across the Irish Sea. In attendance at the meeting that night was a woman whose commitment to such ties of solidarity would change the course of her political career: Sylvia Pankhurst, the radical scion of the revered suffrage family.

An instinctive ally of the oppressed, Sylvia Pankhurst was unusual among British socialists for her early and forceful support of the entwining causes of Irish labour and nationalism. These interests made her an outlier within her activist family, particularly with respect to her sister Christabel and mother Emmeline, who looked upon Sylvia's increasing social radicalism with dismay and hostility. Since establishing an East London branch of the Women's Social and Political Union (WSPU) in 1912, Sylvia's growing independence from the political line pursued by her sister and mother in the campaign for women's suffrage generated significant tension.

Sylvia's appearance on the Royal Albert Hall platform, where she stood in solidarity with a cause distinct from the narrower quest for women's votes at Westminster, proved the final strain on an already taut familial and political link. Sylvia and her East London branch were expelled from the broader WSPU. The family rift would never truly heal. Freed from familial oversight, Sylvia Pankhurst could pursue her own radical schemes in one of the major world hubs of revolutionary activity: London's East End. If the theory of Pankhurst and her comrades in the British socialist movement held true – that *class* could supersede the divisions of nationality in uniting the oppressed people of the East End against the system holding them in subjection – then her East London Federation of Suffragettes would become one of the major sites of cross-community collaboration and resistance. Extracted from the dominance of a sister and mother who deemed such radical dreams a diversion from the practical aim of women's suffrage, Sylvia's revolution began in earnest.

3

Some months after the Albert Hall meeting that led to Sylvia Pankhurst's rift with her family, on International Women's Day in March 1914, a new socialist and feminist journal debuted on news stands in East London. Assertively titled *The Woman's Dreadnought*, the paper gradually extended its readership from beyond its East London base, moving along the shipping routes of the British Empire. It would circulate among Irish nationalists in Paris and make its way into the hands of anti-colonial revolutionaries before becoming one the main papers of the British revolutionary movement. Under Sylvia's editorship, the socialist ideal of co-operation across the dividing lines of ethnicity would become reflected in the office where the *Dreadnought* was typeset and edited, a room where an Irish journalist and her young Jewish friend began a lifelong friendship.

The origins of Pankhurst's East London organisation were described in an article Pankhurst contributed to the *Dreadnought's* first issue. Pankhurst recalled how, in October 1912, she and her friend Flora Drummond decided to undertake the 'work of arousing the working-women of East London to fight for their own enfranchisement'.[7] On a frosty morning a few months later, with the sun hanging 'like a red ball in the misty, white-grey sky', Pankhurst and another comrade went hunting for a permanent East End office, eventually settling on a location with a broken window held together by putty and with holes in its floor.

Activists intent on fixing a broken world cannot afford to be daunted by minor repairs and Pankhurst settled into her new headquarters despite discomfort and initial local antipathy. The task was clear: stand up, speak up and build a community of women-workers. Nellie Cressall, an East End Christian socialist who knew Pankhurst during this period, later recalled that in the beginning tomatoes and eggs were thrown at the East London Federation's speakers as they stood upon their platforms. But Sylvia kept on speaking. 'You see,' Cressall remembered, 'when you know you're right, you can't be turned aside. And it soon stopped. People came to respect us. After a while you could hear a pin drop at our meetings.'[8]

By the time Pankhurst began organising there, London's East End was already a world unto itself, moulded by the professions and conditions of the migrant communities that populated it. London's bustling ports had long welcomed migrants seeking sanctuary: first the Huguenots, then the Irish and the Jews. Settling not far from the ports at which they first docked, these communities found an escape from hunger and violence, but the conditions were far from ideal. In becoming a destination for these cast-out communities, the East End repelled many who considered themselves part of 'civilised' society. The lurid detail of press accounts described crowded, bustling streets where uncouth customs were practised and incomprehensible tongues were spoken. In the by-ways of these streets, so the public were often told, the outcasts of the Russian Empire were plotting revolution.

Journalists and secret policemen continually pinpointed the East End as a major nexus of violent revolutionary dreaming. With the arrival of 63,000 Jewish migrants from the territories of the Russian Empire by the turn of the century, this single London district became a close-knit world of Jewish refugees, exiles and migrants. It was also a home to many belonging to the movements that the authorities feared: feminists, anarchists, socialists and movements for Jewish liberation. More moderate reformers who had long sought to change conditions in the East End found themselves competing with a more radical generation of activists. These intertwining forces and conditions – the state, the revolutionaries who opposed it and the poverty that provide vindication for their radical opposition – shaped the lives of many who were raised in the tight-knit East End Jewish communities. Among those whose early lives unfurled against this radical backdrop were two girls born to a family of Polish Jews in the 1890s: Nellie and Rose Cohen.

4

In 1884 Maurice and Ada Jacobovsky's journey to East London began with a frightening start at Lodz station when they lost sight of their youngest child. The journey continued with an arduous trip across the European refugee routes. After arriving in London, they, like so many other Jews pushed out of the Russian Empire by antisemitic persecution and dire economic circumstance, settled in Whitechapel, not far from where they first arrived. Here they began their new life with their travelling companions: four young children and Maurice's father, Gediliah. The Jacobovskys' point of departure had been Turek, a Polish town whose Jewish community numbered around two thousand at the end of the nineteenth century, a population that contributed greatly to the prosperity of the area but which would be entirely depleted within half a century, first by emigration and, eventually, through Nazi genocide.

Migrant families sometimes anglicised their surnames to ease integration into their new surroundings. 'Jacobovsky' became the more easily pronounceable (though still recognisably Jewish) 'Cohen'. The first child to be born into the former Jacobovsky family with this new name upon her birth certificate was Nellie Cohen, born in Spitalfields, East London, in 1892. Then along came another daughter, Rose, born two years later in 1894. The strength of their bond in adulthood suggests the two girls were each other's favourite siblings. In addition to their placing as the youngest surviving members of the family, they shared a rebellious streak. Nellie concealed Charles Dickens' novels beneath the table while her father believed she was reading the story of Passover. Young Rose 'was a fighter' with sharp nails that got her into trouble with the boys and which, on occasion, she weaponised against her older sister Nellie.[9] Whirling around them, as they creatively avoided religious instruction and developed offensive tactics against school-yard opponents and older siblings, were the political currents that would shape their family history.

Antisemitic violence and political persecution pushed communities out of the Russian Empire, fostering not only a Jewish community in the East End, but also a world of Jewish radicalism within it. Long before Sylvia Pankhurst was welcomed to the area with edible projectiles, East London became a laboratory where exiles, emigrants and earnest philanthropists tested their own hypotheses of how to build a new world. There were reformers who sought to better the conditions of the working classes through community services and Christian charity. Then there were revolutionaries who wanted to arm the working classes with the theory, the organisational forms – and sometimes the weaponry – that would place them at the vanguard of a total social revolution.

Were the two young Cohens aware of the revolutionaries traversing the streets and carousing in the inns with detectives hot on their tails? Were words like 'Bolshevik', 'Menshevik', 'anarchist' and 'bundist', terms that would become intimately familiar to Nellie and Rose in later life, part of their childhood vocabulary? Such questions cannot be answered by the sources and the possibility seems unlikely. Feminism, however, did take an early hold on the Cohen sisters.

As a young woman, Nellie enjoyed attending open-air suffrage meetings at the Mile End Road. She found herself particularly enthralled by the speeches of Flora Murray, a Scottish suffragette and doctor. At one of these meetings she met a comrade of Sylvia Pankhurst who told her that Sylvia needed a secretary. Nellie told the woman she wouldn't mind filling that role. 'She said I'll intro-duce you,' Nellie told the historian Lucia Jones decades later, 'I said all right and that was that, so I became her secretary.'[10] For the Cohens, this was how involvement in the world revolution arrived: through a job vacancy.

Despite her extraordinary stamina, Sylvia Pankhurst could not have functioned without assistance. Her hectic work schedule involved writing polemics and petitions late into the night while maintaining an international correspondence. Someone had to organise the diary of an activist whose energies needed to be focused on staying out of prison and maintaining lines of communication with a global radical network. Nellie Cohen, by then around twenty-one years of age, received the job and thereby took up an administrative position at the historical crossroads of anti-imperialism, feminism and socialism. As she remembered it, Nellie's initial involvement in Pankhurst's radical world took place between tennis sets in an East London park. Nellie's serves were interrupted by a messenger from Pankhurst's headquarters, who would inform the young secretary that her employer was once more out of prison: time to get back to work. Sometime in 1914, Nellie met a new colleague and comrade in the office: May O'Callaghan, an Irishwoman several years her senior with a love of literature and a talent for languages.

5

In early 1916 Daisy Lansbury, a young activist from a family known in East London for their socialist campaigning, wrote a letter to a friend in New York that playfully revealed some activist mischief. Daisy told her friend that the *Forward*, a left-wing journal, had been suppressed by the censors for printing reports of Lloyd George's interview with workers in Glasgow's Clyde district. 'I have to chuckle every time I think of it,' she wrote. One of her 'pals' named 'Rosie' Cohen had 'stencilled 100 copies from a very dilapidated copy of the *Forward* which managed to leak out and which is now reposing under a glass case'. Daisy also wrote about the 'awful job' it took to get a flat in London's Gray's Inn Road due to the bad reputation of the district. She noted that her father, George Lansbury, later a leader of the Labour Party, had to write and 'convince the damned old ass of an agent that I wasn't being led astray by Miss O'Callaghan & Nellie Cohen, the girls I'm going to live with'.[11]

This letter was intercepted by Scotland Yard and an inspector was posted outside the Gray's Inn Road flat. He reported to his superiors that all three residents spent their days 'engaged at No. 400 Old Ford Road, Bow, the Headquarters of the East London Federation of Suffragettes, the office of the "Women's Dreadnought" (their official paper) and residence of Miss Sylvia Pankhurst'.[12]

This letter and report – the earliest documentary evidence of the friendships and interconnections between May, Nellie and Rose – are two documents contained in a bulging surveillance folder on Rose assembled by MI5 over the course of several decades. The folder, declassified in 2003, stretches to more than three hundred pages. Daisy's intercepted letter is the earliest dated document, while the final documents deal with Rose's 1937 arrest and disappearance in Soviet Moscow.

Sometimes, the secret policeman unwittingly assembles the first drafts of social history. Here, in attempting to find evidence to support a charge of sedition, evidence of a lifelong friendship was provided. It was also indication of an intimate radical network: May and the Cohens made their way each day to their workplace, which doubled as the residence of their revolutionary employer.

At a single East London address, 400 Old Ford Road, the dawning social revolutions converged. Through the development of social amenities including childcare facilities and a cost-price restaurant, Pankhurst and her collaborators set out to build a precursor to the egalitarian society of the future amidst the slum conditions of the East End. May and Nellie frequented the restaurant, whose Scottish chef, Mrs Snedden, was frustrated by the two friends' vegetarian diet. Snedden would serve them both rice pudding. Many decades later, Nellie could still recall the rich taste of the pudding, a side effect of being left in the oven all morning. Despite the overcooked pudding, Nellie remembered Pankhurst's Scottish chef as a 'good plain cook', who could serve up a solid meal for a shilling and was something of a culinary magician. 'The things that woman did with maize was absolutely astonishing,' Nellie recalled.[13]

One observer described Pankhurst's organisation as an ersatz government with a 'Distress and Welfare Bureau'.[14] At one point in late 1915, a women-dominated mock parliament was staged in the offices at 400 Old Ford Road. May, serving as MP for an Irish constituency in this parliament from a parallel universe, joined Pankhurst in fomenting a 'great disturbance' in opposing the war.[15]

The women who gathered, worked and lived at the Old Ford Road offices were at the forefront in promoting new models of community organising that filled in gaps in social provision and attempted to organise working-class people and empower them with tools and tactics for their own emancipation. With the form-ation of a 'People's Army' in 1913, Pankhurst and her comrades had even sought to provide the East End working classes with an armed wing.

One revolutionary employer, two job postings, a shared flat and an extended network of East London rebels. This is how Nellie, Rose and May first met. History is built on such contingent moments captured in snapshots, seemingly ordinary occurrences whose extraordinary repercussions can only be faithfully rendered against the backdrop of a world historical canvas. Although the revolu-tionary ideology that would fasten their bond had not yet taken its most potent form, Nellie, Rose and May were already attuning themselves to world events. This was a natural outcome of time spent with their employer, Sylvia Pankhurst; a revolutionary who personally knew many of the most prominent figures in the revolu-tionary worlds of feminism, Irish nationalism and international socialism. Their shared home and workplace would provide them with a unique vantage point for the opening act of a wartime insur-rectionary wave.

In early 1916, as these friends made their way to and from 400 Old Ford Road, revolutionaries in May's native Ireland were planning a rebellion. May and the Cohens likely realised that their own organisation was in many ways reformulating itself in response to events in Ireland. The People's Army of the East End was not unprecedented: a month before its formation in 1913, workers in Dublin organised the Irish Citizen Army as a means of defending themselves from police offensives during the 1913 lockout. Three years later, the Irish Citizen Army was one contingent of the wider rebel forces that attempted an armed insurrection against British rule in Ireland. The Easter Rising of 1916, as this uprising became known, would prove a miserable military failure but an enormous symbolic victory. Pankhurst's East End organisation responded immediately to the events – in no small part influenced in its response by the presence of Irish voices on the pages of the *Dreadnought*.

Rebel Ireland and the New Russia

1

Meeting beneath clouds of tobacco smoke in the back rooms of cafés and restaurants across Europe, revolutionaries discussed moving from theory to action. There was at least one English-language newspaper that held the lofty ambition of tracking these movements, from nationalists drilling between Irish hedgerows to veterans of Siberian exile crossing borders with pamphlets sewn into waistcoats: the *Dreadnought*. In 1917, as the undercurrents of radical changed surged ever more strongly, it was retitled the *Workers' Dreadnought*. But already by early 1916, Pankhurst's East London Federation of Suffragettes defined itself explicitly as a 'working class organisation', fighting for votes for all people disenfranchised by their class position.[1] Spending their days in the *Dreadnought*'s hectic East London offices with the paper's tireless editor, May and the Cohen sisters would soon come face to face with many of the leading insurgents battling to remake their world.

Although their office in East London was, in pure geographic terms, far from the insurrectionary cities of Europe, it was connected to these places by the travelling revolutionaries who passed through the office, carrying first-hand news of astonishing political transformations. Although it must have initially struck observers as thrilling chaos in the immediate moment, the Irish Revolution that began with 1916 and the Russian Revolution of 1917 unleashed historical forces that set the stage for the lives of our protagonists.

The revolutionary wave of the war years first crested in Europe's west: Ireland. On the morning of Easter Monday, 1916, members of the Irish volunteers, its women's auxiliary Cumann na mBan and the Irish Citizen army, a socialist militia, marched through Dublin, occupying several locations in the city centre. The British Army moved to quell the uprising. Although the insurrectionaries tried to hold out against a foe with overwhelming strength, the forces they faced were ultimately insurmountable. The leaders of the Rising announced a surrender after six days of fighting. Upon emerging from the rubble of the city centre, rebels were arrested en masse. Those whom the British pinpointed as the rebellion's leadership were sentenced to death. James Connolly, who we last saw on stage at the Royal Albert Hall, was among those executed by firing squad. Already badly wounded from the street battles and heavily dosed with morphine, he was restrained to a chair so the executioners could effectively carry out his death sentence. It was one among many moments of pathos that helped turn Irish public opinion in favour of the rebels' cause.

The Rising fits neatly into a general equation that can be applied to most Irish insurrections and many left-wing conspiracies: over-whelmingly trounced rebels plus time equals symbolic victory. In a lead article published less than a week after Irish republicans surrendered in Dublin, Pankhurst declared: 'Justice can make but one reply to the Irish rebellion and that is to demand that Ireland shall be allowed to govern herself.'[2] The article set the tone for the *Dreadnought*'s coverage of the land its journalists termed 'Rebel Ireland'; at once both sympathetic and grounded in the deep personal connections stemming between the *Dreadnought*'s writers, its readers and Ireland.

Alongside the editorial, the *Dreadnought* published May's pen portrait of one of the Rising's more striking insurrectionists: Constance Markievicz. She was a familiar figure in press reporting of the Irish Revolution due to her diligent curation of her own public image. Well-publicised photographs from the era show her in Irish republican military uniform and brandishing a pistol. May's article was accompanied by a less militant photograph: Markievicz in the countryside with her beloved dog Poppet. In her profile,

May described Markievicz as one 'who has sacrificed everything for her country'.[3] After a concise account of Markievicz's life, May offered a wry summary of the British response to the Irish insurrection: 'Britain, true to her history in championing the cause of small nations, turned machine guns loose on them.'

Although the events of Easter 1916 are often marked as the beginning of the Irish Revolution, in truth this moment had a long gestation. May and the other *Dreadnought* writers were attempting to offer on-the-fly analysis of a major juncture in a long, complex story, one which encompassed the revolutionary currents sweeping across the Atlantic in the late eighteenth century, from France to Haiti, and the catastrophic Irish famine in the 1840s. The famine's impact on Irish politics was seismic. British culpability in the famine's cataclysmic death count – around one million – further radicalised Irish nationalism. The Irish cause had also gained new international resonance through the migrant dispersal caused by the famine. Part of that dispersed and radicalised Irish migrant community settled in East London.

Migrants from Ireland – both recent arrivals and the descendants of those displaced by the famine – filled the East London streets where young women, some of them Irish themselves, sold copies of the *Dreadnought*. It was precisely this symbiosis between the paper's staff and audience that allowed this small leftist journal to secure a scoop: the first eyewitness account of the Rising published in the international press. Patricia Lynch, a working-class woman from Cork first drawn to Sylvia Pankhurst's politics when she saw Pankhurst speak about the plight of 'poor working women', reported to 400 Old Ford Road shortly after learning of the Rising.[4] Lynch, young, Irish and unknown to the authorities, was one of the best-placed *Dreadnought* writers when it came to breaching the military cordon that surrounded the Irish capital.

Lynch's report from her expedition to a city in ruins proved a major coup for the *Dreadnought*. The issue carrying the article sold out and had to be reprinted several times.[5] One contemporary testified to the issue making its way through the colony of Irish expats in Paris.[6] Following this success, coverage of Ireland appeared regularly in the *Dreadnought*.

When, in 1917, Pankhurst learned of a co-operative knitting factory established in Dungloe, a town in Ireland's north-west, she dispatched May and Nellie to investigate. In her front-page report of the trip, May described homesteads by the lakes dotted through the countryside and railways built between 'high walls of rock, magnificent and weird'.[7] The journey took the two friends through land undulating with hills and absent of people as they travelled by ferry, foot and post cart before arriving at the factory. It must have been striking for Irish country folk to meet an Irishwoman and her friend from the Jewish East End, both so far from home. Ireland's Jewish population, never large, was at this time largely confined to the cities of Cork, Dublin and Belfast. Unlike other journals of the British left whose understandings of Irish realities were often far from the mark, the *Dreadnought*, through Irishwomen like May, gave its coverage a ring of authenticity.

Events in Ireland brought a new vigour to the journal's pages. Finally, a tremor heralding the shake-up that would upend British imperialism could be felt. Yet the global collapse of the British Empire still seemed far away in 1916, when each day brought news reports of more lives senselessly lost in a conflict between duelling imperial powers. A year later, however, everything changed. Events in the Russian Empire would fundamentally transform radical beliefs in the possibility of total social transformation. The friendship between May, born and raised in Ireland, and Nellie and Rose Cohen, the children of the Russian Empire's outcasts, was set to become a metaphor for the insurrectionary potential of what could happen when revolutionary movements joined forces.

2

The tributaries flowing into the events that finally brought down a dynasty that reigned over the Russian Empire for three centuries had many originating points. We could begin with the 1905 revolution that forced the Russian autocracy to institute limited reforms, or stretch back to the 1790s, amid the revolutionary waves that made ripples even in Russia under Catherine the Great. But the people who made and witnessed the Russian Revolution did not necessarily experience it as an event hundreds of years in the making. Most accounts emphasise instead the astonishingly rapid pace at which the gears of the popular uprising began to turn.

The revolutionary wave began to crash forcefully over Russia on the eve of International Women's Day in 1917, when thousands of striking workers from the Putilov metal works in the Russian capital of Petrograd were locked out of their workplace. Since 1913, Russian socialist women had celebrated International Women's Day on the last Sunday of February, following socialist women in New York, Vienna and elsewhere who first popularised the celebration. The day following the lockout, the strikers of Putilov joined thousands of women workers taking to the streets of Petrograd to protest a bread shortage.

Although these events had something of a spontaneous character with no central party co-ordinating the women workers and the Putilov strikers, the protests would nonetheless prove the beginning of an unstoppable revolutionary momentum. The Bolsheviks – the revolutionary movement that would eventually come to direct this momentum – gave their party organ an anticipatory title: *Iskra*, meaning 'spark'. This 'spark' of revolution was long-awaited among the Russian exiles living in Europe and America, and in the radical underground. But when it finally arrived, it came unexpectedly – certainly for the Bolsheviks, whose leadership followed the initial events of the Russian Revolution from cities like London, New York and Geneva, rather than on the Petrograd streets. Many of the professional revolutionaries of the underground were disconnected from the day-to-day lives of the working masses of the Russian Empire they sought to mobilise. This was not by choice: the Okhrana, the tsarist secret police and the authoritarian state they defended pushed much of the movement beyond the Russian Empire – and continued to pursue them even beyond its borders.

A day after International Women's Day, a mass of strikers marched into Petrograd city centre from the districts beyond, symbolically moving from the industrial surroundings where they toiled and into the palatial surroundings of central Petrograd. Red flags and banners calling for an end to the war and tsarist governance fluttered and bellowed above crowds that rapidly swelled to include wider sections of society. Students and the middle classes joined the protests to stand alongside their fellow citizens. They flowed over the bridges spanning the canals and took shortcuts across the ice of the frozen River Neva.

The Sunday following the Putilov lockout, soldiers fired on demonstrators; that evening, soldiers in the industrial districts were met with stones and even pistol shots. One revolutionary, making his way through the city streets, learned from passers-by that demonstrators were constructing barricades from tram cars and telegraph poles.

Armed repression was the most effective move the government could make. Corpse-strewn streets were visible after the smoke of rifle fire dissipated. But the atmosphere was distinct compared to other moments of violent repression. Defiance, even optimism, coursed through the democratic forces, especially when they witnessed disorder and disquiet among the soldiers tasked with dispersing them. This time, things would be different. On Monday the first regiment mutinied. Rifles previously trained on the protestors were now slung over the shoulders of people marching alongside them.[8] A general rule of modern revolutionary history came into play: when the soldiers join the side of a popular revolution, the days of the old regime are numbered. The Romanov dynasty was in checkmate.

Less than a fortnight had passed since the Putilov lockout when Tsar Nicholas II abdicated. A new provisional government was formed from the opposition parties in the duma, a constrained parliament that the tsarist regime had permitted following the 1905 revolutions. Meanwhile, workers and soldiers began to elect their own representatives to the Petrograd Soviet, a council of deputies that enjoyed the popular support the duma politicians could not muster. Soviet, a word which would later become synonymous with an entire system and way of life, translates as 'council'. These councils, or soviets, soon emerged across the rapidly fraying Empire.

Did May and the Cohen sisters have time to absorb the news that was making its way over the frontiers of the dying Russian Empire as they helped to keep the gears turning in Pankhurst's many radical initiatives? Certainly, as staff on the *Dreadnought*, they would have been well placed to read over the reports that Pankhurst received from the revolutionary exiles she encountered in London. A December 1916 copy of the *Social Democrat*, a paper printed by exiled Bolsheviks in Geneva – Lenin among them – was clearly well thumbed by someone in 400 Old Ford Road, and the *Dreadnought* published two lengthy extracts from it.[9]

One of the earliest references in the paper to the events of the revolution arrived in the 'Parliamentary Notes' section of the *Dreadnought*, usually compiled by May. It reported on 24 March 1917 that the 'abdication of the Czar and the Russian Revolution were announced by Mr. Bonar Law' in parliament. It was a demure reference to an event that would soon take over much of the *Dreadnought*'s column inches and transform the lives of May, Nellie and Rose.

3

Leftists and anti-imperialists across the world responded to the Russian Revolution with astonishment and euphoria. Suddenly, the Russian Empire, which had appeared to many outside observers as an immovable despotic force, was no more. Even more astoundingly, the people responsible for its dissolution were *the people*, rather than foreign invaders or a palace coup. Over the trenches that now criss-crossed the continent a more beautiful future unexpectedly dawned. Few people were more surprised by the coming of the revolution than those whose names are today remembered as deciding its fate. On that morning in March 1917, as the newspapers first brought news of street protests and soldiers' mutinies in Russia, Vladimir Lenin was preparing for a day at a Geneva library as his wife, Nadezhda Krupskaya, washed the dishes. The arrival of the revolution that would transform their entire lives caught them off guard.[10]

In few other places beyond the Russian Empire was this unexpected news of liberation more widely celebrated than in London, a waystation for generations of refugees from tsarist repression. In the London 'colony', a normally internecine world of Russian political exiles with outposts in Hampstead and the East End, the euphoria temporarily subdued factional fighting. Ivy Litvinov, an English novelist who had married into the colony, recalled how political adversaries from the wider revolutionary world, who would normally be engaged in 'shouting and banging their chairs around my fire hearth', instead embraced when they met and parted 'like brothers'.[11] In the emanating heat of the revolutionary furnace, old divisions melted away and new political fusions could be born.

Ivy's husband, Maxim Litvinov, a political exile from a Lithuanian Jewish family, asked his wife to type up his immediate impressions the day after news reached him of the revolution. Too anxious to sleep, Maxim got out of bed at 6 am and eagerly awaited the arrival of the first newspapers. When he finally had them in his hands, he was so excited that he was unable to read in sequence. He looked to the end of one column, then glanced to the middle of another. It was 'as if I would make one mouthful of the whole paper', Maxim noted.[12] Distractedly attempting to go through his morning routine while digesting the news of this 'real People's Revolution', Maxim tried to shave himself with toothpaste and got into the bath without turning on the tap.[13] Even before Russia's Provisional Government announced its amnesty for those accused of political crimes, exiles like Maxim became fixated on returning and participating in the revolution. This fixation on reaching Russia would gradually also become an aim of the revolution's foreign sympathisers.

Few images depict the shock and excitement of the moment better than the vision of a Bolshevik sitting in a bathtub in North London, awestruck, naked and smelling of toothpaste. Yet people waking up to the news of revolution across the city were struck with similar feelings of awe. Soon, meetings were being organised to mark the event. In late March 1917, representatives of the East London Jewish Community hosted one such meeting, advertising the gathering in support of the Russian Revolution in English and Yiddish-language posters. It was the kind of event that May and the Cohens would have likely attended together. Indeed, the paper that employed May and Nellie reported on the gathering enthusiastically.

The *Dreadnought* evoked scenes of political intoxication as crowds broke forth 'into cheers and cries of enthusiasm for the coming freedom or groans of hatred and contempt for the tyranny that is overthrown'. According to the *Dreadnought*'s reporter, the crowd's response to the first speaker, an English aristocrat, was more measured than the 'infinitely greater enthusiasm' for the female speakers who followed him. Although unnamed, the report described the women as an East London comrade and an Irishwoman, whose legitimacy to speak at such a gathering was rooted in how she too 'belonged to a race which is oppressed'.[14]

Why was this gathering – where an East London woman, an Irishwoman and an aristocrat welcomed the Russian Revolution – organised by a Jewish organisation? Because the tsarist regime now overthrown was, for many East London Jews, the same avowedly antisemitic regime that had first cast them out of their homes and the same regime that threatened, through its wartime alliance with Britain, to have them deported to Russia to serve in the meatgrinder of its army. The Russian Revolution thus had a particular valence for East Londoners who were, like the Cohen sisters, Jewish migrants from the Russian Empire. It represented the possibility that their ancestral homes might finally welcome them. The revolution could replace autocracy with democracy, but it might also turn a place of great violence into a site of sanctuary. And for an Irishwoman like May, it was easy to perceive how the crumbling

Russian Empire might act as a progressive vision of what lay in store for the British Empire: the destruction of an old regime and the subsequent emancipation of the nations it held in subjugation.

The outcomes of the Irish and Russian Revolutions were, in a word, divergent. One instituted a partitioned island ruled by Catholic social values on one side of a border and Protestant dominance on the other side. The other created a socialist regime that ruled over an amalgam of ethnicities across a sixth of the earth's surface. Reflecting on the revolutions a century on, you may be forgiven for believing that their only shared outcome was a global reputation for uninspired cuisine. But in the closing years of the war, the revolutionary future seemed more expansive and capable of hosting multiple projects for liberation. There was room for the differing ideological tapestries of the Irish and Russian Revolutions to become interwoven.

Such Irish and Eastern European collaborations – or conspiracies, in the fearful eyes of the British establishment – were largely intimate in nature, taking the form of Russian and Irish revolutionaries sharing office buildings, train carriages or conference meeting halls. The first Soviet historian of Ireland, Platon Kerzhentsev, for example, learned of the 1916 Easter Rising's importance from an Irish literary couple with whom he shared a New York boarding house in April of that year. The history of global radicalism in this era is littered with such seemingly spontaneous moments where radicals came together in shared spaces of exile. The Hotel Lux, where all the protagonists of our story would eventually converge, was a striking example of such a revolutionary transit station, but it is not the only one in our story. Already by 1917, European socialist movements had built an informal 'underground railroad' of sorts that stretched from San Francisco to Siberia, its stations the safe houses, lodgings, libraries and meeting halls frequented by travelling radicals. Sylvia Pankhurst's headquarters at 400 Old Ford Road became one of the stations along this railroad, where adherents of the Russian and Irish revolutionary movements often converged.

Within a couple of years after their first meeting in Pankhurst's office, major world events conspired to turn the friendship between

May and the Cohen sisters into a neat symbol of the forces set to remake Europe. In a rebel fairy tale that May composed for a 1917 issue of the *Dreadnought*, the Irish migrant writer, clearly enthused by the revolutions at home and in Russia, reshaped the Irish myth of Tir na nÓg according to the future as she saw it. Meaning, in Irish, 'Land of the Young', Tir na nÓg is a supernatural realm of eternal youth found in stories from Irish folklore. In May's retelling, a British politician spends more than a thousand years in Tir na nÓg before returning to the world he left behind in 1917. Speaking to the children of the future, the politician recounts for his audience how, in his time, women 'had only been discovered' and the meaning of the Bolshevik revolution's challenge to capitalism was yet unknown.[15] The Irish rebels, noted the politician, 'who you have celebrated in history and songs as heroes and forerunners of the new era', were oppressed by the British. May's prophecy was a tale of intertwining forces; the women's movement, the Russian revolutionaries and the Irish were creating a harmonious future together.

A fairy tale rather than a manifesto, May's story was not intended to disentangle the many complex threads of the political moment. It was published in the *Dreadnought*'s Christmas edition, which ended a year of publishing during which the paper and its writers constantly sought to parse the news coming from Petrograd and Moscow. An entirely new organisational vocabulary needed to be learned in addition to an ever-expanding cast of *dramatis personae* that would leave even veteran consumers of Tolstoyan epics befuddled.

A single movement emerged from the fray to seize control of the revolution's direction: the Bolsheviks, originally the result of a split within the Russian Social Democratic and Labour Party, eventually known as the Communist Party of the Soviet Union. Of course, for radicals responding in the moment far from the streets where the direction of the revolution was being decided, it was often easier to collapse this complexity into a single cause to be celebrated: the dawn of freedom, variously and expansively defined, in the Russian Empire.

The mass meetings that arose in European capitals to welcome the revolution in 1917 were moments of political solidarity. Far from being something that obfuscated the reality of the revolution, heightened emotion, and even euphoria, was perhaps its most vital export. The Russian Revolution, coming as it did after years of unimaginable violence, was a means for people across the world to re-enchant themselves with the future. Even in the cataclysms of the twentieth century that followed, there were still many who held on to that memory of 1917, when belief in human possibility returned with such force.

In contrast to the disorienting complexity of later events, the over-throw of Tsarism, so astonishing in its rapidity and total in its effects, demonstrated that all had changed, and all could change elsewhere. The conviction which carried people from around the world to ulti-mately converge on destinations like the Hotel Lux emerged, in part, from that belief in the possibility of a beautiful future that was vindic-ated for many by their own experiences of 1917.

When, in November of that year, the Bolsheviks seized power in Petrograd in an event that would ultimately become known, following the pre-revolutionary calendar, as the October Revolution, the *Dreadnought* declared its support. In a lengthy editorial published less than a fortnight after the Bolsheviks stormed the Winter Palace, Pankhurst hailed the 'Lenin Revolution' as an event that ensured workers would 'no longer be disinherited and oppressed'.[16]

The October Revolution fundamentally altered the landscape for international supporters of the Russian Revolution. It was a Rubicon that once crossed ensured that nobody could prevaricate on *who* and *which* programme in revolutionary Russian politics they supported. The revolution contributed to a sense of revolu-tionary immediacy in the minds of its global sympathisers, many of whom sensed their own storming of the Winter Palace lay in their near future. A year after the Bolshevik seizure of power, British authorities intercepted a letter from Sylvia Pankhurst to a friend in Glasgow. 'I expect the Revolution soon,' Pankhurst wrote, 'don't you?'[17]

4

In February 1918 the Irish feminist Hanna Sheehy-Skeffington told an audience in East Harlem that 'the Russians, the Jews and the Irish' were the 'three great revolutionary forces that would, in truth, make the world safe for democracy'.[18] On the other side of the Atlantic, in East London, a small office occupied by the Russians, the Jews and the Irish had undertaken this ambitious task. In the first of a series of organisational name changes, the East London Federation of Suffragettes had become known as the Workers' Suffrage Federation, whose aims were to secure the vote for every adult man and woman and 'to win Social and Economic Freedom for the People on the basis of a Socialist Commonwealth'.[19] Despite this broadening of aims, the organisation was still women-led.

While retaining a commitment to suffrage, the leftward move turned 400 Old Ford Road into an ever more frantic hub of subversive activity and itinerant revolutionaries. One woman who always stuck in Nellie Cohen's mind was Eugenie Bouvier, a Russian immigrant who helped translate the foreign news that came into the *Dreadnought*. 'I'll never forget her,' Nellie noted decades later, 'she was an astonishing creature.'[20] Bouvier had the kind of transnational biography that marked out many of the women who surrounded Sylvia Pankhurst. Born in St Petersburg into a wealthy family and resident in London from the late nineteenth century, Bouvier was one of the first suffrage militants to participate in window-breaking in Westminster in 1909. In 1917 she enthusiastically welcomed the Russian Revolution, telling one counterpart that Russian authorities ought to have taken away her family's wealth 'years ago, and from all those of us who lived on the backs of the people'.[21]

Along with the Russian-speaking Bouvier, Sylvia Pankhurst tasked Nellie Cohen and May with working on the People's Russian Information Bureau, an outfit of propaganda and counterpropaganda that received support from London's resident Bolsheviks. May became its manager. Scotland Yard paid attention to the activities of the People's Russian Information Bureau, which they believed capable of 'certainly doing harm'.[22] The offices of the Bureau were shared with Pankhurst's printing operation, the Agenda Press. After battling with a heavy sliding door at the entrance, May and Nellie made their way up a dark and narrow staircase above a tailors' store to reach their new workplace on 152 Fleet Street.[23]

In an unpublished memoir of this period titled *Red Twilight*, Pankhurst later recalled May's talent for managing the office and her skill at plundering second-hand stores for workplace decorations.[24] After Pankhurst appeared acquiescent in front of Theodore Rothstein, a Soviet representative who complained about staff productivity, May took Pankhurst to task for not standing her ground. 'Why do you permit him to adopt that tone?' May said to her boss, 'I would not tolerate it. I am surprised at you!'[25] I always treasure these small fragments when I find them: minor hints towards lives only preserved because the obscured person worked or lived closely with someone better studied. This moment of May's reported speech suggests the independent-minded personality that would later draw her towards and help her navigate Soviet Moscow.

Among the Bolshevik contacts that Bouvier, May and Nellie encountered through their work on the *Dreadnought* and the Information Bureau was the aforementioned revolutionary and by now Soviet diplomat Maxim Litvinov, husband of the novelist Ivy. Maxim was deported to Russia in September 1918 and reunited with Ivy and his children there a few years later. One of the first publications that the People's Russian Information Bureau released was a 1918 address by Maxim on the situation in Soviet Russia. Later, as members of the Moscow political elite, the Litvinovs would once more cross paths with some of the people they encountered in London, including May.

Pankhurst's Information Bureau was a small strand in a wider world of revolutionary activity. Small it must have been, for its funding came from a mix of sources: subscribers, Bolshevik representatives in London and even salary cuts that May and Nellie volunteered to support the effort.[26]

It was likely around this time that May made a decision that changed the course of her future: she decided to learn Russian. Her tutor may well have been Eugenie Bouvier, whose adverts for Russian-language tuition appeared in the *Dreadnought*. In any case, May would not have lacked Russian-speaking conversational partners in post-war London.

To be able to move between languages was a vital skill in the radical circles of the early twentieth century. In March 1919 the Communist International, the organising body of world communist parties, was formed in Petrograd. The call went out across the world for radicals to form national communist groups that could affiliate with the Comintern, as the International became known. The Comintern was designed to be the guiding light of the world revolution – a kind of administrative centre of global insurrection that would direct and inform those intent on following the Bolshevik example, while also training and guiding future generations of revolutionaries.

Attendant to the desire for a global network of revolutionaries, the Comintern also required people with a specific skill set to occupy its headquarters. Like the League of Nations, its rival in the dream of becoming a world governing body, the Comintern needed multilingual workers who could handle typewriters and understand shorthand. But unlike the League of Nations, for the Comintern it was actively desirable if these workers also boasted experience of the political underground. As it transpired, Sylvia Pankhurst was providing a circle of women in East London with an astonishingly effective training course in administering the world revolution.

5

The People's Russian Information Bureau was one of many radical initiatives launched in the aftermath of the Russian Revolution that remained distinct from the communist parties, whose aims they nonetheless largely shared. There were significant differences between communist *sympathising* organisations and communist parties – one of the most important being the idea of the Party 'cell' and the kinds of discipline it demanded. The Party 'cell', imagined by Lenin during his long pre-revolutionary exile, was designed as a solution to the in-fighting that was endemic to Russian political refugee communities. Political bickering was so common-place that it had its own Russian-language word: *skloki*. The Bolshevik resolution to the perennial leftist dilemma of indecision was ruthless centralisation. This restriction of political pluralism within the movement made natural sense to veterans of the petty interpersonal vendettas and secret police infiltration that dogged Russian political refugees in the decades before the Revolution.

But leftist revolutionaries in Ireland, Britain, the US and elsewhere brought different traditions and experiences to bear on their own national communist parties. Many struggled to emulate Bolshevik practices of conspiracy and organisation. Communist parties beyond Russia were, in their early years, often strange combinations of social worlds, not all of which would remain within the Party fold as the movement developed. The Communist Party of Ireland, first established in October 1921, was a case in point. A year into its existence, the Party described its own original membership as a mix of 'good proletarian elements' muddled together with feminists, trade union 'sycophants' and a cohort of 'budding intellectuals and dashing young revolutionaries'.[27]

It may seem strange that May and Nellie, despite being convinced supporters of the October Revolution, never actually joined a communist party in these years. But party commitment was more than simply the signing of a form and the payment of dues. The Bolshevik model of organisation specified a form of discipline that absorbed enormous amounts of time and energy. Radicals often decided they could better serve the revolution *outside* of the party, in satellite organisations like the People's Russian Information Bureau. Communist sympathisers could navigate worlds and retain roles that card-carrying party members would have needed to renounce.

The two women may have also hesitated in choosing party member-ship because there was more than one communist party formed in

Britain in the early revolutionary years. The East End organisation that employed them became the nucleus of one of these groups, although not the one that ultimately succeeded in receiving Moscow's recognition and support. In the immediate years after the Russian Revolution, Sylvia Pankhurst advocated what many of her comrades regarded as a fatally 'extreme' pathway to British revolution, particularly her rejection of engaging with the British parliament. Pankhurst found herself in an increasingly isolated position on the British far left as various factions worked towards forming a united communist party in 1920. In the summer of that year, Pankhurst formed the Communist Party (British Section of the Third International). Although it was officially formed at a meeting held in the International Club in June 1920, some sources suggest a preliminary meeting that helped lay the foundations of Britain's first communist party was held in a flat on the Gray's Inn Road.[28] This was the very same flat May shared with Nellie and Rose Cohen.[29]

A Moscow archive contains what may well be the only surviving membership cards of Pankhurst's communist organisation. The cards belonged to a Jewish revolutionary named Polya Solovitchich, who was born in Odessa in 1891 and spent more than a decade in London before returning from emigration around 1920. The list of objectives outlined in young Polya's blue membership booklet included the fostering of the 'Social Revolution, which shall dispossess the capitalists without any compensation.' Membership was open to anyone over eighteen, so long as they desired 'a Communist order of society and are prepared to work for a revolution which shall secure it.' If you wanted to overthrow the existing order but were under the age of eighteen, you could join the group's 'junior associates'.[30] Confusingly, Pankhurst's Communist Party (British Section of the Third International) was not actually an official member of the Third International, as the Comintern was also known. It became only one of a wide number of radical groupings that ultimately folded into Britain's longest-lasting communist party in the twentieth century: the Communist Party of Great Britain.

Given the crowded field, it may have been easier, at this point, not to plant your red flag too firmly in any one organisation, since the convulsions of the international movement could lead to yesterday's vanguard party becoming tomorrow's outpost of renegades. The survival stories of those who threw themselves into the revolutionary tumult of the early twentieth century are often of people with good instincts for the right time 'to join' and the best moment 'to leave'.

As May and Nellie's energies were focused on the People's Russian Information Bureau, Sylvia Pankhurst steered the *Dreadnought* in a direction that led her into conflict with her counterparts in the nascent British communist movement. The *Dreadnought*, as a result, became something of a sounding board for those dissenting from the international communist movement's emerging orthodoxies.

One of those dissenting voices was a young writer named Liam O'Flaherty, who wrote for the *Dreadnought* under the pseudonym 'Wobbly'. He would, in time, play a role of major importance in May's life and, through her, in the life of Nellie Cohen. Liam was a founding member of the Communist Party of Ireland. His brother Tom was a founding member of the US Communist Party, forced initially to title itself the 'Workers' Party' to avoid government suppression in the febrile atmosphere of the first American 'red scare'. Both were born and raised in a tiny cottage on the small island of Inis Mór, located off Ireland's rugged western coast. Irish communists would come to regret accepting Liam into their ranks in the early 1920s and by the late 1920s Tom also found himself expelled from the party he helped establish. Less than a year after joining its initial roster of cadres, Liam left the Irish organisation behind and made his way to London. Here he began to seriously pursue a writing career. The *Dreadnought* published some of his first writings to find their way into print.

In deference to convention, let us introduce Liam further by dwelling on the feature that many memoirists and contemporaries took some time to describe: his blue eyes. Chester A. Arthur III, the IRA-supporting queer grandson of the twenty-first US President, encountered Liam in Dublin in the 1920s and found himself seized by the 'electric flashes' from Liam's 'sea-blue eyes'.[31] The islander's eyes evoked another nautical reference point for Francis Stuart, Irish writer and Nazi propagandist during the war years, who compared them to the piercing eyes of a seagull.[32] Ethel Mannin, prolific English novelist and one-time anarchist, described Liam's eyes as the core of his legend, 'for it was said of him that he had only to turn his intensely blue eyes on a woman for her to fall into his arms'.[33] 'I had always wanted to meet him,' Mannin continued, 'to prove that it was not necessarily so.'

It is not clear when exactly May and Nellie first looked into Liam's electric, gull-like, entrancing blue eyes. Was it in 1922, when he arrived in London and briefly became attached to the *Dreadnought*? More likely it was later in the same decade, when we know for certain that Nellie succumbed to Liam's legendary powers of seduction. We can assume, however, that the two women probably heard of the act for which he became known in 1922: a quixotic attempt to hasten an Irish workers' revolution by seizing a central Dublin concert hall.

The Rotunda

1

On a Wednesday afternoon in January 1922, with the semi-independent Irish state only a few weeks old, a band of roughly one hundred men entered the Rotunda, a large building in central Dublin, ostensibly to attend a meeting of the unemployed. When time allocated for the meeting expired, Mr Kay, the venue manager, attempted to clear out the attendees. But rather than leave the premises, the assembled men insisted on seizing the building, flying a red flag from a window and declaring a Council of the Unemployed. 'All of our people were working men,' remembered one participant in the seizure (except for 'one minor crook').[1] Of all the means to extend a venue booking, declaring the meeting room the nucleus of a Soviet Republic was one of the more inventive methods.

There was no shortage of the curious or outlandish in Dublin city in 1922, a year that saw British soldiers finally departing their garrisons while a formerly insurrectionary faction of Irish nationalists became the latest contested authority to govern the capital. A movement once united behind an overall goal of ridding Ireland of British rule became divided over the terms of a treaty between the British government and representatives of Irish republican forces signed in December 1921. The treaty, in the arguments of its ultimately victorious defenders, brought limited independence for Ireland. However, the 'anti-treaty' forces – which included Ireland's fledgling communist party – viewed the treaty as a betrayal that subjected Ireland to continued subjugation under British imperialism. High-stakes political ideas coursed through an island with a tightly interlinked population. This fostered an Irish public well accustomed to attending rallies in support of their cause or denouncing the causes of others. People continued heading out onto town squares and city centres as the country moved towards the island-wide Civil War that would erupt in the summer of 1922.

Months before the Civil War began, the Irish penchant for political spectacle brought a steady stream of onlookers to the Rotunda. Inside, men could be heard drilling and even holding impromptu concerts. One reporter entered the building on the Thursday morning to find the men 'being marshalled by their section leaders', one of whom, 'Mr. Liam O'Flaherty', had been styled 'the "Commander-in-Chief" by his followers'.[2]

Liam O'Flaherty's biography before he walked into the Rotunda as the would-be leader of a new Irish insurrection included a failed vocation in the priesthood, soldiering in Belgian trenches, direct impact from an explosion, the onset of shell-shock, a round-the-world trip, a stint in an American rubber factory, numerous roles on ships, the burned manuscripts of his attempted novels, radicalisation towards anarchism, radicalisation towards socialism and radicalisation towards communism. It was a lot to have experienced before the age of twenty-five.

2

No cottage on the Atlantic seaboard contributed more to the world revolution of the early twentieth century than the O'Flaherty homestead on the island of Inis Mór. Nestled between pathways with names that make your tongue roll about your mouth, like Meenabool and Ballinacregg, the thatched cottage faces towards the mainland. It was under this thatched roof in 1896 that Liam entered the world, one of two boys and seven girls born to a Catholic father and a Protestant mother on the largest of the three Aran islands. His older brother, Tom, born in 1890, would prove an important influence on Liam. Maidhc, their father, was an agitator who spent time imprisoned for his violent contributions to the Irish Land War. Liam remembered how their mother, Molly, when combing the hair of her two boys, would recount her marriage like a fairy tale: the story of a handsome man travelling to a house by horseback to steal his lover away in the night and marry her by dawn.[3] But the fairy tale, it seems, ended shortly thereafter. Molly, Tom later wrote in a piece of autobiographical fiction, did not understand that she had fallen in love with and married 'an incurable rebel, and not an ordinary husband'.[4] Raising incurable rebels, and not ordinary sons, must have only compounded her situation.

A schoolmaster sent over from the mainland was the first to cultivate the intellectual talent of the two O'Flaherty boys. The teacher may well have been shocked by the results of his encouragement. In an autobiographical note describing his path to becoming a writer, Liam described his first attempt at fiction. It was a story he wrote for the schoolmaster when he was around seven years old. The tale described a husband murdering his wife for the infraction of bringing him cold tea. The point of the story, as Liam later remembered it, was that the murderer could not fit his wife, 'who was very large', into the concealing place of her corpse.[5] Liam also claimed that, aged eleven, he decided to write a novel together with his brother Tom. In what would become something of a pattern, Liam then decided he would do it all himself and upended the collaborative project.

Early political influences were absorbed from their rebel father and the entire family were raised as republicans. Liam claimed that Tom became a socialist even before leaving Inis Mór. Upon hearing that the Pope had denounced republicanism *and* socialism, Tom, already a republican, decided to be a socialist too. In his late teens Tom left the island, bound for the US. He soon became a familiar figure in Chicago's circles of socialist journalists and radical barflies.

Meanwhile, Liam was educated in Rockwell College in Tipperary and later Blackrock College in Dublin, elite Irish-Catholic schools that cultivated many of their students for the priesthood. Liam was both rebellious and literary-minded. In one alleged incident recorded in O'Flaherty family lore, the teenage Liam horrified Aran-bound ferry passengers by reading aloud the scene in Dostoevsky's *Crime and Punishment* where Raskolnikov murders the elderly pawnbroker.[6]

After secondary school, Liam attended University College Dublin, where he studied during the early years of the First World War. 'They were very exciting times in Dublin,' Liam remembered, with everyone 'enthused with some sort of war mania'.[7] He described his politics in these years as a mix of Irish republicanism and anarchism. Without finishing his degree, Liam enlisted in the British Army in 1916 under his mother's surname, Ganly. He served with the Irish Guards on the Western Front. In an unconvincing justification, Liam later claimed that he joined up 'with the intention of deserting to the German army' since he believed, as did some other Irish nationalists, that the Germans, as opponents of Britain, were ultimately fighting towards similar ends.[8] Even for someone as unpredictable as Liam, joining the British Army to fight the British Army seems like a bizarre move. A need for employment, his lifelong inability to remain in one location for long and a related desire for adventure were more likely motives.

As a rule, Liam's autobiographical writings must be treated with scepticism. His self-narratives traced his evolution from a wild child of Ireland's West to the bad boy of radical London letters. But they were often sensational stories designed to construct Liam as a rebel and rogue; and only rarely did they reveal his vulnerabilities. Many of these can be traced to an experience in September 1917 when Liam survived a shell hit in Langemark, Belgium. Invalided out of the war, he developed 'shell-shock', what we would now term lifelong post-traumatic stress disorder. The legacy of Liam's war was a profound psychological wound. In the trenches, the boy of Aran became a damaged man.

Liam's suggestion that his wartime service was a moment of deep importance in his political development is, however, more believable than some of his other tall tales. He recalled that he met a fellow soldier from Scotland, a socialist, who converted Liam to a world view he described as a 'faith'.[9] In the trenches and the internment camps, Liam mingled with an array of working-class men; French soldiers, English soldiers, German prisoners and troops from more distant corners of the British Empire recruited into its defence. 'I attribute the awakening of my conscious mind to this experience,' Liam noted in 1926.[10] Upon his return to Ireland after his injury, he spent some time recuperating at home on the Aran Islands before wanderlust set in once more and he left, in his own words, 'to conquer the world'.[11]

Working in a variety of jobs, from foreman in a brewery to dishwasher, pastry chef, dynamite handler and biscuit-factory worker, Liam's travels left behind a global biscuit-crumb trail across many nations, including Italy, Turkey, Greece, the US, Brazil, Belgium and the Netherlands. In the US he reconnected with his brother Tom, who introduced him to American radical circles, settling Liam more firmly with his latest political conviction: communism. According to an unreliable source, himself, Liam spent several months at home in early 1921 mediating on the 'uncertainty of life'.[12] Seemingly having failed to find resolution on life's uncertainties, he set out travelling once more. He returned to Ireland again at the end of 1921 and joined the newly formed Communist Party of Ireland. The world unconquered, he set out to conquer a Dublin meeting hall.

3

On the second day of Liam's occupation of the Rotunda, curious onlookers gathered to read the manifesto posted on the entrance and doors of the building. Jim Phelan, one of Liam's co-conspirators, was particularly enthused by the manifesto, stating that a work of its like had not been seen 'since the days of the American War of Independence and the first French Revolution'.[13] The author of the document, naturally, was Liam O'Flaherty.

As the manifesto was seen on walls throughout the city, a red flag fluttered from an elevated window of the Rotunda. A local tobacconist passed cigarettes through to the occupiers and a bakery supplied bread to the hungry insurrectionists. But as the men tucked into their solidarity loaves inside this small, smoke-filled nucleus of a workers' republic, clouds of hostility gathered outside. While the supply lines into the Rotunda suggest some sympathy among Dubliners for the occupiers' aims, this solidarity did not manifest where it mattered most: on the streets outside.

Initially, there had been a wide welcome for the Russian Revolution in Dublin, with thousands reported in attendance for a 'Russian Republic Reception Meeting' in 1918. Yet the political dynamics of popular revolt in Ireland were divergent from what the Bolsheviks found in the Russian Empire, as Liam and his comrades should have surmised from the confrontational crowd gathering outside the Rotunda by the third evening of their occupation. While the Russian Revolution was first welcomed by many in Ireland as a broader blow against imperialism, reports of Bolshevik anti-religiosity were already beginning to find an audience among the majority-Catholic and largely devout Irish population. According to his own memoirs, a few months after the occupation, Liam overheard a woman telling a companion that O'Flaherty, the man who shot those who refused 'to spit on the holy crucifix' and 'tried to sell Dublin to the Bolsheviks', had been killed in a conflagration during the opening salvos of the Irish Civil War.[14] The rumour was erroneous in all its details, but Liam nonetheless took it as a sign that prospects for an Irish workers' revolution had all but vanished.

On Friday, the third day that the red flag flew over the Rotunda, a sizeable hostile crowd gathered outside. The first signs of an impending attack were stones thrown through the windows, which left the meeting-hall floor covered with broken glass. The offensive began falteringly when a young man attempted to capture the red flag but fell from the building. Once a party from the assembled strike-breakers had carried their failed flag-taker to a nearby hospital, another attempt on this symbol of the unemployed was undertaken. This time they were successful. Following their capture of the red flag, the attackers, reported as three hundred in number, stormed the building. Fist-fighting between the occupiers and the intruders ensued after a makeshift barricade set up by the garrison of the unemployed was quickly destroyed.[15] The Dublin Metropolitan Police, supported by the army of the young Irish state, managed to push the crowds back to adjoining streets. Another red flag emerged from a different window to replace the flag that was seized.[16] Before midnight on Saturday, the Council of the Unemployed disbanded and its foot soldiers dispersed through a side door under cover of darkness. The leaders of the occupation, the last to leave, marched slowly out of the Rotunda.

The red flag had been flying from the window of the Workers' Republic of the Dublin Rotunda for little more than four days. One of the red flags flown during the occupation was wrapped up and posted to New York, where Liam's brother Tom helped to offer it as a reward in a raffle to support communist prisoners.[17] The Rotunda occupation failed to inspire the flame of proletarian insurrection that enveloped other European capitals. Ireland lacked the kindling necessary to spark a widescale workers' revolt despite the sincere anti-colonialism that forcefully made its presence felt throughout the country. Yet, for all its seeming futility, the 'Rotunda Comedy', as one newspaper revealingly titled it, found a central character in our story exiting through a side door and onto the stage of Irish history.[18] With all the tenacity and bluster that would characterise his later career, Liam O'Flaherty debuted something that carried much of the tempestuousness of a workers' revolt: himself.

His superiors in the Communist Party of Ireland were not impressed. A report on 'The Case of O'Flaherty' was dispatched to Soviet Russia for perusal in the headquarters of the world revolution. Penned by one of Liam's former comrades, the report censured his 'childish actions', depicting Liam, with some justification, as an intemperate rogue whose interest in the revolutionary movement extended no further beyond an interest in himself. Among Liam's other infractions listed in the report was how, following the Rotunda occupation, he relentlessly argued that the 'time was ripe' for an armed communist militia in Ireland.[19] The Party relented and agreed to the plan, only for Liam to immediately resign when he was not elected as an officer. Insubordination was clearly a problem for the young party. In a pointed jibe at undisciplined cadre, the Irish communist paper the *Workers' Republic* printed a satirical guide to being a revolutionary in 1923. 'Dream of yourself as the coming Lenin,' the paper quipped. 'It's a helluva lot easier than doing his work.'[20] Liam's actions led to his suspension from the Party and, after participating in the early part of the Irish Civil War on the side of the anti-Treaty IRA, he departed Ireland for London.

Liam O'Flaherty entered each new chapter of his life illuminated by the flames of bridges burning behind him. Profound character flaws metastasised inside him and were transformed into a kind of personal magnetism. He was a brilliant writer liable to say and do objectionable or downright appalling things, yet his personality nonetheless drew people towards him. What made others forgive him his many flaws? Was it his clear talent? Or was it an impression that behind his attempt to make himself a protagonist of his century lay the fact that he was, already, one of its victims? 'One couldn't help liking O'Flaherty,' wrote the actor Constance Malleson, and that, she imagined, 'was the whole trouble'. 'Maybe,' she wondered, 'what he was in need of was a good murdering.'[21]

Arriving in London in 1922, Liam set down more seriously to write and finally moved towards something approximating a settled life. He began work on the first of his published novels and wrote political articles for radical journals, including the *Dreadnought*. In a strange and unreliable memoir published in 1930, he suggested that he first encountered the *Dreadnought* on an earlier foray in London during his wandering years. He viewed it as a 'series of badly written but vituperative articles denouncing individuals and groups who held practically the same opinions as itself'.[22] If this was his impression of the *Dreadnought* when he first perused the publication, it did not stop him from contributing his own vituperative articles. In this way Liam joined the chain of itinerant writer-revolutionaries who, like May and the Cohen sisters, encountered Sylvia Pankhurst and her East End women comrades and ensured the *Dreadnought* continued to find its way into the hands of readers.

A Nest of Revolution

1

In a 1920 book titled *The Red Terror and the Green*, the anti-socialist writer Richard Dawson interlaced insider knowledge from British intelligence with undiluted paranoia and antisemitic canards. The aim of Dawson's terrifying tapestry was to depict for his readers a red-green web of collaborations between members of the Irish nationalist movement Sinn Féin and Russian revolutionaries that he termed the 'Sinn Féin-Bolshevist conspiracy'. Inviting his readers to peer inside the offices at 400 Old Ford Road, Dawson unveiled Sylvia Pankhurst's 'nest of revolution': home of a conspiracy connecting together Irish feminists, Russian radicals and domestic revolutionaries.[1] What made Pankhurst's organisation so threatening in the eyes of some opponents was precisely what made it such a vibrant world for visiting revolutionaries: its internationalism, which was rooted in the migrant London district where it first made its mark.

One radical who testified in more grounded terms to Pankhurst's capacity to draw in visiting revolutionaries from across the world was Claude McKay, a Jamaican writer best known for his contributions to the Harlem Renaissance of the 1920s. At the time that Claude McKay encountered Pankhurst's group, it was known as the Workers' Socialist Federation, another name change and another step beyond its origins as the WSPU, East London Branch. Each transformation resulted in a loss of certain members and the gaining of others, particularly as the broader aims of the organisation beyond suffrage drew in further acolytes and frustrated those committed primarily to feminist ends. But there was always a corps of dedicated members who worked alongside Pankhurst, from the launch of the *Woman's Dreadnought* into the final years of the *Workers' Dreadnought*. Among them were May, her Russian-born colleague Eugenie Bouvier and Norah Smyth, a wealthy Pankhurst acolyte from a well-heeled Anglo-Irish family who was once observed by a Special Branch agent pronouncing before a small audience at 400 Old Ford Road that she would welcome a revolution, 'a bloody one if needs be'.[2]

Claude McKay's thoughts on the coming revolution were that it needed to be an anti-racist one. On Pankhurst's paper, he found a welcoming platform from which he could make his argument. Black sailors were often present on the East End docks and sometimes the victims of racist hostility. The *Dreadnought* took an editorial line against these attacks. In 1919, before he arrived in London, the paper published McKay's famous poem responding to the US race riots 'If we must die'.[3] In his first contribution to the *Dreadnought*, published in January 1920 and titled 'Socialism and the Negro', McKay argued for English socialists to understand the importance of anti-colonial nationalism within the wider scope of the worldwide socialist revolution. He called particular attention to English radical antipathy towards the Irish cause as a result of it being 'nationalistic'.[4] He would develop this argument and take it all the way to Soviet Russia as a delegate to the fourth congress of the Communist International in 1922.

The *Dreadnought*, as scholar Anne Donlon points out, was 'exceptional among left British publications for its inclusion of black writers and attention to African and African-diasporic viewpoints'.[5] For May and Nellie, this exceptional figure of a Jamaican writer regularly hitting away at his typewriter in their shared office surely made an impression. Towards the end of her life, when Nellie was in her eighties, she could not recall McKay's name but remembered the 'West Indian' who once frequented the Fleet Street offices.[6]

McKay, for his part, later recorded some impressions of this London radical world in an article published just after his return to the US in which he described a particularly vivid moment in the summer of 1920 when he stood in Trafalgar Square selling a pamphlet that included articles on Ireland written by May and Pankhurst. All around him, supporters of the Irish cause were gathering to hear a rally addressed by Irish republicans. McKay, wearing a green necktie, was greeted enthusiastically by the attendees as 'Black Irish' and 'Black Murphy'. 'For that day at least I was filled with the spirit of Irish nationalism – although I am black!' McKay reported.[7]

2

In March 1921 McKay reached out to a young friend whom he heard was making his way to London. McKay wanted to advise him on how to enter the London radical scene and wrote, 'If you ever want to meet some real proletarians in London who have no regular passport to intellectualism, I know of a club in City Road where you could drop in.'[8] The International Club was a 'real den for revolutionary working folk', McKay observed, 'quite rough but once in a while one meets "artists" and "intellectuals" there'.[9] The recipient of the letter was Joseph Freeman, by then a rising talent on the New York left-wing literary scene.

When I first encountered this letter in a California archive, it set my imagination racing. Joseph Freeman was the very same young poet whose 1936 account of life in Soviet Moscow had first set me in search of May. This letter from a Jamaican writer to his fellow migrant poet and friend was a tantalising suggestion that years before befriending one another in the Hotel Lux, Joseph and May could have brushed past one another in London's revolutionary haunts. This brief glimpse was a keyhole into a profoundly inter-linked world. Even in a global radical network, people were constantly connected by small degrees of separation.

McKay's impressions of life in radical London in his letters and articles reflected something that authorities feared and which, in fact, existed: plans for revolutionary activities. These plans were being hatched in the same offices where more quotidian-seeming activities were being carried out, such as translation work, news-paper editing and pamphlet printing. May and Nellie were certainly aware of the conspiratorial activities of their boss, if not actual participants in Pankhurst's revolutionary scheming. Certainly, the two friends witnessed some of the consequences. Nellie recalled a police raid on Fleet Street that took place when she was in the office alone. Four detectives arrived to take away items that might be used as evidence, including Pankhurst's duplicator machine. 'It was great fun,' Nellie remembered.[10]

Around this time, in October 1920, Sylvia Pankhurst was arrested under the Defence of the Realm Act and spent six months imprisoned for publishing articles in the *Dreadnought* deemed to be seditious.[11]

By the time of her imprisonment in late 1920, Pankhurst's red star was no longer ascending. The personnel file on Pankhurst in the Comintern archives is surprisingly slim for a woman who once held a formidable reputation as a British revolutionary.[12] Among the few documents that I found relating to Pankhurst in the Moscow archives was a declaration of solidarity with Pankhurst from the 'Women Workers of Moscow', likely dating to the period of her imprisonment. The document asserted: 'We, full-fledged citizen-women workers of the workers' republic, the first in the world, send fiery greetings to the chief enemies of the capitalists, the landlords, the rich: Comrade Sylvia Pankhurst and the English women workers and working men, who we exhort to insurrection.'[13] Pankhurst's insistence on a political line independent of that suggested by Lenin (who, in contrast to Pankhurst, believed British communists should engage with parliament) made her position in the fledgling British communist movement untenable. She was expelled from the Communist Party of Great Britain in September 1921.[14]

Pankhurst's expulsion reflected both a major organisational strength of the Comintern that distinguished it from its rivals and something that would gradually repulse, and even endanger, many of its members: its disciplined adherence to a defined political course. Interested in militating for nothing less than a worldwide revolution, the Comintern anticipated that its leadership would become that revolution's general staff: a kind of global secretariat directing the new revolutionary states towards communism. The scars of the Bolsheviks' exile experience fostered their devotion to the notion of 'iron discipline'. Already by its Second Congress, the Comintern adopted a list of twenty-one conditions of admission for parties seeking to join the organisation, which included undertaking a commitment to purging their membership of 'unreliable elements'. But some comrades later cast off from the movement for their 'unreliability' would read the real reason for their expulsion as being their independent-mindedness.

May and Nellie appear to have drifted from Pankhurst's orbit during her imprisonment. As Pankhurst set out, after her expulsion, to pursue dissident communist politics that critiqued the Bolshevik model from the left, May and Nellie did not follow her. Both women ended up on the margins of the circles that folded into the Communist Party of Great Britain. It was this party, and not Pankhurst's organisation, that would receive official recognition from the Communist International and remain aligned with the Soviet Union to the bitter end. Although not card-carrying members nor workers for the party, May and Nellie did know someone at the heart of Britain's nascent movement – indeed, someone who appears to have been close to the hearts of many of its leading figures: Nellie's younger sister, Rose.

3

A photograph from 1916 captures a parade of young women participating in a spring pageant organised by the East London Federation of Suffragettes, the original incarnation of Sylvia Pankhurst's East End group before its journey through revolutionary politics. In a memoir of the war years published in 1932, Pankhurst recalled the scene, her memory drifting to the 'two pretty Cohens, one as slender as the lily she represented and the other, Nellie, my secretary, glowing ripe as a peach'.[15] At least three of the women in the photograph eventually found their way to Moscow. Two would live and work in the Soviet capital. One, Rose Cohen, the woman whom Pankhurst described being 'as slender as the lily she represented', died there.

Often remembered by contemporaries as intelligent and charming, Rose was a bright young star on the early communist scene. Her entry into political life came through attending classes at the Workers Educational Association and a job on the London City Council. She then left her council role for work with the Labour Research Department, a small outfit that supplied British communism with some of its first intellectual guiding lights. The Christian socialist Maurice B. Reckitt, who passed through this social world, recalled Rose Cohen later in his memoir. He described her as one member of a small socialist milieu that often gathered at the private residence of a comrade in the London borough of Kensington. Among them was Norman Ewer, later a Soviet spy, Daisy Lansbury, former flat-mate of May and the Cohens, and a young Oxford dropout from a wealthy Liverpool merchant family named Hugo Rathbone.

Reckitt remembered Rose as a 'girl of great vivacity and charm', with 'black hair and a fresh complexion';[16] she 'was probably the most popular individual in our little movement'.[17] Much as her tragic fate would later unsettle him, Reckitt considered it 'natural' that someone with her 'ardent spirit' plunged into 'the Communist tide which flowed so strongly in 1920'.[18]

That tide, as it became increasingly clear, was carrying its international adherents in one direction: towards the crucible of the world revolution – Moscow. Initially, Petrograd rivalled it as the destination of choice in the young workers' republic, but soon the organs of the international communist movement became centralised within the new capital that also housed the major seat of Soviet power, the Kremlin.

Paris, Berlin and Amsterdam, where the Comintern maintained western outposts and circles of employed revolutionaries, were also important destinations for the emerging class of border-hopping activists. Rose Cohen visited many of these revolutionary hubs in the years following her entry into the British movement as a founding member of the Communist Party of Great Britain.[19] Yet Moscow would become the most important city in her political life.

In the regal and repurposed surroundings of former palaces and grand imperial halls, revolutionary travellers made the case for why their movement should be regarded as *the* official banner holder of Bolshevism in their home country. Radicals carried references to ease their passage through the underground. One such reference I found in a Moscow archive belonged to a member of Pankhurst's communist group named Frank Saunders. Comrade Saunders was despatched to Soviet Russia in late 1920 to act as the organisation's representative to the Comintern. On cloth paper, the national secretary of the party wrote: 'The bearer of this credential, comrade Frank Saunders has been chosen as representative of this party at headquarters of Communist International. All Communists are asked to aid him on his journey.'[20] Using various pathways, by land and sea, individuals figured out ways of being the first among their comrades to visit Russia or return from political exile to post-revolutionary homelands. Out of the women who shared a flat on the Gray's Inn Road in central London, it was young Rose Cohen who won the race to reach the Soviet capital.

In the summer of 1923 Rose wrote letters to a young man back in London. Esmonde Higgins, an Australian communist who joined the young British Communist movement after returning from a 1920 trip to the Soviet republic, had become enchanted with Rose. It is clear from a July letter that 'Hig', as Rose knew him, had confessed his feelings. The romance, alas, was unrequited. 'We were such comrades and there it seemed to begin and end,' Rose wrote. 'Hig, I'm most frightfully sorry – more sorry than I can say – but it really is impossible,' she continued, before bringing the letter to a close with an olive branch: 'There's no reason why we shouldn't continue to be chums, is there? But don't write if you would rather not.'[21] At the top of the letter, Rose Cohen listed her address as the Hotel Lux, Moscow.

A Tomb of Revolution

Moscow, September 2018

3. Former site of the Hotel Lux, Tverskaya, 2018. Author photograph

1

In the soft heat of an Indian summer in Moscow, I stood before the crumbling walls of a former hotel. Sticking my head through the iron grate that guarded the entrance, I listened to the sound of drills and hammers echoing through the void of a building site. A poster on the wall declared that a new hotel was under construction, but the estimated completion date was already years in the past. There was nothing – not even a small plaque – to mark the fact that this site, once intimately known to radicals and the secret police who trailed them across the globe, was once the location of the most remarkable hotel in modern history. For decades, this building was more than simply a hotel – it was the living quarters of the international revolutionary elite: the Hotel Lux.

If you had arrived at this building at number thirty-six on Moscow's Tverskaya Street at any point from the years after the Russian Revolution in 1917 until Hitler's invasion of the Soviet Union in 1941, you would have encountered far more than simply an empty shell. Above the door, the hotel's name was listed in both the Cyrillic and Latin alphabets. Passing through to the foyer, a stern clerk would have greeted you with a brief interrogation, asking for your name, the name of the person you were visiting and handing you a time sheet to be filled on entry and exit. If you had even the slightest curiosity about the task of building a revolutionary world order, you would have gladly accepted the receptionist's demands.

The variety of human life that flows through hotels makes them ideal settings for tales of romance and political intrigue. The Lux, a premises that was already decrepit by the time the earliest revolutionary migrants arrived, was closer to the dingy surroundings of Joseph Roth's Hotel Savoy than the glamorous residences frequented by Agatha Christie's Miss Marple. But even a novelist would struggle to imagine a hotel where the political wrangling was more subversive and the relationships more intense than the Lux. Diversity defined the residents, but they did have one thing in common: they were all communists. Nowadays, it can be hard to recapture the sense of hope that underpinned this grand human project to which so many once dedicated their lives. The Berlin Wall came down and, eventually, the old Lux fell into dereliction. Yet you do not need to travel far from the hotel's former site to find documents that help us to imaginatively reconstruct this building and recapture the extraordinary idealism that ensured the hotel's near-constant full occupancy.

A marble Lenin leans out of his seat on a nearby square, poised as though the pigeons congregating on his head have just awoken him from his slumber. He guards an imposing institution almost as old as the revolution he led. Here, in the Russian State Archive for Socio-Political History, founded in 1918, archivists maintain the final remains of the last great attempt to incite and direct a world revolution. Miles of methodically organised boxes preserve statements of love, betrayal, insurrection and intense bureaucracy.

Taken as a whole, these documents form the archive of the Comintern. For most of the twentieth century only leading Communist Party members, secret police and trusted students of Marxist-Leninist history were permitted to pass beneath the imposing facade of Marx, Engels and Lenin that stands above the building's entrance. But restrictions reduced dramatically following the Soviet collapse. The eyes of historians swept like searchlights over tens of thousands of documents, illuminating a past that few believed would emerge from darkness in their lifetimes.

Most researchers with the patience to navigate Russian visa bureaucracy could access the archive from the 1990s onwards. I was among those who believed this arrangement would remain in place indefinitely. I was also among those who believed that the era of full-scale land warfare in Europe had ended. At the time of writing, the Moscow archives are much more difficult to access for most western researchers.

But when I arrived in September 2018, the portents of a darker future for Russia were difficult for me to discern. Moscow and several other Russian cities had just hosted the FIFA World Cup. The fans of national teams brought a greater vibrancy to the capital. The after-effects of that excitement and cultural diversity still lingered in many parts of the city when I arrived. It is only in hindsight that I have been able to notice the kinds of historical remembrance that, although perceivable in Moscow in 2018, would, within years, become taboo and even illegal.

Much of Moscow seemed familiar. Even before the world watched France beat Croatia in the Luzhniki Stadium, decades of post-Soviet transformation had westernised much of the city. The metro stops were announced in both Russian and English, the fast-food options were mostly recognisable and the Russian term for 'flat white' was pronounced 'flat white'. While in the queue for Lenin's mausoleum in a morning before an archival session, I realised that one of the few recognisable Moscow sights common to both myself and the people from my research was Lenin's preserved corpse. Nonetheless, I tried to retrace, to the best of my abilities, the footsteps of the political emigrants who came to Moscow in the 1920s. Each day I walked home from the archives on a similar route to that followed by the Comintern workers as they made their way to their offices: from the Lux, by the Kremlin and into the Comintern headquarters on Mokhovaya Street.

2

The journey from the Hotel Lux to Mokhovaya took me a brisk thirty minutes on foot. In the 1920s it would have been easily traversed by tram, taxi or *drozhki*, horse-drawn carts. The apartment where I was staying was a further walk from the old Comintern building, near the metro station for Gorky Park. When I arrived in Moscow the capital was preparing to celebrate its 'city day'. Stages and barriers were being prepared. Large sections of Tverskaya Street, the wide avenue that slopes down towards Red Square, were due to be pedes-trianised for the occasion. An old Soviet guide book published in 1925 informed me that Tverskaya, in addition to the Lux, was also the address of the Central Office for Emigrants and home to a mural of the executed revolutionary Rosa Luxemburg, adorned with the phrase: 'The Revolution is a storm which blows away anything that stands in its way.'[1] Neither sight survived the almost-one-hundred years between the guide book's publication and my visit.

Further down Tverskaya from where this mural would have stood, I passed Moscow's Central Telegraph Building. This signalled the point at which Gazetny Street angled off from Tverskaya. On one walk, I fulfilled a favour that a friend in Ireland had asked me to carry out on Gazetny. Mairead, a woman I met through my research, had asked me to visit the final Moscow address of her father and remember him there. Born in Belfast in 1937, Mairead was the daughter of Irish radicals who met in Soviet Russia. Her parents, Patrick Breslin and Daisy McMackin, are known to Irish historians both for their translation work from Russian and the tragedy at the heart of their love story. Patrick was one of only three Irish victims of the Stalinist terror. Arrested in Moscow in December 1940, he died in 1941 in a prison camp near Kazan. He never met his daughter, Mairead.

At the time of his arrest, Patrick's registered residence was an apartment on this side street by Moscow's Central Telegraph building. As I approached Patrick's building number, I saw a sign with an Irish flag jutting out of the wall. The accidental poetry of the universe had placed an Irish pub called the Stag's Head opposite a Moscow address where an Irishman spent his final years in the 1930s. I stood on the street and took in the moment, thinking through the layers of time that separated the city from the Moscow of Patrick Breslin.

While Breslin's final Moscow address was marked only by an Irish pub, an accident rather than any intentional commemoration, the last addresses of many other Moscow residents imprisoned and executed during the Stalinist purges were physically marked on buildings with small steel plaques. The plaques were the initiative of the Russian NGO Memorial, whose work focuses on investigating human rights abuses and on commemorating the victims of Soviet political persecution.

Posledny Adres, or 'Last Address', is the name given to Memorial's plaque project. Each plaque contains the name and dates of an individual, their profession, the date they were arrested, the date they were executed and normally the date of their posthumous rehabilitation. An empty square in each plaque evokes the small portrait photographs that the secret police took of arrestees. The Russian word *rasstreliat* is featured on many plaques. When pronounced, the first syllable of the word whistles like a bullet cutting through air: it translates as 'shot'. The blunt phrasing pierces through the obfuscation implicit in the Soviet-era textbooks and biographical entries that give someone's year of death as 1937 without a clear indication of why so many lives were cut short in those months.

Like the *Stolpersteine*, concrete cubes laid on streets across Europe to mark the former addresses of victims of Nazism, the Last Address plaques plot the path that repression took through the topography of urban life. The plaques also reflect the Soviet practice of *memorialnaya doska*, the wide-scale erection of plaques marking major and minor points in revolutionary history ('Lenin slept here on this date', 'Lenin met comrade so-and-so here on this date').[2] The Last Address plaques are, in a sense, *memorialnaya doska* taken to their logical conclusion. What would a city look like if it marked every moment of heroism and tragedy experienced by every actor in the drama of its twentieth century? I did my best to pay attention to the plaques I encountered and visited one that marks the life and death of a young writer who features on these pages.

Moving along the Moscow city walls pockmarked with memorials to heroism and tragedy, I walked further away from the archives down the lengthy street. The Kremlin's red walls came into sight as I reached the bottom of Tverskaya. At this spot, so my old Soviet guide book from the 1920s told me, a statue of a tsarist general had been replaced with an obelisk commemorating the October Revolution and a bronze plaque engraved with the first Soviet constitution. I saw that neither tsarist nor Soviet history were now marked on the same spot.[3] All I could see were advertisements, traffic and the imposing walls of the Kremlin complex, its ochre brickwork rising from the Alexander Garden. Here, the road branches in two directions, along Teatralnaya Street, which curves passed the Bolshoi Theatre and finishes where the tragic final acts of so many lives were plotted: the Lubyanka building. Since the early years of Bolshevik rule, this building has stood to many Moscow residents as a symbol of state repression. Throughout the Soviet era, it hosted Soviet secret police operating under their various titles: founded in 1917 as the Cheka, the force became known as the OGPU in 1923, which was absorbed into a broader force called the NKVD in 1934, which was then retitled the KGB following Stalin's death. Today it is owned by the FSB (Federal Security Service), the KGB's modern-day successor.

But my journey home took me down the other route: along Mokhovaya Street rather than Teatralnaya, and thus away from such ominous surroundings. Wide and clean like so many central Moscow streets, Mokhovaya is lined with imperial buildings. One of these buildings, the old Comintern headquarters, once hosted the most virulent scourges of international capitalism to have ever gathered on one premises. Now it contains a gift store selling generic Moscow tourist tat. Through the gift store windows you can see the Russian State Library, still referred to by locals as the Lenin Library.

Before I walked the final stretch of road to my apartment, I would often spend the evening in a reading room of the Russian State Library overseen by yet another marble statue of a seated Lenin. One evening I recognised a colleague sitting at one of the desks; another historian whom I knew from my university. We spoke quietly as I stood by her table in the reading room, surprised to cross paths so far from our usual haunts in the libraries of Oxford. She invited me to join her at a lecture taking place that evening, hosted by Memorial in their Moscow office.

We returned our books to the desk and took a taxi together to the venue. Although it was difficult to keep up with their conversation, I understood that my colleague and the taxi driver, a middle-aged man, were discussing Putin's rule. Experiences like this made me feel as though I was in just another normal European society. Sure, there were restrictions here and there and a heavier police presence, but ultimately Russia seemed like a place where you could at least criticise your leaders, if not easily vote them out.

Arriving at the Memorial building, I learned the subject of the lecture was the mass arrest of Polish nationals during the 1930s terror. Although I once more struggled to keep pace with the lecturer's academic Russian, I was content to simply sit in a room of people seriously attempting to make sense of the past. I felt (and still believe) that a serious and self-critical reckoning with a darker past is important for all nations and movements.

In October 2021 Memorial organised a screening of a film about the Holodomor, the 1932–3 famine in Ukraine. The screening was held in the same building where I heard a lecturer speak on Polish victims of the terror in 2018. A mob of thirty people interrupted the screening. This was followed by a police raid on the Memorial offices.[4] When I visited the offices only a few years before, I felt no fear of any unwanted intrusion. The prospect of being unlawfully detained by police also seemed remote. In Moscow, I would learn, history always moves at a rapid pace. It is true: ominous clouds were already gathering in 2018. But I would not have believed then that Russia's full-scale invasion of sovereign Ukraine would be the storm that finally hit.

Progress is never linear nor inevitable. As I write this chapter, in the summer of 2023, the 'Last Address' plaques are being removed from the walls of buildings in Moscow. The lives of those remembered in them – so many of whom were sincere believers in the idea that a new and more beautiful future was being built around them – are being dismembered once more by the paroxysms of the alternative future that emerged in the wake of their emancipatory projects.

Yet commemoration takes many forms beyond the erection of physical monuments. To write about the people of the past is to remember them in the original sense of the term: to *re-member*, to put back together what has been torn apart. I realised in my walks through Moscow how one of my tasks as a historian of these complex revolutionary lives was precisely that: an act of *re-membrance*. The former site of the Hotel Lux does not have any plaques to remove. Perhaps the pages of history books can fill some of those absences.

3

On days when I was not scheduled to visit an archive or library, I headed out to different parts of the city. I always took the Moscow metro, marvelling at the design of each station, testaments to an unrealised vision of luxury and bounty for all. One day I took a train to the Moscow suburbs to see the Shukhov Tower, a work of modernist architecture built in 1921 as a broadcast relay for the Comintern Radio Station. On another evening I travelled to the right bank of the River Moskva so that I could look back on the skyline from Sparrow Hills. As I marvelled at the city extending before me, I thought about the famous scene from Russian revolutionary history when, in the early nineteenth century, the young radicals Alexander Herzen and Nikolai Ogarev embraced one another on Sparrow Hills and took an oath to dedicate their lives to the cause of freedom. The late-Stalin-era towers of Moscow State University rose up behind me, their edifices illuminated by rows of spotlights.

Not all my visits were so suffused with the romance of radical history nor surrounded by such halting views, however. As part of my exchange, I was also encouraged to visit the university that sponsored my visa: the Moscow State Institute for Foreign Relations. The university is a training school for diplomats, foreign policy experts and – so I was told – spies.

I had arranged to meet a staff member, a Russian academic, who brought me through the late-Soviet architecture of the university, guiding me towards an open and bright library. Standing before a display case containing histories of Russia's imperial past, she turned to me and asked: 'So who are you for, the Bolsheviks or the Romanovs?' Taken aback by this question, I mumbled something about how, as a leftist, I was for the Bolsheviks, though there were complexities to my position. She nodded and seemed nonplussed. We continued to a magazine rack and she pointed out some English-language academic journals.

My chaperone's question, however, continued to turn over in my mind. Slotting figures from the past into two columns, one labelled 'heroes' and the other labelled 'villains', is poor history. And yet, prevarication and fence-sitting does not make for good history either. Ultimately, you must pick a side and state your case. Our privilege as historians and writers is that we usually get to qualify our choice with thousands of words.

If I was better prepared for the question, perhaps I would have answered something like this:

> the Soviet experiment inaugurated by the Bolsheviks was the culmination of many projects for revolutionary emancipation that arose in nineteenth-century Europe. For better or worse, I consider all those emancipatory projects a part of my political ancestry. This is a messy inheritance, one that includes revolutionaries embracing one another in enthusiasm for a shared dream and former comrades sentencing one another to death in service to their cause. At the most basic level, the Romanovs did not want the world that I and others like myself desire. The Bolsheviks sought what I seek: equality. Therefore, when presented with this choice and within this context, I am for the Bolsheviks.

Perhaps, though, such a fluid response would have been even stranger than the stark binary question.

As I made my way through the Moscow archives, libraries and streets during that uncharacteristically warm September in 2018, my thoughts continually came back to the question which seemed to intersect with multiple lines of my historical enquiries. When you commit yourself to becoming a partisan for the cause, how does that shape your self-perception and the ways in which you interpret the world around you? Was there a political route through the twentieth century that came without profound moral compromises? When I chose to remember my political ancestors, what were the stakes of that remembrance?

4

These were among the questions that I took with me to the archives, along with my passport and a letter of introduction from my faculty. Each day I gave a friendly nod to a security guard who let me pass into a building filled with documents that foreign spies would have once risked their lives to read. I passed a display case containing Joseph Stalin's Communist Party membership card, turned left at a statue of Lenin covered in a white tarpaulin sheet and ascended to the fourth floor in an elevator decorated with a safety notice that opened with COMRADES! Working on a cryptic schedule, archivists retrieved documents from the depths of the archives and left them to be retrieved from a spacious locker located at the end of a dimly lit corridor guarded by a blast-proof door.

By the time I presented my credentials in bumbling Russian to the archival staff, much of the groundbreaking exposures in the history of the world communist movement had, it seemed, already come to light. Nowadays, we know that the purges of the 1930s were to a great degree (but not entirely) the product of Stalin's paranoid world view. With some confidence, we can state that the International Brigades who fought in the Spanish Civil War received a great deal of direction from Moscow, but that this story alone could not account for the idealism that compelled men and women to fight. The last great mystery hidden in the building, it seemed to me, was figuring out the length of time between ordering documents and their appearance in my locker.

For two weeks, I made my way through the Comintern's personnel files, folders where personal material relating to comrades and enemies of international communism was collated. I struck up an acquaintance with another English-speaking researcher who regularly visited Moscow to work with Stalin-era materials. This researcher, I learned over coffee breaks, supported a resolutely hard-line form of communism. This gradually became clear over coffee-break discussions of our research topics. 'Stalin was a man of great depth,' he told me as I sat, disconcerted, before a disappointing cappuccino.

With one part of my mind thinking over the steel Memorial plaques that I constantly saw on the walls of Moscow residential blocks, our conversation turned to 1937 and the Great Terror. For those who saw communism as a dead idea, it was not merely *the* Great Terror but one of *many* inevitable red terrors. Violent oppression was, according to this theory, the unavoidable outgrowth of left-wing ideas. They could not be fulfilled without it: radical levelling required violent purging. Such determinist readings, including those made by proponents of a teleological Marxism, always seemed unconvincing to me through their wilful blindness to the extraordinary range of possibilities that exist in the past. In our conversation, my coffee-break companion appeared to share with the anti-communists a belief in the inevitability of terror. He differed only in his approach to its desirability. He upheld the orthodox communist line: yes, mistakes were made, but the terror was ultimately necessary to defend socialism: counter-revolution needed to be met with all-encompassing violence.

This interpretation of the terror, one I have encountered occasionally in left-wing circles, seemed to render socialism a cruel idea. Yet I needed to confront how many of those I wrote about and researched, people whose lives seemed to me so full of sympathetic moments, accepted similarly cold logic. Before coming to Moscow I had found it easier to see 'my people' as those who courageously faced the firing squads without renouncing their ideals. But now I could see more clearly that our political ancestry is never so neat. This was an admission that I tried to keep central in my mind once I returned to my work. I continued parsing through fragments from a time when other paths seemed open, when dreams were not yet vanquished. I was learning to become more comfortable with the murky moral complexity of revolutionary lives.

5

Back in the archive after a round of bland coffee and extreme opinions, I found a Comintern personnel file that I had ordered a week previously awaiting me in my locker. I was close to reaching the end of my time in the archives and, although I had found enough interesting material to justify my visits, there was nothing which shattered my existing perceptions. Beneath the ever-present eye of a CCTV camera, unknotting the string that held the file closed, I opened the folder to find a covering sheet with the name of the file's subject alongside the Russian phrase, *sov sekretno*: top secret.

Turning to the sheet placed at the start of each file for every researcher to sign, I noticed that I was seemingly the first person to call up this document since a bureaucrat had confined it to the archives sometime during the Second World War. The folder bulged with more than two hundred pages of documents dating from the mid-1920s to the early 40s. Generally, the bulkier the folder, the more suspicious the Soviet authorities were of the individual described within. A file of this size generally indicated the subject had been placed under investigation or even put on trial.

But I could not have predicted what I would find inside. Contained within this folder were the protocols of an investigation, trial and verdict. It was not, however, a person under interrogation, but a book. My fellow researcher, who shortly before had been sitting in front of me in a nearby café (approvingly) outlining Stalin-era political economy and (disapprovingly) describing Khrushchev-era political economy, passed by my desk. He pushed up his glasses and looked at the pages laid out on my table. 'Now that,' he said, 'is a find.'

PART II

Revolutionary Dreams
at the Hotel Lux

1923–1929

Checking In

4. Hotel Lux, Moscow, c. 1930s, University of Oregon Special Collections. Ruth Epperson Kennell Papers, Ax 872, Box 4, Folder 21

1

In November 1922 a journalist for a Boston newspaper was granted access to the Hotel Lux to visit Bill Haywood, an American labour leader who dodged criminal charges in the United States by fleeing to Soviet Russia. The reporter was greeted in the lobby by a sign announcing 'the coming of the world-wide revolution' in bright English lettering. Bringing his readers along the hotel corridors to

the room occupied by the fugitive 'Big Bill', the journalist wrote:
'You walk up a flight of stairs and encounter a second-rate hotel
reception room, decorated in the best red plush motif, with a few
stray tiger skins prone upon a rather gaudy carpet. You turn down
the broad corridor and stop at No. 12. You knock.'[1] This walk was
the one experienced each day by the foreign technical workers who
lived in the Lux during the 1920s. While the description does not
suggest a refined interior design sensibility, the decor does evoke
a visual metaphor: in the Lux, the vestiges of the old world, such
as tiger-skin rugs, were trampled over by the people ushering in
the new.

Peering back into the dynamic past of the Hotel Lux, our
perspective is not unlike that of the clerks who sat in the reception
watching the comrades come and go. We can find the names and
room numbers of the residents. We can understand where and how
they spent their hours outside of the hotel. But unlike the clerks,
we can also use an array of sources that would not have been left
behind at reception to reconstruct the kinds of discussions that
took place inside the rooms. Over this central act of our story, we
will trace life in the Lux according to an ordinary day in the
Comintern: from work to recreation. We will follow a select group
of residents across their day, from breakfast in the hotel, taken in
the canteen or cooked over their own personal Primus stoves, on
to work in the headquarters of the Comintern or within the ornate
halls of the nearby Kremlin Palace. Afterwards, we will delve into
the vibrant social life of the Lux, attending gatherings fuelled by
vinyl records, high ideals and supplies grabbed last minute from
the co-operative store across the street. But first, let us imagine
ourselves outside the Lux, looking up to its neoclassical facade,
and ask: what was its own story?

Initially opened in 1911 by a branch of the Fillipovs, a family
that ran well-known Moscow bakeries, the Lux was one of several
hotels and palaces in Moscow that the Bolsheviks requisitioned in
the early years of Soviet power. Expedient to the need for housing
supply in the crucible of the world revolution, these buildings were

converted into 'Houses of Soviets'. The Lux, like other Moscow hotels, offered the facilities the Bolsheviks required: a location close to the centre of power in the Kremlin, dining and banquet halls that could be repurposed for congresses and rooms to house their revolutionary 'guests'. Its conversion into the Comintern's living quarters took place in 1920.

The Houses of Soviets usually functioned as dormitories for high-ranking Bolsheviks, but these rooms were also earmarked for foreign radicals making their way to Moscow.[2] Among the most luxurious of the Moscow dormitories was the Hotel Metropol, a residence reserved for Soviet officials and foreign visitors (including visiting dignitaries and respected journalists) whom the Bolsheviks wanted to impress. The Metropol still functions as an upmarket hotel in central Moscow, its outside walls covered in plaques marking the major meetings in Soviet history that took place inside.

Other Moscow hotels, like the Bristol and the National, were similarly sought after as more comfortable places to stay than the cramped, communal apartments occupied by most Moscow residents. The anarchist Alexander Berkman, deported from the US to Soviet Russia in 1919, discovered that foreign visitors boarding in the Houses of Soviets, including the Hotel Lux, received special supplies of food that were unavailable to the average Soviet citizen.[3] Such divergent privileges in the supposed land of equality were easily explained by the ideologically committed. Party members understood that the future of abundance for all was being worked towards, but it had not yet arrived. In the time of struggle *towards* communism, certain privileges needed to be granted to those carrying out the most important work. Thinking along these lines, foreign communists accepted privileges as recognition of the important task that fell on their shoulders: bringing through the world revolution that would rescue the Soviet state from isolation and 'capitalist encirclement'.

As the Comintern dormitory, the Lux was in a category of its own. While the hotel bar of the Metropol would have been recognisable as just another European hang-out for gossiping journalists, the Lux canteen served up unique sights. Nowhere else could you find people wanted on multiple counts of sedition in their home countries, spoon in hand, creating red whirlpools in bowls of borscht, or leading figures of revolutionary movements queuing for a shower. Although more desirable than the average Moscow housing set-up and connected with prioritised supply lines, the Lux was already run-down by the time visitors started reporting on its conditions in the early 1920s. By all accounts, standards of hygiene and comfort seem to have only worsened as the years progressed.

The Houses of Soviets had a longer history rooted in the experience of political exile in Europe and America. Pre-revolutionary models of communal living were developed not only by the victorious Bolsheviks but by organisations like the Mensheviks and the Jewish Labour Bund whose contributions to the liberation struggle were eclipsed in the wake of the October Revolution. However, after the Bolsheviks seized power, they became the chief importers of old habits, good and bad, into the new society. Historian Faith Hillis has traced the rich emancipatory projects crafted in the foreign 'colonies' of Russian exiles in the decades before 1917.[4] In cafeterias, libraries and meeting halls, a revolutionary generation carved out concrete utopias in the immigrant districts of cities like London, Paris and New York. Places like urban communes, the Hotel Lux and other Houses of Soviets transplanted these communal models shaped during the exile experience to the society under construction by the triumphant Bolsheviks. Wilfully or not, the Bolsheviks, in housing the global revolutionary elite across a handful of central Moscow hotels and the Lux in particular, recreated precisely the same hothouses of radical theory, practice and argument experienced in the exile colonies.

Yet, as Hillis' work also reveals, the pre-revolutionary worlds of the Russian exiles were not only places where grand dreams became small-scale realities. They could also foster oppressive and violent atmospheres. Ferocious ideological conflicts were common and the tight-knit social networks of the exile colonies made them ideal targets for penetration by tsarist police informants and agent provocateurs. In response, the Bolsheviks developed obsessions with discipline and mutual surveillance, fixations which seeped into the foundations of life in the Hotel Lux. During the paranoid years of the late-1930s terror, the fact that many foreign communists lived together in a single building in central Moscow would make it easier for the NKVD, Stalin's secret police, to move room by room, arresting radical emigrants falsely accused of spying for foreign governments.

The divergence in experience between the Lux residents of the 1920s and the 1930s can be demonstrated in a short history of the hotel's 'NEP wing'. An old building on the side of a courtyard, it was so named because during the period of the New Economic Policy in the 1920s it was opened to regular paying guests to generate income for the Lux. This measure was an example of the limited market economy that the NEP policy re-introduced to Soviet society in the spring of 1921. With the NEP, the familiar 'bourgeois' comforts of the old world became more accessible to foreign visitors in Soviet Moscow. In the late 1930s, the role of the wing changed once more to accommodate another Soviet policy shift. Wives and children who previously lived in the main building of the Lux were re-billeted to the wing as husbands and fathers disappeared into the terror.[5]

Much of what happened in the wake of Stalin's rise to power was unimaginable to the first generation of Lux residents. Often blind to the repressive apparatus being built around them, they found the beginnings of a beautiful society rather than its horrifying negation within their rooms. Just as visiting radicals had once ventured into London's East End to feel the reverberations of a radical underground rising to the surface on the migrant streets, foreign radicals sensed that post-revolutionary Moscow was a space of limitless potential for social experimentation. The Russian Revolution made the abstraction of theory accessible in a living and breathing society, one that could be reached with increasing ease as the Soviet state got on firmer footing following the tumult of its early years.

As the Lux began to fill up with visiting rebels from across the world, the hotel became one experiment in the wider Soviet laboratory. Within its walls, political migrants could work out the models of community, which they could then bring back to their own movements. Overseeing all of this was a Soviet regime that grew increasingly suspicious of the ideas being imported from outside its borders and ideas found beyond the pages of its canonical texts. Yet, for a brief window in time, rebels thinking through ideas like anti-colonialism, queer emancipation and radical cultural expression sincerely believed that Soviet Moscow was a canvas upon which they could outline an entirely new world. As the Frankfurt School philosopher Walter Benjamin noted, Moscow in the 1920s provided an urban schematic of the human future, a map pointing to a range of human possibilities: 'above all, the possibility that the Revolution might fail or succeed'.[6] Occupying its rooms, the guests of the Lux ensured that the hotel acted as a catalyst for an unprecedented experiment in revolutionary living. The results were as extraordinary as they were unpredictable. To invite ourselves into this world with a personal guide, let us follow the first of the Gray's Inn Road comrades to arrive in the Lux: the young, idealistic and much-desired Rose Cohen.

2

Rose first crossed the Soviet frontier by train on 21 May 1923. Upon arrival in Moscow, she was billeted to room 32 in the Hotel Lux, though she would later be moved to room 144. She began work as a stenographer in the English section of the Comintern's press department.[7] Unlike May, who would arrive later, Rose did not remain in this role for very long. Rose spent most of the 1920s among the class of Comintern workers who shuttled between

Moscow and other European cities, entrusted with regular travel in service to the revolution.

The dry, factual details of Rose's initial stint in Moscow can be gleaned from her personnel file held in the Comintern archives. The folder's contents are eclectic, ranging from straightforward biographical facts to secret police surveillance and paperwork relating to her posthumous rehabilitation in 1956. Among the documents there is a yellowed envelope that contains a small black-and-white photo of Rose. It seems to have been taken in the early 1930s. No emotion is betrayed by her face. Around her neck she wears a patterned scarf. Her hair is neat. Dark, sunken eyes stare directly into the camera.

Thousands – potentially tens of thousands – of such photographs are held in the Comintern archives. In many cases, they may well be the only surviving portraits of these migrant radicals, mostly from working-class backgrounds, who passed through the halls of the Comintern headquarters and the corridors of the Lux. Neutral faces frozen at what must have been a moment of enormous importance. Standing before a photographer shortly after their first arrival into Soviet Moscow, the new employees of the Comintern would have months of adaptation ahead of them. They would need to acclimatise to a new language, a hectic pace of work and the often-harsh realities of a society undergoing an unprecedented transition. But the rewards, so many felt, were worth it: the opportunity to feel as though you, a single person, were part of a community that was tipping the balance in the scales of history.

Victor Serge, a Russo-French participant in the revolution and a Comintern worker whose writings provide rich impressions of the period, described the typical 'militant comrade' of international communism in his memoirs. 'All we lived for was activity integrated into history', he remembered, 'we changed our names, our postings and our work at the Party's need; we had just enough to live on without real material discomfort, and we were not interested in making money, or following a career, or producing a literary heritage, or leaving a name behind us; we were interested solely in the difficult business of reaching Socialism.'[8] Such a life was difficult to sustain and required enormous sacrifices; from relationships with family and friends to personal safety. In truth, there was a spectrum and variety of typical 'militant comrades' to be found in Moscow. The people described by Serge, those who eradicated their own sense of self to fuse with the collective ideology, did exist among the political emigrants in Soviet Moscow. But the kinds of foreign communists unwilling to let the 'difficult business of reaching Socialism' get in the way of their personal relationships and meaningful cultural experiences were also a common sight. Among them was Rose Cohen.

Returning to the letters Rose wrote from Moscow to her admirer Esmonde Higgins, we find a woman walking an interpersonal tightrope. Rose was attempting to foreclose any romantic potential without severing the possibility that she and 'Hig' could be comrades building the new world together. The situation had, it seems, even reached the stage of a marriage proposal. Rose replied in an August 1923 letter that her 'pen is stammering & spluttering, because I can't bring myself to tell you the blunt truth'.[9] 'Oh it's horrible', she continued, 'to tell you a second time (to sort of rub it in) that I can't marry you.'[10] The topic of the unrequited romance continued to arise. In an October letter she offered to stop writing if 'it would be easier' for Higgins simply not to hear from her. Nonetheless, she underlined how she wanted him 'very badly for a comrade'.[11]

The world revolution could help to disentangle the knot of love and comradeship that tied together Rose in Moscow and Higgins in London. Rose tried to place things in perspective. She counselled him not to let his love for her intrude on his life, especially his role in the coming revolution. 'There are big things ahead,' she stated '& you are going to play a vital part in them.' Underlining the point, Rose asserted to Higgins in the closing lines of the same letter: 'You're a damn sight more important than you think. Please forgive me.'[12] The curious alchemy of revolutionary life could take something as recognisable as the romantic rejection letter and infuse it with a political charge. It was fortunate that Rose was skilled in the art of saying no to insistent communist men. Higgins would not be the last suitor that Rose would need to rebuff.

Amid the emotional turmoil she was doubtlessly inflicting on her unfortunate correspondent, Rose also took up space on her letter pages to describe the extraordinary events she was witnessing in Moscow and hinted at exciting happenings. 'I am writing this in the big gilded hall of the Kremlin, at the First World Conference of Peasants,' Rose wrote in one message. She described a 'big contingent of Russian peasants – lovely bearded things in their long coats & high boots, smelling of the land'. Rose also saw delegates from Asia: Mongolia, Japan and China, along with large European delegations from France and Germany. The organisers were 'partic-ularly anxious to have someone from Ireland', Rose noted, 'but they seem to be a feeble lot over there' (to be fair to the Irish peasantry, they were contending with the immediate aftermath of a civil war).[13] The whole experience of being at the first of such congresses was the 'sort of thing one will tell one's grandchildren', Rose believed.

Although Rose's experience at the peasant congress must have reflected a truly internationalist revolution, already, by the time she was writing, the tide of the revolutionary surge in the wider world had turned. In Lenin's era, now coming to a close, the Comintern laid its hopes on a series of revolutionary upheavals in the wider world, especially Germany, that would prove abortive. As Lenin's health was failing, the capitalist system was stabilising. These events fundamentally determined the direction of the Comintern. The Soviet Party, as the only communist party still overseeing a revolutionary state, became dominant. In turn, wider Comintern politics became entangled with the inner-party struggle as the Bolsheviks decided upon a successor for Lenin.

Whether such macro-level politics impinged on Rose's day-to-day life in service for the Comintern is unclear from her letters. Apologising for her delayed reply in one letter to Higgins, Rose noted that she had been 'away on an important mission'.[14] The details she gave were vague, perhaps deliberately so, and she suggested to Higgins that he would hear all about it in person from a mutual friend. Whatever the task was, it had taken her beyond Moscow and even across the Soviet frontier into Scandinavia. When she eventually travelled home from her stint in Moscow she hoped to return via northern Europe. 'The glimpse I had of the fjords and mountains has given me a thirst for it,' Rose noted.[15] Later in the 1920s, after her time in the Lux, she would be tasked with undertaking 'illegal work' by the Comintern. These were underground activities that were given to trusted comrades, which stretched from relatively mundane yet important tasks such as acting as a courier smuggling documents and money to more high-stakes actions like instigating insurrections.

However, it was not all excitement and adventure: Rose, like many foreign communists, found learning Russian hugely difficult. A few months into her residence in Moscow, she finally felt as though she were making headway. 'But Jesus,' she noted, 'as you've no doubt already discovered for yourself, it's a hell of a job.'[16] A 1932 pamphlet released by the publishing house for foreign workers in the USSR contains a lengthy vocabulary list, which suggests the specific vocabulary that communist students of Russian were advised to learn. In place of vocabulary lists that you would normally find in language textbooks like 'At Home' and 'At Work', the pamphlet organised its vocabulary under sub-headings such as 'The Forces of Imperialism and the Forces of Revolution' and 'Imperialism and the Downfall of Capitalism'.[17] Learning Russian to live and work in Moscow as a foreign communist in this era was not simply about grasping the language's case system, but interpreting the highly specific terminology of Russian as it was spoken by the Bolsheviks. Learning Russian is difficult. Learning *Bolshevik* Russian introduced further complications.

Knowledge of the Russian language was an important skill for workers in the Comintern's press department (*Otdel Pechaty*) such as Rose. One of the first bureaus formed following the founding congress of the Comintern in March 1919, the press department's initial title gives a more holistic sense of its purpose: the International Propaganda Department.[18] The department was tasked with organising communist propaganda and publishing documents relating to the Comintern and the Soviet Communist Party in different languages. Within the department, there were four language sections, each reflecting the most important linguistic spheres of Comintern activity: Russian, German, English and French. Much of the staff was made up of secretarially trained women with a flair for languages, precisely the kinds of activists that Sylvia Pankhurst had attracted and cultivated in her cosmopolitan East London world of suffrage, socialism and publishing.

Despite the necessity of grappling with the Russian language's notorious genitive plural case, Rose had gradually eased into an entirely new world upon arrival in Soviet Moscow. For foreign communists like Rose (particularly those from parties whose prospects for insurrection receded along with the revolutionary wave of the post-war years) visiting Moscow often provided a flood of optimism. From attending peasant congresses to carrying out clandestine tasks, experiences in Soviet Russia were far removed from the endless political debates about affiliation to the Labour Party that characterised political life back home in London. Yet precisely because the British party was still finding its place among the British labour movement, Rose could not remain in Moscow indefinitely. She was a valued Party member; intelligent, energetic and determined. Stints in Moscow were a kind of apprenticeship. Once skills were attained, the parties in the periphery called their comrades back from the centre. By the spring of 1924, Rose Cohen had added an education in the Comintern's internal workings to her radical repertoire and it was now time for her to return to London.

Throughout the existence of the Comintern press department, four different women from East London worked within it. Rose would be the second. But only one of these veterans of Pankhurst's East End movement would become head of a department translation team.

3

May O'Callaghan, who would rise higher in the Comintern apparatus than any other former member of Pankhurst's world – or any other Irish person, for that matter – entered the department shortly after Rose Cohen left it behind in 1924. It is possible that she arrived to fill the vacancy Rose's departure created. On 4 July 1924 Harry Pollitt, a British communist who would also receive rejections from Rose to his marriage proposals, wrote to Esmonde Higgins. He noted that May was departing for Moscow the next day. By this point, Rose was already back in London. She had returned to the Gray's Inn Road flat she shared with her sister and Irish friend since at least 1916.

May's departure for Moscow that summer left open a room that would be occupied by yet another amorous young radical: Hugo Rathbone. Known to his friends as 'Rath', Hugo belonged to the same leftist London social circle as the Cohens, Higgins and Pollitt. A few weeks after May left England, Pollitt wrote to Higgins that 'Rath has gone to live at the Cohen–O'Callaghan flat and is I hope living the simple life.' Yet there was a problem: 'in view of the direction I am informed his affections lie', Pollitt continued, 'I do not think that this can be looked upon as being a good move.'[19]

It is unclear whether Hugo's affection lay in the direction of Nellie or Rose. My own evidence-informed speculation would suggest that his affections, in truth, lay in two directions: Nellie *and* Rose. No wonder Pollitt suspected this was a bad move. In time, however, Hugo distinguished himself as the only British communist to propose marriage to a Cohen sister and receive a 'yes' in return. Hugo, in turn, would eventually depart the Cohen–O'Callaghan flat, making his way to Sweden before finding himself yet another guest at the Hotel Lux.

If May felt sore leaving behind her room in London, she would have found some comfort upon learning where she was to stay in

Moscow. According to several impressions, the Lux room where May lived was one of the hotel's more envied options. May's Lux apartment, room 5, looked out onto Tverskaya Street, the main thoroughfare for parades and celebrations. The bedroom was also occupied by May alone, a privilege that was not guaranteed in the Lux. It was a perfect vantage point to watch a city and a community in transition. Just as she turned forty-three, May was beginning the most exciting years of her life. She was also about to make friendships that would prove enormously important for an unpredictable reason: in the Lux she met two Americans who would preserve the letters she wrote to them, ensuring that May, an obscure worker in the world revolution, could eventually speak stridently into the historical record in her own voice.

Several months before May's arrival, in January 1924, Vladimir Lenin died at the age of fifty-three on his estate outside Moscow. A cortege of Bolshevik Civil War veterans carried the deceased leader through a snow-covered field to the railway station to be transported back to Moscow. One witness recalled bonfires burning as seemingly endless lines of people marched by to pay their last respects.[20]

May arrived too late to witness the scenes of mourning after Lenin's death, but not too late, strangely, to see Lenin. It was a bitterly cold January when Lenin died, even by the standards of a Moscow mid-winter. In the sub-zero temperatures, the corpse of Lenin decayed at a slower-than-normal rate, granting his comrades time to develop a novel idea: their leader's body would go on public display in perpetuity to allow generations of visitors to visit and mourn the departed leader.

With Lenin lying deprived of organs but invested with symbolism in a mausoleum on Red Square, the fate of the revolution now hung on the question: who would succeed him? May would extend her stay in Soviet Moscow far beyond the initial year she planned; so long, in fact, that she would personally witness the debates that provided an answer to the question of succession. As a Comintern worker, she occupied a front-row seat in the unfolding drama.

Sweeping Away the Old Order

1

In November 1924, months after Lenin was placed on display in Red Square, a sense of excitement coursed through the Hotel Lux. Beyond its walls, preparations were under way for the seventh anniversary celebrations of the great October Revolution – the momentous event that had, in one way or another, brought everyone in the hotel together.

In the days before the parade, citizens in the city were granted time away from their labours. For two days the streets were quiet and free from the ringing bells of the trams that normally made their way up and down the broad avenue outside the Lux. With the canteen closed, each of the Lux residents was required to gather provisions to see them through the weekend before the celebrations began. But as they awoke on 7 November, the residents discovered that the engines of the city were once more at work.

Everyone, from those operating the printing presses to the Bolsheviks in the Kremlin Palace, was busily preparing for the momentous day ahead. News stands carried the latest issue of *Pravda*, with its bold typeface confidently declaring: 'Class Comrades! Friends In Europe And America! Slaves Of The Colonies! Are You Listening To Us? We Are Growing! We Are Getting Stronger! We Are With You!'[1] Beneath the headline, an illustration showed three workers, two men and one woman, ascending a staircase with determination, each step labelled with a year since the Revolution and a quote from Lenin. A long article by Grigory Zinoviev, a leading figure in the Comintern who had recently found himself an unwitting antagonist in British politics, pronounced that this seventh anniversary was the first year where the October Revolution would be celebrated 'without Ilyich'.

One foreign witness to the festivities was a young American librarian named Ruth Kennell who had recently been assigned a room in the Lux. It was a fateful placement. Ruth would become close to many other Lux residents. Indeed, she would develop an intimacy of such intensity with the bob-haired Irishwoman who lived downstairs from her that rumours would begin circulating that the two were something more than simply friends. It was Ruth Kennell who, largely unwittingly, did more than anyone else to ultimately spare her friend May O'Callaghan from historical oblivion.

Through May's letters to Ruth, I discovered the first details to lure me into the drama of May's life and that of her comrades. For now, however, Ruth lived only a staircase away from the woman who would become her closest confidante in the Soviet capital. The pair had no reason to write to one another. We must rely on Ruth's own voice, preserved in letters she sent to a boyfriend and her family, to trace the contours of their shared world and the early days of May's life in the Lux.

Although it was her first time living in Moscow, Ruth had, in fact, already been on Soviet soil for some time. In 1922 Ruth and her husband Frank travelled to Kemerovo, an area in remote Siberia, alongside other immigrants from across the United States. Their destination was the Kuzbas colony, an autonomous community organised along socialist principles. Life in Kuzbas had given Ruth a first taste of what Soviet-style women's emancipation looked like in practice. Here, she sought to be treated as an equal partner in the building of socialism rather than simply being siloed into a conventional domestic role as wife or mother.

Ruth's time in the colony also coincided with a breakdown in her marriage. On her first day of work in Kuzbas, Ruth met Sam Shipman, an engineer from the US who seemed to her both young and sophisticated.[2] Amid the heavy snow and romantic aura that loomed over life in the Siberian colony, Ruth gradually gave in to temptation and started an affair with Sam. By late 1924 Frank briefly returned to the US. Sam, meanwhile, joined Ruth for a blissful month in Moscow. Writing frankly to her mother about her waning desire for her husband and infatuation with Sam, Ruth noted that by 'all the rules of the old-fashioned morality, we should have parted forever with the memory of our "three weeks" to comfort us in the years to come – but I don't think I can be satisfied with memories'.[3]

With Sam setting out on a return journey to America, Ruth remained in Russia. She would need to either rely on her memories or perhaps seek out new encounters in the bustling Soviet capital. Ruth maintained a lively correspondence with her husband, her lover and her mother while pursuing her life as a single, emancipated woman in Moscow. Like many other women motivated by similar desires for an independent life, she looked to the crucible of the revolution for fulfilment in both her career and sex life. As historian Julia Mickenberg notes, after two years in Siberia, Ruth threw herself into life in the Soviet capital, which was 'dazzling with energy, culture, and activity.'[4]

There were also more mundane benefits to life in Moscow. Although residents of the Lux constantly referenced its poor sanitation and growing population of cockroaches, for Ruth – who had spent much of her time in Russia in a lodge-style dwelling in the Siberian wilderness – the accommodation was exceptional. Here, she could avail of hot-water showers and boiling water on tap to make strong tea. These positives appear to have outweighed the major negative of Ruth's early life in the hotel: her Russian roommate, a woman who smoked incessantly and insisted on closing a small inset window whenever Ruth opened it to refresh the air in the room.[5]

Hotel security, represented by the infamous *propusk* (meaning 'pass'), was complex. 'The Lux is carefully guarded as persons of the greatest revolutionary importance from foreign countries stay there,' she noted in a letter home: 'It is necessary for a person visiting a friend in the hotel to present identification papers and get a pass to go in which is signed by the resident he is visiting before leaving.'[6] Only after surrendering this pass at the entrance did the visitor have their identification papers returned to them by the receptionist-slash-guard in the foyer.

An even more severe version of the same security process was observed at the nearby headquarters where Ruth was employed: the Comintern buildings on Mokhovaya Street. A brisk thirty-minute walk from the Lux, one easily collapsible by tram, the Comintern headquarters were located within the yellow walls of an imposing neoclassical building. Ruth described her workplace as a 'madhouse of clicking typewriters and hurrying footsteps.'[7] Women and men from across the world gossiped with one another in a babel of languages in this workplace located a short walk from the Kremlin. Staff frantically pounded the corridors carrying typescripts to the correct offices for translation from and into the major working languages of the international communist movement: Russian, German, English and French.

More than simply banal stenography reports, these transcriptions of discussions among leading revolutionaries were sometimes akin to the epistles shared among the early Christians. Devotees across the world eagerly awaited the good news from Moscow. If the translations were inaccurate, then the faithful abroad risked adopting an incorrect revolutionary line. The work was intense and technical but absorbing. After all, few other typists in the world could claim that every press on their keys represented a further tiny crack in the fortress walls of global capitalism. Ruth informed her mother that she had made a 'very good friend' through this work, a fellow Lux resident and the boss of her typing section, a woman named Miss O'Callaghan.[8] This was the first of several winters that May would spend in Moscow. It was also her first experience of an October Revolution anniversary celebration in one of the central theatres in which the action had taken place.

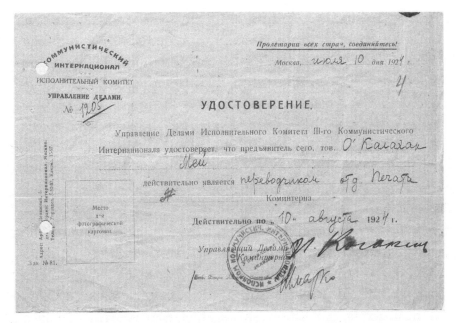

6. May O'Callaghan's Comintern Press Department permit, July 1924. RGASPI

On the night before Moscow toilers marked the October Revolution with celebrations, Ruth stayed late in the Comintern building where she and May worked. She emerged as the first snowflakes of winter were falling and discovered that the 'city had suddenly turned red'. Politically speaking, the city had turned red almost exactly seven years before, but this time the urban landscape had *literally* turned red. The globes of streetlamps were covered in red, casting the boulevards in the colour of the revolution. Red banners streamed down the front of the Comintern headquarters and garlands of fir were placed across the facades of the imperious buildings of Soviet government. A red flag was always flying from the dome of the Kremlin Palace. At night, whenever it was caught in the glare of a searchlight, Ruth thought the flag looked like a 'flame of fire'.[9]

In shop windows, busts of the Soviet leaders and the philosophical forefathers of Marxism sat atop red tablecloths. One window display featuring a strange mixture of oil portraiture and cardboard modelling was drawing a particular amount of attention as Ruth made her way back to the Lux. Peering into the window, she saw a cardboard figure seated behind a table and dressed in a brass-buttoned uniform. Lit by a table lamp, the figure was positioned in front of a wall of photographs depicting Lenin and other eminent Bolsheviks. This revolutionary, Ruth noted, 'seemed to be the favourite of the people, although he is not given much publicity, perhaps intentionally, because they are afraid he will be too popular'. Anyone reading the history of the Revolution backwards from 1953 might hazard a guess that this cut-out Bolshevik inspiring an incipient personality cult was Joseph Stalin. But it was, in fact, the figure who would emerge as Stalin's arch-nemesis: Leon Trotsky.

In these crucial years after Lenin's death, the decision as to who would become his successor was being debated. Upon whose shoulders this mantle fell would decide the very future of the Revolution itself. But in the buoyant atmosphere of the Lux ahead of the anniversary celebrations, the emergence of factional fighting that would split the world communist movement apart must have seemed unlikely. For the time being, the watchwords in the Comintern were 'international solidarity' and the 'united front'.

Awakening the next morning to find her Lux room-mate in atypically buoyant spirits, Ruth made her way to the Moscow Immigrants Club, where the various national sections of the Comintern were gathering and assembling their banners for the great anniversary celebration march. Throughout its history, an estimated 160,000 communists worked in some capacity for the Communist International, with roles ranging from secretarial work to the assassination of political opponents. Of this mass of humanity, roughly 600 worked in the Moscow headquarters of the Comintern at any one time. The social world of this select few revolved around the government buildings where they worked, the Lux where most of them lived and workers' clubs and canteens such as the Immigrants Club, where they socialised and organised.

The largest contingent marching on the 7 November demonstration was the German section. In the years following the October Revolution, the Bolsheviks fervently prophesied that revolutionary workers were poised to seize power in Germany. Hand in hand, the industrialised German Soviet Republic and Soviet Russia, economically backwards but possessing a base of skilled cadre, would then proceed to spread the revolution across the globe. This was not mere propagandistic flourish. Initially, the Soviet leadership had good reason to believe their own prognostications of an impending German revolution. The German Social Democratic Party, founded in 1863 and known as the SPD, was a hotbed of creative polemicists throughout the nineteenth century. From the party's mass membership arose influential leftist thinkers such as Rosa Luxemburg and Clara Zetkin, both of whom opposed the war and advocated a revolutionary transformation of Germany. Luxemburg paid for her activism with her life while Zetkin, a major contributor to the debates surrounding the 'woman question' in socialism, would become a leading figure in the Women's Section of the Comintern.

German communists regularly traversed the transcontinental land routes through the Polish–Soviet frontier to reach Moscow, where they received training and direction on how the Communist Party of Germany, known by its German-language acronym KPD, should resurrect the thwarted revolutionary moment. Ruth and May would befriend several women from among the German émigrés resident in the Lux during the heady years of the mid-1920s.

As the October Revolution anniversary parade of 1924 passed the German embassy, the gathered German emigrants registered their distaste with hisses and jeers. With the Germans constituting the largest foreign group in the vast parade, it seemed likely that they would be the first contingent to enter their Moscow embassy as emissaries of a new Soviet republic. Keeping spirits high were the Italian communists, who spent the entirety of the parade singing revolutionary ballads in their lyrical native language. Not far from them marched the English-speaking section, which included Ruth and May, whose musical offerings paled in comparison.

The British émigrés had reason to be dispirited. In the 1924 British General Election, the Conservative Party returned to power with a resounding majority. Ever since the days that Marx had hunched over a desk in the British Museum, revolutionaries had

anticipated that the British workers, perhaps spurred by their insurrectionary counterparts in Ireland, would topple their monarchy.
But with this recent election result, the idea of a guillotine being
hastily erected in Trafalgar Square appeared more remote than ever.
Ruth wrote to her mother that 'even some of the most sceptical of
the Communists I meet in the Comintern were surprised at the
overwhelming reactionary vote'. The election results were shaped
by a forged letter published in the *Daily Mail* that purported to be
sent to the Communist Party of Great Britain from Grigori Zinoviev.
Marching defiantly through Moscow only weeks after the election,
the British political emigrants carried above them a banner declaring
'Forged Letters Won't Save Capitalism', which showed a capitalist
escaping a hangman's noose by throwing himself into the sea with
a lifebelt labelled 'Zinoviev Letter'.

To march among the masses as a communist was a means of
communing with the wider revolutionary project. The waves of
people waving banners – an unceasing flow passing through the
streets – must have seemed an unstoppable force. So vast was the
parade that Ruth estimated that it took six hours for the crowd to
file past Lenin's mausoleum in Red Square. One diarist who
witnessed the spectacle recorded that the elements must have
favoured Russia's new rulers, for at one point during proceedings
the sun illuminated the Kremlin and the square in front of its walls
while the banners were waving in the air.[10]

In the evening following the parade, Ruth and her new friend
made their way to the Red Club, a new workers' theatre established
inside the impressive department store GUM. May had been fascinated by theatre since at least her days in Vienna. Post-revolutionary
Moscow was the epicentre of experiments in drama – a fact that
May exploited to the best of her ability, often bringing friends like
Ruth along to various performances. Here, in the Red Club, the
two friends watched the 'living newspaper', a kind of live newsreel
where headlines were acted out by performers, part of a wider early
Soviet effort to make informed citizens out of the Soviet peasantry
and proletarians, many of whom were illiterate.

Heads emerged from slits in the theatre curtains and delivered the headlines. Then actors with the flags of America, Britain and France fastened to their coat-tails held a mock conference about their designs on Asia, represented by two circular disks painted with dragons. 'At the side of the stage Soviet Russia was represented by a big Red Star,' Ruth noted, 'and in the midst of the conference, a Red Soldier appeared and broke it up.' As they emerged from the theatre, the two women observed a picturesque scene. Writing to her mother of what she witnessed outside the theatre, Ruth evoked the strange beauty of a city transitioning between two worlds, where every friendship, work of art and corner of the architectural landscape seemed charged with a revolutionary energy:

While we were inside the snow had been falling and all the square had turned white. The cobblestones were covered over with the new snow, it touched the mausoleum of Lenin where lights glowed softly, and the red banner fluttered like flames through the thick snowflakes. The air had turned warmer, and the people were wild with delight, they would slip and fall on the streets and then lie pretending to be unconscious, and get up laughing all covered with snow. Coming before the Square of the Bolshoi theatre, which you know is beautiful under any circumstances, I thought here was the most beautiful picture of all – the buildings skating the square were outlined with red lights, one of the stores had a red light in every window of its six stories. Across the columns of the theatre was stretched a big painting entitled 'Capitalist Democracy'. In the centre stands the Statue of Liberty, with the sign of fascism on her breast, on a green monster with open jaws; below the wretched people (immigrants, I suppose) are trying to escape the yawning jaws.[11]

Hindsight may compel us to ask: had political migrants like May and Ruth merely thrown themselves into the yawning jaws of something more violent than the worlds they had left behind? But in the afterglow of a triumphal demonstration, as snow fell outside the Bolshoi theatre, future tragedies must have seemed far less likely than a vision of lasting social harmony for all. The revolutionary socialist city of the early twentieth century provided something that most Western societies were unable to outpace: a sense of belonging to a societal project, one that offered a particularly potent promise of women's emancipation. Crucially for women like May and Ruth, this promise was not merely a distant dream, but a partly realised present.

2

Some years before May and Ruth joined the minor wave of female migrants seeking employment, independence and meaning in Moscow, Clara Zetkin, a prominent German communist, had informed the Third Congress of the Comintern in 1921 that those who ignored the value of women in the movement were, in fact, 'conscious saboteurs of the revolution'.[12] Zetkin's assertion that women would play a crucial role in the revolution was by no means axiomatic to socialists. The international communist movement inherited from its nineteenth-century predecessors an attitude towards women's issues that was often dismissive and sometimes outright suspicious. Marxist antipathy towards feminism was based in part on a notion that the women's movement was at heart opportunist: its 'bourgeois' leaders would abandon working women as soon as they made gains for fellow bourgeois women.[13]

Even more common was the notion that feminism was simply misguided: class, not gender, was the real axis of oppression and therefore once the divides of class were transcended women's emancipation would be secured in tow. In this understanding, causing a fuss over something like votes for a bourgeois parliament was a waste of time that could be better spent preparing for class war.

Despite the frustrations that activists like Zetkin faced in arguing that women's emancipation was a central part of the world revolutionary programme, some of the most radical twentieth-century re-imaginings of women's place in politics and society arose from the international communist movement. Women were prominent in several of the revolutionary movements that arose in the Russian Empire before the rise of the Bolsheviks. Activists like the Menshevik Vera Zasulich and Ekaterina Breshko-Breshkovskaia, the world-travelling Socialist Revolutionary, were well-known symbols of women's revolutionary agency well before October 1917.

Women like May and Ruth would have been aware of such revolutionary forebears before their arrival to the Lux. In Western cultural representations, Russian emancipatory movements were sometimes represented through the figure of the woman revolutionary. May, as a connoisseur of Irish theatre, would have surely known of Oscar Wilde's first play, a tragedy centred on the actions of a Russian revolutionary named Vera Sabouroff, potentially a fictionalised Vera Zasulich. Certainly, May would have known certain works by the leading Soviet theorist of women's emancipation, Alexandra Kollontai, whose pamphlets were published in translation by the same Fleet Street press May had helped manage in the years before she left for Moscow.

Alexandra Kollontai, the St Petersburg-born daughter of an aristocratic family, already had a long record of work in the revolutionary underground before 1917. Her writings would prove influential in determining the most radical aspects of the Soviet Family Law Code of 1919. Divorce was liberalised, abortion was provided in safe clinical settings, the category of childhood illegitimacy was abolished and all laws rendering women the property of their fathers and husbands were eradicated. For at least two women in our story, these laws, particularly the abolition of illegitimacy, would prove important.

Kollontai considered these reforms part of a wider programme that would liberate women and set them on equal standing with their male peers. Another crucial strand of Kollontai's formula for women's liberation, ultimately never realised in the Soviet era, was the socialisation of all domestic and childcare duties that kept women tied to the household. Kollontai, in her personal life and writings, also modelled a form of sexual freedom. Her writings developed an expansive vision of emancipation with a still-discern-ible influence in modern feminist movements. In contrast to many more reform-minded feminists elsewhere in Europe, Kollontai understood the necessity of transforming ideas about societal gender roles *alongside* reforming the legal position of women.

In what would become something of a pattern, international communists resident in the urban centres of Soviet power like Moscow and Leningrad benefited more from these policies than those beyond the major cities, who were more likely to witness the negative consequences of rapidly introduced reforms. Historian Kristen Ghodsee notes that by 1926 many women, 'especially in the rural areas, were clamouring for a return to the old ways' as men used eased divorce to abandon women as soon as they became pregnant, sexual liberalisation combined with poor access to birth control and limited state resources resulted in large numbers of homeless children, while poor wages did not afford women the ability to support children as single mothers.[14] Kollontai's vision of emancipation achieved some legislative successes, but patriarchal attitudes were deeply engrained in Soviet society, as elsewhere.

Nonetheless, the experience of emancipation that proved intoxic-ating for many women who made their way to the Soviet state, especially in its early years, was based on real opportunities and rights that were often unavailable to these women at home. For international sympathisers of the Soviet experiment, women's emancipation was one of the aspects of the new society that could easily be spoken about with pride. This is precisely why it came as such a blow to many in the international movement when, in the mid-1930s, the Soviet commit-ment to women's emancipation was rapidly de-prioritised and certain reforms, notably the liberalisation of abortion law, were reversed.

But as Moscow residents in the years of the revolution's most fervent commitment to political experimentation, May, Ruth and their fellow political emigrants of the 1920s lived within a particular window in revolutionary time that would not be repeated. Some could see that the window was gradually closing. Already by 1924 the concept of 'Socialism in One Country', which Stalin would uphold as a central tenet, was being developed. This doctrine called for the re-orientation of the international communist movement away from its focus on spreading the revolution internationally and towards the defence of socialism within the borders of the USSR. The hope that ascendant Workers' Republics in Europe would rescue the Soviet Union from its isolation was dashed by the failure and collapse of communist experiments in countries like Hungary and Germany. Only by lionising and defending the 'achievements' of Soviet socialism would workers elsewhere be encouraged to overthrow their masters, so the thesis stated. The ultimate adoption of this idea as orthodoxy set the communist movement on a path towards a near-hegemonic level of Stalinist control, opened the door for Russian nationalism to replace internationalism and stifled attempts to suggest any path forward other than that adopted by the Soviet politburo.

The mid-1920s, with the calamitous war conditions a few years behind and the onset of Stalinist orthodoxy still some time ahead, was the twilight of the revolution's most imaginative period. The public theatre of regular demonstrations occasionally passed by the street-facing windows of the Lux as thousands of people – workers, foreign delegates, old revolutionaries and migrants from the coun- tryside – wound their way down Tverskaya Street to celebrate various holidays. Writing to her boyfriend, Ruth described 'how fortunate' she was to be able to watch the 1925 May Day march from May's room on the second floor, which overlooked the wide street: an ideal vantage point.[15] On another day of festivities, the two women prepared dinner on a small oil stove in May's room. The noise of bands and marching feet outside continually brought them away from the stove and towards the window to look out. After finally managing to cook something, May and Ruth dined together to the sounds poured out by the musicians among the marchers.[16]

New cultural forms blossomed while the classics were yet to be regarded irredeemably bourgeois. May, a vegetarian since at least her days in the suffrage struggle, ate regularly at a club devoted to the ideals of the writer Lev Tolstoy, whose political vision advocated pacifism and cruelty-free diets. Ruth regularly joined May for meals and the two women, in Ruth's words, would 'almost talk ourselves to death'. At one point, Ruth realised she had not eaten meat for five months, not through a conscious decision but simply through becoming so close to May. One evening, the pair marked Tolstoy's ninety-second birthday at the Tolstoy Club. A pianist played some of Tolstoy's favourite compositions and the attendees heard from the great novelist's former secretary, who spoke about Tolstoy's views on women and the 'sex question'.[17]

As May and Ruth whiled away their evenings with comrades in the Hotel Lux and among vegetarian diners at the Tolstoy Club, they encountered a city that provided unprecedented freedoms not only for single women like themselves, but for many others from the margins of pre-revolutionary society. In the mid-1920s the Soviet state was developing its 'techniques of hospitality', the practice of touring foreign visitors around model institutions where the working and peasant classes were educated and accommodated. In November 1925 Kennel wrote in a letter to her boyfriend that she had spent the previous Saturday with May and a close German comrade of her Irish friend at a home for peasants that had previously been 'Moscow's finest hotel'.[18] The German comrade, Kennel noted, was a woman called 'Leonard', the 'wife of Edo Fimmen'.[19]

'Leonard', really Emmy Leonhard, was not, in fact, the wife of the then internationally famous Dutch trade unionist Edo Fimmen. However, she had given birth to his daughter in a hospital close to the Kremlin Palace a few months before. In any other European state, Emmy and Edo's relationship would have cast their daughter as 'illegitimate'. For women like Emmy, however, part of the appeal of living in Soviet Moscow was precisely that such a stigma could be avoided. This November 1925 letter from Ruth to her boyfriend is the earliest existing source that points to May's friendship with Emmy Leonhard. These two women, upon meeting in Moscow in 1925, began a friendship that would outlast decades, ideological crises and a world war.

What explains this friendship's durability and intensity? Multilingualism would have been an initial connecting point: both women had a flair for learning languages. May was fluent in German.

Emmy, a German native-speaker, was already experienced in English. Another factor in their friendship was surely May's refusal, in all the sources I have encountered, to ever cast judgement on Emmy's romantic arrangements as a legally single woman raising the children of a married man. Even though the two women crossed over in the Lux for less than a year, May constantly sought ways of supporting Emmy and her young family in the decades to come. These supportive ties, which remained unbroken for the rest of Emmy and May's long lives, started from the very moment Emmy welcomed her first child into the world. In turn, this friendship and its unusual legacy would prove pivotal in allowing me to piece together the wider story told within this book.

7. The Kaemmerer Children, Leonhard Fimmen Papers. Standing (L–R):
Bruno and Heinrich. On the floor (L–R): Joachim and Elisa. Emmy is seated
in the chair. Hamburg, late 1890s. Leonhard Fimmen Papers

Before she came to know the precarious nature of a life dedicated to revolution, the young Emmy Leonhard experienced a childhood surrounded by fabulous wealth. Emmy was born in May

1890, the first child of Georg and Alida Kaemmerer, members of a powerful Hamburg banking dynasty. Four more children would follow little Emmy: first Heinrich, then Bruno, Elisa and Joachim. A studio photograph – an artefact that itself reflected the family's status – finds all the children neatly dressed. Emmy, perhaps in recognition of her seniority, is the only one seated in a chair, her flowing blonde hair moving through a white bow and her face resting in her palm.

The grand home where Emmy and her siblings spent their childhood was in Heimfeld, then a rural district of the city of Hamburg. The residence must have been enormous, with the family photo album revealing that there was a second garden building on the spacious grounds that complemented the impressive neoclassical family home. Emmy would leave it all behind: the home, the titled 'von' in her surname and eventually the family name itself, preferring instead to be known to her revolutionary comrades as 'Leonhard'.

This, too, is the name and context by which I know her best. Emmy became politically active in her mid-twenties, finally leaving home in 1915. An assiduously staged photograph of Emmy as a grown woman finds her in a thoughtful pose, her head resting lightly on her hand, mirroring the pose from her childhood family portrait. There is a smile on her face, suggestive of the optimistic outlook that she would maintain even amid the harrowing experiences of the decades ahead. The photograph dates from 1916, the same year she lost her mother. It was a deep loss for the then 25-year-old Emmy. She counted her mother as an early inspiration for her commitment to socialism. Two years after this photograph was taken, a revolutionary fervour erupted in Emmy's city.

On 6 November 1918, responding to a wave of insurrection that would topple the German monarchy and install the Weimar Republic in its place, a group of armed sailors occupied a printworks in Hamburg and issued the first edition of a new revolutionary paper, *Die Rote Fahne* (*The Red Flag*). 'This is the beginning of the German Revolution, of the world revolution,' the paper confidently declared: 'Hail the most powerful action of the world revolution!

<8. Portrait of Emmy Leonhard, 1916. Leonhard Fimmen Papers>

Long live socialism! Long live the German workers' republic! Long live world Bolshevism.'[20]

First ascending to power in port cities such as Hamburg, these revolutionaries, inspired by the Bolshevik model, set about dissolving the traditional institutions of the state. Workers' and soldiers' councils replaced senates, 'red guards', composed of mutinous sailors, replaced police forces. But in Hamburg, this Bolshevik arrangement proved particularly short-lived, with the old administrative organs being re-established mere days after their dissolution. According to family memory, Emmy participated in the workers' councils that emerged in this revolutionary moment.

After the German revolutionary wave ebbed, Emmy continued her political activity and was elected to Hamburg parliament as a member of the SPD, the German social democrats.

Historians of obscure revolutionaries must accept the limitations of the archive. My knowledge of Emmy's life is fragmentary. In certain periods I can write of her actions with extraordinary specificity; in other instances I know frustratingly little about how she navigated years of revolutionary turmoil. What, for example, did Emmy make of the crises that wracked her country as it fitfully transformed into the Weimar Republic at the close of the First World War? I know only that she grew steadily more politically engaged and more revolutionary.

After her tenure as a member of the Hamburg parliament, she was involved in trade union affairs in Germany and drew towards the German communists, the KPD, one of the most important national parties working within the Comintern. Before she joined the party in July 1923, she spent two years in Amsterdam within the International Transport Workers Federation, known as the ITF. It was almost certainly through this work that she met the man who became her life partner: Edo Fimmen, the imposing and determined Dutch leader of the ITF.[21] Almost nine years her senior, Edo was already a leading figure in the international trade union movement. He was also already married with two children when he met Emmy. Nonetheless, the tall, voluble trade unionist and the young idealist were drawn to one another.

Although more radical than many of his trade union comrades and a convinced anti-imperialist, Edo always maintained a distance from international communism, in ideology if not in love. Despite political differences, Emmy and Edo became romantically involved – a partnership that would last until his death. Their dedication to one another fostered the deeply inadequate role Emmy would come to play in the historical record: the life partner of a leading labour figure. Edo was separated but not legally divorced from his wife, and his marital status would have repercussions for how Emmy navigated interwar radicalism while raising their two daughters.

When Emmy first became pregnant, Soviet Russia was the one country in the world that granted full legal equality to the children of married and unmarried couples. This may well have been the reason why she chose to have her first child there, rather than remain at home to give birth in more familiar surroundings. In the latter half of 1924, already in the early stages of her pregnancy, Emmy arrived in Moscow. She was assigned Hotel Lux room 14, close by the one occupied by a woman who would have a profound influence on the direction of her life and that of her daughter: May O'Callaghan. Although Emmy's main work was within the Profintern, the trade union wing of the Comintern, she also spent some time translating in the same department where May managed a team.

By the summer of 1925 May was beginning her rise in the Comintern offices. Her command of the organisation's most important working languages eventually eased her into a managerial role in the press department's English section. On 30 May 1925, when Emmy went into labour, it was May who provided the cab fare that allowed her to reach the Kremlin hospital, where she gave birth to her first daughter, Elisa. This moment, with its dramatic setting, became part of Leonhard family lore. May's role made her an important part of this story too, surely helping to establish her as both a lifelong friend to Emmy and, later, a recurring and important figure in the life of her daughter.

Born in the Soviet state, young Elisa spent her earliest moments free of the legal category of 'illegitimacy' that would be placed upon her when mother and daughter returned to Berlin. Elisa's surname was first registered not as her mother's family name nor her father's, but her mother's chosen pseudonym, 'Leonhard'. She was born into the revolution and fittingly took the name her mother used to navigate it. Many decades later, a friend of Elisa's remembered how, in philosophical conversations that continued into the early hours, Elisa would sometimes mention that she was born close to the Kremlin. It was an unusual beginning that, in ways that would take decades to become clear to Elisa, determined the arc of her life.

Elisa spent her first months in the Hotel Lux, surrounded by her mother's revolutionary friends. The population of the Lux had increased almost sixfold from a reasonably comfortable 160 guests in 1921 to more than 600 by the end of 1925.[22] Living conditions transitioned from cosy to cramped. The populations of bedbugs and rodents increased as a result, but so too did opportunities for new comradeships. The dominance of the German community in the Lux began to be diluted by men and women arriving from English-speaking countries such as Ireland, Britain and the US. The contained social world of the Lux grew wider and more vibrant, just as the factional debates over the future of the world revolution became sharper.

9. Emmy Leonhard and baby Elisa, Moscow, 1925. Leonhard Fimmen Papers

The Language of Revolution

1

In the spring of 1926 the Aran Islands-born communist Thomas J. O'Flaherty, known to friends as Tom, arrived in Moscow to participate in a time-worn leftist tradition: factional in-fighting. Already, as he became familiar with the rooms and residents of the Hotel Lux, Tom was being introduced as the brother of someone more famous. Back home in Ireland, his younger brother Liam was making a name for himself (and not always a good name). While Liam wrote fiction and scandalised literary Dublin, Tom rose through the ranks of the Workers' Party of America, the name given to the 'surface' wing of the Communist Party.

As a native Irish speaker born in Ireland, Tom was – in a curious way – a typical American communist of the early 1920s. This was a world dominated by foreign-born immigrants where native English speakers were a minority. *The Patriot*, a British far-right journal, paid attention to the O'Flaherty brothers in 1923, identifying Liam as a founding member of the Irish Party and signalling out Tom as one of a 'large number of Irishmen' in important positions within 'the American revolutionary ranks'.[1] Irish-born radicals were certainly present among the American comrades, but their numbers were scarcely 'large'. *The Patriot* was, at the very least, right in pointing out that Tom O'Flaherty was important.

When Tom arrived in the Lux in early 1926, he was part of a delegation of US communists appearing before the Comintern executive to iron out fierce internal disputes. From the mid-twenties onwards, American communists became a regular sight in the Hotel Lux as the Comintern sought to provide resolutions. 'Geese' versus 'liquidators', 'Lovestonites' versus 'Fosterites' – the American party was riven by factions with names of varying inelegance. As Stalin continued his ultimately victorious pursuit of power during these same years, he deftly played Bolshevik factions against one another to his own benefit. Because Comintern politics, with the failure of the European revolution, was now increasingly beholden to the fate of the inner-party struggles among the Bolsheviks, Stalin's ascent within his own Party would be accompanied by the dominance of the Stalinist line within the Comintern. Thus, by the late 1920s, there was only one faction that could win in an American inter-communist dispute, or any other debate within a Comintern-backed party: the faction that ultimately sided with Stalin.

But the Comintern was not only calling American communists to Moscow to hear the case put forward by its warring sides. Another major issue that required Comintern intervention was the US party's approach to its various wings organised around language and ethnicity. In the early 1920s American communism boasted an astonishingly cosmopolitan membership. The December before Tom O'Flaherty arrived in Moscow, the American commission of the Comintern learned of a party group in New York where eleven separate languages were spoken among only *thirteen* members.[2]

A rich, multilingual media offering was spearheaded by communists in early 1920s America, which included papers in Yiddish, Lithuanian, German, Polish and Ukrainian. In these years, there were no fewer than three daily communist newspapers published in Finnish in the US, such was the appetite for radical news among migrant Finns.[3] Often, these papers were just one part of a wider radical cultural world, with the various ethnic groups within American communism also forming orchestras, acting troupes, clubs and schools.

The party press was considered central to the coming American revolution and Tom O'Flaherty played an important role within it. Tom was, like his brother, a writer. As a high-ranking staffer on the *Daily Worker*, the main US communist English-language newspaper, and editor of its publication for prisoners' causes, the *Labor Defender*, Tom appears in numerous reflections on radical life in 1920s America.

Charles Shipman, a New York-born radical who also went by 'Jesus Ramirez' and 'Manuel Gomez', remembered Tom when he first met him in the early 1920s as a 'free-swinging revolutionary columnist' with a 'barbed humour' and a 'complex of talents'.[4]

Whittaker Chambers, the one-time literary star of American communism and later intellectual light of anti-communism, recalled Tom more dourly as a 'big unhappy Irishman, who lived sadly in the shadow of his celebrated brother'.[5] Yet in his autobiography, Chambers also memorialised Tom in affectionate tones. For Chambers, Tom was a man of 'gifts' who bore a 'heavy cross for a Communist': a sense of humour. Another contemporary noted that Tom's writing for the party press, with its wit and light touch, stood out amid the 'sea of hyper-revolutionary, thunderous class-angling of every event reported by the paper.'[6] Often written with real verve, Tom's reports and sketches for the *Daily Worker* aged better than much other communist writing of the era.

Yet, as Chambers' mention of Tom's unhappiness reflects, humour in a world of self-regarding ideologues was not the only cross he bore. Both O'Flaherty brothers balanced their talents with a tendency towards self-destruction. In the prohibition era US, Tom drank his way through dives and speakeasies, occasionally requiring comrades to bail him out when he lacked the dollars to foot his bills. In Chicago, his stomping ground for much of his radical career, his landlady, a motherly retired teacher, helped Tom 'when he needed it most'.[7] Sometimes, Chambers would find Tom lying on Union Square, completely inebriated, in front of the *Daily Worker* offices. 'So he would be roughly lugged inside,' recalled Chambers, 'amidst taunts and remarks of disgust, by men who were not worthy to touch him.'[8]

If May and Ruth were exposed to any of Tom's demons when they met him in the Hotel Lux, it is not conveyed by Ruth's light letter to her boyfriend Sam describing the fun to be had with Tom and his fellow delegates in their rooms. All indulged in a 'peculiar kind of nonsensical American humour' into the late hours.[9] Ruth described Tom as 'a nice fellow, the brother of Liam who wrote several notable novels'.[10] Fuelled by the cheap alcohol received in exchange for his delegate's allowance, he regaled Hotel Lux guests one evening with a comedy sketch about the happenings among the delegates and his new friends during his weeks in Moscow.[11]

During working hours, however, conversation was less light and humorous, more hyper-revolutionary and thunderous. Tom and his comrades attempted to argue out a path forward for the party, all under the watchful supervision of the Comintern executive. Tom's circle, although known in a barbed joke as the 'drinking faction', was the nucleus of what would become America's first circle of communists to back Leon Trotsky in his showdown with Stalin before Trotsky's exile from Soviet territory.[12] But all that lay ahead of Tom in early 1926, when the contours of the debate that would result in Trotsky's removal from the Communist Party, and thus Tom's own, were only just becoming clear.

Attendant to the growing influence of Stalinism in Soviet communism, the Comintern increasingly pushed its member parties towards centralisation, or 'Bolshevization'. One of the frontlines of this fight was a war against linguistic diversity in the US Party. The Comintern executive was opposed to American communism's many language groups, seeing within them a threat to political unity. Though the lively and multilingual communist press was arguably the central means by which ordinary migrants and American citizens came to learn of revolutionary ideas, the Comintern had identified a real problem: you cannot organise the proletariat if they cannot understand one another.

While in Moscow, Tom had his own personal encounter with the perils of multilingualism. Ever attuned to where levity could be found amid interminable ideological wrangling, one evening Tom set out to attend a Moscow play with a promising title: *The Mad Monkey*. He was disappointed to discover that his Russian interpreter had, in fact, mistranslated the title of Eugene O'Neil's play *The Hairy Ape*. Nonetheless, he sat through the entire production out of what he described as 'a sense of decency'.[13]

The Comintern was always concerned with what might be lost in translation and attempted to refine the interpretation process at its meetings. The place of Russian as the language of communism – reflected today in kitschy backwards Rs printed on the title of any vaguely Soviet book, movie or product – was by no means a given from the outset. German was dominant at the First Congress in 1919. French and English asserted their presence at the second in 1920. But after 1923, with the failure of the German Revolution, Russian became ascendant as the primary working language of the Comintern. International communists were encouraged to learn it as the auxiliary language through which they would conduct their revolutionary work.

Yet it was only by the Fifth Congress, in July 1924, that Russian became the primary language of Comintern proceedings. May O'Callaghan, English native speaker, fluent in German and Russian, arrived just as the Fifth Congress concluded, well placed to contribute to the Comintern's translation needs. Not only was she linguistically talented, but her years working on the *Dreadnought* gave her experience of navigating an office filled with rambunctious radicals, most of whom were younger than herself. As someone in her forties, she was on the senior end of the Comintern workforce. It is perhaps this seniority, in addition to her skillset, which eased her ascent to a managerial role.

By early 1926, when Tom and his fellow delegates arrived, May was managing one strand of the Comintern's elaborate translation process. Historian Brigid O'Keeffe describes it as a system of 'consecutive interpretation', where after every speech 'congress delegates who required translation would reconvene in their various "language groups" to meet with the appointed interpreters'.[14] Stenographers (workers who could write in shorthand) made notes of the speech; the script was passed through to the translators and then the transcript was delivered in the delegates' own language. It was down to a middle-aged Irishwoman and her translation colleagues to lead this process as the US delegates – along with delegates from many other countries in Europe, Asia and the Americas – entered the halls of the Kremlin Palace to try and work towards a common language of revolution.

2

Delegates would often wait quite some time to listen to the speeches they wanted to hear as the words made their way through the flow of consecutive interpretation. Bolshevik speech-makers were not known for brevity. Trotsky, in a showy display of the language skills he honed through study in tsarist prisons and in his pre-revolutionary exile, once famously broke the six-hour mark in a single speech he personally delivered in Russian, German and French.[15] But while the life of a Comintern translator was intense and often tedious, it could also prove vindicating and even exhilarating. Hearing so many languages spoken all at once provided a living example of communism's promise of internationalism. The surroundings where these languages were spoken and translated contributed enormously to this overall impression.

While some of the most exciting tasks were carried out in the Kremlin Palace during official Comintern gatherings, more humdrum work took place in the nearby Comintern headquarters. Shifts in the Comintern headquarters were divided into a six-hour working day: clocking in at 9 am, breaking for food in the canteen by 11 am and tying up work at 3 pm. This six-hour working day was, as historian Brigitte Studer has noted, 'genuinely revolutionary'.[16] One of May's employees described the office of her department in the Comintern building on Mokhavaya Street as a well-lit space, spread out over two rooms. Here, the employee remembered, 'various documents, appeals, speeches and articles originally written in Russian, French and German' were translated into English. This same employee recalled his surprise upon learning that the 'most confidential Comintern documents' were handled by employees like May who did not hold party membership cards. Party members were constantly recalled back to their home countries, while non-party migrant workers could remain in the Soviet state and thus commit themselves to one role. The 'fastest, most prolific, most efficient translator' on the team was reportedly a lapsed Menshevik, an older woman with white hair who had lived in

London and who would, according to this recollection, lambast various Bolshevik luminaries in frank terms during the working day, casting out remarks that would infuriate May, now the manager of the English section.[17]

During the most intensive periods of Comintern work when international delegations converged on Moscow, May, Ruth, and their colleagues were given passes to join the delegates inside the Kremlin Palace. For those who often faced persecution for their political ideals at home, gaining access to the most vaunted corridors of power based on those same ideals was often a deeply moving experience.

Each day, after showing their passes to the layers of security guarding the entrance to the Kremlin compound, the Comintern workers headed towards the grand palace. The palace stands within the walls of the Kremlin complex, overlooking the River Moskva from which the city takes its name. Built in the mid-nineteenth century, the palace was decorated with material from every corner of the vast Russian Empire. Throughout the Comintern's existence, major events of the Comintern congresses and the smaller gatherings of delegates known as 'plenums' took place within the throne room, known as the Andrievsky Hall. Loudspeakers were placed at intervals along the seating to broadcast the speaker's voice along the long hallway. The stenographers sat below the stage from where the delegates addressed the room of revolutionaries, the same room in which tsarist emperors once addressed their subjects.

Most of the Comintern workforce remained in the smaller though no less ostentatious room beside the hall where the Tsar once sat upon his throne, the Alexandrovsky Hall. The room's large windows frame a panoramic view that takes in the Moscow cityscape on the bank of the Moskva opposite the Kremlin. Although the two rooms were merged into one in the 1930s, with the Romanov throne replaced with a statue of Lenin, in the years that May and her team worked during Comintern sessions the Alexandrovsky room still retained much of its pre-revolutionary trappings.[18] High ceilings were inlaid with gold, marble fireplaces and a large mirror were set into the walls and six golden chandeliers lit by electric lighting hung over the translators and typists. For John S. Clarke, a leftist author and lion-tamer who attended the Second Comintern Congress, the interiors of the Kremlin Palace 'spoke eloquently of the utter wickedness of a social system which bestowed such privileges upon the sickliest and most stupid creatures on earth (monarchs)'.[19]

For those more accustomed to incarceration than candelabras, it must have prompted a kind of political vertigo. Ruth Kennell suggested as much when writing excitedly to her mother after her first stint as a typist in the palace:

It seems incongruous to enter this place and see a score of men and women busily at work, fifty typewriters clicking madly, and a dozen translators dictating to the typists, the mimeograph machine with all its papers, black ink and disorderliness cluttering up one of the alcoves, and all this noise merging in the vast hall into a loud buzzing sound – a staff of men and women from every country of the world, many of them from the prisons of those countries, and the majority of them having known persecution and poverty in the old world, and here we talk in many languages with a feeling of perfect security. What a paradise Moscow is for the rebels and outcasts of the capitalist world![20]

Nonetheless, for Ruth, at least, the novelty of working in the palace eventually wore off. Her second round of work within these ornate halls took place during the early 1926 Comintern gathering, when May and Ruth would have first met Tom O'Flaherty – a session that devoted a great deal of time to the row between the duelling American factions. It was also a moment for the Comintern to take stock of broader prospects and tactics. While Western Europe had evidently failed to live up to its revolutionary expectations by early 1926, demonstrations and strikes by worker and student movements in China revealed an emerging revolutionary situation.[21] During the sessions, the Comintern executive directed its members to draw more people towards revolutionary ideas through further work alongside non-communist organisations, such as nationalist groups fighting imperialism. An important example of this 'united front' approach was the alliance between Chinese communists and China's nationalist movement led by Chiang Kaishek. These two forces would ultimately oppose one another in a long civil war that birthed today's contestation between China, the People's Republic of China, and Taiwan, the Republic of China. As the translators and typists in the Kremlin Palace grappled with terms like 'united front' and 'mass organisations', they were juggling the concepts that major political forces would use to reshape modern history.

3

10. Tom O'Flaherty, c. 1910s. Joyce Rathbone Papers

The year 1926, with its decisive discussions in the Kremlin Palace, was, as always, a year of movement at the Hotel Lux. Tom O'Flaherty returned to the US once his role as a delegate concluded. He made stops in Ireland, where he 'discussed the futility of things' with Dublin's 'cynical intelligentsia', and London, from where he despatched reports on the General Strike.[22] But before setting out on his circuitous homeward journey, Tom spent his final evening in the Lux at a gathering in the room of an old comrade. 'Big Bill' Haywood was a long-time resident of room 12 and still a legendary figure of the American left. A photograph captures Tom in Moscow, standing behind Haywood, possibly taken in Haywood's room on that very evening. Tom is dressed neatly in a suit and tie. As Tom left the gathering, Haywood asked him to pass on his regards to friends back home and encourage them in the fight. There was, Tom remembered, a sadness about the moment.

His health failing, Haywood seemed to recognise that he would never again see some of the American visitors who came to his room at the Lux.[23] Tom, in turn, would never again see Moscow. In truth, Tom himself had less than a decade left before his own early death. Yet there was another reason why Tom never returned: taking the side of Leon Trotsky, he became persona non grata in Moscow circles. The tribalism that had characterised pre-revolutionary life in the revolutionary exile communities was manifesting once more in the Soviet Communist Party. But the factional struggle had yet to take its most lethal form.

For now, Moscow still had the aura of a revolutionary sanctuary. This was certainly the experience of a new addition to May's team in the Comintern. Joseph Freeman was approved for onward travel to Moscow by superiors in the US party in April 1926.[24] A 28-year-old radical poet with deep-set eyes and equally deeply-held ideals, Joseph's trip from New York to Eastern Europe was almost a journey of ancestral return. Born in 1897 in Piratin, a village in Poltava, Ukraine, the first son of Jewish parents, Isaac and Stella, Joseph and his family moved to New York in 1904. His memories of childhood in Ukraine veered from absurdly picaresque moments – being tossed in the air 'like a ball' by visiting Cossacks – to darker imagery that evoked many other Jewish family histories of the era: the 'fear of pogroms' hanging 'like a black nightmare' over the village.[25]

Joseph came of age in a migrant world, Jewish Brooklyn, with many similarities to the Jewish East End of Rose and Nellie Cohen.

In both cases, there was a mix of languages, tenement blocks and Irish people. But Joseph, who retained memories of his own early life in the Russian Empire and had a more intimate experience of tsarist antisemitism that the Cohen sisters, born and raised in London, could only have learned about through family stories. It was this intimate experience that Joseph would later remember moving him to tears during a work day with his translation and stenography colleagues in the Kremlin Palace.

Joseph was seated beneath the platform at a session where the Trotsky and Stalin debate was playing out in the throne room, likely during the same late 1926 Comintern plenum where Ruth finally grew tired of her plush surroundings. Taking leave of his workstation close to the orators, Joseph made his way to the adjoining Alexandrovsky Hall with its tall windows looking out onto the river Moskva. Here, Joseph spotted a boy, the son of a Jewish colleague, playing in the room where his fellow technical workers sat before their typewriters. Tears came into Joseph's eyes, 'tears of joy and recompense', as he watched this 'little Jewish boy playing freely in the palace of the czars'.[26]

Beside the hall where the revolution was being outlined in theoretical abstractions, Joseph found the revolution's promise of liberation reflected in a boy who reminded him of his younger self. 'The Revolution seemed justified on the deepest emotional level', Joseph recalled, 'it had redressed a wrong which had affected me – and in that little boy I saw a radiant future for the new generation he represented.' Joseph realised, too, that 'never before' in his life had he 'found so complete an acceptance by a community or believed so completely in its creed – never, that is, since my Ukrainian childhood'.[27] Here in Moscow, Joseph befriended 'people in all ranks, for rank had not yet begun to count'.[28] During the year he spent in Moscow, a period it took him a lifetime to fully understand, he made many deep friendships in the rooms of the Lux. It was a moment of safety in a century that offered few.

Mixing Poetry and Facts

1

Guests in the Lux brought with them their traditions and social habits from home. Christmas, for example, was a time of relaxation and recreation, just like elsewhere. Friends gathered for drinks. Meals were shared. On May and Ruth's second Christmas in the Lux in 1926, when Emmy was still there but Joseph was yet to arrive, Ruth told her mother 'we had many parties, at which the English speaking comrades met one another socially for almost the first time and we discovered how clever and nice we are'.[1] At Lux parties, there was singing and dancing and cheap wine. There was conversation spoken over the crackling music emitted from a phonograph. And there were elements of all the prominent aspects of Lux life in the twenties, which one former resident listed as 'fun, fights, storms, celebrations, conspiracies, disclosures, jealousies, the clash of national customs, and such a variety of appearance that variety itself became commonplace and hardly noticeable'.[2]

There was also, of course, politics, of both the revolutionary and personal varieties. The distinction between the party (a disciplined organisation composed of a cadre who considered themselves the vanguard of the socialist revolution) and a party (an often unruly assortment of people socialising together) became blurred at evening gatherings in the Hotel Lux.

Thrown together by circumstance and compelled to negotiate basic human needs like eating, hygiene and sex, Lux residents were at the forefront of thinking through the question of how the revolution would reshape personal life. And what could be more personal than bonds of friendship, love and attraction? Having checked in and followed the working day of those who resided at the Hotel Lux, it is time for us to spend more time with the guests during their evening schedules and, where the sources allow, follow them into the night, peering behind a few bedroom doors that the diligent use of archival fragments can help us set ajar.

In the Lux, people made friends they considered to be a chosen family. Affairs were not unknown, even common. This could all be told as a recurring story about people of a similar age living together in proximity, often thousands of miles away from their families back home. But it can also be seen as the product of a movement that gestured towards an all-encompassing idea of revolutionary liberation. Because the contours of that revolution were still flexible in the 1920s, many found licence to cast out 'bourgeois' mores in favour of dissident models of family, sexuality and romance.

Some of these radicals were politicised in a context where 'free love' was a maxim that encouraged them to view interpersonal jealousies as harmfully individualistic. But Soviet theories of the place of sexuality under socialism, crafted in the austere years of the Revolution and Civil War, rarely aligned neatly with more bohemian models imported from abroad.

Although, for reasons that will become clear, May remained above the fray of dating in the Lux, she developed intense friendships with people whose romantic attachments were complex and, in a few cases, overlapping. Two of her earliest friends in Moscow were in relationships that would have been more fraught to navigate elsewhere. Emmy Leonhard lived with her 'illegitimate' daughter Elisa while Elisa's father, Edo, travelled across Europe on trade union work. Ruth, meanwhile, remained open to amorous advances in the Lux while simultaneously maintaining a correspondence with her boyfriend *and* her husband Frank, by then returned to Siberia with their son Jimmy. Towards the end of her time in Moscow, Ruth told her mother such 'freedom exists here between men and women that they never feel tied to one another by anything but their own wishes'.[3] Some, like Ruth, found liberation from the romantic jealousies and

familial expectations of their old society in revolutionary Moscow.
But for others, it was all a recipe for heartbreak.

2

When I started searching for the identity of an anonymised
Irishwoman, whose life in 1920s Moscow I found referenced in an
out-of-print autobiography, I expected to find an interesting story.
But I was not optimistic it would be a story I could tell in her own
voice. The writings and letters of Joseph Freeman were the second
part of the equation, which, along with Ruth's voluminous archive,
would eventually allow me to piece together a vivid sense of May's
personality.

In time, as I delved deeper into Joseph's story in my search for
May, I realised that he almost certainly spent longer analysing his
time in the Lux than anyone else who ever passed through its walls.
He was fascinated by Freudian psychoanalysis from early adulthood.
In the deeply self-reflective boxes of material he left behind, now
held in a basement in California, it really showed. For Joseph, his
time in the Lux – only eight months in total – was not just a transformative experience of confirmed convictions and revolutionary
living: it was the story of a messy break-up. I began to understand
how his book *An American Testament*, the autobiography that
started my research journey, was partly a tribute to people like May
who shaped him, but also a retaliation against a different woman
in Moscow who, frustrated with Joseph's lack of ambition, left him
for another man. The 'other man', in this case, certainly did not
lack ambition. Indeed, Joseph's romantic competition in the Lux,
Manabendra Nath (M. N.) Roy, became one of the major figures
of the Indian independence movement.

When Joseph arrived at the Lux, his first port of call was room
288; the residence of Luise Geissler, the woman who would become,
albeit briefly, his girlfriend. He first met the woman he knew as
'Lou' in a Japanese restaurant in New York, early in 1926 before

he came to Moscow. That evening, Joseph was struck by Luise's 'bright blue eyes' and her close-cut hair, parted on one side with the long end framing the right side of her 'handsome, intelligent, sensual' face.[4]

Though a couple of years younger than Joseph, Luise was far more experienced in revolutionary affairs. Born to a German father and a mother with Sinti and Roma heritage, young Luise became a member of a radical left movement by the age of seventeen and worked with the leadership of the short-lived Bavarian Soviet Republic. Some years after the Munich-centred workers' republic collapsed, she made her way to Moscow to join the Comintern apparatus in 1921.[5] Following an apprenticeship in Comintern roles ranging from stenography to involvement in the German Party's 'secret military apparatus', she travelled to New York in April 1925 to work with the German section of the US party and the American Negro Labor Congress.[6] For Joseph, she was 'the real thing, a militant bolshevik'.[7] He was smitten. In May 1926, Geissler swapped New York for Moscow. A couple of months later, Joseph did the same.

While Joseph's mother tongue, Yiddish, provided a linguistic bridge to understanding German that eased his entry into Luise's circle, he also arrived in Moscow just as the number of English-speaking residents was expanding. Regular evening parties at the Lux brought these Anglophone residents closer together during the early months of 1926, fastening another friendship circle that welcomed the charming Joseph upon his arrival.

When Joseph received his room assignment in the Lux, he learned that he would share number 349 with another comrade, Hugo Rathbone. Hugo, of course, was already familiar to the transplants from London before his arrival. Since taking May's room in the London flat she shared with the Cohen sisters following her initial departure for Soviet Russia, Hugo spent time in Sweden before travelling to Moscow.

In Moscow, Hugo took up a role in the Comintern generating specialist reports, including analyses of the Indian anti-colonial struggle. It was likely through this work that Hugo developed his strong admiration for his room-mate, Joseph's romantic rival M. N. Roy. Joseph regarded the Rathbone–Roy friendship through an orientalist lens, seeing Roy as playing the guru to Hugo's seeker-after-truth.

The photograph of Hugo that I found in his Comintern personnel file depicts a sharply dressed young man with a serious gaze and an understated handsomeness, his dark hair neatly parted. Later, the grand-niece of someone Hugo had once set his heart on – Luise Geissler's younger sister, Eva, who also spent these years in Moscow – sent me a copy of the same image. By now, you may be getting a sense of how love life in the Lux, if represented through a diagram, would be a series of interlaced lines.

11. Hugo Rathbone, c. mid-1920s. Courtesy of Pia Backhaus

Hugo's political path contrasted starkly with his own family's political tradition. He worked for the revolutionary destruction of the British Empire, while his father, Hugh Rathbone, was the former Liberal Party MP for Wavertree. Even with this stark political distance between generations, Hugo's elite background was evident in his mannerisms, something that people like Joseph, May and others noticed as soon as he began speaking. Before Joseph's arrival,

Hugo became a regular at the same parties of the English-speaking Lux guests frequented by May and Ruth. Often, Ruth, May and Hugo would have breakfast together in May's room before work began at the Comintern. The trio also spent Christmas of 1926 together with some other friends. Hugo supplied the gathering with a pungent concoction he devised from cheap wine, oranges and lemons. 'He is the type of Oxford man whom we burlesque on the American stage,' Ruth told her mother, 'but a splendid fellow in spite of the English accent.'[8]

Joseph found his English room-mate an amiable if somewhat intense companion. He described Hugo as a 'tall' and 'dreamy' omnivorous reader, who would sometimes 'catch himself reading Stendhal or Tolstoy' before throwing the books to the floor and declaring that he 'must read for profit, not for pleasure'.[9] The depiction rings true. Judging from his own published Marxist analyses, Hugo was doctrinaire and single-minded. Even so, he would later resign from the party in 1937, around the same time that his sister-in-law was arrested in Moscow by the NKVD, Stalin's secret police.

But such dark ends were scarcely imagined in the atmosphere of hopeful beginnings that pervaded life in the Lux at the time that Hugo and Joseph were getting acquainted with their shared room. It was large, with a bed for each of the resident comrades, and had two windows. To reach it, you needed to cross the courtyard from the pre-revolutionary main building of the Lux to the hotel's 'NEP wing' originally opened to generate currency from paying visitors. Clearly the demand for housing in Moscow meant that the NEP wing was now being repurposed for Comintern workers like the rest of the premises.

Although the simple fact of sharing a residence and a common language would have led them to cross paths, it is possible that Hugo made the initial introduction between May and Joseph. In any case, Joseph would soon be brought into her circle and become one of her closest friends in Moscow. For Joseph, May became a respected mentor in his attempts at literature and love. May, in turn, adopted a maternal relationship with the sixteen-years-younger

Joseph, enlisting him in a circle of intimate friends she began to refer to as her 'family' and whose male members she affectionately claimed as her 'boys'.

Because they shared not only a residence but also an office, their friendship was given ample time to develop. He knew her as O'C. She knew him as Joe. In his descriptions of May in his autobiography, Joseph recorded May speaking in both extended monologues and shorter, sharp remarks. Remember: it is by no means common for the people of the early twentieth century to speak directly into the historical record in their own voice, or even someone else's impression of it. Many records – censuses, birth certificates, court documents and so on – can give us a glimpse of a person, but it requires personal documents and memories for us to imagine we can hear them. As I trawled through the vast archive of life in the Lux that Joseph gathered, I began to think of him almost like a stagehand crawling through the rigging of a theatre, lowering a microphone down towards a cast composed of people whose voices would otherwise only resonate faintly in the historical record, if at all.

12. Joseph Freeman, c. 1926. Hoover Institution Library and Archives, Joseph Freeman Papers, Envelope C

3

'Say that in your sonnets, but don't mix poetry with facts,' Joseph recalled May telling him whenever he grew too enthusiastic about life in the Soviet capital.[10] Poetry and facts: these two concepts would become central to how Joseph understood life in Moscow. What were the facts of the revolution? They included its programme for the seizure of power, the rules of conspiracy, the long balance sheets outlining factory production and the dry reports on the iniquities of capitalist economy. There was also the fact of the ever-expanding powers of the Soviet state security apparatus, rarely acknowledged by those who lived in the Lux. In the 1920s, this silence was probably fostered by naivety, but in the 1930s, as some began to suspect listening devices were hidden throughout the hotel, it was predicated more on fear.

What was the 'poetry' of the revolution? For Joseph and his comrades in the Lux, this amounted to the artistic experiments that emerged in the revolution's wake, readily perceivable in the bold new dramatic forms exploding onto Moscow stages, and the attempts to reimagine a more equitable vision of how people related to one another as family, friends and lovers. Contrary to May's advice, it was impossible to avoid mixing the revolution's facts and its poetry.

For Joseph, even their very friendship was evidence of this. For her dear friend 'Joe' Freeman, May stood as one example of what he described as an obvious notion: in the 'communist movement, as everywhere else, our ideas and attitudes are influenced not only by theses and slogans, policies and reports, but also by warm human relationships'.[11] Although this fact was already 'obvious' to Joseph writing in the 1930s, the crucial role played by interpersonal relationships in determining the successes and failures of political movements is too often overlooked by historians.

May related to both her friends and the project of international communism in a similar mode. As we will see when physical distance between May and her friends led her to write letters that still survive, May was often direct and brutally honest, delivering both criticisms

and praise with a view towards encouraging the personal development of her friends and the political development of the Soviet state
she called home. Joseph recalled how May and Ruth – who almost
always moved through Moscow as a tittering duo – would vacillate
'between romantic adoration and bitter despair over the Soviet
system'.[12] Lux accommodation issues, such as issues with running
water or the grossly inadequate provision of bathing facilities (two)
for guests (three hundred plus), would cause the two friends to
'bitterly attack bolshevism from the day Lenin learned to say *mama*
to the particular episode which galled them' while a 'stirring'
performance or a parade of red-scarved young Pioneers would,
Joseph recalled, make them 'bubble over with joy and praise'.[13]

When did Joseph find the opportunity to make these character
observations? It was in downtime following Comintern shifts that
the guests of the Lux found space to talk with one another unin-
hibited (and sometimes inebriated). The long evenings were, in
theory, free for the workers to spend as they wished. However,
communist party members usually faced hours of meetings. One
former Lux resident recalled that sometimes the Comintern workers
even held after-work meetings in their rooms 'or were swotting over
reports, drafting resolutions and thesis and heavens knows what
until all hours of the night, with a minimum of relaxation'.[14]

Nevertheless, even for dues-paying party members like Joseph
and Hugo, time for gatherings, parties and spectacles elsewhere in
the city could still be stolen from the hours remaining once
drawn-out discussions on international issues and trade union practices finally finished. Even late meetings in the Lux, if Comintern
business was tied up early, could descend into a party, with furniture
pushed back to the walls to make way for dancers and residents
belting out popular songs like 'It's a Long way to Tipperary', 'When
Irish Eyes are Smiling' and 'Loch Lomond'.[15] If time for relaxation
was at a minimum, then many Lux guests exploited this minimum
to the best of their ability.

Joseph was a regular and commanding presence at parties in
the Lux. He was, in the words of scholar Alan Wald, famous for his

'irrepressible and irresistible charm'.[16] In what amounted to one of the most flattering contemporary comparisons imaginable, two of the women who fell for Joseph in the 1920s compared his looks to those of Rudolph Valentino. An early star of silent cinema, Valentino was one of the first global celebrity sex symbols of the twentieth century. The author photograph of Joseph, prominently placed on the front cover of his autobiography, is curiously like a well-known image of Valentino. In both, there is a similar seductive gaze and a high-collared white shirt worn in the same manner with top buttons undone.

13. Joseph Freeman's 'militant bolshevik' crush: Luise Geissler, first woman from right, Russia, c. 1926. Courtesy of Pia Backhaus

4

Although May gained several new friends in Moscow in 1926 – the most intimate of whom was 'Joe' Freeman – one of the women closest to her departed the Lux sometime around the year's beginning: Emmy

Leonhard. In September 1925, with her daughter Elisa only a few months old, Emmy wrote to Berlin requesting an extension on her time in Moscow. She argued her case: she could enhance her Russian abilities and work where she was needed. 'The Press department continues to urge me to stay here,' she wrote, 'as there is a great shortage of manpower for translating into German and editing the German documents.'[17] It is possible that, behind the scenes, May was using her role in the press department to try and help Emmy lengthen her stay in Moscow.

Nonetheless, Emmy's request to be granted more time in Moscow was evidently refused. More than a month later, she wrote to the Comintern secretariat to formally request her dismissal from work in Moscow. The German party, she wrote, had demanded her 'immediate return'. 'Moreover', her baby Elisa, now several months old, made it 'impossible' to effectively carry out Comintern duties. Emmy recommended an alternate comrade for her translation work. 'As a replacement,' she wrote, 'I propose to employ Comrade SABO, Berlin, who has a perfect command of English.'[18]

When I first encountered Emmy's letters navigating her return home in the Comintern archives, it was the last line that struck me most. If, as the line suggested, Emmy played some role in bringing 'Comrade Sabo' to Moscow to continue her translation work, then this revealed an unexpected connection between two threads of my research. I knew exactly who 'Comrade Sabo' was: Elise Saborowski, known in wider Comintern history largely through her underground activities in the 1930s, which saw her operating in Shanghai, China, and Rio de Janeiro, Brazil.

In 1926, May – and especially Joseph – would come to know Sabo too. And it was through my research into their lives that I came to know a different Elise Saborowski to the militant revolutionary of Comintern histories: not the willing tool of a conspiratorial network, but a deeply conflicted and sensitive woman, at first falling in love with and then coming to terms with her unrequited passion for Joseph. I wondered: had Emmy unwittingly helped set Sabo on her collision with Joseph?

There was one clear connecting point between Joseph and Sabo: the woman he first set eyes on in New York, Luise Geissler. In Joseph's archive in California there is a handwritten invitation addressed to him in a teasing, almost flirtatious tone. The sender was Luise. 'Dear Joe!' she wrote, 'Do you think it is very nice to let us wait more of an half an hour. So we finally decided to go without you (our heart is bleeding but who cares?) What about tomorrow at 8 o'clock in the morning at Sabo's Room 350, I will come there too. Now don't let us wait again.' She continued, 'Breakfast you can have here,' noting that 'Sabo' wanted to invite him. She did not 'want to compete' with May, Luise noted, hinting, perhaps, at a sense of possessiveness. She signed off: 'So long, Lou.'[19]

I found Luise Geissler's invitation misplaced in a folder of letters sent to Joseph from Sabo. Like Luise and Emmy, Sabo came to Moscow as a Comintern worker from the German communist party. She was born in November 1886 in Borzymin, a village then located in East Prussia and today part of modern Poland. Sabo had met her husband Arthur Ewert in Berlin and together they spent time in Canada after the war, where they helped found the Communist Party of Canada. Life in Canada also gave Sabo an opportunity to develop her abilities in English. Following their return to Europe in the early 1920s, Sabo and Arthur became prominent members of the German communist party. Upon meeting Sabo in Moscow, Joseph was impressed by her revolutionary credentials. The two also connected over their shared literary tastes.

Someone, either an archivist or perhaps Joseph himself, arranged his folder of letters from Sabo in chronological order. Soon after opening the folder, I found the invitation note, sent during his first encounters with Sabo in the Hotel Lux. At the end of the folder is the final letter Sabo sent to him in 1938, shortly before her murder. She wrote it in pencil, on the poor-quality paper she was given as an inmate in a Nazi concentration camp near Wittenberg.

What made Lux friendships and relationships so meaningful for many who lived there in the 1920s was a sense – readily perceivable in memoirs and later traceable in the structure of archives themselves – that this was the crossroads of so many lives and movements. All paths to the future still seemed open. More terrible outcomes remained unimaginable. As another Lux guest from the time put it: 'none of us in the years '26 and '27 were thinking of anybody's demise on the date line of fate'.[20]

The Family

1

By the beginning of 1927, Moscow was regaining its standing after the lean post-revolutionary years. This, at least, was the perception among some of the comfortably accommodated residents of the Lux. The previous summer, repairs had been carried out in the hotel. Ruth remembered how many of the tenants escaped to dachas (summer houses) outside the city to avoid the plaster, ladders and workmen crowding every corridor as 'foundations were torn up and roofs down and community kitchens were built on each floor'.[1] She lived on one of the upper stories of the Lux, on a corridor filled with young families, though she could easily escape downstairs to the relative calm of May's room.

The renovated Lux could better accommodate residents and their invited guests. Sometimes, these evening visitors included luminaries of the Bolshevik revolution. One resident recalled post-work meetings in her room that would be attended by the likes of Nikolai Bukharin, an eminent Bolshevik theorist, Osip Piatnitsky, head of the Comintern's international department, and Vyacheslav Molotov, the high-ranking Soviet politician who later had an incendiary cocktail named in his dishonour.[2]

Just as exciting – at least for literary-minded radicals – were the invitees appearing at the soirées hosted by May in her Lux apartment. May's foremost interest was always more literary than political. Sylvia Pankhurst recalled that May 'prided herself upon her compatriotism' with the Irish-born playwright and socialist George Bernard Shaw, 'regarding him in some subtle fashion as a piece of her own property'.[3] Pankhurst was perceptive. May liked to 'take in' intellectuals, gathering them like a collection of rare books that she could lift from a shelf and show off to acquaintances.

Sometime in late 1926 May began to assemble around her a circle of Soviet intellectuals who each shared a common fascination with English-language literature, especially contemporary fiction. This was the modernist era of James Joyce, Virginia Woolf and Gertrude Stein. It was also the decade that saw a new literary star in ascendance, Liam O'Flaherty. Less interested in formal experimentation than many of his peers, Liam O'Flaherty's work was closer to the direct, realist prose of his American contemporary Ernest Hemingway. Around this time, May began reading Liam's writings. She would come to regard him as among the most brilliant writers of his generation.

In Soviet letters, this was a time of sharp disputes over the political ends that literature should serve. The point of contestation was not necessarily form but intent. Even if the stakes of the literary debate differed, there was mutual interest between Western authors and Soviet intellectuals. Scenes from this cultural encounter would play out in May's room. For the Soviet writers and thinkers who befriended her, May and her foreign friends in the Lux were living bridges to the bohemian worlds of Paris, New York and Dublin described in their favourite novels. For May and Joseph, this gathering of Muscovite brainiacs became a link to the most vaunted heights of the Soviet cultural set. This was also the case for Ruth, though she also found opportunities for something more than friendship with her Irish friend's new companions.

2

In early 1927 May arrived back to the Lux after a trip to Vienna. It must have been a nostalgic journey: she would have traversed the same palatial streets she walked as a young woman entering adult life at the beginning of the century. Ruth remembered May returning to Moscow 'enthusiastic' about her time in Austria, bringing with her knowledge of how to dance the Charleston and a green dress with 'three stripes of yellow, orange and brown at the edge' as a present for Ruth.[4] At that time, Ruth recalled, May was 'continually meeting interesting Russians', who were 'inaccessible' to the average Lux resident – perhaps because they lacked the Russian language skills to make the initial connection.[5]

One evening May phoned Ruth to inform her that two 'professors' were coming to visit her in the Lux. It was a time in Ruth's Moscow life when she needed a diversion. She had passed through a traumatic ordeal at the end of 1926: Graft, a Georgian manager of the Siberian industrial project where she once worked, sexually assaulted her in his Moscow office. She brought charges against him. In the draft of an unpublished memoir, she recounted this terrible experience in detail. Sitting in the room as her rapist attempted to besmirch her character during a hearing, she recalled thinking how 'alike men were the world over' as she looked at him 'in contemptuous silence'.[6] Her charges were upheld but, as historian Julia Mickenberg notes, it must have been 'small comfort'.[7] Graft was imprisoned. Writing about the events many years later, Ruth's account gives a sense that she felt uneasy about this outcome.

The opportunity to find new friendships as the sharp Russian winter receded from the city must have felt like a distraction from these difficult events. After hanging up the phone, donning her new green dress and making her way down to May's room, Ruth was introduced to the writers Sergei Dinamov and Ivan Kashkin. She noted the two men were 'excessively young, tall and good looking and serious minded'.[8]

Soon after meeting Sergei and Ivan, Ruth described them affectionately as two 'big kids'.[9] May took to calling them her 'boys'. They were twenty-five and twenty-eight respectively, in contrast to Ruth, in her late thirties, and May, approaching her mid-forties. In her autobiography, Ruth recalled a summer scene in a village outside Moscow when the friendship between all four was just blossoming: Ivan and Sergei pelted one another with pine cones from behind tree trunks as their two foreign friends watched, May growing steadily colder in a linen dress and Ruth tiring after turning somersaults in the soft grass.[10]

Sergei and Ivan, who were learning English and German respectively, found the two women 'worth cultivating'.[11] As tutors, May and Ruth had their work cut out for them in Sergei's case. He spoke softly in a form of English that Ruth described as 'quaint'.[12] But this underplays the reality. Sergei's English could be almost lyrical in its disregard for linguistic conventions. Letters he wrote in the late 1920s included phrases like: 'I drink wine very much now' instead of 'I drink a lot of wine'; 'I was very wonder' when he meant 'I wondered'; and 'It is the book on the sex-life of our young people' when he intended 'this book is about young people's sex lives'.[13]

But his friends were clearly capable teachers. By the early 1930s Dinamov could fluently explain a delayed reply with the unusual explanation: 'I have been seriously ill with typhus for many weeks and am far behind in my correspondence. Now I am feeling much better.'[14]

Soon after these two young Soviet academics first arrived at May's room, there was another intellectual for Ruth to meet in room 5: the art critic Osip Beskin, a prominent figure in the State Publishing House and the editor of a magazine on Soviet cinema. He was a colleague of the 'boys' and a few years older than Sergei and Ivan. Osip was also much more tightly interlinked with the leading figures of the Soviet cultural avant-garde. A photograph from 1925 captures him among a crowd of artists in the apartment of the then world-famous poet Vladimir Mayakovsky. Standing alongside Beskin are the likes of Sergei Tretyakov, a well-known playwright, Lilia Brik, an author whose face adorns one of the most famous pieces of early Soviet art propaganda, and Boris Pasternak, later to achieve fame as the author of *Doctor Zhivago*. To the extreme left of the picture is Mayakovsky himself, cradling a cat. Soon, some of these luminaries would become May's acquaintances too.

Writing home, Ruth told her mother that 'some new influences have been coming into my life'; a 'new circle of friends, Russian literary people'.[15] One of them, Ruth described, had become what she described as her 'special friend'. Ruth believed he was 'so far superior' to her 'intellectually' that it was 'painful' and declared that 'there isn't anyone in America as wonderful as he is, so there!'[16] 'His first name is Osip, and his last name I won't write,' she added. Perhaps we do not need to be so discreet: it was Osip Beskin.

May was gathering the circle she called her 'family' in Moscow: a combination of her new Soviet literati friends and fellow Lux guests like Joseph and Ruth. May's nickname reflected the intimacy of the group. Her parents no longer alive and distant from her Irish siblings – geographically and, one can assume, politically – in Moscow she could play the role of an older sister, even a mother, to those around her.

Evenings in May's rooms must have provided an unusual scene: a literary salon, mainly composed of precocious twenty-somethings, presided over by an older Irishwoman with fluency in several languages. Some nursed wounds from past bouts with typhoid, tuberculosis or the White Army. All discussed the avant-garde future. At least two of them had a crush on Ruth.

Joseph was a regular attendee. He befriended May's Russian 'boys' – Ivan, Sergei and Osip – through the parties in her room and recorded some further sights one could encounter there. Osip would reminisce about his bourgeois childhood and threaten 'to write a novel about it'. The red-haired Ivan would arrive at the Lux dressed neatly in a grey overcoat and black muffler – what he believed to be 'the English fashion'.[17] He had never left Russia, so he could only assume. Confused by the American slang he encountered in novels, late in the evening Ivan would call on Joseph, the hotel's resident New Yorker, to ask: 'What to hell mean this? And this? And this?' pointing at words like 'cahoots', 'dicks', 'stick-ups', 'fifty-fifty' and 'gazump'.[18]

In an album Joseph devoted chiefly to portrait photographs of close friends there is an image of a boyish Sergei on sepia-toned paper. He signed it: 'To Joseph, as a sign of our friendship.' It is a portrait of a young intellectual who could easily be imagined grappling with Shakespearean English in a Moscow university. More difficult to imagine is how this same bookish individual, at the end of his teenage years, had served in the Red Army. Enlisting during the Russian Civil War, it is likely he witnessed its brutality. Indeed, the recent pasts of all these Soviet intellectuals could be threaded through the country's fraught and violent history. Their starry-eyed memories intrigued May and her immigrant friends. After all, May, Joseph and Ruth were not on Soviet territory during the earliest years of the Revolution and relied on these personal witnesses to recall that time of feverish idealism.

14. A portrait gifted to Joseph Freeman by Sergei Dinamov around the time of Joseph's departure from Moscow in March 1927. Hoover Institution Library and Archives, Joseph Freeman Papers, Folder fMM

Although they shared past experiences, not all agreed on the revolution's path forward. Take, for example, Lydia Gasviany, a Georgian woman in her early twenties and a friend of Sergei's, who worked with the State Publishing House. Joseph devoted several paragraphs to her story in his autobiography, where she appeared under the pseudonym 'Tamara'. After her work organising women in Muslim-majority regions in the Caucasus, she was attached to Soviet trade missions abroad and developed abilities in English and German. By the time she crossed paths with the radical expats of the Lux like May and Joseph, she was an outspoken supporter of the Soviet Communist Party's 'left opposition', centred around Leon Trotsky. Joseph was one of her many admirers. Though he declared their relationship was nothing more than comradely in his autobiography, he confided in a later diary entry that Gasviany allowed him a kiss 'and no more'.[19]

3

By the time Joseph befriended the Soviet additions to May's family, his romance with Luise Geissler was over. She had left him for M. N. Roy, the Indian revolutionary whom his room-mate Hugo so deeply admired. Joseph's explanation for Luise dispensing with him was that she saw him as an unambitious scribbler of verse, not a leader of nations. His depiction of Luise in his autobiography is unflattering, even embittered. He would later have a chance to apologise for it. This would be a rare opportunity: several of the Lux residents and visitors whose personal and political deviations were described frankly in his autobiography would be executed within years of its publication.

Joseph suggested that May was never enthusiastic about his relationship with Luise. May, he wrote, was 'positively savage on the subject'.[20] He described how she once 'threw back' her 'bobbed hair' and told him 'grimly' that if he stuck around with Luise he would learn all he wanted to know 'about the so-called new life'. 'Mary Pickford may be the sweetheart of a nation,' May added sharply, 'but your little friend is the sweetheart of all nations.' Still, May admitted, she admired Luise and found her 'charming'. 'If I were a man, I'd fall head over heels in love with her', she told

Joseph. Nonetheless, he was, in May's estimation, a 'damned fool' to have fallen for someone she regarded as fickle.

The 'new life' May referred to in her takedown of Luise was a broad concept that included within its definition a new sexual way of life. Many young Soviet citizens considered themselves as the vanguard who would liberate sexuality from the old mores. As the scholar Gregory Carleton notes, Soviet youth, the generation upon whom fell the task of leading the 'world to communism, transferred their iconoclastic enthusiasm to questions of sexual behaviour'.[21] For many young communists, the revolution 'became invested with meanings and values that outstripped the relatively straightforward intentions of the Bolshevik old guard'.[22] In the late 1920s, many of these tensions between differing revolutionary conceptualisations of communist sexuality were encountered in novels. One of the most provocative and popular was a novel called *The Moon on the Right Side*, written by Sergei Malashkin and first published in 1926.

The novel uses the letters and diaries of a fictional young communist named Tanya Aristarkhova to depict the downfall of a young woman who gets swept up in the 'sex crisis' of promiscuity that older revolutionaries feared was sweeping through Soviet youth.[23] Tanya is kicked out of her rural home, moves to Moscow where she meets factory workers, joins a commune formed in a university, rapidly passes through a series of relationships with different men, stages an orgy, has a crisis of faith in her own sexual licentiousness and ultimately sets out to try and recapture her lost innocence. The book was one of a trio of works that caused *Pravda* to bemoan in December 1926 that 'women's underwear occupies an unnaturally large place in our literature'.[24]

May had to have a copy, though she initially found it difficult to find one. The store of the State Publishing House where some of her friends worked was 'cleared out', but by 'mere luck' she happened upon it in a 'tiny shop'.[25] May told Joseph that the book-seller straight away 'offered me another "very sought after" book!!'[26] But the book left a bad impression: it was 'poor pornography', she observed, and 'still poorer reality'.[27]

Sergei Dinamov was also fascinated by this literary trend, sending Joseph several letters describing impressions both of Malashkin's work and the wider discussions of sexuality it reflected. Sergei summarised the book for Joseph in his unique English: when Tanya was 'in the village, she was good' but when she moved to Moscow, 'she was become the time of bad roads'. Sergei continued, noting the 'heroine of the novel has sometimes 6 men in the night'. He did not believe the novel was an accurate picture of young communist lives. 'Of course,' he wrote, 'we and young communists have some elements of decay because we live in the crossing period – but the pictures by Malashkin are not true in whole.'[28]

In another letter to Joseph, Sergei summarised the famous Bolshevik 'glass of water' polemic on sexuality – the notion that sex under socialism could be as accessible as water – 'when I am thirsty – I drink; when I want the women – I have them'.[29] Sergei did not approve of such an idea, but nonetheless granted that, so long as private life did not upset radical commitments, people could do as they please. 'Communist can has 1, 2 or 3 or more women,' Sergei told Joseph, 'communist can drinks, communist can dresses well, if it does not destroy the revolution.'[30] This debate was not without precedent, he noted: 'In the days of revolution 1905 we had no the sex-problem but after our defeat (1907 etc.) we had it.'[31] May, as we will learn, was more circumspect on the socialist sex problem than some of her peers. For May, private life and revolutionary commitment were inextricable – one *must* inform the other.

After its publication in 1926, *The Moon on the Right Side* unleashed a wave of intellectual dispute that receded by the end of the decade. A few years before its publication, a literary storm of an entirely different magnitude was kicked up by an Irish author on the other side of Europe. Copies of James Joyce's *Ulysses* made their way to Soviet Russia not long after its publication, though it would not appear in a full Russian translation until 1989, just before the Soviet collapse. The book had several admirers among May's 'family', including Joseph and May herself. Around the same time she read Malashkin's tale of Komsomol orgies in Moscow, May was also reading Joyce's experimental account of a day in the life of Dublin city. *Ulysses*, and Joseph's fondness for it, would play an unusual role in sparking one of his most intimate and long-lasting relationships of his Moscow days.

4

On one particularly bitter winter's night, one of the 'boys' was due to give a lecture on the American writer James Branch Cabell. The speaker was Ivan, the red-haired professor who could sometimes be found at the door of room 349 asking Joseph to explain words from American literature like 'banjo' and 'saxophone'. Ivan encouraged Joseph to attend his lecture. Joseph decided to bring along a friend. His companion for the evening would be Elise 'Sabo' Saborowski.

While his relationship with Luise frayed and she became set to leave Joseph for M. N. Roy, Joseph grew closer to Sabo. Reading between the lines of the letters that survive, it seems he unloaded his heartbreak over Luise to Sabo. In one undated letter, Sabo appeared tired of this dynamic, writing to Joseph: 'I start to be fed up with this atmosphere of petty intrigue' and the 'bed and tongue praxis'.[32] But she was patient with her younger friend and soon felt so intimately connected with him that she imagined him almost as a twin sibling.

On the night they made their way from the Lux to the university for the lecture, the snow, Joseph remembered, 'was heavy white in the streets' and the pair could 'hardly see a foot in front' of them. Nonetheless, they safely made it by tram and got comfortable against a wall in the lecture hall. After surveying the room, Joseph and Sabo observed to one another that 'exactly the same type of men and women came to literary lectures in Moscow, Berlin and New York – pale, dreamy, almost unworldly'.[33] At that moment a woman walked into the lecture hall and caught Joseph's attention. In a typescript composed in the mid-1930s, Joseph described this experience: the moment he first set eyes on Ivy Litvinov. He did not record whether he found her pale or dreamy, but she certainly seemed like a being from another world.

Under her 'black hair shone a pair of black eyes, startling in their luminous intelligence', Joseph wrote. 'Her features were regular, bold yet delicate in their modelling,' he continued, 'and her mouth was frank and warm and firm.' Partway into Ivan's lecture, she looked up from her notes and surveyed the room, holding her gaze on Joseph to smile 'enigmatically'. After the lecture finished, Ivy walked through the departing attendees, heading towards Joseph and Sabo. She had recognised Joseph's shirt as US army issue from across the room and pinned him for an American. Joseph recalled her opening line: '"Tell me" – she said in pure English, looking first at Sabo, then at me, "and do they read *Ulysses* in America?"'[34]

15. Ivy Litvinov, mid-1920s. Hoover Institution Library and Archives, Joseph Freeman Papers, Folder fMM

Ivy Litvinov, whom we last met in Hampstead in Part I recording her husband's awestruck response to the first news of the Russian Revolution that reached London, had, by this point, lived in Soviet Russia for four years. Unlike the other English expats in Moscow, Ivy Litvinov was not slumming it in one of the Tverskaya Street hotels like the Lux or the Bristol. As the wife of Maxim Litvinov, then assistant Commissar of Foreign Affairs, she was granted residence in a mansion built in the late nineteenth century by a Muscovite millionaire. It was here in Moscow that she first read *Ulysses*. She told a friend that although Joyce wrote at length about toilets and erections she did not 'in the least object', considering the Irish author's 'enormous talent' and 'power of convincing'.[35] On the sharp winter's night in the lecture hall, Ivy learned that Joseph shared her admiration for James Joyce's masterpiece and duly invited him to her home, along with his companion Sabo.

Joseph and Ivy became intimately close. They would remain so, if not always in a romantic sense, for many years. Both shared a fascination with literary and sexual experimentation. As a free-thinking young woman in London, Ivy had declared that her 'chief interests' were 'sex and literature'.[36] In contrast to her husband Maxim, more than a decade her senior and busy leading the Soviet foreign service, the charming Joseph Freeman provided her with an opportunity for sex *and* literature.

Ivy Litvinov's first biographer would later describe Ivy's love for Joseph as perhaps 'the deepest passion she ever felt for any man'.[37] Writing to a friend in England in February 1927, she mentioned about her new 'friend' Joseph. 'There is real sympathy between us, and we like each other's writing,' she noted, though it was 'all very complicated'. 'So you see,' she continued, 'taking it by and large, your Ivy is launching out into life. I put it all down to *Ulysses*. I do really.'[38] With its tremendous experiment in form, *Ulysses* was liberating minds.

On Joseph's first visit to Ivy's home with Sabo, the trio drank vodka and shared *zakuski* – hors d'oeuvres traditionally washed down with alcohol. Ivy treated them to a reading from the last chapter of *Ulysses*. 'Can you imagine translating *Ulysses* into

Russian?' Joseph recalled Ivy saying. 'I wish they would translate it into English first.'[39] That night, Ivy let Sabo borrow her copy. It was an encounter that Joseph would continue to turn over in his mind for decades to come, particularly as the course of world events pushed these two women, whom he cared for so deeply, closer to life-threatening danger.

I found this memory of the evening when Joseph first met Ivy during the weeks I spent immersed in his archive. Trawling through boxes of material, I realised that if Joseph's reflections on life in the Lux had an over-arching theme – aside from how *not* to get over a break-up, it was the story of how his closest friends saved him from what he termed a 'fate worse than death': becoming a politician rather than a poet.[40] In a letter from 1958, Joseph listed those who saved him from this fate: May, the circle of Soviet writers whom she introduced to Joseph, Ivy Litvinov, and an 'extraordinary Polish girl': Sabo.[41]

16. Elise 'Sabo' Ewert (*née* Saborowski), mid-1920s, Hoover Institution Library and Archives, Joseph Freeman Papers, Folder fMM

For Joseph, these friends became his most important guides through the political eruptions and his own personal tumult of being at first in love in a revolutionary city then heartbroken as he left it behind. His self-seriousness, both in this moment in the mid-1920s and in his later reflections, belie the fact that he was relatively young and ill-experienced in matters romantic, poetic and political when he first checked into the Lux. He was still coming of age in Moscow. Even after he left, Joseph was not a convinced convert to the Bolshevik ideal as he made out in his autobiography, but still someone caught between 'bourgeois' attachments to the old world and the radical demands of the new. He would be far from the only radical of his generation whose claims to have discarded past patterns of life and thought were simply untrue.

Sabo left Moscow, and Joseph, around the start of 1927. In a letter sent in early January, she confessed to Joseph that she stood alone on the Moscow train platform for minutes, 'looking out for something like a furry cap and a pair of dark eyes underneath'. But Joseph was unable to make it to the train station to bid farewell to Sabo before her return to Berlin. The train moved on, she wrote, and she said her 'silent good bye' without seeing him on the platform.[42]

Sabo must have known Joseph's homeward route would take him through Berlin, so they would see one another again soon. She wrote frankly in her letters to him about the profound impact he had on her personally. Ever since arriving in Germany, Sabo noted, she wrote letters in her head to Joseph, but was glad she did not actually commit the thoughts to paper. 'You surely would have thought me crazy,' she admitted.[43] Nonetheless, some unguarded comments still passed her internal censor. The 'close contact' they shared in Moscow, she wrote, broke down a protective barrier she built around her inner self.

One moment of their 'close contact' would leave an especially strong impression on Sabo. In the years to come, she would sometimes refer elusively in her letters to a political prophecy made by Joseph. At some point in Moscow, Sabo and Joseph were together in his office – surely the room in the Comintern building where he worked under May's direction. He translated for Sabo a piece he found in the Yiddish-language socialist paper *The Forward*. The article described the internal party debates between Stalin and Trotsky. It prompted Joseph to confide in Sabo something serious: doubts about the revolution's future under Stalin's leadership. A year after she left Moscow, Sabo already felt too cautious to discuss this explicitly in her personal correspondence. 'But of course, if you at all know what I mean,' she wrote, 'keep it to yourself and do not talk about it – to nobody.'[44]

These Russian Boys Think Being
Irish So Wonderful

she
never kneeling at his shrine
sees what is great in lenin and man
measures this age
with the vast gauges of her nature

These lines formed part of a poetic portrait of Sabo that Joseph composed in Moscow. He showed the poem to Sergei Dinamov and May, who, along with Sabo herself, was one of the few people in the Lux whose understanding of poetry Joseph trusted.[1]

Sergei, committed to the idea that the working class should invent their own artistic forms, 'shook his head sadly' and declared Joseph 'an impressionist'.[2] He cautioned Joseph to spend less time with comrades from the old world and gain more experience with those shaped by life in the crucible of the revolution. May responded similarly, giving Joseph some practical advice on finding poetic inspiration closer to the revolutionary wellspring. If he was interested in the 'so-called New Woman', she told him, then he should not 'fiddle around with shadows'. 'I'll introduce you to the real thing,' May promised him.[3]

The 'real thing' May referenced was a woman named Olga Minskaya, one of her more remarkable Russian friends. At the time that Joseph was guided into May's room for his meeting with Minskaya, she was a student in the Moscow Military Academy of the Red Army. By this point, May had already known Minskaya for several years and had even helped her navigate the loss of a child. Clearly intending to make an impression, Minskaya met May's young

American friend armed and outfitted for battle, wearing close cropped hair, a neat military uniform and a Sam Browne belt. She was carrying what Joseph described as an 'enormous revolver'.[4]

One historian of Soviet fashion lists Minskaya as a textbook example of the 'Red Commanderess' style of the 1920s, typified by military uniform, naval or leather jackets and 'scandalously short, boyish hair'.[5] Joseph, whose descriptions of women were sometimes heartfelt but usually emblematic of the male gaze, claimed that her outfit 'did not entirely conceal a graceful body, at once vigorous and voluptuous'.[6]

Where did May befriend the impressive Minskaya? Her friend Emmy Leonhard had a theory. Many decades later, Emmy remembered soldiers fetching herself, May and a woman 'who later fell as a victim of the great purge' to bring them to the 'big army camp near Moscow'. Emmy and the other woman 'used to have a good gallop in the camp' while May, reluctant to ride on a horse, 'sat all the time in the officers' mess'. Emmy believed it was here, as she mingled among the officers, that May first met Minskaya, who became 'her lasting friend'.[7] No letters between May and Minskaya survive. It is only the memories of their mutual acquaintances that provide evidence for this friendship, unusual in a world where Lux guests tended to maintain social circles bounded by their Comintern work.

Both Joseph and Ruth published accounts of meetings with Minskaya. These encounters appear to have taken place in May's company, either in her Lux room or on the encampment where Minskaya lived.

Born in Moscow around the dawn of the century, young Olga Minskaya was enthused by the October Revolution in 1917 and found herself in Budapest during the short-lived Hungarian Soviet Republic of 1919. In Joseph's telling, Minskaya followed a man to Hungary rather than arriving there as a soldier. Yet in Ruth's account of her life, Minskaya was sent to Budapest on a mission to provide armed support to the Hungarian revolutionaries. The facts align closer with Ruth's vision of a woman directed by her own agency:

Minskaya first enlisted in the Red Army in December 1918, months before the Hungarian Soviet Republic arose.[8]

One Sunday, likely in the summer of 1927, when Ruth was together with May and Minskaya at the military encampment where she lived, Ruth caught sight of several scars on the inside of Minskaya's wrists. It looked as though 'a red-hot iron had been laid across them', Ruth wrote.[9] Later, she learned the story of the scars. Joseph told a version of it too: after the collapse of the Hungarian Soviet Republic, Minskaya was imprisoned by the counter-revolutionary forces and attempted to take her own life in a prison cell with a piece of broken glass. A prison guard intervened before her action proved fatal. By the time of her release, having survived an insurrection, imprisonment and a suicide attempt, she was eighteen years old.[10]

Minskaya joined up with Red Army forces fighting in Ukraine to impose Soviet control over the country. According to a short biography she wrote for the Soviet women's journal *Rabotnitsa*, her tasks included sweeping forests and villages for hiding *Makhnovtsi* – anti-Bolshevik fighters loyal to the Ukrainian anarchist leader Nestor Makhno.[11] Among a series of curious details, Joseph claimed that during this time she bandaged her breasts, shaved her hair entirely and experienced relationships with several 'sweethearts': women living where her regiment was stationed.[12] With the help of Alexandra Kollontai and then-overall commander of the Red Army Leon Trotsky, she returned to Russia to undertake cavalry training in the city of Oriol.[13]

After the Bolsheviks emerged victorious in the Civil War, Minskaya decided she wanted a child. 'She did not want a lover or a husband,' Joseph clarified, 'she just wanted a baby.' In Joseph's telling, she approached a suitable man in her regiment and declared: 'I don't love you, I don't want to marry you, but I would like you to be the father of my child.'[14] Sadly, the child died in a tragic accident. Ruth remembered the night in the winter of 1925 when Minskaya came to the Lux seeking her friends' support through her grief. 'There must have been something soothing to her about the foreign civilian environment,' Ruth mused, 'she probably wanted to forget that she was a soldier and just be a woman – and a bereaved mother.'[15]

With her second child, things would be different. Now, Minskaya believed that under the 'present conditions' in the long path towards communism, a child needed 'a father, a home, a family'.[16] This was how May and Ruth found Minskaya when they visited her in the summer of 1927 at the encampment: married and caring for her son while simultaneously trying to maintain the obligations of a soldier's life. Parenting, as Ruth observed, was not a part of her military training.[17]

For Joseph, Minskaya personally represented one of the revolution's most extraordinary achievements in the emancipation of women. Ruth felt similarly about May's 'Red Commanderess' friend. But her stories of Minskaya contained more evidence of battles fought on multiple fronts than Joseph's account. Sure, women like Minskaya could join new spheres of the workforce. But if new roles did not go together with women's emancipation from the idea that traditional maternal duties were their destiny rather than a choice, then was that really emancipation? The humdrum but hectic demands of family life continued to pile pressure on the egalitarian sensibilities supposedly underpinning relationships based not only on romance but 'comradeship'.

Communism was both an ideology and a destination, or, as Minskaya told Joseph: 'We are building the future, but we cannot live in it.'[18] What did the revolution have to say about love, which so often complicated relationships between men and women? As the Soviet 1920s entered its final act, even the avowedly single May would be compelled to confront these questions.

2

Joseph's departure from Moscow in March 1927 was a surprise announcement for his friends in the 'family'. Its method, meanwhile, came as something of a sharper shock – for May, at least.

It took some time, and multiple archives, to piece together the chain of events. Eventually, however, using an astonishing letter from May, details from the typescript autobiography of Ruth and a salacious diary entry Joseph composed after a restless night twenty-two years after the events in question, I triangulated the details.

The sequence starts like this: sometime around February 1927, Joseph told his close friends in Moscow, including Ivy Litvinov and May, that he would soon depart Soviet Russia to make his way back to America. A leaving party was arranged for a night in early March. The location: the flat of one of May's Soviet 'boys', most likely Osip Beskin, who lived nearby, in rooms he sometimes shared – on account of the housing shortage – with his ex-wife.

Most of the guests that night were men. Copious amounts of food and vodka accompanied talking, singing and speech-making. Joseph loved them all, he remembered, and he assumed they felt similarly. May was there too. She was in a 'horrible mood', one that undermined her ability to speak frankly with Joseph.[19] There was a conversation she wanted to have with him, but she was unsettled and conflicted over whether she was justified in broaching a sensitive topic. She feared being perceived as controlling.

A few days earlier, Joseph had confided something to her. What precisely he said went unrecorded. Only a handful of details survive: he shared some 'candid hints' to her in a library and his inferences left her feeling frustrated with his approach to sexual relationships. Indeed, this 'confession in the library', as she termed it, festered in her mind. She left the party before its end and did not witness what happened next, but she soon learned of it. And when she did, it prompted her to write a long letter outlining her understanding of sex under socialism.

The party continued late into the night. The host, her friend's attractive ex-wife, whispered something into Joseph's ear: an 'invitation'. Once the party finished, the star of the evening was guided back to the Lux by some of the Soviet intellectuals he befriended through May. Joseph watched them disappear back down the street, then turned around. He walked back to the scene of the party and was greeted by his friend's ex-wife. 'We embrace, kiss, undress, get into bed,' Joseph recalled. After waking up from a (presumambly brief) slumber, they made love again.

'And this', he noted, 'is only the beginning of that last fantastic day in Moscow.' He recalled making love to two further women before he departed the city, one the wife of an English representative to the Comintern, the other a photographer's assistant whom he met while receiving the photographs required for his passport. Thinking back on these events decades later, he confided to his typewriter that he was 'neither ashamed nor proud' of his actions, perceiving 'sensuality' as relatively 'harmless' in a violent world.[20] Joseph left Moscow on a westbound train, travelling first to Berlin before returning to New York. He surely would not have predicted, as the locomotive made its way out of the Moscow station, that he would never again return.

Two days later, he visited Sabo in her office in Berlin. He left an impression there too. Writing in English, she later reminisced about the evening of his arrival; how they went to dinner together and then she wandered back to her office, so distracted that she almost came under the 'wheels from the passing automobiles' because within her 'there was a great singing': joy at having reconnected with Joseph. Although, she admitted, perhaps 'it was also from the wine we drank'.[21] After his departure, she told him that 'even the Berlin heaven somehow felt with me and started pouring rain shortly after you left'.[22] Soon she would seek a cure for her blues in New York. It was a curious inversion of Joseph's own entangled journey: he met Luise Geissler in New York and followed her route to Moscow. Through Luise he met Sabo, who would follow him back to New York.

3

Often, writers of historical fiction will trace a paper trail and seize the opportunity to animate the people of the past in ways that we historians, hemmed in by the limits of sources, can only envy. But occasionally the tables turn, and you find yourself holding a document that reveals a voice so startlingly assertive that it can bridge the decades of separation. Suddenly, that individual who was just a spectral form materialises into a living, breathing figure in your imagination, more vivid than even the most finely drawn character from fiction. They appear more vivid precisely because the typescripts or letters in front of you were once held by that person, the ink from the pen or the typewriter was impressed upon the page by them. I have been fortunate to repeatedly sense that moment of frisson.

After tracing the letters that May wrote to Joseph following his departure from Moscow, I read them with a sense of something approaching awe. Now I could *hear* her speak at length. She was talking frankly about things that my training as a historian encouraged me to believe I would only encounter through circumspection and euphemisms. Put bluntly: she was writing about sex. Not only was she writing about sex, but she was also *theorising* it. This was a topic that I believed few Irish people of the twentieth century discussed in anything more than a series of raised eyebrows and blushes that vanished from historical memory as soon as they occurred.

Readers sensitive to the particular circumstances in which May was raised – rural Ireland in the late nineteenth century – will understand my surprise. But perhaps anyone who has ever wondered about the many millions of lives that have simply sunk without a trace into the overwhelming darkness of history will sense something of the thrill I felt in encountering these remarkable and vivacious writings.

Let us take, as an example, the letter May wrote to Joseph over a few days at the end of March 1927. Before she wrote it, May had learned that Joseph spent his final night in Moscow in the bed of their mutual friend's ex-wife. This was, as she knew only too well, far from his only indiscretion. Holding the pages, you can feel the thin, brittle paper and see closely spaced handwriting on grey pages. Perhaps, as she began to write the letter in question, she was inhaling the cigarette smoke of her lifelong addiction, dressed in a favoured waistcoat she often wore in Moscow. When she hand-wrote her letters she liked to lounge, whereas the typewriter compelled her to be seated at a desk. On a Friday, possibly lounging in her Lux room on an evening after work, she took up her pen and began to take her friend to task on sex, socialism and destiny:

Dearest,

I wonder where you are or what you are doing – I fear I shall know no peace until I hear of your arrival home – will I know peace then of course is another question – at the moment I'm just impossible both for myself & others. So harassed by regrets about my weakness on that *fatal* Tuesday. I should have been the typical woman & tried to interfere with your liberty – but for that I'm not only filled with contempt for those who do so, but also too damned proud. To what purpose your confession in the library? Where by candid hints you have given an idea of licentiousness – I more or less forced the facts from [Ruth] but I must tell you frankly I'm disappointed. *There was no earthly reason* for this confidence (which I'm convinced will not be betrayed) *for God's sake grow up.* When you were with me I have never seriously taken you to tack on this subject – simply because of a certain inability to be quite objective. Now I realise that our friendship *justified* me in doing so and I'll now try to make up for what I consider a sin of omission.

Our senses and emotions are strange things which we rarely understand – passion is so inexplicable – it is a thing which only fear or reason can keep within bounds: it is preferable that reason should act as a brake, for after all we are supposed to be creatures with reasoning powers. Excess in drink dulls the brain, a bout of rage tires out the system, too much freedom in sex blunts the instincts and undermines the human machine. We must be discriminate or how else can we expect a man or woman to be *everything* to us – for that relation there must

always be *respect*. Can there be respect when we get the reputation any trousers attracts her – any petticoat attracts him.
This lowers our human relations to a purely animal level – I
would say even lower – I know the reply arguments 'so & so
was only a slut' – 'I wanted to try this experience, but *now*
I'm really serious.' There are ideas about what the mother of
our children should be – if they still prevail they apply doubly
to the father. This is moralising.

Materialistic viewpoint: are we fit on the morrow to create
or work as we want to or should? If we are able to accomplish
anything great in life – and I know someone *who can* – this
is a very vital matter – think it over at leisure and let me have
an opinion. Women are as a rule much more sensitive creatures
than men and lose in my opinion more quickly than men –
instincts get blunted more quickly & naturally frequent
changes are disastrous both mentally and physically. Final
question: if everything in our lives has its time and place why
not also sex relations.

I know that in the specific case about which I am thinking
that a period of schooling is necessary – that sudden restraint
will do more harm than good – we cut down on cigarettes
gradually – no fine sounding resolutions, no asceticism, but a
slow return to 'normalcy' and perhaps by that time a *real woman*
will have appeared on the scene. That friend 'Beyond. . .' [refer-
ring to herself] is of the opinion that there is a rare happiness
in store for the woman you *really* love, provided she is capable
of appreciating the luck fate is giving her. The most unkind blow
fate ever dealt that friend was to overlook the fact that *twin souls*
should be born *together* just as twin bodies – I do not hesitate
to say that had that been the case then the problem of that 'real
woman' would have been more or less solved, because if fate
had done to make sure that physical attraction would also have
been there. Well, life is like that and regrets *cannot* help where
real fundamentals are at stake, but why have regrets about details
which are avoidable. Forgive me, this would not have such a

prosaic aftertaste had it been verbal but there never seemed to be the time or opportunity.

Continuing, she referenced recent discussions of sexuality in the *New Masses*, the US left-wing periodical that Joseph helped bring out and to which he often contributed:

[The] March *New Masses* sex explanations are enough to give a sane being belly ache – The fundamental error is the *terminology* – Bourg[eois]. & Proletarian – why not natural & unnatural – do we want to set up an interregnum in such matters or do we want to put the whole business on a sane permanent basis? We have convinced ourselves that Revolutions are made in order through the Dictatorship of the Proletariat to attain a *classless society* – in industry we actually know the methods that are likely to be permanent: machines, electricity – everything that will make for the lightening of toil and the ennobling of man – in art and literature *some* of us know that the term 'proletarian' is illogical (I will spare you infantile details)! But in sex and the family, we are forced to be shackled with a 'proletarian' brand! They don't even talk of sex under socialism! You remember Osip & those two years of War Communism – how this factor faded in a world of equality & opportunity – & to work for the whole or what you may wish to style it – doesn't that suggest that what we are seeking is a restoration of a healthy relationship where there will be no question of gain, where we stand to live or die sexually on our natural qualities, where the present-day-much-denounced idea of affection will dominate – where it will be decisive factors & no tinkering as to whether this is bourgeois or proletarian.

Birds in their natural state may contribute something: they mate and are faithful till the family is *feathered* and ready to fly – such constance may not be necessary for mere humans *when* there is a state to act as nest and nursery – remember Minskaia – now a family is unavoidable in this stage of transition.

What was May describing? There are some cryptic phrases, references whose precise meaning has been lost to time. Yet the crux of May's thinking can be discerned. It pivots around two words, really an instruction: 'remember Minskaia'. Drawing Joseph back to the example of her Red Army friend – who experienced the tragic loss of the child she sought to raise alone then set out to model a conventional marital arrangement for her second – May was making the point that now, in this moment of transition between the old world and the new, people could not simply live as though an era of unhindered liberation – in the spheres of sex and all others – had already arrived.

This may seem a conservative point – even prudish in comparison to the lived reality of her friends with their frequent affairs – but it reflected prominent currents in revolutionary thinking. It was closer, in many ways, to the orthodoxy within Soviet Communism than the 'free love' concepts that many political emigrants brought with them from their left circles at home in Berlin, New York, London and so on. Yet by eschewing terms like 'proletarian' and 'bourgeois', she was searching for a vocabulary that could outline a revolutionary vision of sex and the family without leaving her cold.

Looking towards the future when 'the present-day-much-de-nounced idea of affection will dominate', she gestured towards a *transformation* of familial bonds rather than their eradication. It was not the abolition of the family she wanted, but rather the transformation of the very concept itself. On the one hand, capitalism distorted intimacy and familial bonds. Adoption was often about inheritance and legacy rather than care. Marriage could be a means of increasing wealth and social prestige and not about love. Socialism would, bit by bit, remove these distortions, eventually eroding the need for such outdated formulations and rituals altogether. Putting it simply, the leading 'Bolshevik feminist' Alexandra Kollontai had told an audience in Sverdlov University in 1921: 'The stronger the ties of all members of the collective, the less the need for the creation of strong marital relations.'[23]

3

But where did May's own affections lie? Did she have any desires to put into practice her ideas about sexuality and the family? Or was she content for 'family' in her life to simply remain an affectionate metaphor for the polyglot intellectuals who gathered in her room? May and her contemporaries left us with a few clues to follow in search of answers. Her intense friendships speak to a lasting desire for the company of other women, from her life with Nellie Cohen in East London to her attachment to Ruth Kennell and Emmy Leonhard in Moscow. There is also her suggestive friendship with Olga Minskaya, a woman who upended almost all traditional ideas of femininity. The sources that survive are not explicit about any kind of physical intimacy between May and these women, even if the same sources reveal bonds that were peculiarly intense and long-lasting.

While there is some evidence that May had male suitors, it seems she brushed them off. Referring to some younger men from the US who were drawing towards her amorously, she dismissed their attraction to her as the 'usual love the Americans have for antiques'.[24] On another occasion, during a period when she was both financially insecure and deeply frustrated with the men in her life, she joked with Ruth: 'my only interaction with the male sex will be to get hold of some old bloke with one leg in the grave and lots of money', clarifying that this desire would allow her 'to get even with them some way'.[25] 'Them' in this case being men in general.

Her evident preference for the company of other women did not go unnoticed. May's sexuality was a topic of gossip among some who knew her in Moscow. This was precipitated by her friendship with Ruth, her near constant companion from their first meeting in 1924. In a handwritten note slipped between typescript pages of her autobiography, Ruth later reflected on the depth of their friendship and the salacious talk it prompted, reciting how the 'happiest hours' of her life had been spent in May's company: 'and yet so rare a thing, from the viewpoint of men is friendship between women that whispers reached our ears from the "Comrades" – prompted, perhaps, by a desire to be even with us for our aloofness from themselves – about the nature of this friendship, suggestions which shocked and disgusted me, since I was still rather ignorant of the intricacies of such matters, more familiar phenomena to a European.'[26] The 'more familiar phenomena' being gestured towards was physical intimacy between the two women.

A hint towards the rumour can even be found in a book by the then revered American novelist Theodore Dreiser published in 1930. In his short story 'Ernita' – really a fictionalised biography of Ruth – Dreiser concluded the story with a note about how, in Moscow, his main character 'shared everything' with an Irishwoman: 'room, bed, past, and present troubles'.[27]

Unlike Ruth, May appears to have been nonplussed by the gossip, even amused. She once told Ruth how she had been corresponding with Emmy Leonhard, who asked to 'be remembered' to Ruth. Clarifying why she found this amusing, May typed in her trademark quirk of pressing down again and again on the exclamation-mark key: '*they all think* we are together!!!!'[28]

Beyond May's own often opaque and joking comments, these are outsider perspectives: the reflections of a historian or the gossipy whisper of contemporaries. Interestingly, however – *extraordinarily,* even – May composed a short prose poem that attempted to reconstruct her own internal monologue during a moment of soul-searching about sexuality.

During the same weeks that she was turning over Joseph's confession and her own inability to bring him up on what she saw as his harmful promiscuity, she wrote a short prose poem called 'Thoughts Mind Flashes'. She described this as her own personal attempt to write in the style of *Ulysses*.[29] Like many pages of *Ulysses* it contains sentences that can be read multiple ways, literary allusions and a free-wheeling approach to syntax. This remarkable fragment survives among the letters she sent to Joseph.

May's minor piece of modernist experimentation begins with a farewell on an evening in early March 1927. The scene setting is

172

opaque, but it appears to be the final meeting between Joseph and May before he departs Moscow, apparently at the train station from where he will begin his journey to Berlin. He tells her she was 'very nice' to him.

By the time the narrator develops the right response, it is too late to tell him in person and she can only address these thoughts to the page: 'Noon 12. 3. 27. Nothing like as nice as you deserve or I would have liked – those stupid feelings choke me I have no voice to say my thoughts that station scene was typical – there is a degree of love that numbs us.'

Now the clock turns back and May finds herself at a gathering, likely Joseph's goodbye party. Osip Beskin recites a sentimental poem by the Russian Romantic poet Mikhail Lermontov and it causes the 'floods to open' and our narrator starts to weep. 'I suppose I have not read Adler for nothing,' she writes, citing the Austrian psychoanalyst Alfred Adler before launching into an analysis of her own interiority:

I wonder does J[oseph] think I can be. Probably possible. . . The world is mad and people and feelings why can't I be natural this absurd shyness where I love. Also an inheritance. My mother never showed her feelings to us kids. All these damned complexes are Irish of our type these Russian boys think being Irish so wonderful, etc. and the pain of longing and regret we all have – rot.

After these brief thoughts on inherited complexes and an inability to be 'natural', our narrator evokes past desires after what appears to be a short reflection on the sexual adventures of Joseph's final days in Moscow:

Is it possible to f— as he did these last days. In the early days I wanted it every day but always the same one – makes a differ-ence. That Sunday business it was that Sen—— woman of course it might have been the French, but what matter – I wish I'd asked was she willing. In another I'd feel indignant just because he's such a thoroughly good kid – feel it's not part of him. R[uth] is kind she doesn't understand me real American with – out fine feelings – I suppose I'm mistaken again.

Reading between the lines, the composition appears to be May attempting to express her interior life; a kind of counterpoint confession to Joseph's own, but marked by a fundamental perplexity regarding her own desires. Even though it is rare to find ordinary people from the past in such a reflective mode, any impulse to bundle up her sexuality in a concise phrase like gay, lesbian, or heterosexual is still defied by these lines. Perhaps the term queer, which gestures towards a vivid spectrum of identities, is the most apt label for May. But there is another option: to define her as someone living at a time where everything conspired to leave her with only 'this absurd shyness where I love' – to borrow her own choice phrase. It was her fate to be a single woman surrounded by romantically intertwined friends, a fact which surely encouraged her to remain attentive to the role sex played within the personal and political dynamics of those closest to her.

If May believed that Joseph's orgiastic departure from Moscow would be the final time the entangled love lives of her friends brought turbulence to her own plans, she would be sorely mistaken. An unexpected whirlwind of events swept through her life during her final year in Moscow. In rapid sequence, all the threads of her life since leaving Vienna for London as a young woman became unexpectedly interwoven. The precipitating factor for these events was the return of the Cohen sisters, Rose, and particularly Nellie, into May's life. There was also a harbinger of the coming storm in a letter she sent to Joseph shortly after her epistle on socialism and sexuality. Writing in early April 1927, May told Joseph about a letter she received from an Irish novelist, one whose brother she recently met in Moscow: Liam O'Flaherty. 'The letter was a scream, such high-sounding foam,' she wrote, 'it makes one more anxious than ever to meet him.'[30]

The New Stars and the Smaller Lights

17. Nellie Cohen, passport photograph, 1920. Joyce Rathbone Papers

1

Nellie Cohen's passport from the 1920s survives in a plastic storage box that I found in a Cotswolds home. The pages, covered with stamps from various European frontiers, reveal the journeys of a well-travelled and independent woman. Some of the markings hint towards the unsettled continent she was traversing, such as the stamp declaring in block capitals: 'TRAVELLING TO GERMANY – NOT VALID FOR OCCUPIED GERMAN TERRITORY EXCEPT FOR ONE JOURNEY IN TRANSIT'. Many more of the passport's stamps were from the desks of Soviet consular officials and border guards. Reflecting the bureaucratic practice oft bemoaned by Lux guests of *propuski*, regular identity checks and passes, there are stamps for nearly every stage of the journey: the initial clearance for travel at the Soviet embassy in London, disembarkation from the boat at Leningrad and departure from Soviet territory. Stamps from the People's Commissariat for Foreign Affairs add colour to the passport; green 25-kopek stamps depict workers greeting one another beneath the Soviet emblem, orange one-rouble stamps are illustrated with a hammer and sickle and a globe sandwiched between two ears of wheat. It is certainly a contrast with the stamps elsewhere on the passport depicting King George V in imperious profile.

The passport markings from Nellie Cohen's Soviet travel provide some of the few fragments of evidence for her month-long visit to Moscow in the summer of 1926. Her sister Rose was undertaking special Comintern assignments elsewhere in Europe at this time, so a primary purpose of the trip must have been a visit to May. The visit was likely the first time that May and Nellie enjoyed each other's company since the summer of 1924, when May left behind their shared apartment on London's Gray's Inn Road to take up her own personal room in the Hotel Lux. Letters between Nellie and May from this period do not survive, but the ease with which Nellie connected with May's new friends and her decision to travel to Moscow suggests they remained close throughout May's Moscow years.

The two women had a lot of catching up to do. Nellie had carried on much the same as before: working in secretarial roles in London. Her employer after Sylvia Pankhurst, who had by this time swapped East London for a cottage outside Epping Forest, was the head of the London Guild of Builders, a man she found 'horrid'.[1] He tried to fire and rehire her on worse terms but she resisted the move. She was a member of the Clerks Union, an organisation she remembered as being 'very wishy-washy about it all' but found an ally in a former conscientious objector named Malcolm Sparkes. He set up his own guild for builders and took on Nellie as his secretary. Here, she continued the same clerical work that defined her adult career. These may have been routine years, but Nellie would soon experience a dramatic change in her circumstances that transformed both her life and May's Comintern career.

2

Rose Cohen, meanwhile, was living a much more adventurous life than her older sister. Due to the nature of the work Rose was carrying out, it is impossible to tell exactly how much her sister Nellie knew about Rose's movements. In the years since she left the Lux in 1924, Rose Cohen fulfilled both 'open' and 'underground' roles in the communist movement. The 1925 letter heading for a communist-directed relief organisation lists Rose as a member of the executive committee for the group.[2] The minutes of a meeting of the St Pancras Branch of the Communist Party held in January 1926 find Rose informing her comrades 'that most industrial unions definitely excluded clerks' – perhaps with her sister's recent employment troubles on her mind.[3] But a report from later that year by a Soviet secret agent attached to the Foreign Service of the OGPU (Joint State Political Directorate) finds Rose someplace else entirely.

When I encountered this report in Rose's Comintern personnel file, I was surprised to find it. I was told by colleagues that material relating to clandestine activities would not be delivered in Comintern archives. But here, in Russian, was a 1926 surveillance report on Rose, ready for my perusal. It was a brief glimpse into a world that still remains elusive to historians: the overlap between Soviet secret intelligence and Comintern activities beyond the Soviet Union. This, however, was not an account of Soviet intelligence's collaboration with Rose but, more unexpectedly, evidence of their suspicious tracking of her movements.

In the summer of 1926 an OGPU agent reported back to Moscow about the alarmingly shoddy counter-espionage tactics of English communists under their watch, including Rose. A Scotland Yard agent by the name of Hughes was in Paris, the Soviet officer reported, and this British agent was on the hunt for one Comrade Max, a Comintern emissary attached to the British Communist Party and close to Rose.

A Soviet agent tailed Comrade Max through the city streets and found both Max and Rose, then acting as his secretary, paying visits to English communists who, 'in the majority of cases do not know the elemental rules of conspiracy'.[4]

In the opinion of this OGPU agent, 'Comrade Max' had been rumbled by British intelligence.[5] Hinting towards the deep paranoia festering within the Soviet security apparatus, later to metastasise and consume countless lives during the Stalinist Terror of the late 1930s, the Soviet watchmen were watching the watchmen. Rose would have understood that her activities were clandestine and that Western authorities wanted to track them, but she was surely unaware that the Soviet state, which was, nominally, on her 'side' and that of the Comintern, was also tailing her.

British sleuths, already aware of Rose, were struggling to decipher the precise identity of 'Comrade Max', the man she was accompanying. They nonetheless knew this figure was important in the networks linking the Comintern in Moscow to revolutionaries in Britain. MI5 began to assemble a file on him. Also known in his revolutionary work as Bennett, Goldfarb or 'the big nose', 'Comrade Max' was known to many of his British comrades as David Petrovsky, a mixture of his actual first name and the name he assumed in the underground.

Born to a well-to-do Jewish family in Berdychiv in Ukraine in 1886, Petrovsky began his political life as Dovid Lipets, a prominent activist in the General Jewish Labour Bund. Known simply as 'the Bund', this revolutionary movement went from humble beginnings as a Marxist party formed by thirteen Jewish activists in an attic in Vilna in 1897 to become a formidable revolutionary movement among the Jewish working class during the terminal decades of the Russian Empire. The Bund distinguished itself from wider social democratic currents in the Russian Empire through its insistence that questions of Jewish emancipation required discrete answers that needed to be articulated by a distinctly Jewish revolutionary movement. As a gifted speaker and organiser, Petrovsky agitated along the routes carved out by the Bund across the 'Pale of Settlement', the territory where tsarist authorities allowed Jews to settle, before taking up work for the movement in New York. Here, in early 1917, he shared a house in the Bronx with another Ukrainian-born Jewish socialist who went by the name Leon Trotsky.

The country of Petrovsky's birth, Ukraine, would, as historian Joshua Meyers notes, become especially important to his story. In March 1917, after the February Revolution, he returned from exile to participate in the transformation of his homeland. Following the October Revolution, he took an anti-Bolshevik stance, even organising to resist the imposition of Soviet power in Ukraine in 1919. This was a year of chaos and pogroms across Ukraine amid fighting between Ukrainian national forces, the monarchist White Army, the Bolshevik Red Army and other smaller militias. Although all major forces in the Civil War carried out pogroms in Ukraine, the national army of the Ukrainian Directorate was culpable for most of what Meyers describes as the 'antisemitic carnage' of the period, including a pogrom in Proskurov in February 1919 that left somewhere between 1,500 and 2,000 Jews dead after a three-hour rampage.[6]

In the face of this violence, Petrovsky turned his back on the Ukrainian Directorate and aligned himself with the forces he believed best placed to advance the socialist revolution and stop the ferocious violence against Jews: the Bolsheviks. After a short but prestigious career in the Red Army working under his old housemate from the Bronx, Petrovsky was dispatched to London in 1924 to work for the Comintern under the pseudonym A. J. Bennett. It was likely here that he first met the woman who would become his wife: Rose Cohen.

3

'You remember Nellie,' May wrote in a letter to Joseph Freeman that she sent from Moscow in April 1927. Joseph and Nellie evidently crossed paths during Nellie's brief visit to the Lux back in 1926, not long after Joseph had first arrived at the hotel. 'Well her sister has arrived to work,' May continued. 'I rather think you heard something about this at one of our parties.'[7] May told him that his old room-mate Hugo 'is very glad to have such an old friend here'. Continuing in a mischievous tone, she implied to Joseph that there was – or at least had once been – something more to this friendship between Rose and Hugo, telling him 'this is a friendship that would be too much for you, and overthrows all your principles and theories'.[8]

Rose Cohen and David Petrovsky returned to Moscow to work together in the Comintern in 1927. Within a year Petrovsky became head of the Anglo-American Department of the Comintern, a role that placed him on the organisation's executive committee and granted both Petrovsky and his soon-to-be wife Rose a vaunted position in the Moscow political elite. Although Rose seems to have spent some time at the Lux in 1927, she eventually graduated to a more spacious and comfortable four-bedroom apartment.[9] One English communist visiting Moscow in late 1927 crossed paths with Rose at a historical opera.[10] It was a long way from the tenement-lined streets of Whitechapel.

If May and Rose ever compared how far life had brought them since they shared a London flat, going back and forth from Sylvia Pankhurst's fierce but embattled suffragette headquarters, there would have been many extraordinary turns of fate on which to reflect. When they met again in Moscow in 1927, both women were travelling on parallel tracks upward into the heights of Soviet society. Rose's path led her deeper into the political life of communist migrants in Moscow. May's journey was taking her into new and exciting cultural worlds.

May's Soviet literary friends – particularly the bespectacled Sergei Dinamov and the balding Casanova Osip Beskin – were her link into the Moscow artistic elite. By April 1927 the relationship between Osip and Ruth had fizzled out. Nonetheless, May's friendship with both was unhindered by its end. For May to take sides in her friend's break-ups would surely have been ill-advised, given her friends' habit of dating each other. Shortly after his break-up with Ruth, Osip moved on to a woman May described as 'the woman of his heart . . . till next time'. To May's displeasure, this woman was the wife of another close friend.

With Osip otherwise engaged, Sergei Dinamov launched his own advance on Ruth. His campaign made some significant advances, but he was forced into retreat when Ruth's husband, Frank, returned to Moscow from the Soviet far east. Frank had something of a trump card over Ruth's sympathies: he was recovering from being shot by Siberian bandits. May's light-hearted references to many of these events in her letters suggest she was simply amused to stand in the eye of the romantic storms whipped up by her friends. Their chaotic love lives did not impinge upon her own desire for new friendships among the Soviet avant-garde – at least not yet.

The world situation, as ever, acted as a backdrop to these personal dramas. Unlike the excitement of personal intrigues within and beyond the Lux, the political situation of the world outside was increasingly becoming a source of discouragement – for May and for many of her comrades. The British General Strike of 1926, initially perceived by many as a harbinger of a coming British revolution, instead resulted in a defeat for the miners followed by the introduction of anti-labour legislation. Yet hopeful eyes remained trained on China, where the united front between the Chinese communist party and the Kuomintang, the Chinese nationalist forces, remained the proof behind the thesis that communists and nationalists could fight an anti-imperialist struggle together. But towards the end of March, May told Joseph that the Chinese revolution 'and a certain scepticism' were disturbing her as of late.[11] If May was hinting towards a dark premonition, she would have been right to sense it: on 12 April Chiang Kai-shek, leader of the nation-alist forces, ordered hundreds of communists murdered, bloodily ending the alliance and inaugurating a campaign of suppression.[12]

Some months later, tragic news once more raised emotions in Moscow. In late August Ruth shared with May the 'feeling on the streets' of Moscow after the newspapers brought news about the US government's execution of Sacco and Vanzetti – two Italian American anarchists whose exoneration campaign had long been a cause dear to many on the international left. On Ruth's way home from the Comintern library, she witnessed people opening the evening papers to learn more about the killings. 'Everyone was standing still, reading, some with tears in their eyes,' she wrote.[13] In contrast to the early post-revolutionary years when capitalism appeared to be entering its death spiral, by 1927 the news was more often carrying stories of setbacks for communists in the world beyond the revolutionary state.

4

If personal drama and international tragedies could cause emotional turmoil, then a retreat into the cultural sphere could provide some respite. On a Wednesday evening in June 1927, May was visiting Osip in his office when one of the leading cultural figures of early Soviet history walked in. Wearing a tweed hat and looking to May like 'a big farm hand', Vladimir Mayakovsky entered the room.[14] By this time, Mayakovsky was one of the leaders of LEF, an avant-garde artistic circle that May began orbiting as an outside observer. Regarded as the 'poet of the revolution', Mayakovsky's poetry cham-pioned the new Soviet way of life and gave it forceful expression. He remains popular in Russia, even as this way of life disappears from living memory. When I visited in 2018, his dark eyes beneath arched eyebrows looked out at me from street art in trendy Moscow districts. Whenever I emerged from the metro station named in his honour, I passed by his statue. When May met Mayakovsky, he was yet to undergo the full force of the canonisation that came after his suicide in 1930, but he was nonetheless one of the most famous and influential figures with whom she crossed paths. 'I just stumble on the great as you see,' she told Joseph.

A few weeks later, she wrote excitedly to Joseph. She began with an apology for her delayed replies to his letters, describing how she had 'so many new experiences I could not get my old brain to gather its old wits together to write sooner'.[15] The 'great event' she wanted to tell him about was that she attended a private reading by Mayakovsky of his poem celebrating the tenth anniversary of the October Revolution, held at the dacha where all the LEF group members gathered on Sundays. The hosts were Osip and Lilia Brik, husband and wife and two corners of the love triangle which Mayakovsky completed. The rest of the guests, May noted, were cinema celebrities, 'painters, the literary lights of the tendency, etc., etc.' She was the 'only outsider', she claimed, and came as the guest of a new friend Olga Tretyakova, wife of the famous playwright Sergei Tretyakov. May was greatly moved by the experience of hearing the poem. Mayakovsky read 'marvellously' and she pronounced him one of 'the greatest orators imaginable'. May told Joseph that she would like to eventually read the poem to him.

After describing another evening spent with the influential photographer-designer couple Alexander Rodchenko and Varvara Stepanova in the same letter, she gestured towards a game of Soviet artistic elite bingo she was playing. May claimed that the cinema director Sergei Eisenstein was the last leading light remaining on her list of personalities to meet, though she was sure they would cross paths soon. She was right. Less than a month later, she told Joseph that she was spending a lot of time in Eisenstein's flat, where her friend Tretyakov was living temporarily. May hinted that she was 'flirting' with the idea of taking the flat for herself sometime soon, as Eisenstein was making plans to leave Moscow for a period.[16]

Boastfully excusing her lack of attention to other friends, she noted: 'I have been so busy with the new stars that I have not seen much of the smaller lights.' But Sergei Dinamov and Osip Beskin remained a regular presence in her life. Both wanted May to carry out work for them. Osip planned for May to write a book on Ireland for the State Publishing House. She agreed and made the case that to write it required a return trip home. Sergei, May complained, was 'simply flooding' her with prefaces to do for translated books commissioned by the State Publisher's Anglo-American section. Sergei also maintained his correspondence with Joseph and expressed his sorrow that Joseph was 'not among us any more', bemoaning that 'our "family"' was now 'strewed'.[17]

The only preface May was really interested in working on for Dinamov was a book by Liam O'Flaherty, a writer who was being name-dropped with increasing frequency in her letters. The two compatriots had begun an epistolary friendship. There were discussions under way for Liam to make a trip to Russia. May told Joseph that if he crossed paths with Tom O'Flaherty, then still an editor of US communist journals, he should tell Tom 'how much these kids' – referring to her Soviet friends – 'want very much to meet' his younger brother. Liam impressed her. She found him clever and was enthralled by his writing talents. However, she admitted his attempts to convey his philosophy in his letters made him come across like 'an awful baby'.[18]

It was an electrifying time in May's Moscow life. There is a sense from her letters that she was finding renewed purpose and meaning as a wandering observer to the artistic elite. She also began working – seemingly informally and voluntarily – as a fixer for visiting Western intellectuals. The first to avail of her services was Roger Nash Baldwin, a founder of the American Civil Liberties Union and its long-serving director, who came to Russia in 1927 to research his book on the Soviet Union. Baldwin served food and chilled wine to May in his unusual Moscow digs: the former rooms of the anarchist prince Peter Kropotkin.[19] Later during his visit, Baldwin came to the Lux on a mission to cook a blueberry pie in a communal kitchen and both Ruth and May took the opportunity to introduce him to their impressive friend Olga Minskaya.

In one letter, written on a day she described as 'tense' due to the funeral of a Soviet ambassador assassinated in Poland, May confided to Joseph: 'I am tired of saving my skin and want to be useful for once in my life.'[20] She intended to spend some time in the US, where she wanted Joseph to help her figure out how 'the wheels go round' in the American daily press.[21] But she planned to return to Moscow afterwards – a city where she felt she could make something of her life. May even suggested that she was 'going native', writing to Joseph that she could not see herself as 'western' anymore.[22] But before she pursued her American dreams and a lasting relocation to Moscow, she left behind her exciting cultural life in August 1927 to travel beyond the Soviet frontier, first to visit her old Lux companion Emmy Leonhard in Berlin and then onwards to her native Ireland to meet her new friend Liam O'Flaherty.

5

May travelled to Berlin from Moscow via Poland. In contrast to the grilling received on the Polish frontier, she found the German border guards relatively relaxed and uncaring about the Russian literature she was carrying. She recalled that their only question for her was whether she was carrying any caviar.[23] For the duration of her time in Germany, May was hosted by Emmy Leonhard and her young family. May's accommodation was palatial: Emmy resided in one of the living quarters of the mid-nineteenth-century orangery built in Sanssouci Park at the behest of Frederick William IV. Emmy placed her guest in the dining room, looking out onto the flowers, trees and water of the park. May found the place unusually silent, even though Emmy and Edo had welcomed another daughter to their family, Alida, born in Charlottenburg earlier that year. Alida's older sister, Elisa, whom May helped bring into the world by providing Emmy with the fare to take her to the hospital close to the Kremlin Palace, was now a 'charming' toddler with a mop of hair. At the age of two, she was already taking gymnastics lessons. 'Every care' was being given to the two girls, May told Ruth in a letter: 'good nurse, maid, etc, etc, everything that is necessary'.[24] Both childcare and accommodation were supported by Emmy's family wealth.

The discordance between the cramped confines of the Lux and this imposing Berlin residence was not lost on May. 'Here I am with my good friend Leonhard and her two babies and husband – in the residence of royalty at Sanssouci,' May told Joseph, 'and I feel lonely for my M[oscow] surroundings and you!'[25] She was working on an exciting commission she hoped to carry out in collaboration with Joseph: the first English translation of Mayakovsky's 'October poem', authorised by the poet himself.

When I visited the Russian State Archive of Literature and Art in a Moscow suburb to look through the small archive of Mayakovsky's correspondence, I found a letter May had written to Mayakovsky from Berlin during this August 1927 visit, misfiled under the name 'Magda O'Callaghan'. In Russian with some minor errors, May addressed the great Soviet poet as 'Comrade Mayakovsky', using the formal address that Russian speakers use when speaking with elders and superiors. She forwarded some translation queries and asked him for a quick response to her in Berlin, care of 'Frau Leonhard' of the 'Orangerie, Sanssouci'.[26]

May's visit to 'Frau Leonhard' coincided with Emmy's partner Edo visiting his family. As general secretary of the International Transport Workers' Federation, headquartered in Amsterdam, his work kept him on the move. Months before May's visit, Edo played a prominent role in a gathering that would later be regarded as one of the most consequential international meetings of the interwar period: the Brussels congress of the League Against Imperialism. The event brought together anti-colonial leaders from across the world, including some who would go on to lead their states in the decades to come.

A photograph from the congress depicts Edo among a small gathering that included Jawaharlal Nehru, later to become the first prime minister of independent India. Elsewhere in the photo is Edo's friend and comrade Willi Münzenberg, a prominent Comintern activist and another key organising figure behind the conference. The 1927 photograph from the sidelines of the Brussels congress captures the smiling boyish Willi and his tall friend Edo. In time, Willi and his wife Babette would also become close friends of Emmy's.

Although not a communist like his partner, Edo was on the radical end of the social democratic left in interwar Europe and proved willing to build coalitions with communists, other revolutionary socialists and those on his right, provided his collaborators were committed to his own primary goal: resisting fascist influence over the European working class. Well travelled and closely attuned to the worlds of the transport workers his union represented, Edo sounded an early alarm to awaken the European left to the threat it faced. In November 1923, two days before Adolf Hitler launched the failed Munich beer hall putsch, Edo was announced as a member of a committee calling for a global anti-fascist campaign.[27]

Anti-fascism became the pillar upon which Edo's activist career stood, eventually placing him and those closest to him in the line of danger. But during May's visit as the final warm summer days of 1927 gave way to autumn, Emmy and her two young daughters, Alida and Elisa, were not yet subject to the cold and hostile atmosphere of living on enemy territory.

18. The Leonhard girls: Alida (left) and Elisa (right), Berlin, c. 1930.
Leonhard Fimmen Papers

6

After leaving behind Emmy, Edo and their two 'charming' daughters in Berlin, May continued to Ireland by way of London, where she spent some time with Nellie. She finally arrived in Dublin in early September. With a general election under way, it was an interesting time to visit. Konstantin Umansky, a cosmopolitan Soviet journalist who lived in the Lux with his Austrian wife and befriended May, told her before she left Moscow that he thought Ireland was, politically speaking, 'the most interesting spot at the moment'.[28] Fianna Fáil, a new political force that eventually dominated Irish politics for decades, was contesting seats for the first time. Earlier that summer, Kevin O'Higgins, a prominent figure in Cumann na nGaedheal, the party that held power in the Irish Free State since independence, was assassinated by Irish republican gunmen while on his way to Mass. A loathed figure among Irish republicans for sanctioning the execution of republican prisoners during the Civil War, O'Higgins is oft-cited by historians for his claim that he and his comrades 'were probably the most conservative-minded revolutionaries that ever put through a successful revolution'.[29]

Yet May, though attuned to a certain religious conservatism in Irish society, nonetheless found the changes in her home country truly transformative. She wrote a letter to Joseph describing how there was much 'more freedom here than in my days', marvelling that she could stand at an election meeting addressed by Jim Larkin, then running on a communist platform, and ride on the top of trams smoking cigarettes without anyone bothering her, presumably with concerns over her stepping beyond the norms of traditional womanhood in her cigarette-scented independence.[30]

In the first and only case of a communist candidate being elected to the Irish parliament in the early twentieth century, Larkin won a seat – though legal troubles meant he was ultimately unable to occupy it. This was not, however, the dawn of Irish communist parliamentary representation in the interwar years, but its nadir. The Comintern soon discovered that Larkin was ultimately impossible to work with. As with Liam O'Flaherty years before, the Comintern learned there was a class of Irish revolutionaries who held the power to melt iron discipline in the heat of their own self-importance. May perceived something of this during her visit, writing afterwards about how, although outsider communists would think Larkin's election a 'great feat', the Irish 'are simply amused'.[31]

The population at large struck her as remarkable. 'These Irish are damned clever,' she told Joseph. 'I used to think I was an exception but I'm out of the running with these!!!!' She gave some examples of the line-delivery she was hearing, describing how locals were 'prepared to believe anything no matter how startling', simply noting in response '"shure an' I wouldn't put it past him"'.[32] This remains a common Irish response to news of grave misdeeds and labyrinthine tales of political corruption.

Ireland, she believed, had many similarities with Russia. There was the same 'largeness of soul and that wonderful fellowship amongst the artist crowd and the national revolutionaries' she found among her Soviet friends.[33] But she found the political scene governed by stark cynicism. Marxist analysis was largely absent. The 'materialist conception of history is as much in place', she claimed, 'as to tell the Laplanders how invigorating back salts are – it's all far too remote'.[34] She joked with Joseph that the whole experience of Irish politics was encouraging her to leave 'thinking politically' behind to 'grow cabbages' instead.[35] May's vision of Ireland at the end of the 1920s, just like her experience of Soviet Russia, was mediated almost exclusively through experiences in its capital city. The personality of her private guide to Dublin, Liam O'Flaherty, certainly coloured her impressions too.

As they spent extended time together, May found Liam to be a 'very charming young chap'. He was 'a real artistic type', she told Joseph, but 'hopelessly irresponsible'. Liam spent the preceding years living between Dublin, London and various states of intoxication. In the Irish capital he was a regular at the kinds of bars and hang-outs that writers, actors and the more progressive political types frequented. He held court at gatherings of the Radical Club, a cross between an avant-garde cultural circle and cabaret-organising committee that brought together many of Dublin's most interesting characters.

His more perceptive interlocutors sometimes saw through his desire to make a startling impression, sensing his troubling reliance on alcohol. The Anglo-Irish actor Constance Malleson was unsettled by her first encounter with Liam around this time, noting that he was 'sliding up and down the polished floor with a lot of under-graduates' at the Dublin cabaret where they met.[36] He promised to seek her out on a visit to London but later confessed that he failed to do so, having spent his time in England 'in more or less the same state' in which she found him in Dublin.[37] This admission, Liam told her, left him feeling like a nun after a 'bad confession'.[38]

Beholden to the emotional ravages of the 'melancholia acute' he developed as a soldier in the First World War – what we would now term severe post-traumatic stress disorder – his working life veered from periods of astonishing productivity to weeks of crip-pling creative paralysis. Between his discharge from the Irish Guards in the summer of 1918 and early 1925, Liam experienced what he described as three relapses, almost certainly referring to mental breakdowns.[39] His doctor described these as bouts of 'severe horrors' and 'exhaustion'.[40] Yet amidst it all, he managed to publish critically acclaimed work, regularly scandalise the Dublin literary elite and even start a family.

With his wife, fellow writer Margaret Barrington, Liam had a daughter, Pegeen, born in April 1926. May met the entire family on her trip to Dublin. But the only Liam O'Flaherty she encountered on this initial trip was the bombastic literary star, not the wounded ex-soldier. Together, the young Irish novelist and this prodigal daughter of Ireland recently returned from the land of the Soviets moved through Liam's literary haunts and walked together in the Wicklow mountains. All the while, they greatly enjoyed each other's company.

During this visit Liam gifted May a copy of his latest novel, *Mr Gilhooley*, and inscribed it to her: 'To May O'Callaghan, with love, Liam O'Flaherty'. It seems May did not finish it, for there is a bookmark, a receipt for a London tea house, lodged halfway into the book. How do I know this unusually specific detail? Because in the most extraordinary online shopping find of my career, I came across May's personally inscribed copy of *Mr Gilhooley* on an American antiquarian bookseller's website. How it made its way from May's personal library and eventually onto the signed book market, I do not know.

As they travelled through Dublin, May was developing plans to help Liam bring his work to wider Soviet audiences through her friends in the State Publishing House. Soon, multiple editions of Liam's writings would be released in Russian-language editions. Liam repeatedly told her, and even his wife Margaret admitted, that May and Liam were much alike.[41] Reciting this to Joseph, May told him that he too had much in common with her. It was a case, she observed, 'of all of us being restless souls with impossible desires'.[42]

The Eternal Propusk

1

Writing from Berlin towards the end of summer 1927, May told Joseph that she was torn between two 'extremes of sentiment: you and Moscow'.[1] She was not the only woman who felt a pull towards Joseph in New York. A couple of months earlier, in June, Sabo chided Joseph about the women from his Moscow days to whom he still wrote letters. 'What does Ivy write you?' she asked. 'And what is O'C doing?'[2] 'Funny', she noted 'that all the women hang on to you.'[3] Ivy, he later replied, wrote him 'sorrowful, witty and sweet words', while May was 'on her way to Ireland to kiss no doubt her native soil and gain new strength for living, as they say'.[4] Sabo would have recognised the pull towards Joseph and New York that May described, for she too was one of the women still 'hanging on' to him. Soon, Sabo let Joseph know that she would arrive in New York in the middle of July on board the ocean liner SS *Cleveland*, sailing from Hamburg and stopping in northern France and southern Ireland before making the transatlantic crossing.[5]

For a third and final time, Sabo and Joe shared a city. It is a paradox for the historian of intimate lives that the moments people spend closest together are often the hardest to reconstruct. People near enough to embrace rarely needed to write letters to one another. An 'x' written on a letter can survive in an archive, but an actual kiss usually disappears into memory as soon as it occurs. It is only when distance was created that historians can pick up the trail once more.

Yet even when Sabo was only a few subway stops from Joseph, she felt an emotional distance that she attempted to bridge through letters. Rejected by Luise Geissler for his lack of ambition, Joseph returned from Moscow intent on making his mark on the movement. The following months and years inaugurated the most intensive periods of his working and activist life, securing his rise within the literary circles of American communism. He juggled his continued writing for the *New Masses* alongside a role with the Soviet press agency TASS and ordinary party obligations. His relationships suffered, as the young poet of the Lux became the loyal cultural theoretician of New York communism.

Already by September, May was complaining to Joseph that she now found the coldness of his correspondence jarring, accusing him of making 'the impersonal note' into a 'fine art'.[6] Sabo's letters, meanwhile, reveal that she too was upset by this change in Joseph. Only for Sabo, the discordance was more acute for she could sense his coldness in person. What she desired from Joseph was not simply the continued warm friendship that May asked of him, but something deeper, a kind of love or spiritual communion that she called their shared 'twinship'. Later, she admitted to Joseph that she felt 'a bit bitter' after the first evening they spent together in New York. 'I was so much looking forward to it,' she noted, that she imagined it as a more perfect occasion than it came to be. 'And as it happened, it was a bit flat,' she wrote, 'and I could not help feeling that our twinship had evaporated and left only a somewhat lukewarm friendship.'[7] Joseph tried to reassure Sabo, telling her that 'despite the uneasiness you've expressed so often I feel about you a good deal the way I always have'. He noted emphatically: 'I am NOT bored with you, but I regret – very much regret – that I am bored with a terrible lot of things.'[8]

But Sabo was clearly thrown into a moment of turmoil by what she perceived as Joseph's disinterest. She feared that Joseph connected her in his mind with the time Luise broke his heart in Moscow. And now, in New York, Sabo wrote 'here I am, reminding you constantly, and you want to get away from it and from me'.[9]

If she were stronger she could weather this, Sabo believed, 'but I am not strong and great'. 'I am a person,' she continued, '[for] whom you have opened a world where I always longed to be and never could be.'[10] Clearly, she hoped to find the same connection with Joseph she had known in Moscow – but he was either too busy or unwilling to grant her the time necessary for such an emotional investment.

Sabo wrote frankly to admit that coming to New York was 'an all around mistake' for her.[11] In this letter she recalled speaking with another friend about May's plans to eventually travel to New York and pondering what, exactly, May intended to do in the city. The friend posed the exact same question to Sabo. She confessed an answer to Joseph: 'I simply could not resist the temptation to come and see you "in your natural surroundings". That was the reason. But I forgot, that by losing my natural surroundings I could not very well see anything in a natural way.'[12] Writing with candour, Sabo admitted that she would only feel 'all right again' when there were '3000 miles between you and me'. She ended the letter dramatically with: 'I will go away again and some day I will be dead and that alone will end this relationship for me. I am quite clear about that to myself. And that I feel this way, that is my fault, my guilt and – my excuse.'[13] 'We met three times, I suppose that is all we ever will have,' she predicted. These lines could be read as Sabo's attempt to provoke Joseph into writing a declarative and reassuring response, but they nonetheless reveal someone in a fragile emotional state.

As I read this letter in its containing folder in an archive in California, I could see that I was well over halfway through the bundle of correspondence between Sabo and Joseph. Clearly, Sabo was right to believe the time of her shared personal intimacy with Joseph was ending. The thinning correspondence reflected their diminishing relationship, as Joseph and Sabo's lives branched off in different directions. Notably absent from these letters are mentions of Sabo's husband, Arthur, who was also in New York with her – at least for a time. Details contained in an MI5 surveillance folder on

Arthur Ewert place him in New York in August and September of 1927, listing him as a Comintern representative in attendance at the Fifth Convention of the Communist Party USA.[14] It is remarkable, given her husband's perilous attempt to navigate Comintern factionalism, that her letters about her time in New York speak more to her personal turmoil over Joseph Freeman than the broader movement's political turmoil over Joseph Stalin.

Sabo's next letters to Joseph were written on board the ship that carried her away from New York that winter. As the last lights of New York disappeared, Sabo walked downstairs to her cabin on board the SS *Deutschland* to find a gift of 'beautiful chrysanthemums' left by a friend, which brought her to tears. She expressed her gratitude to Joseph for his own gift too: a book he inscribed with a note that she would always have an 'eternal propusk' granting her access to him.[15] Using the Russian word for the passes all Lux residents needed to get inside the building, Joseph told her, in his own way, that there would always be something between them. Now, she wrote, 'I am again so near to you as ever,' even though the ship was 'putting mile upon mile between us' and the sound of elevators and subways was being replaced by that of 'wind and waves'.[16] In her next letter written on board, she hinted that something between them *had* changed – at least for her: 'I danced and drank wine last night . . . and was not even thinking of you – and that was new . . .'[17]

The SS *Deutschland* continued its journey towards Germany, carrying people she styled 'glad to be on the way "home"'.[18] As I turned the pages in the folder, the gaps in the chronology reflected the cataclysm that lay ahead: there were some letters from 1928, a couple from 1929 and then a final letter she sent in 1938. Her ability to maintain her friendship and correspondence with Joseph reflected a period of rootedness in her own life that was destabilised by political events in coming years. After she returned to Europe from New York, Sabo's commitment to the cause – despite grave reservations – soon plunged her into a dangerous world of underground activity.

2

While Sabo returned to Europe following her disenchantment in America, May was preparing for a return to Moscow that would prove similarly seismic in its impact on her own life. Delaying her plans to spend time in New York, May returned once more to the Soviet capital. She hoped to offer her talents to Soviet cultural circles rather than focusing her energies on Comintern work. May was also interested in doing some 'work for the old country', something she would achieve through propagandising various Irish writers to her Soviet intellectual friends.[19]

Her time in Berlin, London and Dublin throughout the summer and autumn of 1927 had been productive. She reconnected with old friends, like Emmy and Nellie, and secured a new one: Liam O'Flaherty. Returning to Moscow, she packed for a journey that would take her through Paris, Berlin once more and then on to the Soviet frontier. The train journey from Berlin to Moscow, via Warsaw, took around two days. May was excited to see Moscow once more, where she still had several friends including Sergei Dinamov and Ruth Kennell.

Upon her arrival in the winter of 1927, she discovered that the Moscow housing crisis had worsened in her absence. She was first given a room she believed to be beneath her standing in the Hotel Bristol, located across the street from the Hotel Lux.[20] Though bedbug-infested, the Bristol was still comfortable accommodation by Moscow standards. But she was right to claim that she had gained 'a certain standing' in her circles.[21] If she couldn't use it to get a nicer room, she could at least use it to assist her friend Liam O'Flaherty.

Before her return to Moscow, May and Liam evidently discussed her becoming a go-between to negotiate the publication of his works in Russian and help transfer royalty payments. The arrangement was not without friction. Liam did not blame May for this – though she did catch some of the shrapnel from his explosive moods. 'Dear

O'C,' he opened a November letter, 'For Christ's sake try and get those bastards to send me some money.'[22] Otherwise, he threatened, he was going to come over in the spring, 'blow up' the State Publishing House and 'abduct all the mistresses of the Commissars.' Clearly sensing May was a kindred spirit who appreciated his bombast, he signed off: 'Yours, until we are both properly roasted in hell.'

May's ability to bridge worlds through her expansive network and language abilities also made her a useful point of contact for prominent visitors to the Soviet capital. Her first clients came to her through Joseph, including an American professor whom she brought to meet some Soviet friends. 'I think they have not as yet recovered from it,' she confessed to Joseph in a note describing the visit; 'why are all professors so deadly dull',[23] she wondered.

More exciting visitors soon made their presence known. In November 1927 the celebrated American novelist Theodore Dreiser was approached by a Soviet representative in New York as he prepared for a trip to witness the Soviet experiment in action. The Soviet official, charged with smoothing Dreiser's entry into the Russian cultural set, provided a list of introductions to valuable 'Moscow personages'. The list included Sergei Eisenstein, director of *Battleship Potemkin*, Constantin Stanislavski, head of the Moscow Art Theatre, and May.[24]

Detailed insights into this Irishwoman's astonishing level of access to the Moscow cultural elite can be found in the diaries of Jere Abbott and Alfred H. Barr, two American art historians. More than a year before Abbott and Barr jointly established the Museum of Modern Art in New York, the pair travelled to Soviet Russia to learn more about the artistic experiments under way in the USSR. They checked into the Hotel Bristol in late December, where they met May on their first evening. She made an immediate impression, with Barr regarding her as an 'exceptional person'.[25]

Few visitors to Moscow in 1927 could have anticipated that one of the foreigners best connected to Soviet avant-garde circles was a woman in her forties raised in a coastal village in rural Ireland.

Barr and Abbott found May both unexpected and impressive. She became their guide to the Soviet avant-garde, introducing them to friends and acquaintances that included the photographer Alexander Rodchenko and the dramatist Vsevolod Meyerhold. When required, May translated from Russian.

By early January May was once more back in her old haunt – albeit briefly. In the second week of 1928, Barr wrote in his diary about a dinner with May in her room at the Hotel Lux with the food provided 'by her private cook'.[26] It 'was excellent', Barr recalled, 'though vegetarian'. In his journal entry describing the dinner, Abbott added a short note on his appreciation for May. 'She has been more than kind to us here and is one of the most competent and entertaining people I have ever met,' he wrote. 'She leaves for England soon much to our sorrow,' he added.[27]

A minor 'changing of the guard' at the Lux was taking place: Joseph had left behind room 349 a year earlier, Ruth was ready to finally return to her family in America. Hugo Rathbone was also homeward bound to Britain, having attained useful experience of the Comintern's internal workings. This meal with Abbott and Barr, accompanied by Georgian wine, was to be one of May's last in the Lux. The next decade would see a new cohort fill the halls; many of them fleeing dire circumstances, first in Germany, then in Spain.

After the meal, May invited her new acquaintances to meet some of her old friends: two Soviet intellectuals, who, from Barr's short description, were probably Sergei Dinamov and Ivan Kashkin. Shortly after, the gang – May, Abbott and Barr – had a date with the director Sergei Eisenstein, who showed them reels from his film *October* and *The General Line*, his cinematic exploration of agricultural collectivisation.

Had May paused during this tour to take stock of the cultural connections she had amassed, she would have surely felt her own position to be secure and a further rise in her Moscow career unstoppable. But after her departure from Moscow in January 1928, she would never return to the hotel that hosted so many of her most cherished moments. Never again would she enter the room with its windows overlooking Tverskaya Street where she and Ruth sat as demonstrations flowed by outside, where Joseph met his guides to the world of Soviet letters and where the 'Red Commanderess', Olga Minskaya, astounded her friends. She left behind a residence that must have seemed, given the extraordinary connections she had made in the preceding months, simply another step on a journey towards much more prestigious surroundings.

Soon, however, her ambitions were entirely demobilised and her return route to Moscow indefinitely barred. This dramatic change in prospects was linked to two forceful historical processes that could only have ever collided through May O'Callaghan: the final triumph of Stalinism over its internal opposition and the womanising of one Liam O'Flaherty.

May could not believe herself merely an observer to the lethal animosity between Stalin and Trotsky for much longer. Although it took her time to realise this and even longer to admit it to friends, she was the subject of malevolent gossip. It was something far more dangerous for her reputation than the rumour that she and Ruth were lovers. There was a growing belief in Comintern circles that May was a Trotskyist. This rumour, in turn, determined how she could help Nellie when her friend needed to navigate a fraught situation. Not long after returning to London, May learned that Nellie was facing a moment of personal crisis precipitated by the 'charming' but 'hopelessly irresponsible' Liam.

On with the Dance

1

After only a brief stay in Moscow, May was once more back in London. She was finding it difficult to arrange a return journey to the Soviet capital, and it took her weeks to piece together the reason – that she was the subject of a harmful rumour, which was preventing her from returning. Meanwhile, she was tied to a city she found much less hospitable than Moscow. Despite finding a cause and close friends in the British capital during the suffrage years, she later wrote that getting 'stranded' in London at that time was a kind of 'curse'. The city, she recalled, was a 'soulless desert – full of people, who are no people'.[1] Like many Irish emigrants before and since, she was distressed by a city that was vast, lonely, and filled with English people.

Writing to Joseph after once more becoming an Irish captive in the imperial metropolis, she drew him back to a moment they had shared in her office in the Comintern building, when he had 'impetuously' confided in her that he 'could not live without love'.[2] Here, in London, May confessed, she was 'quite without love . . . I mean there is no atmosphere of love, my spirit is so to speak lonely . . . It is always so in London with the English.' Continuing in a great Irish tradition of honest writing on England and the English, she affirmed: 'Everyone and everything is hard and cold!!!'

Evidently, she was not confined to London through a burning desire to live among the English. Clues pointing towards the reason behind her early return from the USSR can be found in this same letter – although May surely did not discern these hints even as she wrote them. The very details seemed so incidental that May forgot to include them in an earlier letter. 'Your one-time friend Lida,' she told Joseph, had lost her job, along with 'nearly all' of what May described as 'the Trotsky crowd'. 'Lida' was Lydia Gasviany – the beautiful Georgian children's literature expert who once granted Joseph a kiss but nothing more. Sergei Dinamov, a supporter of the Stalin faction and Gasviany's friend, was trying to help her through the situation. 'She was as good as starving' by the time Sergei intervened, May wrote, but sadly 'she was not good enough for his standard of translation'.[3]

Sergei had already informed Joseph about the situation. 'Lida was excluded from the party,' he wrote, before appealing for help from his American friend in his characteristic broken English: 'new your writings send me immediately: I shall give them to her for translation.'[4] 'Poor girl!' Sergei lamented of his Trotskyist friend.

These notes of personal affection already needed to bridge an increasingly deadly abyss created between Stalinism and its political opponents. The same month that Sergei wrote this letter, January 1928, Leon Trotsky was exiled to Alma-Ata, Kazakhstan, ahead of his final expulsion from Soviet territory. What Sergei must have seen simply as a supportive act of friendship was rapidly being transformed, in the eyes of the Stalinist state, into evidence of collaboration with counter-revolutionaries.

May, a veteran but usually aloof observer of left factionalism from her suffrage days onwards, was naive about the seriousness of the situation. Some months earlier she had asked Joseph about his own positioning in the divides with a note of levity: 'I suppose you too are taking sides,' she wrote. 'I should love to know in which mud puddle you find yourself?'[5]

Yet the German members of May's wider circle of friends from the Lux could sense the gravity of the situation. In the wave of expulsions and defections from 1927 onwards, Emmy Leonhard left the Comintern-aligned German communist party. After her return from Moscow in 1926, she drew away from the centralising tendencies of the orthodox communists and became interested in 'left-communist' and anarchist ideas, eventually becoming a Trotskyist.

Many decades later her youngest daughter Alida remembered how Leon Trotsky 'once spent a night incognito' at their Potsdam home. Perhaps, like May, he was put up in the dining room. Trotsky's son Lev Sedov and his girlfriend were also regular visitors, she recalled. The pair were 'much liked' by the two Leonhard children, Alida and Elisa.[6] Due to her political perspicuity but also perhaps partly in recognition of her hospitality, Emmy's rise within German Trotskyism was rapid. By 1931 no less an authority than Trotsky himself, in letters he wrote to Emmy personally, regarded her as a member of the national leadership of his supporters in Germany.[7]

Yet even Sabo – who remained and died a member of the Soviet-supported, and therefore Stalin-aligned, German communist party – was already tracing the contours of the coming catastrophe in 1928. Having settled back into activist work in Berlin after her period of infatuation and discouragement in New York, she was once more writing introspective letters to Joseph. In March 1928 she wrote to him elusively about the divides in the Russian communist party and their impact upon the German movement.

Strikingly and ominously, she was already self-censoring in personal correspondence. 'If I could draw,' she wrote, 'I [would] make a diagram of the situation, but in words which one does not dare to use openly it is hard to speak too much about it.'[8] Relying on insinuation, she once again asked Joseph to remember their conversation in his office in Moscow, when he expressed 'certain reservations' about Stalin – though Sabo only allowed herself refer to him as the '"big man"'.[9]

After her husband, Arthur, returned from Moscow later that year, she told Joseph that 'things look dark'.[10] Sabo sensed a crisis looming in the international movement. She could find little comfort in the 'historical inevitability' of Marxism in the long term when, in her immediate future, she sighted deeply disturbing developments. The dynamics of the revolution, she believed, were now pushing people apart rather than drawing them together. 'In a long perspective,' she reflected, 'to be optimistic when the short one is pessimistic is an art which needs a little mental gymnastics.' 'But for all that – on with the dance,' she concluded.[11]

Joseph, for his part, could offer slim consolation to a woman capable of intelligently disentangling the alternating forces demobilising her movement and setting the stage for a grave historical catastrophe. 'Today is not the last day in history,' he wrote to reassure her, 'you will see other things happening.'[12] But as Sabo witnessed those 'other things happening' in Germany, her pessimism would tragically be vindicated. Still, she remained committed to the party that had absorbed her energies since its founding.

Amid all of this, the dance went on. Right-wing forces metastasised into ever more lethal societal cancers as the international left tore itself apart over the missteps taken and paths unfollowed since 1917. Nonetheless, many retained the vision of a beautiful future that first brought them into the movement. People were still searching for a way to mobilise towards it rather than throwing up their hands in resignation in the face of bleak prospects.

For all her underestimation of the situation and its grave prospects, May, like Joseph, Sabo and others, still drew a sense of purpose from the wider movement to which she and her closest friends had committed their lives. But her intimate relationships would soon upend her prospects for a career in the movement.

2

Throughout 1928 Liam O'Flaherty continued writing his rambunctious and wordy letters to May, still full of 'high-sounding foam', as she once described them. In April he encouraged her to return to Moscow: 'Yes, get back to Russia,' he wrote, 'for it seems there is nothing for Western Europe but the sword of Michael, or perhaps some new avenging spirit of the Steppes – the golden whore of youth emptying the chalice of her lust among the ruins of depravity.'[13] He bemoaned the conservatism of Irish society. 'It's like whipping a dead horse trying to stir up this country,' he told her.[14]

Occasionally, the two met in person. May would travel from London to Ireland to spend time with Liam. She met him at his home in the countryside, where she found him tending his garden while continuing to let his mental garden grow wild. May still regarded him as a 'nice chap', though she thought he was sometimes 'so very difficult' and 'full of moods'.[15] His friends elsewhere occasionally found him hard to deal with too. In London he was a regular at the Progressive Bookshop on Red Lion Street, a literary hang-out overseen by Charles Lahr, a German anarchist who managed the store with his East London Jewish wife, Esther Archer. On one occasion, Lahr and the editors of a newly launched literary journal were obliged to escort a thoroughly sauced Liam back to his London residence where he frantically 'began swallowing eggs'.[16] Liam's London visits provided opportunities for May's circle of friends to interlock. At some point around April or May 1928, it seems May introduced Liam to Nellie Cohen.

This, however, proved to be less a standard meeting of worlds than the human comet of Liam O'Flaherty colliding with an unprepared Nellie. The extent of the impact would only become apparent to May when, in the summer of 1928, Nellie told May a secret. It was the revelation of an affair many years in the making, one whose historical roots moved through all the phases of May's radical career so far and – to some extent – through the major phases of the world revolution itself. All these moments and processes collided for May in a single event.

Sometime around April or May, Liam brought Nellie back to his London hotel room. There, he opened some whiskey, sang Irish songs and the two of them made love. May was surely accustomed to learning her friends had slept with one another. If anything, platonic friendships were the exception in her circle. Yet Nellie's secret was not just about her night with Liam, but about a lasting consequence of their time together.

Soon, May was prepared to share the secret with someone else. May and Ruth had been discussing May's next movements: whether she was finally going to make her long-threatened move to America or attempt a return to Moscow. But Nellie's revelation changed her plans entirely and settled her more definitely on a particular course of action. It is best we learn the news from May herself, writing to Ruth in California on 7 August 1928:

> *Now, I know you have a charming habit of forgetting that things are told you in confidence (this is not meant nastily), but now I want to tell you some one else's secret and therefore must ask you to be specially careful . . . so far I AM THE ONLY PERSON who knows. Nellie like a sweet inexperienced person has 'slipped' and put her foot in it seriously . . . result is that she thought it would be nice to go to Russia where children are not considered illegitimate!!! Have you got me? She had already talked of getting away from this country for a year or so, but NOW SHE MUST!!!!!! Well, I am the friend in need and I do not want her to think that she is hampering my movements in any way as the circumstances are all rather peculiar and I want to think I am in a way an expectant mother by proxy . . . as it MIGHT have been mine!!!!!! Even the prospective father is ignorant of the affair . . . enough said . . .*[17]

A single woman becoming pregnant following a one-night stand was a complex scenario. It was made yet more complicated for Nellie because this was England in 1928, a time and place where possible alternatives such as abortions were criminal acts and where children born outside marriage were placed under their own stigmatising legal category.

All legal distinctions between children born to married and unmarried parents would not be removed in Britain until 1987. In May's native Ireland, the situation was even more dire, with unmarried mothers at risk of being institutionalised within infamous Church-run 'mother and baby' homes until the end of the century.

There was a destination where some of these complications and prejudices could be avoided, Soviet Russia, where Nellie's sister Rose now lived. May would have been well placed to advise Nellie on how other friends had navigated 'unconventional' parental arrangements in Moscow: from Emmy and her daughter Elisa, to her Red Army friend Minskaya and her children.

But the rumour now percolating through May's Comintern circles about her political unreliability jeopardised their ability to reach Moscow. This thorny situation was made even more perilous by the fact that the child's father was not only married but one of the rising stars of English literature.

'So you see,' May told Ruth, 'troubles never come singly.'[18]

Archives at the End of the World

1

By the light of the moon outside the train window, I caught my first sight of the inches of snow that had fallen while I was sleeping – or rather, attempting to sleep – in my upright train seat. I was on board an overnight train taking me from California, northward-bound, over the Cascade mountains. My destination was the University of Oregon in the city of Eugene, home to the Oregon Ducks, the scenic woods of Hendricks Park and, through several turns of fate, more than a hundred letters an Irishwoman sent to her American friend over the course of five decades.

A couple of years before I boarded the train for Eugene, a staff member at the University of Oregon first sent me scans of May's letters to Ruth – the letters that proved the key to unravelling so many mysteries of her life. These letters provided the first evidence I found that Liam O'Flaherty and Nellie Cohen had a child. They were also the first documents that revealed details of Emmy Leonhard's life and her close connection to May.

I remember the feeling of discovery when I read May's letter asking Ruth to keep Nellie's secret. I had to stand up from my desk and pace outside. I was excited about the possibility the sources presented to me: that although May never had children of her own, she was close to friends who did; Emmy and Nellie. Perhaps these children, or their children, were still around and still held on to further documents of that world of 1920s Moscow that so fascinated me, sources that slipped beyond the reach of conventional archives.

But it was not a search for living descendants that brought me to Oregon. I was on a quest to see what I could find by rooting through all the other boxes of material I could not reasonably ask an archivist to spend days photocopying and scanning. In any case, I was excited to work with the personal archives of someone whose life I found so fascinating. And so, only a couple of months after my return from Moscow in September 2018, I began my long research trip to the US west coast. There were two collections that I was especially excited to explore: the personal papers of Joseph Freeman, which had ended up in the archives of the Hoover Institution at Stanford, California, and the archive of Ruth Kennell, held somewhere in the snow-covered city that greeted me as I disembarked the Amtrak Coast Starline train and made my way towards my accommodation in Eugene.

There were still some hours before I could check in, so I visited a café near the station to dodge the cold. Another customer approached me to ask me questions about the book I was reading. *Friendly people*, I remember thinking. The impression was confirmed further by my taxi driver, who invited me to join him for an evening of board games after I settled in. Keen to experience the forest and wild turkeys that I knew you could find in Eugene, I had booked to stay with a woman living in the hills outside the city. I did not expect to see much of my host, Bobbie, as every day would be devoted to archive work – or so I thought. Instead, I would get to know Bobbie quite well, because we were about to get snowed in together. That evening, as the weather grew worse, my taxi driver messaged to inform me that board games were cancelled. I read it as a bad omen for the accessibility of the archives.

When I woke up the next morning, the first thing I saw outside my window was mounds of snow piled up. This was not just a typical Eugene winter's day, I learned, but the most significant snowstorm in a generation. Soon, the heating cut off. And then – even more worryingly for me – the Wi-Fi went. Using my phone, which still had reception, I checked the website of the archive I was due to visit. No news yet. But I did have a message from Bobbie inviting me to come up to the main house, where there was food, a fire and two of her friends, Mark and Geoff. We sat together in the kitchen while outside a scene of extraordinary natural beauty unfolded; redwood branches became burdened with snow, a hummingbird flirted with a bird feeder and wild turkeys sporadically gabbled into the cold air.

Later in the day, over a reheated Chinese takeaway, I told this small gathering about my research. Mark, a curious type, took notes on a piece of paper both on my own biography and my research topic. Occasionally, I would stand up from the table to find cell phone signal and check the University of Oregon's social media. I wanted to learn when, or if, I would be allowed into the archives. A closure was announced. Disappointed but deciding to make the best of it, I headed out into the mounds of snow with Bobbie and went sledding for the first time in my life, passing by downed trees and vehicles abandoned beneath feet of snow.

Finally, the archives opened for a brief window. Mark let me borrow his boots and I began the mile-long walk downhill, carefully navigating icy roads that were only traversable by foot, sled, or ski. Upon arriving at the archive at the university, a librarian generously provided me with several boxes of material at once (rather than slowing me down by delivering the items folder by folder). I immediately set about photographing everything I could. When I left at the end of my first day, a staff member commented he had never seen someone take photos so rapidly. Although I took this as a compliment, it was not how I liked to work. I wanted to 'commune' with the archive material rather than simply convert it into photographs that I would eventually stare at, bleary-eyed, on a computer screen.

Unlike the Moscow archives, created by the Comintern itself for purposes ranging from information-gathering and internal surveillance to insurrection, personal archives are structured by different desires. One of the reasons we engage with the past, notes the historian Catherine Hall, is to grasp how the lives people pursued and 'the conceptual frameworks that were open to them produced distinctive ways of seeing'.[1] In my work, I find the best way of accessing a 'distinctive way of seeing' is to spend an extended amount of time working with material from a vast archive assembled over a single lifetime. I have, on a few occasions, been fortunate enough to be granted the time to do so.

Although my ticket for onward travel to Portland and Seattle soon forced me to tie up my time in Eugene, I managed to photograph enough documents from Ruth Kennell's archive to count my trip as a success. When I finally had a chance to look through the material in detail, I was able to get a sense of the world of 1920s Moscow as seen through Ruth's eyes. Preserved in folders contained in the brown boxes were details like the sounds and sights of translation work in the Kremlin Palace, an account of Tom O'Flaherty's visit to the Lux and so many reflections on the romance and friendship this one woman found in Moscow. One of the more unexpectedly moving documents that I came across was a single photograph of Ruth and May together.

19. Ruth and May on the Novodevichy walls, 1927. University of Oregon Special Collections, Ruth Epperson Kennell Papers, Ax 872, Box 4, Folder 21

The photo might seem undramatic. Yet in its staging it suggests much about what made the period, the city and this friendship so remarkable. The two women are seated on the wall of the Novodevichy Convent, a religious complex located outside Moscow. The moment was captured in 1927. Both women are enigmatically facing away from the camera. The image struck me because of a detail I had learned about May's family; that her sister became a nun. Yet here was May in the mid-1920s, sitting with her friend on the wall of a convent that the Bolsheviks converted into a museum of women's liberation. This photo reflected the determination, even courage, that was common to those who ended up in the Lux in the 1920s, all of whom shared this common experience: against the conventions of their own societies, they chose a self-invented life. They took on the risks and sought the rewards of a path dedicated to transforming the world. That made them participants in aston-ishing events while all too commonly bringing them, and those they loved, closer to danger. Sometimes, you find one letter, diary entry or photograph that justifies an entire research trip by itself. For me, the photograph of May and Ruth on the walls of a convent outside Moscow was one such document.

2

During my time in California on either side of my own personal Oregon trail, there was never a risk of being snowed in. But I discovered the atmosphere in the Bay Area was far more harmful to ordinary human beings than the blizzard-bound foothills of the Cascades. Shortly after my arrival in Palo Alto, the city beside Stanford that became my base during my time there, I was greeted by an ominously orange sky. Smoke from wildfires made the air toxic to breathe and painted the entire area in an apocalyptic hue. Fortunately, I would be spending most of my time in an archive with filtered air. Many of the state's workers, I learned, were not afforded the same privilege.

My workplace for most of my time in California was in the basement of the Hoover Tower. The structure soon becomes visible as you travel the long tree-lined driveway towards the Stanford campus. Each day I entered the Hoover Tower and made my way to the archives located on the lower floor, a repository whose collection remit is described as anything related to revolution, war and peace. Quite broad, in other words. Here, in an archive that includes both Hitler's marriage licence and an ordnance manifest for the flight that dropped the atom bomb on Hiroshima, are boxes of letters, journal entries, photographs and family documents gathered by Joseph Freeman over his lifetime. I found my time among the many fragments of his life a welcome respite from the dystopian scenario outside.

In total, Joseph spent less than a year in room 349 in the Lux. He arrived in the summer of 1926, pursuing his political ideals and love. He left the Lux in the spring of 1927, heartbroken. His ideals, meanwhile, were altered but intact. In the closing decades of his life, Joseph would spend many evenings parsing through memories of his time in Moscow. In correspondence, history books and memoirs, he tracked the afterlives of those whom he came to know in the Hotel Lux. He cultivated and curated his own personal archive, with many of the documents and photographs relating to that one moment in his life: Moscow, 1926–7. Making sense of that year, what he termed his 'year of grace', became a lifelong obsession.

Historians are generally fond of researching fixated people like Joseph Freeman. Many of us find a sense of comradeship with these past obsessives. What could be more recognisable than someone with a singular focus on a narrow set of events and people? On a practical level, those who are invested in their own personal histories tend to diligently maintain material. Joseph Freeman is a case in point: it took me more than a month to wade through the many boxes of his material, all lovingly maintained, before it passed to its eventual archival home. True, such dedication to the debris left behind by your own life can be a mark of narcissism: you generally must believe your life will matter to future historians to hold onto documents and seek their preservation. But what I found in this archive was not egotism – or, at least, not *only* egotism – but a kind of devotion to past friends and a long act of mourning for a lost cause.

Immersed in Joseph's archive, I learned that holding onto all these yellowing letters was a means for Joseph to keep his friends from Moscow present in his life; in some cases, years after they met dark ends. Beyond preserving the letters sent to him by those whom he had loved and befriended in the Lux, Joseph also believed that writing them *into* history granted them a kind of immortality. In long, sprawling diary entries, autobiographical fiction and lengthy letters to those who sought his memories of the era, he wanted to rescue his old comrades – with their all of their quirks and vulnerabilities – from becoming subsumed within the broader story of a mass movement. 'I do not live abstractly,' Joseph told one interlocutor he met towards the end of his life, 'because my relations are with life and the living and the dead who can never die for me.'[2]

Joseph's vast paper trail is often rambling, frequently disjointed and threaded through with his own, sometimes mediocre, often maudlin verse. But historians searching for the remaining memories of the Hotel Lux must be grateful for this enormous body of manuscripts all the same. Joseph had an eye for the novelistic detail that other chroniclers might miss: the small blemishes in an otherwise beautiful face; the exact jazz record that was playing at a particular party; and the moments of doubt expressed, sometimes silently in a facial expression, by the otherwise ideologically resolute.

In contrast to my Oregon trip, my time in Stanford was the longest I ever spent working with a single set of papers left behind by one individual. I was so immersed in Joseph Freeman's world that I developed the illusion common to historians that I understood not only how his contemporaries perceived him but also the rhythm of his innermost thoughts. That opportunity to become close to the people of the past is the kind of experience I always crave in research. It was something the Moscow archives, for all their revelations, could not provide. Assembled by the Comintern, the central insight they granted was how a vast institution operated. They could not tell me what made someone's heart tick.

3

Friendship, I realised through my work in Stanford and Eugene, sometimes continues posthumously. The final act of devotion that Ruth Kennell and Joseph Freeman performed for May – along with a whole cast of other minor figures from the revolutionary drama of their lives – was to preserve the letters sent to them and eventually leave these documents someplace secure from the ravages of time. I was trained to treat archives with circumspection. Lecturers told me the archive was often a place where state power manifested. Archival material was gathered according to authoritarian impulses; it was needed for surveillance and control. But such conditioning prepared me better for the Comintern archives than the boxes of items collected by Joseph and Ruth over their lifetimes. In all my years of training to be a researcher, nobody ever emphasised to me that love and human warmth also determine what gets left behind.

Still, Joseph and Ruth's documents were preserved because they had, in their own circles, come to positions of relative prominence. Where is the personal archive of the truly obscure? The survival of cherished letters and photos belonging to people like May and Emmy Leonhard – activists who, before I found mention of them in other people's letters, no historians had ever written about in any kind of detail – is a more fraught process.

Before, during and after my time in Moscow, California and Oregon I was also searching after a real rarity: the attics, somewhere in Europe, where material belonging to people like May, Nellie and Emmy may have ended up. Finding those archives, if they existed, could bring me closer to an understanding of how human intimacy and affection often determines the survival of documents. Living descendants do not, as a rule, approach their household clutter like an archive does – they do not have budgets devoted to preserving the boxes their loved ones leave behind or temperature-controlled rooms in which to store them.

Was there a younger generation that cared for Emmy, May and Nellie enough to hold onto such material? Were there, perhaps, some people alive who remembered them? Even if the truth of the matter was that everything I was searching for had been dumped into refuse sacks years before, I needed closure.

Fortunately, I eventually learned that a treasure trove of documents survived. The first clue that led me to finding all that material, first in an attic in the Cotswolds and later in a garden shed in northern Spain, was something May revealed in her letters to Ruth – the letters I first opened on my laptop screen in 2016, and which I finally held in my hands in the aftermath of a blizzard several years later. That clue was the name of Nellie Cohen and Liam O'Flaherty's daughter.

PART III

The Found Generation

1929–1945

The Time of Bad Roads

1

In defying the stigma of 'unmarried motherhood', Nellie Cohen could draw inspiration from her former employer. In 1928, shortly before she departed England with May, Nellie called on Sylvia Pankhurst in the small, dilapidated cottage on the edge of Epping Forest where she settled after closing 400 Old Ford Road.[1] Beside the residence was a tearoom built by Pankhurst's partner Silvio Corio, an Italian anarchist with whom both Nellie and May had worked in the Fleet Street office of the *Dreadnought*. Earlier that year, Sylvia and Silvio welcomed another addition to their Epping Forest retreat: a son, Richard. During Nellie's visit, Sylvia told Nellie that she should have a baby too. Evidently still feeling guarded, Nellie chose not to reveal that she was in fact pregnant.

May and Nellie would not have required a whisper network of fellow veterans of the East End struggle to learn about Sylvia's new arrival. They simply could have opened the *News of the World* on Easter Sunday 1928 to read the headline: 'EUGENIC BABY SENSATION. SYLVIA PANKHURST'S AMAZING CONFESSION.'[2]

Pankhurst's recent biographer Rachel Holmes delicately disentangles the word 'eugenic', which may disturb modern readers, from the headline. The early twentieth century saw many social reformers and progressives advocating eugenics: the idea that population growth should conform to a plan that encourages the 'fit' to reproduce while discouraging the 'unfit' from producing children. 'The loaded question was, of course, who decided who was "fit" and who was "unfit",' writes Holmes.[3] In the US, eugenics acts, upheld by the US Supreme Court in 1927, targeted mentally disabled and institutionalised women and compelled them to undergo sterilisation. The Nazi German state would later construct its mass-murder campaigns on eugenically motivated policies.

Holmes argues that although Pankhurst's language of eugenics is 'distasteful to the modern ear', in the 'context of the times, defending the right to be an unmarried mother at forty-five and celebrate maternity as a positive choice would have been heard and understood differently'.[4] Certainly, race science was not part of Sylvia Pankhurst's political imagination. She would spend much of her activist career in the 1930s organising within anti-fascist movements. A crucial motive in the choice of language was, it seems, financial: Sylvia and Silvio needed money as new parents and the tabloid press in Britain were on the lookout for a 'eugenic baby' story. That it involved a well-known name like Pankhurst was a bonus.

What is revealing, in this respect, is the fact that the *News of the World* interview was a reprint of an American press interview released a day earlier. A few months before Richard Pankhurst was born, the New York tabloids created a press sensation after revealing the birth of a 'eugenic baby' born to Grace Burnham, an activist in the US communist party. Remarkably, May and Nellie knew the tabloid 'eugenic' babies on both sides of the Atlantic. Feverish speculation on the identity of the father of the communist baby in New York led fingers pointing in the direction of Joseph Freeman.

May knew Grace Burnham through her Moscow circles and directed a jibe in Joseph's direction about his alleged involvement in the affair. Her understanding of the pregnancy better reflected the reality than tabloid references to 'eugenic' children. 'I understand that a friend of yours', May wrote 'has gone and enacted' the *I Want a Baby* 'stunt'. Here, she was referencing a controversial play written by her friend Sergei Tretyakov about a Soviet woman who sets out to become pregnant by a good socialist worker and then live independently after the child is conceived.[5] May told Joseph that she wondered whether 'you confined your activities merely to propaganda or whether according to Communist theory you developed propaganda to action!'[6]

This was May's typically tongue-in-cheek way of enquiring whether Joseph was the father (he was not). But it also gestured towards a political framework that could vindicate raising a child outside of a conventional marital family structure.

'Remember Minskaya,' as May once implored Joseph in her discussion of sex under socialism. Olga Minskaya had first set out to become pregnant by bluntly informing another soldier she wanted a child with him but nothing more. A widely known example of the same principle of voluntary motherhood could be seen in the life and writing of Alexandra Kollontai, whose influential feminist writing we encountered earlier. Kollontai raised her own son, Misha, with the help of another female comrade.[7] In her 1923 novel *Red Love*, Kollontai's protagonist leaves her male partner without informing him of her pregnancy and sets out to raise their child with the help of a collective of women she is helping to construct.[8]

2

Nellie did not have a revolutionary women's collective to help her through her pregnancy and the early stages of motherhood, but she did have May. Their shared ideals supported the unconventional project they were about to attempt: raising a child together as two single women, in defiance of society's prejudices. Could there have been something more dissident about this arrangement? Were Nellie and May a couple? There is little evidence to suggest this. The normally and sometimes ostentatiously frank May betrayed no hints that her bond with Nellie, like her connection to women like Ruth and Emmy, was anything other than an intense friendship.

While Nellie's pregnancy was, unlike those of Sylvia Pankhurst and Grace Burnham, an accident, there was, in a different way, an element of choice. May and Nellie must have discussed the possibility of reaching Soviet territory for a safe abortion. Writing to Ruth,

May listed several factors that made it 'impossible to get way for any operation of that sort', including the late stage at which May was informed of the pregnancy, along with the illness and death of Nellie's mother, Ada.[9]

Nonetheless, crossing the Soviet frontier still meant reaching territory where illegitimacy was no longer a legal category. But, alas, this plan would prove impossible too. May was refused a visa to return to the USSR. It was a decision beyond her control that must have proved just as destabilising to her future plans as the news that Nellie was pregnant. May believed the refusal was due to her rumoured Trotskyism. Not yet able to admit this to her friend, May cryptically informed Ruth that there had been a personal disagreement with 'the people here' and she was 'for the moment' cut off from Moscow.[10]

Yet Nellie and May still wanted to get out of the country, even if this meant remaining under capitalist rule elsewhere. Perhaps London, where one could find the prying eyes of Nellie's extended family and the whispering world of Liam O'Flaherty's contemporaries, seemed like a claustrophobic setting in which to have her child. Nellie could rely on her sister Rose, at least for moral support. She arrived to see Nellie in London, but she had her own life in Moscow and could not join May and Nellie for their planned trip.[11]

As Rose returned to Moscow, May and Nellie re-oriented their direction of travel across the Atlantic to New York. For May, this was almost a return to course: after all, she was first en route to America in 1914 when the outbreak of the First World War rooted her in London and led her to seek employment on Sylvia Pankhurst's journal. Now she had something new in New York: a network of revolutionary American friends to ease her landing. Similarly attuned to her own political ideals and shaped by first-hand experience with Soviet mores, May's small network in New York would provide Nellie some degree of sanctuary from the societal prejudice of 'illegitimacy'. She also hoped her contacts would help her secure fulfilling work.

May and Nellie booked a berth on the comfortable SS *Berengaria* on its late-September transatlantic crossing. The closer the *Berengaria*'s departure date became, the more May felt her spirits rise, despite the unsettled political winds blowing her westward.[12] She was both excited to discover what kind of impression New York would have on her and eager to reconnect with Joseph.[13] Thinking about introducing Nellie to Joseph, May let her imagination wander – although she ultimately concluded they would make a poor match. 'If my friend Joe were not such a flirt,' she wrote to Ruth ahead of the journey, 'it would be nice' for him to marry Nellie. He wanted a Jewish wife, she continued, 'and I doubt if he could find a nicer one!!!!!'[14]

More pressing than matchmaking were May's concerns about Nellie's pregnancy and the prejudices it might elicit. May was anxious about the medical examination that Nellie would be subjected to on board and confided in Ruth: 'I shiver in my shoes that they may find out N's state and decide she is an "immoral woman".'[15] 'God what a world!' she wrote. Finances would also be an issue. May would soon be providing for herself, a mother and a child. Given her recent employment history, she would need to find work someplace that considered the Comintern a respectable past employer.

3

Bonds between communists were shaped by a vast array of personal interdependencies in addition to political commitments. Interwar communism's hold over its adherents lay partly in its powerful creation of networks of practical support, able to provide everything from food and childcare to safe houses and forged passports in any location where communists arrived. Loyalty to the ideology thus acted as a movable reference check. Assuming you passed these checks, a plethora of provisions were opened to you and a series of obligations fell upon the communists stationed in whatever outpost was due to welcome the travelling comrades. As historian Brigitte Studer persuasively argues, the Comintern offered an 'opportunity for a social and geographic mobility that would otherwise have remained inaccessible to most'.[16]

International communism beyond the Soviet Union, especially in the 1920s and 30s, can be imagined as a 'diaspora' community of a similar mould to the great historical Jewish, Irish and African diasporas. Like ethnic diasporas, communists held an idealised image of their political homeland in their minds, tended to gather in particular neighbourhoods wherever they found themselves and shared cultural reference points.

The communist diaspora even spoke a language that was often unintelligible to the outsider listening in – whether that outsider was simply someone overhearing communists gathered in a bar or a secret police agent attempting to penetrate a cell. Informers who installed themselves within radical circles could be rumbled through their lack of fluency in the communist tongue. This language was a political creole: a mixture of the speaker's native tongue with phraseology rooted in Marxist theory, Soviet practice and conspiratorial codes.

Examples of this language included the Soviet Russian habit of abbreviation according to word components rather than acronyms, a method with at least one term still in use: the term 'agitprop' for 'agitational propaganda'. Adoption of this linguistic convention beyond the USSR once led Tom O'Flaherty to sardonically propose to a strait-laced superior that the *Daily Worker* should refer to the United Councils of Working Class Housewives as the 'Uncopwokwifs'.[17]

Tom's wry proposal suggests how 'speaking Bolshevik' could twist tongues. Yet the phraseology of leftist theory – 'proletarian', 'materialist', 'bourgeoisie', and so on – percolated in the daily conversation of communists precisely because these terms helped people make sense of the chaotic world around them. The communist creole was thus a multifunctional revolutionary tool: a protective measure, a test of political reliability and a means of revealing the historical processes at play in the class struggle.

Even though rumours of her Trotskyism were already at work undermining May's position within broader Comintern networks, her friendships still allowed her and Nellie to situate themselves within the New York branch of the communist diaspora. In one of her first letters sent after their arrival in October 1928, May claimed: 'at every step I seem to be meeting my old friends from Russia'.[18] Jere Abbott, the art historian who had crossed paths with May during her last weeks in Moscow, invited her out to lunch, as did Roger Baldwin, the ACLU founder who once hosted her in Prince Kropotkin's former rooms. Joseph was, of course, one of the first New Yorkers May sought out. He brought May and Nellie around Harlem and took them house-hunting, after which they soon settled on a set of rooms in Chelsea. Writing to Ruth shortly after they reached New York to note their safe arrival, Joseph told her that May 'looks well' though she was 'a little fatter than in Moscow'.[19]

May soon had some impressions to share of Joseph. She confided in Ruth that Joseph had 'become so sober and strange that I do not recognise in him the charming boy of Moscow days'.[20] May became another victim of Joseph's intensive focus on political work that had so disquieted Sabo a year before. Nonetheless, she continued to meet him in New York, including visiting his home and meeting his younger siblings.

What did these two radical women, making their way in a vast and unfamiliar city, look like to outside observers? Usefully for our story, there was an informer – of sorts – dispatched to report on May and Nellie shortly after their arrival in the city on board the SS *Berengaria*. Before departing Moscow to return to California, Ruth Kennell had begun an affair with Junius Woods, a correspondent for the *Chicago Daily News*. When Ruth's new lover informed her that he was passing through New York, Ruth implored him to check in on her friends May and Nellie. Ruth wanted a status report on May, who had been uncharacteristically silent in her correspondence since arriving in the US. She also encouraged Woods to introduce May to some of his journalistic contacts.

In the afternoon following his arrival in the city, a few weeks after May and Nellie arrived, Woods took his overcoat from his suitcase and walked out onto the chilly New York streets. He headed in the direction of May's address, given to him by Ruth. Woods was not a communist and he apparently did not enjoy the company of the ideologically committed, whom he regarded as suspicious and single-minded. Ruth, his latest infatuation, was the exception.

On the walk over, 'between dodging taxis', he had second thoughts about meeting May. Writing to Ruth, he revealed that he was under the impression that May was probably in league with Soviet intelligence so decided it was not worth his time 'hobnobbing' with her.[21] This was not a suspicion directed particularly against May but a common impression those outside the communist fold had of those within it.

He walked to her street and decided to turn around without calling on May. He wrote to tell Ruth that her friends were staying in what he described as a 'nice and clean' house on Manhattan's West 24th Street, 'a block from the piers on the Hudson'.[22] But Ruth was not happy with mere geographic notes from her boyfriend. Clearly chastised by his girlfriend for not calling on May as she asked, he soon agreed to visit May, despite his reservations. After dropping in once more a few days later, he was greeted by May in the lobby of the building. He found her 'quite impressive' as she came into the lobby to meet him 'with a nonchalant cigarette in a long holder'.[23]

But here, his impressions turned sour as this lackey of the capitalist press was forced to spend an evening with a willing dupe of the Bolshevik menace. May, he claimed, attempted to impress upon him her view that there was 'no difference between the two political parties in the United States' and then talked about what he described as 'the usual hooey of a high society matron'.[24] May revealed no hostility in her own descriptions of meeting Woods. Quite the contrary: 'we had a lovely evening together', May told Ruth, 'perhaps this was due to the fact that we had cocktails, wine and liqueurs'.[25]

Later, when the two went to what Woods described as a 'swell restaurant', he found May hesitant. Speaking in a mode he considered indirect, she told him she had come to New York with 'an English girl' and was living close to 'an American girl'.[26] Over dinner, however, it was Woods who claimed to be the subject of suspicion. He joked that May's coyness was well founded, given she was 'in proximity to one of the minions of the Capitalist enemies': himself.[27]

Only on the walk home did he finally warm to his deeply politicised companion who, for the sake of his affection for Ruth, he was willing to spend time with. As the mismatched pair walked back towards May's building, she spotted the 'English girl', mentioned obliquely over dinner, passing on the street opposite. She called Nellie over and introduced Woods, although he already knew some details about her, including her 'secret'. In any case, according to Woods, it was no longer a secret. Nellie, he reported to Ruth, was 'large' and unmistakably pregnant.

Woods then witnessed something that caused him to concede that May had 'her fine points' even if he still believed her guilty of thinking she was always right.[28] As Nellie joined May and Woods for the walk through the Manhattan streets on that early November evening, out of the corner of his eye, Woods would notice May carefully taking Nellie's arm to help her over rough spots in the path. All the while, May spoke to her pregnant friend in a 'motherly tone of voice'.[29]

This was a moment of real affection – the kind that too rarely makes it into the historical record. Yet it was also a symptom of the peculiar intensity with which a shared political passion could bind two women to one another. Woods later dismissed May's argument that Nellie and her child required 'international support' as 'a comedy', but in doing so he revealed his failure to understand the meaning May and Nellie found in their shared commitment.[30] As part of a global network of activists, individual members of the movement were vindicated in their personal sacrifices by a vision of interdependent humanity. Such a vision would, in time, come to contrast starkly with the cynical realpolitik of Stalinism. Yet just because the grand dream of a world commune remained an aspiration does not mean it never materialised in small-scale realities. The act of living selflessly for others was a core tenet of radical commitment in the early twentieth century that could take a multitude of forms; from laying down your life on the barricade to undermining your own personal ambitions and guiding a friend along the perilous path that lay ahead.

4

Junius Woods may not have simply been projecting his hang-ups about communists onto May when he found her guarded. When they met, May was beginning to learn more directly about how her own past associations were shaping her present predicament. Shortly after arriving in New York, May and Nellie headed to a communist party rally, where they ran into a party activist named Gertrude Haessler. They ran into her literally, it seems, as Haessler was, in May's words, 'dashing round . . . in her element arranging the procession with no time or eyes for anybody'.[31] Later, Gertrude Haessler phoned up the Chelsea apartment to arrange a meeting with Nellie but emphasised that she wanted to meet Nellie alone. 'I am not broken-hearted,' May told Ruth. She was, nonetheless, perturbed by the snub. Just before departing for New York, May admitted to Ruth that she believed she had some rivals in the wider Comintern world. Her role in the Comintern headquarters in Moscow had now been filled by an American communist named Mary Reed, May observed, and she was suspicious that Reed played some role in getting May recalled from Moscow.[32] On 10 February 1929, a few months into her and Nellie's life in New York, she finally addressed her worries in simpler terms in a letter to Ruth. Bram Fineberg, a communist veteran of East End socialism, was visiting New York. May confessed that he was 'avoiding me like hell', suggesting that there was talk in 'the Party here that I am helping the Trotsky faction'.[33]

The exact same letter carried momentous news of an entirely different variety. Something happened that proved more impactful on May's future than the rumours of her Trotskyist sympathies. The previous evening, around five, May took Nellie to the Park Avenue Hospital where, shortly after midnight, Nellie welcomed her daughter into the world: a hefty new arrival weighing in at eight and a half pounds. May was particularly pleased with the doctor, 'really a fine chap'. 'Imagine,' she noted, 'he is arranging the birth certificate so that everything will be quite "legal".'

Of course, it was not the first time May played a pivotal role in helping a close friend bring a daughter into the world. Curiously, May's Comintern career was book-ended by two births: Emmy Leonhard's first daughter, Elisa, born in a hospital near the Kremlin in May 1925, and four years later Joyce Isabelle Cohen, born on Park Avenue in February 1929. These were years that saw May's gradual ascent in the Comintern world followed by the collapse of her ambitions. On a less intimate scale, between these two dates lay decisive years when the future of the world revolution was set on an inexorable course. Nellie's daughter Joyce entered the world on the eve of a new decade, one that would bear witness to a darkness from which Joyce would be largely shielded. Her Kremlin-born counterpart Elisa would, however, be raised under its shadow.

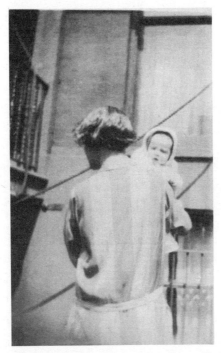

20. May with baby Joyce, New York, 1929. Joyce Rathbone Papers

Proust for Breakfast

1

While his second daughter acclimatised to the world in a hospital on New York's Park Avenue, Liam O'Flaherty was drinking, horse-riding and upsetting his wife in the south of France. These details can be gleaned from letters that Ione Robinson, a young Portland-born artist, sent to her mother during a European journey that brought her briefly and perilously into Liam's orbit. After arriving in Cagnes-sur-Mer, a picturesque coastal town then haunted by artists and White Russian refugees, Ione wrote to her mother that the 'only artistic person' in the town 'who shows any enthusiasm for real fun is an Irish writer named Liam O'Flaherty, and even he drinks too much'.[1]

On 5 February, less than a week before May brought Nellie to the hospital to give birth, Ione visited Liam and his wife, Margaret, at their *pension* – a large home with a garden covered in grapevines. Ione and Margaret drank tea while Liam bounded across a field on horseback. Liam did not partake in the tea-drinking. 'He would die, I believe, if he drank anything with water in it,' Ione told her mother.[2]

In 1929 Liam was at the peak of his literary powers. Several acclaimed novels were already gathering glowing reviews across the literary pages of the Anglophone world and two of his greatest works, *Skerrett* and *Famine*, would gestate in his mind in the subsequent decade. Interest in translations rights for his works now extended beyond Russia and there was talk of theatre and cinema adaptations.

Just as he would have wanted, Liam was garnering eminent fans and prominent enemies. When discussing Liam in a private communication, one Irish government minister made the case that there was now a 'short cut to being recognised as a great writer by favouring Communism and stressing filth'. 'I think if you eliminate Bolshevism and muckraking from Liam O'Flaherty,' the minister continued, 'you have a very unimportant writer left.'[3] There was no love lost between the writer and the state. Though Liam still called Ireland home, he detested its governing regime.

Ione quickly realised Liam's writing career was on more steady footing than his family life. On a visit to a racing track in Nice with Liam, Margaret and their daughter Pegeen, Ione witnessed Liam gradually becoming too inebriated to even see the horses. Meanwhile, Margaret cried openly and little Pegeen simply stood watching the horses outpace one another.[4] It is an image of a woman at the end of her tether with an irresponsible partner. Within a couple of years Margaret and Liam were separated. They never legally divorced. Following their separation, Margaret left behind Ireland to continue her writing career in London under her maiden name Margaret Barrington. She took Pegeen with her to England.

Despite her parents' troubled relationship and Liam's long absences from her life, Pegeen remembered Liam as a 'marvellous' and 'devoted' father. It was partly a symptom – so I was told by one of Pegeen's close friends – of Liam being the parent who would show up out of the blue, full of imagination and fun, in contrast to her more constant and responsible mother, Margaret. Pegeen's earliest memory of her father took place on an evening in the south of France: a Corsican nanny carried her to the terrace where her parents were having dinner. Her mother said it was bedtime, but her father argued for indulging little Pegeen. 'I know that my father gave me an experience of the joy of being treasured so strong that I still remember it,' Pegeen wrote many decades later.[5]

21. Liam O'Flaherty and Pegeen, mid-1930s. Courtesy of the
National Library of Ireland

In February 1929, as he fascinated Ione Robinson, charmed his
daughter and unsettled his wife, Liam was just over a year away
from his long-planned trip to Soviet Russia. His intention was not,
as he had once threatened May, to abduct the mistresses of the
commissars and blow up the State Publishing House, but more
prosaically to write a book on the journey. Books about the Soviet
Union were in vogue in the UK and US publishing worlds. The
most popular publications took the form of travelogues that featured
the author returning from the land of socialism either terrified or
enchanted with the future of humanity, but never unmoved by the
experience.

Speaking with his young painter friend in his Cagnes-sur-Mer
home, Liam boasted to Ione that he had an invitation from the
Soviet government to visit and claimed he could arrange a similar
invite for her. But Ione had other plans: she wanted to travel to
Mexico to paint frescoes. Liam thought her 'crazy' for not wanting
to go to Russia, where, he argued, there was a 'modern renaissance'

under way. Still, Ione found the politics of the Russian Revolution difficult to parse and already admired artists at work in Mexico. She went against the Irish writer's advice to follow her own instincts.

After arriving in Mexico, a country recently emerged from its own revolutionary upheaval, she met the painter Diego Rivera, who suggested she take up residence in the apartment of Tina Modotti. It was here, in the apartment of the Italian revolutionary photographer, a gathering point for radical artists passing through Mexico city, that she first met a handsome Ukrainian-born American writer: Joseph Freeman. 'I was terribly affected by the glint in his eye when we met,' she recalled, 'you would think he was a brother of Rudolph Valentino by the shape of his head, his eyes.'[6]

This was not the first time Joseph was compared to Valentino, the prototype Hollywood sex symbol. Sabo, in a poem about Joseph composed during their time together in the Lux, wrote of '*Joe's dunkle Valentinoaugen/ Die so gut für's Lieben taugen*': 'Joe's dark Valentino eyes/ They are so good for loving.'[7] A few years later, those same deep-set eyes ensnared Ione. 'I have a feeling that I'm falling in love with Joe,' she told her mother not long after she met him in the apartment she shared with Tina Modotti.[8] Unlike Sabo, however, Ione soon learned her feelings for Joseph were reciprocated. Soon, Joseph and Ione would celebrate their marriage in a New York synagogue.

I gasped and muttered *no way* to myself in the Stanford art library when I first read Ione Robinson describing her encounters with Liam O'Flaherty. I had sought out Ione's letters, collected and published in 1946, for details on what it was like to be married to Joseph Freeman. I never suspected Liam would show up out of the blue, despite his well-evidenced ability to do exactly that.

This may seem like an extraordinary set of circumstances: the transatlantic and cross-continental itinerary of a single young artist moved from one moment I was trying to uncover to the other moment I initially set out to find. Although extraordinary, it was not chance. It was the kind of discovery that spoke to the profound interconnectedness of the world I was researching, a world where everyone was rarely more than two steps of separation from anybody else. After all, if you belonged to a certain class of activist or artist in the 1920s, you could step into a hotel in Moscow, an apartment in Mexico, or a café in Marseilles and be entirely unsurprised to spontaneously encounter a close comrade.

2

When Joseph met Ione, he was visiting Mexico as part of his work for the Soviet press agency TASS. Although Mexico experienced years of revolutionary struggle after the First World War, the state birthed from the process was tilting towards conservatism by the end of the 1920s. In late 1929 the *New Masses*, the slickly produced leftist journal that Joseph helped edit, announced on its pages that 'the revolution is over in Mexico'.[9] To grasp the future potential for Marxism in Mexico, Joseph embedded himself among the beleaguered activists of Mexican communist party, founded in 1919 by, among others, Joseph's one-time romantic rival in the Lux: M. N. Roy.

Although the Mexican political currents were heading rightward by 1929, the artistic vibrancy that arose from the struggle in Mexico remained alive. Alongside the photographer Tina Modotti, Joseph and Ione navigated a world populated by the likes of Diego Rivera and Frida Kahlo, figures better known today for their art than their revolutionary politics. As a committed party member, Joseph found Rivera politically suspect. He was also jealous of his new love Ione's closeness to Rivera, a suspicion that Rivera's lover Kahlo would, in turn, hold against Ione. Even though Ione's letters reveal she was thinking over the revolution since her time in France with Liam and considered herself 'a red', she was disinterested in Marxist theory. In a bad omen for the future of their relationship, she decidedly rejected a central tenet of Joseph's world view: that art should always serve the revolution. Joseph himself would eventually jettison this view, although much too late to salvage their relationship.

That the more politically flexible Ione should fall for Joseph exactly when he was at his most ideologically fixed speaks to the strength of his charm. But charm was not enough. Their doctrinal differences would ultimately lie at the heart of a personal rift that ensured their marriage was a brief one. Stephanie J. Smith, a historian who has explored the marriage of Joseph and Ione in detail, writes that though Ione respected Joseph's 'dedication' to his cause, 'she quickly grew to resent his insistence that all art, including her own, should be political in nature'.[10] Then there was the discordant matter of Joseph's conventional understanding of marriage, which contrasted starkly with his advocation of revolutionary societal transformation.

The long hours of political work since his return from the Hotel Lux seemingly did little to resolve for Joseph the question of how matters of love should relate to revolutionary commitment. Ione's correspondence with her mother, sent after her return from Mexico with Joseph, reveal him to be single-minded, sentimental and often contradictory. In other words: much the same young man who both frustrated and charmed May, Sabo, Ivy and other women from his Moscow years, but with added self-seriousness. What distinguished Ione from these women is that she learned from experience what he wanted from marriage.

The signs that Joseph wanted a traditional marriage, not a radical attempt to redefine the age-old institution, were clear from the outset. For all his forthright opposition to international capitalism, Joseph buckled before his parents, Stella and Isaac. He asked Ione to pretend she was Jewish, knowing that his parents, already disappointed with their son for becoming a communist, would be 'heartbroken' to learn that he was entering a 'mixed' marriage.[11] This subterfuge required quick thinking on Joseph's part. To explain Ione's inability to speak the languages of the Old Country, he told his parents that her family had emigrated so long ago it was all forgotten. When the rabbi at their ceremony asked Ione for her parents' Hebrew names, Joseph interjected with two invented names before Ione needed to answer.[12]

This son of a Ukrainian village and his wife – the supposed daughter of the *shtetl* of Portland, Oregon – moved into an apartment together. Located on the fifteenth floor of a recently constructed building in Manhattan's Murray Hill area, their new home had a view overlooking the East River. Shortly after settling in, Ione sat on a soapbox surrounded by Joseph's stacks of books, writing to her mother to tell her how glad she was to be married. 'Being settled will give me a chance to see what sort of artist I am,' she noted.[13] Being settled would have precisely the opposite effect.

Although Ione had some real affection for the Freeman family, her husband's friends proved more trying company. 'For dinner', she told her mother a few weeks into their marriage, 'we always have some rabid revolutionist as a guest.'[14] Ione found several visitations unpleasant, including the communist author who sat in an expensive chair smoking and dispensing his ashes onto the floor, a correspondent who returned from Mexico with a bag of dirty socks he asked her to wash and a radical artist whose main inspirations were industrial objects like bridges and factories. 'I think these Communists take themselves too seriously,' Ione observed.[15] Her husband also revealed some trying habits, like an insistence on starting each day reading aloud from literary classics. In a line that effortlessly conveys a sense of intolerable tedium, Ione wrote to her mother: 'Every morning at breakfast, Joe still reads Proust.'[16]

Just over a month into their marriage, Ione knew things were going badly. At the time, she blamed it on Joseph's women friends. 'They are all so much older than I,' she noted, 'and they are all people who have done some extraordinary work for the Revolution.'[17] She ultimately intuited that she needed to make a choice between her constrained married life and the artistic career she deeply craved. Joseph, notes Stephanie J. Smith, 'realised his expectations of a deeply affectionate partnership and a comfortable, shared home would not materialise with Robinson, and soon distanced himself emotionally in the same ways Robinson moved away physically.'[18] He was guilty of several transgressions besides requiring his wife to lie to his parents about her family and continually bringing home ill-mannered radicals. When Ione was hospitalised that winter, he did not visit her and – to his own mother's outrage – hosted another woman in their flat.[19] Soon, Ione left for California and the couple began living separate lives, eventually culminating in divorce proceedings in 1931.

At least one of Joseph's 'women friends' in New York appears to have known little of the turmoil in his personal life and was unaware that this new relationship was already reaching its end. Writing to Ruth in California after Ione's hospital stay, May noted that Ione proved 'not equal to the climate here' and had returned 'to California at the doctor's orders'. 'So,' she added, 'poor Joe has bad luck.'[20] Next time, Joseph would be luckier in love. His marriage to Ione Robinson was at first intense, then unwittingly comic, finally bitter and ultimately brief. Yet, even fresh from their divorce, he wrote to her to emphasise: 'really pure and deep feelings come to us very rarely in life; and when I look back on those four months in Mexico I feel that my life, in this respect, has not been at all empty'.[21] Even as he wrote this letter, he was under the sway of similar 'pure and deep feelings' once more. In fact, he was already corresponding with the woman who would become his second wife, Charmion von Wiegand, as his divorce was under way. Unlike his partnership with Ione, this marriage lasted until his death.

3

As Joseph settled uneasily into his ill-fated first experience of married life and drew closer to his more successful second attempt, elsewhere in New York, May was dealing with domestic tribulations of a different kind. Having lived without familial obligations for her entire adult life she was now, at the age of forty-eight, jointly responsible for a newborn with the much younger Nellie. While always aware Nellie would need help, May had hoped New York could be a launching point to place her career on more steady footing after being recalled from Moscow. But much of her energy became consumed by the demands of parenting. Her search for work became a series of frustrations.

During her early months in New York, May tried to maintain her literary contacts in Moscow. She hoped her friends back in 'the beyond', as she sometimes called Russia, would bring in lucrative translation commissions. But May sensed a coldness from her old friends and heard from them infrequently. She suspected the rumours about her political unreliability played a role in this.

Baby Joyce, though demanding, was nonetheless cherished by May and provided a welcome distraction. At eight weeks old, May found Joyce already anxious to play and often caught the baby smiling. Joyce seemed to her more interesting every day, despite giving May what she described as 'a hell of a lot of work'.[22] Although Ruth was in California, her own son Jimmy, who had spent part of his childhood in the Lux, was now in New York with his father. Sometimes Nellie and May would bring Joyce to visit Ruth's family in the city. 'You would have been delighted if you had seen your son and Joyce playing together on the floor,' May wrote, noting that Jimmy provided Joyce's first experience of 'playing with a being not too giant-like for her'.[23]

In addition to contributing to the ever-rising laundry pile and requiring round-the-clock attention, Joyce made demands on the household budget. Here, evidence from intelligence agencies suggested a wider network of female comrades in Britain assisted Nellie and May. From the mid-1920s onwards, British intelligence was intercepting the correspondence of many in Rose Cohen's orbit. In addition to opening letters, MI5 also established phone taps on some of her contacts in Britain. The officers produced summaries of the contents of the conversations and kept photocopies of the intercepted correspondence. It is difficult to ascertain whether MI5 believed this group of women on both sides of the Atlantic, sharing news about a baby girl, posed any threat to national security. But the cross-references to other folders and the terse summaries typed up by MI5 staff make the mundane letters seem much more thrilling and suggestive than they really were.

Clearly suspecting their communication was under surveillance, the Cohen sisters wrote to one another using pseudonyms in some of the letters intercepted by British intelligence. One letter from 'Mablay' to 'Dinah' – actually a letter from Nellie to Rose – gives an impression of Nellie and May's strained financial circumstances in New York. Nellie told Rose that she was now living on money sent by Rose after exhausting another loan of $150. The situation was so bad she was contemplating a risky step. If 'Dinah' were to go to London, 'perhaps she could get hold of L.O.F' to tell him about Joyce and their 'straitened circumstances'.[24] In pen, someone had spelled out Liam O'Flaherty's name for any MI5 colleagues confused by the initials. Some months later, British intelligence picked up another reference to Joyce's father, who clearly did not yet know he had another daughter. Writing from New York to a comrade in London, a former housemate of Rose's named Eva Reckitt, Nellie shared news of a 'rumour' that Liam would be arriving to the US for a book tour sometime soon. 'He may get the shock of his life,' she wrote.[25]

When exactly Liam received this shock is impossible to pinpoint. Perhaps it came to him through the ordinary exchange of gossip. After all, Nellie and Liam's circles in London and New York were interconnected. Of course, Joyce had family elsewhere in the city: Liam's brother Tom, though he likely never learned of his niece in New York. For Nellie and May, reliant on a network of support tightly interwoven with Comintern networks, to have approached a 'renegade' like Tom would have been unwise. In a statement published a few months before Joyce was born, Tom declared: 'After studying new material on the question of the Trotsky line in the CPSU [Communist Party of the Soviet Union] and the Comintern, I have come to the conclusion that the line of the Russian Opposition led by comrade Trotsky is the correct Leninist line.'[26] He was duly removed from his position on the *Daily Worker* and expelled from the party.

Fortunately for Nellie and May's financial situation, the rumour that May took a similar line did not prohibit her from finally getting some steady work through Amkino, an organisation promoting Soviet films in the US. Rose in Moscow made enquiries about May's status when May first realised there were rumours spreading about her. The prominence of May's friend from the East End, in addition to the important role played by Rose's husband Petrovsky in Comintern affairs, may have stood to her credit when she was later considered for Amkino. There was also the simple fact that May was *not* a Trotskyist – nor a Stalinist or a Bukharinite or any other specified -ist or -ite. May remained as she described herself on her Comintern questionnaire in 1924: *bezpartinaya* – without party membership. Aside from her lack of firm devotion to any 'line', party membership entailed a commitment in both time and dues payments. Candidacy for membership would also have entailed an examination of her 'political reliability' that she would have likely failed. At one point May feared she would be formally denounced, and Joseph counselled her that she would do 'more harm than good' by 'taking notice of it', perhaps by mounting a pre-emptive defence.[27]

The most likely explanation for this muddy scenario was the one May herself believed: it was a symptom of Comintern office politics blending with actual politics. Her position as manager of a translation department in the Comintern was an enviable one. Circulating the rumour that a work rival was politically suspect was an efficient, if cynical, tool for career advancement. May did not help her situation by maintaining close friendships with those who belonged to opposition groups. The most damning relationship, in the eyes of an orthodox Stalinist, would have been her continued closeness with Emmy Leonhard, not only an active member of the communist opposition in Germany but the partner of Edo Fimmen, a major figure in European social democratic currents that the Comintern was beginning to denounce with ever more venom by the late 1920s.

All of it – the rumours, the struggle to find meaningful work, the late nights caring for an infant – turned New York into a city of disenchantment for May. Baby Joyce, at least, brought some silver linings to the experience. In her letters to Ruth, May provided regular updates on Joyce. 'Of course *I* think her very clever,' she wrote when Joyce turned one, 'but I imagine even an impartial observer who would see her at her tricks would also think her bright.'[28] To May, Joyce had 'the most delightful ripple of a laugh' and an early musical flair: her first intelligible sounds were the opening bars of a nursery rhyme. May believed Joyce was developing a striking resemblance to her father – and was just as brilliant.[29] Liam, it seems, was no longer in contact with May, but she spent much of her days with a laughing, crying, living reminder of their friendship.

22. Joyce and Nellie, c. 1931. Joyce Rathbone Papers

4

The dawn of the 1930s found many of the Hotel Lux 'alumni' whom we have followed throughout our story struggling with various forms of family. Like Joseph and May in New York, those who remained in the European waystations of the world revolution – such as London, Berlin and Moscow – navigated the trials of personal life, from the mundane to the momentous, against a rapidly shifting world situation. In late 1929 came the Wall Street Crash, inaugurating an economic depression that would set much of the world on what seemed an unpredictable course. Yet Comintern theoreticians believed that the future of world capitalism was rendered vividly clear by this economic devastation. A year earlier, they had confidently announced that the victory of socialism predicted by Marx was now at hand. Capitalism had evolved into a final incarnation – its 'third period' – that would give way to the delayed world revolution. The reality, as historians Kevin MacDermott and Jeremy Agnew have noted, could 'not have been more devastating or unexpected: the Nazi rise to power, the brutal destruction of the mighty German labour movement and the resultant imbroglio of communist theory and practice'.[30]

Attendant to this macro-economic analysis were a series of tactical shifts in Comintern policy, including a disastrous push towards stark political sectarianism that demobilised any incipient collaborations between communists and other movements. Ahead of the predicted revolutionary surge, anyone to the right of communists, including the still-powerful social democratic parties of Europe, was to be branded as 'social fascists' regardless of their actual political persuasion. It was a dim-witted analysis with catastrophic results. This total rejection of compromise or political pluralism radiated outwards from internal Soviet politics into the global movement. Historians of communism have extensively analysed how 'third period' doctrine shaped the ability of German communists in particular – a genuine mass movement – to counter the rise of the Nazis. There is something of a consensus: the call from Moscow to break all ties with any forces to the right of the communist movement was a disaster, undermining any hopes for a decisive and united anti-fascist front within Germany.

Throughout 1928 and 1929, the dominant Stalinist faction in the Russian communist party designed plans for rapid industrialisation and collectivisation pushed through by 'unprecedented levels of coercion', while undermining any remnants of opposition within the organisation by denouncing these elements as a 'right-deviation' from the party line.[31] There could be little doubt that Stalin, whose capriciousness Lenin warned against in his testament, was a deft manipulator of the party machinery he had inherited and came to control absolutely by the end of 1929. 'You tricky bastard' was how Sheila Fitzpatrick, one of the great historians of the Soviet century, surmised her response to encountering Stalin through his own archival trail.[32]

Noxious ideological rigidity soon poisoned the atmosphere in all major international communist parties. The German communist party was the first to be impacted. In December 1928 leading German communists were brought before the Comintern executive. Stalin made a personal intervention in the discussions, accusing German communists he disliked of betraying the 'iron inner-party' discipline required of them by allowing a 'rightist' faction to develop within the party. Between these 'rightists' and the Stalin supporting cadre were a group that Stalin denounced as 'conciliators'. The right was to be expelled and the conciliators 'given a most serious warning'. Among those accused of being a 'conciliator' was Arthur Ewert, Sabo's husband.[33] With her partner denounced from on high, Sabo watched as a political storm whipped up in Moscow made landfall in the German party.

In May 1929, a month before Joseph's departure for Mexico where he met and fell in love with Ione, Joseph heard once more from Sabo. This communication would be her final surviving message to him for many years. It conveyed a sense of deep foreboding. People like May and Joseph, whom Sabo knew from the Lux, were too caught up in their own personal dramas to discern the political winds, but Sabo, exposed to the political elements, could not avoid making a forecast. 'Joe,' she wrote, 'we are living in very difficult times – so difficult, that one must take ones Heart and Courage in both hands and go the road, which is at present full of mud and stones and thorns.' Sabo confided that she was now, 'more than ever', thinking on Joseph's 'prophecy', which he confided to her in Moscow. 'It is as if a bad spirit would be working with the one aim to destroy what has been built since decades full of fight and blood, only to satisfy some dark cravings for power,' she continued. It was a revealing line, one that emphasised how Joseph's prophecy must have spoken vividly to the sense of trepidation Sabo felt about Stalin's rise.

However, this line was not as revealing as her next sentence: 'I somehow can wonderfully understand Brutus.' Sabo, it seems, sensed a tyrant asserting control over the movement. She sought reassurance in those whom she felt thought similarly. 'Dear Joe, let me hear from you,' she wrote, tying up her letter with a question: 'do I still have the "eternal propusk?"' His response, if he found time to write one, does not survive. The next letter from Joseph to Sabo was sent almost a decade later in 1938. By that point, Joseph and Sabo were already living witnesses to the tragic fulfilment of their darker prophecies.

Leaving the Land of Sorrows

1

A short drive from Oxford, in a beautiful old vicarage converted into a home, I found May's personal copy of Liam O'Flaherty's Soviet travelogue *I Went to Russia* on a tall bookshelf. There is an inscription on the inside: 'To O'C, with love & good wishes from Nellie & Joyce, as an advance birthday present.' Published a year after a short 1930 trip, it is a wholly unreliable account of Soviet life at the time of his visit. It is written in a similar voice to that used in his two books of memoir: verbose and cynical. In addition to unflattering depictions of May's literary friends, there are undercurrents of antisemitism.

Aside from Liam's own strange testimony there is only one contemporary impression of the author in Russia that I have found. It was almost inevitable, given their mutual friends and shared literary tastes, that Liam and Ivy Litvinov would meet in Moscow. His allegedly irresistible allure nonetheless proved resistible to her. Her judgement was concise and damning. 'Conceited boor, I think,' she wrote to a friend in England. 'He tried to persuade me that London was utterly effete, corrupt, Lesbian & what not.' She conceded that he had a 'general eloquence & looks' but 'resented' that these were offset by 'his complete lack of bottom row front teeth'. The encounter ultimately led her to ponder in this message to her friend how 'ill-bred & gossipy *literary* men tend to be'.[1]

The year following his return from Russia, 1931, on a trip through New York, Liam also crossed paths with Joseph Freeman. The available sources do not reveal whether Liam knew by this point that one of his recent creations was a toddler living elsewhere in the same city. Joseph meeting Liam was a connection May had long imagined. If she was aware of the encounter, though, she would have been disappointed with the results. Liam made an even poorer impression on Joseph than when he had tried to convince Ivy that London was irredeemably lesbian. Joseph had read Liam's book on Soviet Russia and resented the Irish writer's depiction of his and May's friend Ivan Kashkin. It was, Joseph typed on an unpublished page of his autobiography, 'an antisemitic and ignorant book about his brief alcoholic visit'. When Joseph and Liam met in 1931, Joseph recalled observing Liam's 'inebriated lyricism and self-adulation', which convinced him that Liam could not be relied upon for an 'objective description' of 'anything'.[2] There may have been a further personal animosity: Joseph believed Liam and his first wife, Ione Robinson, had a brief affair, albeit before Joseph met her in Mexico.

May's own copy of *I Went to Russia* is full of underlined sentences and exclamation marks. She, too, would have surely been sensitive to antisemitism in the book, having spent much of the last decade in the close company of Jewish friends. However, it is impossible to discern precisely what she meant by the various etchings. This copy of the book, like the woman who owned it and the friend who gifted it to her, eventually found its way from New York to England. May and Nellie struggled for years to find a more stable life in New York, but ultimately conceded defeat and returned from America. Nellie took Joyce back to England in 1931, the same year Liam visited New York. May followed a couple of years later, turning away from what she came to describe as a 'land of sorrows'.

The years between Nellie's return home and May's return to London are poorly documented in both of their lives. Surviving sources paint a picture of May finding little more than career disappointment. Back in England, Nellie settled into a steady routine, eventually finding secretarial work with the Soviet embassy in London, thanks to Rose's eminent husband.

May's final attempt at an American career came about after she learned that Maxim Litvinov, then Soviet Commissar for Foreign

Affairs, was travelling to negotiate US diplomatic recognition of the USSR. May wrote to Joseph, attempting to find a role for herself on the delegation. Although she suspected Litvinov was unaware of it, she told Joseph of her time working for Sylvia Pankhurst's People's Russian Information Bureau. 'I held the fort when he was in London and sat in a Fleet Street office and faced Scotland Yard daily,' she wrote. 'Ivy knows me,' she continued, but 'has no cause to love me.' Any sources revealing the intricacies of Ivy Litvinov and May's relationship have, it seems, now been lost. May asked Joseph to put in a good word for her. 'All these requests are based on our friendship of 1926,' she wrote.[3] It is the final surviving letter in the folder of correspondence between them. She does not seem to have worked with the Soviet delegation. Soon after this letter was sent, she sailed back to England on board the SS *Manhattan*.

Her journey having come full circle, May joined Nellie to shelter together in the confines of middle-class British socialism. Their shared task of raising Joyce was now the priority, not revolution. Having reached her early fifties, May's life within Comintern networks was over, demobilised by a confluence of factors including harmful rumours and the demands of childcare. Yet even as May and Nellie lived quietly in London, they continued to maintain intimate connections to those still honing their political survival skills including Rose in Moscow, now married to David Petrovsky and raising their son, and Emmy Leonhard, who was embarking on a years-long exile from her native Germany to shelter her daughters on the refugee routes of Europe. For now, let us leave behind May, Nellie and Joyce, comfortably ensconced in a domestic existence and removed from the political tumult of the wider world, to turn our attention to those standing before the coming avalanche.

German Family Robinson

Bild vom Tage

Die Familie im Grase

23. The Leonhard Family (L–R): Elisa, Emmy and Alida, Montana, c. 1936.
Leonhard Fimmen Papers

1

On a few occasions in the sources I found, Emmy Leonhard hinted that the essence of a person – something akin to a spirit – could be carried within the next generation. She wrote that her mother, who first inspired Emmy's interest in socialism, lived on through her after her mother's death in 1916. This was the year Emmy believed her life really began, it was the year following her first involvement with the workers' movement in her native Hamburg and two years before revolutionary railway workers in the same city voted her onto their council. Over the next decades, Emmy lived as a 'soldier' in the international workers' movement, to use her own phrase.[1] The 1930s proved her most perilous period in the struggle. As a revolutionary socialist and the partner of a prominent organiser of anti-fascist resistance networks, she often lived dangerously.

One of her most urgent tasks was finding sanctuary for her two young daughters, Elisa and Alida. On the other side of the period when – to paraphrase Brecht – the Leonhard family changed their country more often than their shoes, Emmy typed a short message to her daughters. It reflected the bonds of devotion that helped them navigate life as a refugee family and suggested her vision of immortality. '*Solange ihr lebt, lebe ich*,' Emmy wrote: so long as you live, I live.[2]

Emmy did not hide the world's darker realities from her two daughters. Both were raised to understand the forces at work around them and to value a life of political commitment. Meanwhile, their father Edo's prescient reading of world events always kept his family one step ahead of those who wished them harm. As the general secretary of an organisation whose influence could be felt in every major port in the world, Edo held the power to move cargo of all kinds across frontiers, ranging from arms and illegal literature to refugees, anti-Nazi operatives and his own family.

For all their parents' remarkable ability to keep them safe in a decade of state-sanctioned massacres, Elisa and Alida nonetheless bore the marks of their unusual upbringing throughout their lives. Their father could never be a constant presence during their childhoods, though he tried to ensure his daughters felt beloved. He remained separated from his family out of a concern for their safety and a desire to commit himself to work that he believed would determine Europe's future. His base until the eve of the Second World War was Amsterdam, while Emmy and the two girls moved through Germany, Switzerland and France. If Edo had chosen another path through the decade, perhaps he may have lived to see Elisa and Alida become adults. But he chose a life guided by firm convictions in an era when the pressure of living by those principles ultimately proved fatal to him.

2

Naturally, a life rooted in one place is easier to recover than one lived constantly on the move. It can be difficult to write about the intimate worlds of a refugee family whose existence depended on being able to relocate at short notice. Those sources of subjectivity that the historian sifts through – letters, diaries, and so on – are often left behind in hastily planned exits. Historical sources are always as vulnerable as the people who create them.

Most of the letters that revealed, in the words of Emmy and Edo themselves, the adventures and trauma of these years were consumed by the events of their era. In 1934 the Gestapo turned over the Leonhard family home in Potsdam.[3] If they did not destroy the documents shortly after combing through them, then the material almost certainly disappeared into the vortex of the Nazi bureaucracy or later vanished into the archives of the conquering Red Army.

Other material created and collected by the family over the years after their flight from Nazi Germany went underground – literally – on the eve of France's fall to the westward-marching Wehrmacht. Emmy and her two daughters gathered the material they wanted to preserve and placed it in a metal barrel. Among the documents were hundreds of letters Edo sent to his children and thousands that he sent, almost daily, to his partner Emmy. This barrel was then buried in a garden south of Paris owned by the family of the philosopher Simone Weil. When Emmy returned to excavate her past, she could not find the material she had tried to barricade from discovery. Her daughter Alida believed it was dug up by someone else in search of treasure.[4] Or, perhaps, Emmy misremembered the precise location. Maybe the barrel is still in that back garden in the Ile-de-France, awaiting a historian with time, patience and a shovel.

Despite the intervention of the Gestapo and, possibly, a French local with a shovel, these years in the lives of Emmy, Edo and their daughters can be traced with sometimes extraordinary specificity.

Edo's anti-Nazi activities can be followed through the resistance literature his network smuggled into Germany and the vast archive of his union, the ITF. Using these and other documents, scholars have traced Edo's formidable organisation and its activities. The most detailed study of the war against fascism conducted by Edo and his comrades was written by the scholar Dieter Nelles, although historians of transnational anti-fascism and anti-imperialism have recently taken notice of his circle's activities.

Until now, however, little has been known about Edo Fimmen's personal life during this period. Edo's family were an important source of practical support, particularly when his health declined sharply on the eve of the Second World War. Emmy, as an independent political thinker in her own right, should be considered a radicalising influence on Edo, whose instincts were more moderate than those of his partner. Emmy and their daughters did not merely provide a domestic subplot to Edo's thrilling tale of anti-fascist operations. They were, in many ways, an integral part of his story and are the focus of ours.

Against all odds, a striking set of documents charting the Leonhard family's history did survive the years of displacement and war. For our ability to uncover this personal story of love and resistance, we owe our thanks to Edo himself. The exigencies and dangers of simultaneously leading a global trade union and operating a clandestine resistance network required Edo to remain constantly on the move. From the start of the 1930s until Hitler's rise to power alone, Edo undertook organisation work in Spain, Belgium, Denmark, France, Germany, Japan, China, England and Ireland. He visited a number of these countries several times in these years.

Yet even amid all this travel, his children were a constant presence in his life – in his thoughts, at least, if not in person. Every fortnight for several years, Edo's daughters handcrafted an illustrated newspaper and sent it to their father. Edo preserved each issue of his children's journal, which Elisa and Alida initially titled the *Alpenpost*. When he was forced to evacuate his headquarters in Amsterdam, he took his collected volumes of the newspaper with him to London, then Mexico. Many decades later, the near-complete collection of the *Alpenpost* and its successor publications made its way through a line of family inheritance to a coastal villa in Galicia. That is where I eventually found the volumes among the remnants of the Leonhard family archive.

Most of the *Alpenpost* – a handwritten, richly illustrated 'newspaper' recounting exile existence as seen through children's eyes – was contained in a blue folder when I discovered it. The two girls decorated the folder with a drawing of a tall sailing ship, the kind you might find adorning a children's book set during the golden age of piracy. I soon interpreted a further significance to the illustration as I leafed through the pages. Not only did the illustration hint towards the seafaring activities of their father's resistance collaborators, but the ship was seemingly a metaphor for the family's refugee journey. During their exile, Elisa and Alida possessed a children's edition of *Robinson Crusoe*, the eighteenth-century story of a sailor who lives on a tropical island for decades before returning home. It was evidently cherished, as the exact copy is still sitting on a shelf in the home of their descendants. Like the fictional Crusoe, Emmy, Elisa and Alida lived as castaways.

Growing up with parents who sensed that Europe was grinding towards another calamitous war must have made for an intense upbringing. It must have been only more intense to have a father who believed he held the power to prevent the coming disaster. Surely this grandiose sense of purpose emerged not only from the vast network of loyal cadre working alongside him but also from the revolutionary intellectual circles within which both Edo and Emmy moved. Later, when the Leonhard girls became women who understood that their childhood took place at the crossroads of European history, Elisa and Alida would realise that the people who passed through their youthful memories, the same men and women who sometimes featured in cartoon illustrations on their homemade newspaper, were among the major figures of the radical world.

3

Among her early childhood memories, Alida Leonhard remembered the long discussions between Edo and Emmy when her father would reflect on his 'bitter disappointment' with the course taken by the Soviet revolution. Edo always pursued an idiosyncratic political path – too revolutionary for fellow social democrats but too moderate for most Bolsheviks. His unusual amalgam of ideas was rooted in his own past membership of the Salvation Army and early interest in utopian anarchism, experiences which inspired in him a religious devotion to his cause, a suspicion of bureaucracies and a messianic faith in the eventual coming of a just world. Meanwhile, his work in ports revealed the unequal flows of colonial trade, inspiring an anti-imperialist conviction that would lead his union, the ITF, to be among the very few in Europe to take an actively anti-racist stance in the interwar years.[5] He was charismatic, effortlessly multilingual and loyal. These traits shaped his resistance work. Although Emmy and Edo were dedicated to both theory and praxis, Edo always sought methods of action while Emmy focused on political ideas.

While few of Emmy Leonhard's writings from this period have survived and historians of Edo Fimmen's world have overlooked her as an intellectual influence, she did write a revealing letter in 1931 outlining her politics in forceful language. This letter survived because its recipient, Leon Trotsky, maintained it during his own life in exile.

In 1931 Emmy was assisting the dissident revolutionary Victor Serge, then still in Soviet Russia, in finding a German publisher for his works. That summer she wrote personally to Trotsky, then in Istanbul, seeking help with the task. He was happy to help. In his letter signalling his assent, Trotsky added a postscript asking Emmy to explain to him 'in a few words' some recent internal eruptions within the German Trotskyist movement. 'This is all absolutely mystifying to me,' he wrote in the same postscript, declaring that never, 'not even in the worst times of the emigre struggles' had he witnessed 'such customs, such dispositions, such methods' of factionalism.[6] This was a grand statement, given the pre-revolutionary exile community's legendary capacity for in-fighting.

Emmy did not explain the situation to Trotsky 'in a few words', as he requested. In true radical fashion, she sent several thousand closely typed words instead. First, she opened with an apology.[7] She blamed her delayed response on sickness, work commitments and 'existential struggle', the latter perhaps a reference to some form of depression. Now, however, she found it 'impossible to remain silent any longer' in view of the 'appalling exacerbation of the German situation, which makes the failure of the Left Opposition a historic catastrophe'. As embittered internal fighting continued within the left opposition, street fighting between Nazi paramilitaries and fighters loyal to the Comintern-backed KPD led to lethal violence in Berlin. All the while, the Nazi party was on the electoral warpath towards the early 1932 presidential election that would see Adolf Hitler poll in second place.

'Once again,' Emmy wrote, 'as in November 1918, and in January 1919, as in March 1920 and July 1923 in Germany' the old regime was dying and the people were seeking a weapon to strike a death blow. But the revolutionary leadership was unprepared. 'Once again the blackest counterrevolution will be the beneficiary.' Over the sixteen pages of her letter, she sought to diagnose the ideological currents and failures of revolutionary leadership that had, since the turn of the century, gradually pushed Western Europe's largest workers' movement to the brink.

Her analysis was fluent in historical reference points and revealed a deep immersion in decades of socialist polemics. It was also, like many of these polemics, starry-eyed about the real potential for a worldwide proletarian revolt that existed in the years after the First World War. For Emmy, the present impotence of anti-Stalinist revolutionaries was rooted in the notion of 'the Party' itself. Emmy confidently told Leon Trotsky that the basic 'fundaments' of how a revolutionary movement should organise itself needed to be subjected to 'a relentless strength test once again'. If, as Emmy and Trotsky agreed, a future just world must be classless and without borders, then, she argued, 'our organisations, not only in order to be suitable carriers of the coming order, but also as weapons against the present one, must realise these two principles here and now in their own structure'.

Emmy argued that the opposition should 'mercilessly' fight the centralising tendencies of Stalinism. While she still retained a faith in certain Bolshevik precepts, like the notion of a 'vanguard party', she wished for a return to the idea of small-scale workers' 'soviets' or councils that animated so much of the revolutionary movement of 1917, and which she witnessed in her own native Hamburg in November 1918.

In effect, Emmy sought an organisation that could uphold the spontaneity and genuinely grassroots character of a people's revolution in its early stages beyond the initial upsurge. Such political activity required intensive physical energy and intellectual enthusiasm.

Emmy was likely breathing in the atmosphere of the contemporary German revolutionary left beyond the Stalin–Trotsky divide. The twilight years of the Weimar Republic provided a greenhouse-like atmosphere for the growth of new leftist organisational forms. This period saw the birth of movements like 'the Org', a semi-clandestine group of former communists who saw the KPD response to Nazism as myopic, and the ISK, an idiosyncratic, radical sect that advocated Esperanto, vegetarianism and the rigorous but cult-like indoctrination of a socialist 'elect' to rule over society. Presaging the 1960s birth of the 'new left' and its frustration with the stuffy bureaucracy of the 'old left', these movements made the case, according to one scholar, that 'the form your organization took determined the fate of your politics'.[8] It was precisely these hyper-committed and conspiratorially trained agitators whom Edo would come to rely on while expanding his anti-fascist resistance network into hostile territory.

Approaching the final pages of her letter, Emmy assertively told Trotsky: 'we are not a playground for dilettantes, but a force in battle'. Emmy, Edo and the people they called their friends were exactly the kinds of intensely focused and committed people who could comprise such a fighting force. Perhaps this is why she held such a strong conviction that there were many more like them. The coming months in Germany and the darkening of the night into which the world was plunging surely shook this confidence. Instead of 'the proletarian tidal wave' that Emmy dreamed would 'sweep over the rotten, rudderless ship of the capitalist government together with its decomposed reformist and fascist guards', the onset of Nazi rule was rapidly approaching.

Unlike May, Emmy was deft in articulating revolutionary political theory. Nowhere in her long missive to Trotsky, however, did she talk directly about her family's situation. This was unsurprising: Emmy was writing about how, 'in defiance of all the powers from Hitler to Stalin, and the risk of our lives', the left could save Germany from an approaching nightmare and build a new world. She was not updating Trotsky on family affairs. Yet that personal life was present, if mostly between the lines. After all, she had cited the pressures of her situation in explaining her delayed response.

Remaining an active voice on the revolutionary left while raising two small daughters when their father was only occasionally at home was surely a balancing act. May suggested this when she asked one of her famous acquaintances for a translation commission for Emmy. Writing to the American novelist Theodore Dreiser, whom May first met in Moscow, she asked if he would consider a friend of hers, 'an excellent linguist and writer', for any forthcoming German editions of his works. 'Germany is not exactly a good place to live just now and added to that she cannot take a job away from home as she has two small children,' May wrote in this letter from early 1932. 'For your *private* information,' May continued, 'she is the "morganatic" wife of Edo Fimmen of international fame.' In conclusion, May affirmed that 'my friend' Emmy is a 'most ardent supporter of the unpopular cause, which you have been so courageously espousing', meaning, in this case: communism.[9] May was evidently eager to help her dear friend from the Lux, even while she faced her own struggles navigating the tribulations of life in New York.

4

When discussing the nature of Stalinism around the dinner table in Potsdam, the question of bureaucracy would have provided a point of agreement between Edo and Emmy. Political points of difference, as Emmy's letter to Trotsky suggests, were surely argued out in detail. Both Emmy and Edo shared a lifelong interest in the kinds of decentralised movements favoured by anarchist political currents. This mode of organisation would become particularly important to Edo as he began to design a movement resistant to Gestapo penetration.

Yet the political questions raised in private must have received differing answers from another couple whom their daughters remembered visiting their childhood home: Willi Münzenberg and Babette Gross. Münzenberg, whom we last encountered collaborating with Edo on the League Against Imperialism, was perhaps the single most important activist in the Comintern beyond the USSR, and certainly within Germany. The mastermind of a vast array of organisations devoted to everything from creating revolutionary cinema to supporting the victims of political persecution, Münzenberg, more than any other activist, was responsible for some of the Comintern's most effective and influential initiatives of the interwar years. His wife, Babette, was a constant counsel and companion to her husband until Willi's mysterious death. A tall, elegant and even-tempered woman, she was a dedicated activist who had joined the communist movement in 1921.[10]

On Edo's regular visits to Berlin for political work and to see his family, he often met with Willi Münzenberg in a small tavern on Dorotheenstrasse. Edo enjoyed the food and atmosphere, even though most of the other regulars were minor nobility. Here, the 'two men talked endlessly about the "Russians"'.[11] Münzenberg, Babette recalled, 'was the cooler, more realistic of the two'.[12]

These revolutionary couples, Willi and Babette, Emmy and Edo, felt themselves drawing closer to danger as the Nazis marched towards total control of the German state and a divided left failed to effectively resist the fascist takeover. The friendship between them – one couple nominally 'Stalinists', the other composed of a 'Trotskyist' and a 'social-fascist', according to Comintern parlance – was not the kind that we, as historians of the left, expect to find. Often, however, the overly neat categories that ideologies and states tried to impose, and which historians inherit, dissolve on an intimate level. Maybe young Elisa and Alida heard more notes of unity than discord over dinner at their home outside Berlin.

We can assume at least one topic discussed by Edo and Emmy, Willi and Babette, something that would provide the couples with reason to collaborate in the years to come: escape routes. On a morning in late February 1933, the shouts of newspaper boys alerted Babette to the burning of the Reichstag and the danger now facing her and her husband. Hitler would soon use the fire as a pretext to complete his assumption of power. Hunting out resourceful opponents was an early priority of Nazi rule. Babette awakened their driver, intercepted her husband on his way to a café and began planning their next steps. After making their way across the Saarland, territory then still under League of Nations control, the couple reached Paris.

Shortly before – and possibly during – the opening moments of Nazi rule, Edo was in Berlin, although by the first days of March he was back in Amsterdam. As a Dutch citizen, he was relatively safe from the danger of becoming trapped in Germany. His partner and young daughters were less secure. If Edo had divorced his wife and married Emmy, she would have assumed Dutch citizenship. Through legal recognition as 'legitimate', Elisa and Alida would also have become Dutch citizens. Together, they could all have simply crossed the border into safety in the Netherlands. But this was not the case: Emmy and her two daughters were German citizens and therefore vulnerable.

Edo and Emmy surely sensed the profound risk of staying in Berlin. According to family memory, Emmy nonetheless remained in Germany for some weeks after their friends' rapid departure, long enough for Emmy to be arrested by the Gestapo before being released for lack of evidence. The situation, however, was untenable. Her grandson recalled that Emmy's decision to flee Nazi Germany with her children was less about her own activism and more about a fear that the Nazis would eventually use her as leverage against Edo by holding her as a prisoner.[13]

In any case, their departure was soon arranged, almost certainly through Edo. A Dutch diplomat managed to get Emmy, Elisa and Alida out of the country, with one of the girls disguised as a boy for reasons of subterfuge now lost to time. In a later drawing, Elisa, the eldest, would illustrate this border crossing, emphasising the covert element. In the picture, we see Emmy being guided through a forest at night. Behind a tree, a shadowy figure stands waiting with a gun.

van Duitsland naar Holland

24. Illustration by Elisa Leonhard, 1940. Leonhard Fimmen Papers

The Leonhards safely crossed into the Netherlands. From there they travelled to Switzerland, where they found a home in the Alps, in Montana, today part of the Crans-Montana municipality, a couple of hours by train from Geneva. It was here that Emmy, Elisa and Alida settled into their lives as refugees or, in the children's imagination, their time as castaways.

Far from their mountain home – though not so distant that he could never visit – their father Edo remained in Amsterdam. Moving via the ports and rail routes of Europe, he began assembling a determined network of anti-Nazi activists. It was the beginning of a campaign that would earn him an unintended accolade, one that any believer in a just world would have worn with pride. Addressing trial proceedings against German resistance fighters in 1938, one Nazi prosecutor declared: 'Edo Fimmen is Germany's greatest enemy.'[14] His two daughters would spend the same years working on a homemade newspaper with one central message: that Elisa and Alida were their father's greatest supporters.

The Leonhard family, through their own intelligent reading of the world around them, positioned themselves well for posterity as opponents of both Hitler and Stalin. Yet the devoted and single-minded revolutionary commitment that was common in their circles almost always entailed a series of moral choices that modern readers will find unsettling. It would be heartening – but obfuscating – to chart the rest of this decade solely through the lives of people like the Leonhards: activists who arrived at conclusions that most of us find sympathetic.

We will soon have reason to return to their story, for it reveals much about the necessity of thinking and the pursuit of righteous action in perilous times. But if we are to take the communist project of the twentieth century seriously and encounter it on its own terms, then we must turn our attention to those whose own commitments entailed starker ethical compromises. Often, individuals proved willing to make these compromises due to coldly calculated ideological commitment. Yet fully understanding these choices requires us to confront the much messier fact that decisions are often made amid the fear and confusion of living through the chaos of a rapidly unfolding present. The clarity of hindsight usually burns away the jagged edges in our image of the past, but perhaps those blemishes, when returned to view, can heighten our ability to understand the choices people made.

Belomor

1

In 1934 an unusual and infamous publication was released in the Soviet Union: *The History of Construction of The White Sea Canal.* The product of more than a hundred Soviet writers who took a journey on the canal after it opened for traffic, the work is a paean to the glories of socialist construction in Stalin's USSR and the potential for re-engineering wayward human souls though communism.

The book stands out among twentieth-century literature as a work that could only have been produced by the cultural project of Stalinism. It is, in essence, an illustrated justification for the use of forced labour as a praiseworthy step on the path to a workers' paradise. This singular work of Stalin-era propaganda told the story of the construction of the Belomor canal linking the White Sea in Russia's far north to the Baltic. A terrific feat of Soviet engineering, the canal was trumpeted as a symbol of Stalin's wise guidance of Soviet society during the first of the Five Year Plans. Built under the supervision of the OGPU, the secret police service later reincorporated as part of the NKVD, the canal was constructed by a force of around 126,000 prisoners consisting of both common criminals and political prisoners. It was a prototypical example of the vast architecture of repression known as the Gulag, a term derived from the acronym for the Soviet administration for labour camps.

Ferried through orchestrated meetings that concealed the 'deprivation, loss of life, and terror that inmates endured', some writers attached to the *History of Construction* project were reportedly sceptical enough to doubt the official image presented to them.[1] However, enough accepted the story that an ambitious propaganda effort resulted from this journey.

The Russian-language edition of this collectively authored and state-sanctioned book on Belomor has its own history cast in the shadow of the terror. Originally handed out to delegates to the 1934 Communist Party Congress, copies of the book were being destroyed and pulled from library shelves by 1937. The reason? The Stalinist purges consumed some of the books' authors, two of its editors and entire upper leadership of the Belomor construction project, including its supervisor Genrik Yagoda, the organiser of a 1936 show trial and then a defendant in a show trial staged two years later.[2]

In the book, the canal's construction was depicted as a foresighted experiment. The watchword of the experiment was *perekovka*, which can be translated as 'reforging': labour would remake the criminal into a 'new person' worthy of participation in the Soviet project. This was the official story of what was happening along the canal work ways, but unofficially, as historian of Belomor Cynthia Ruder notes, 'convicts came to be viewed as cheap, infinite sources of labor who could be corralled into working on projects to which other workers could not be lured without force'.[3]

It is troubling but important to recognise that forceful socialist arguments – visions of a world without hunger, war and servitude – were once articulated by many who also saw Stalin's Soviet Union as their guiding light in forging that world. This was the same Stalinist state whose policies starved millions during the collectivisation drive of the early 1930s, a process which impacted Ukraine with ferocity during what has come to be known as the 'Holodomor', the same state that – as the Belomor canal project demonstrated – brutally pursued its economic plans through forced labour.

Measuring the everyday complicity of ordinary people in the violence that enabled the political systems in which they lived – or which they advocated – can draw us away from the task of understanding and into the terrain of judgement. Yet the threads of violence that bound together Soviet society cannot be disentangled from the lives of those I have explored elsewhere on these pages.

I realised this early on in my research when, as a graduate student browsing the Soviet history shelves of my university library, I came across the English translation of the infamous propaganda history of the Belomor canal's construction. This translated edition was published a year after it first reached Russian-speaking audiences and two years before it was pulled from Soviet shelves due to its inclusion of 'enemies of the people'. Opening the book, I was astonished to find printed on its opening pages a publisher's note mentioning a name I recognised. The publishers expressed thanks to 'Miss May O'Callaghan for her invaluable help in the work of collating the translation with the Russian edition, and checking and reading the proofs.'[4]

It was slight but striking evidence of a wider reality that continues to unsettle me as a historian of communism: the people whom I research, whose hopes mirrored my own in many ways and who were enthused by basic principles I share, were implicated in complex connecting chains of complicity. Encountering this note of thanks to May was intriguing, if also troubling. I was searching for precisely such a catalyst to think over these questions of everyday complicity. A historian could spend an entire career thinking over these complexities. Some do.

Over the following chapters, as we delve into those aspects of Stalinist society that directly impacted those who feature on these pages, these questions will repeatedly arise. Ultimately, the exact reasons why May came to be involved in this project remain unknown. Perhaps she was trying to reingratiate herself after the rumours of Trotskyism. Maybe it was the kind of project, involving prominent Soviet writers, in which her sense of pride would have made her an eager participant. It could have been a combination of the British publishing house requiring someone with certain editorial skills and May needing money. In any case, it was the kind of murky entanglement between Western observers and the arms of Soviet propaganda that would become increasingly frequent and disquieting as reports emerging from within the Soviet Union grew ever more disturbing.

2

Although May, along with most foreign residents of Moscow in the 1920s, had been aware of the atmospheric presence of Soviet security services, she, like others, did not find their presence suffocating or threatening. Nor did she or her Lux friends need to adapt to the survival techniques required of the Soviet friends they left behind, or the later waves of political emigrants. And unlike Mary Reed, the American communist who had stepped into May's Comintern role and who she believed had played some role in pushing her out, May never learned through intimate experience the realities of the Soviet labour camp system. There was a fundamental breach in political emigrant experiences between the 1920s and the 30s, a change which must, in the final analysis, be rooted in the totalising conformity demanded by Stalinism, which permeated all aspects of Soviet life, from politics to culture and everything in between. Some, like Ivy Litvinov or Rose Cohen, remained on Soviet territory long enough to experience this transformation in person.

With all the defining junctures in the history of the Stalin regime there are at least three stories that we must juggle to understand how these events and ideas were encountered in the contemporary moment by communists within and beyond the USSR. Firstly, there is the story told by the Soviet state. Archival discoveries have revealed how, to an extraordinary extent, this was a narrative personally edited by Stalin himself, a man who wielded his power with extraordinary vengefulness and cunning. Secondly, there is the story of the darker realities that the Stalin-approved story attempted to conceal or deny.

And then there is another story, usually distinct both from the stories Stalin's politburo told about the path toward socialism and the history of repression upon which this path was paved: the tales about Soviet society that individual communists told themselves. This was a story personal to each person, composed from an amalgam of theory, experience and intuition. Lisa Kirschenbaum, a historian whose work disentangles this process, notes that the issue is 'less one of accuracy than identity'.[5] The peculiar intensity of communist belief allowed individual communists to both encounter 'unpleasant or dissonant realities' while also learning to 'observe in particular, mediated ways'.[6] A non-communist observer could baulk at the use of slave labour in Belomor, but someone committed to the idea that the 'general line' was ultimately correct could soothe their conscience by deferring to the external authority of the Party and imbibing the propaganda about 'reforging' errant citizens.

This willing suspension of critical thought seems like self-delusion to modern eyes. But for ordinary people caught up in Stalinist society, it was not only a means of negotiating acute cognitive dissonance but a technique that aided survival in a time of paranoia. While the stakes were drastically lower for communists abroad, they, too, risked exile from their social worlds if they let the evidence of experience overwhelm their beliefs. The 'breaking point' for many activists was determined not only by a willingness to open their eyes to uncomfortable truths, but a calculation of the real social and psychological costs that came with such an acknowledgement. As the intimate networks that always tied together international communism brought ever more news of disappeared comrades, the moral stakes of continued commitment rose and the rationality of dismissing all evidence as 'anti-Soviet propaganda' decreased.

Just as the Comintern and Soviet society both became solidified within Stalin's ultimate control, Nazi control over Germany changed the composition of the émigré population in Moscow. German communist refugees sought sanctuary in Moscow, with many taking up residence in the Lux. The Lux retained all the issues of ill-repair familiar to the guests of the 1920s. There was one major structural change: two floors were added. However, the mass exodus from Germany meant these extra rooms did little to resolve overcrowding.[7]

Alongside the arrival of refugees from Germany, Stalin's industrialisation drive created opportunities to expand the Soviet Union's foreign workforce. The economic depression in the West seemed to contrast with the triumphant successes of the Five Year Plans in the USSR, drawing a wave of economic migrants across the Soviet frontier.

To reach some of these migrants, an English-language paper called the *Moscow Daily News* was launched during the first Five Year Plan, its language dictated in part by the prominence of Anglophone journalists in the outfit's early years.[8] Circulated through leftist networks beyond the USSR, the paper also had an eye on a foreign readership. Its staff included the American labour journalist Anna Louise Strong, Mikhail Borodin, a former Comintern emissary who spent much of his pre-revolutionary life in the US, and Rose Cohen, who surely carried some of her experience from the offices of Pankhurst's *Dreadnought* to her work on this Moscow daily paper.

Since marrying her partner David Petrovsky and settling permanently in the USSR, Rose had given birth to a son: Alyosha, born in December 1929. A picture taken around 1932 captures Rose, evidently on a rare trip home from Moscow to London, in a garden with her sister Nellie and their two children. In the photo, Joyce and Alyosha, both born the same year, are still toddlers. The two cousins would be in their fifties before they finally met again.

25. (L–R) Joyce, Nellie, Rose, Alyosha, c. 1932. Joyce Rathbone Papers

When Alyosha was born, Rose was working within the Comintern's Anglo-American Secretariat, the same Comintern department where her husband played a prominent role. She then spent some time as a student at the International Lenin School, a secretive training academy housed in a palatial building in Moscow's Arbat district.[9] Here, students from across the world undertook intensive study in Marxist-Leninist theory and revolutionary practice.

Rose was an atypical Lenin School pupil: in her late thirties, she was older than many other students. Unlike the visiting students, most of whom lived together in the school dormitory, she was permanently resident in Moscow. Few other students could boast her practical experience of conspiratorial work. In a 1930 resumé of her revolutionary credentials, Rose was able to list periods of 'illegal work for the Comintern' in Paris, London and Berlin.[10] What benefit she desired from the course is difficult to tell, but it almost certainly heightened her understanding of Marxist theory in the Stalinist mould. After her course of study at the Lenin School, Rose joined the staff of the *Moscow News*, becoming its foreign news editor.

How did Rose fit into the unusually cosmopolitan staff of the paper? What did she make of Soviet society beyond the world of her work, particularly during the years that witnessed the Stalinist terror grip the city? Rose's letters to Nellie from this period no longer survive, making it largely impossible to answer these questions using her own words. Although we do not have Rose's letters, the correspondence of one of her colleagues, an American journalist named Millie Bennett, did survive. Millie Bennett was a recent arrival in Moscow when she joined the staff of the *Moscow News* in early 1931. She settled into her work in the Soviet capital and found a partner, an actor and Soviet citizen named Evgeny Konstantinov, whom she married around 1932. Bennett encountered Rose regularly through their shared office space and sometimes updated their mutual friend Ruth with impressions of Rose.

The paper's office, as Bennett described it, was formerly a ballroom. 'How it would amuse you,' Bennett told Ruth, to see the 'serried ranks' of Rose Cohen and other paper workers whom they both knew, 'bending over desks' in the 'rapidly fading glory' of the converted ballroom. The conversion itself reflected the premium placed on space in Moscow, where such social activities as dancing needed to make way for more utilitarian usages of a large open space.[11]

As in any workplace, there was office gossip. Unusually for the time and place, however, the *Moscow News* brought together several men whose queer relationships became topics of discussion – in one case openly at a gathering of the paper's staff. Although Bolshevism never offered a coherent plan for liberating those whose sexual preferences transgressed social norms, communism's broad appeal to the oppressed resonated with some queer people. Among the tsarist-era laws abolished after the Revolution was one criminalising sex between men. However, from late 1933, on the initiative of secret police chief and one-time Belomor Canal supervisor Genrik Yagoda, a clampdown on homosexuality began. In March 1934 an all-Union decree against 'sodomy' made the USSR the first state in modern history to *re*-criminalise homosexual acts. Rose Cohen found herself working alongside men who once more found their sexuality the target of state laws in the very place they had sought sanctuary.

In response to the Soviet clampdown on queer life, one of Rose's colleagues, a Scottish communist named Harry Whyte, wrote a defence of homosexuality from a Marxist-Leninist perspective. Along with this analysis, he also detailed attempts to discover what became of his Russian lover, who had been swept up in police raids carried out ahead of the law coming into effect.[12] He courageously sent this document to Stalin himself. Whyte received no response and Stalin, in his characteristic vulgar directness, ordered the letter to be archived after describing its author as an 'idiot and a degenerate'.[13] Millie Bennett's own husband, Evgeny, whom she referred to as 'Zhenya', was also arrested in the summer of 1934 on charges of homosexuality and sent to a labour camp in western Siberia. In a startlingly matter-of-fact opening in a letter to Ruth, Bennett wrote: 'We have had lots of rain this summer. And it may interest you to know that Zhenya is doing three years in an OGPU concentration camp.'[14]

All of this suggests that the *Moscow News* staff became intimately acquainted with the gears that mobilised the terror of the late 1930s even before those same mechanisms of persecution began to grind through society at large. How did Rose interpret all of this? We only have one piece of evidence, from the perspective of Millie Bennett. It is second-hand information from someone who harboured unexplained feelings of hostility towards Rose.

One of Rose Cohen's compatriots on the *Moscow News* staff was the vagabonding writer Charles Ashleigh, who, according to one history of British communism, was 'living openly as a homosexual' by the time he joined the paper's staff in 1931.[15] In early 1934 Millie Bennett informed Ruth that the 'bohemian' Ashleigh had been 'thrown out, cashiered, bounced' from their staff through a 'cleaning' procedure. This reference to 'cleaning' was Bennett's free translation of the term *chistka*, the Russian word more commonly translated as a 'purge'. Ashleigh's *chistka* was carried out before an audience of his colleagues and according to Bennett was a 'sensational' affair with observers waxing 'pale with excitement' as former comrades denounced Ashleigh as someone who was 'perverting Soviet youth' and who came to the USSR to 'carry on his orgies here without interruption'.[16] Bennett claimed she was the only member of the paper's staff who attended Ashleigh's goodbye party. On Rose's response to it all, she noted concisely that she, 'who, I'll admit never made a fuss about him, didn't see him at all'.[17]

If Rose chose to avoid the denounced Ashleigh after his dismissal from the *Moscow News* through concern for her safety, then she chose wisely. At the end of the year, what historians regard as the precipitating event for the Great Terror took place: the assassination of Leningrad party boss Sergei Kirov. One Mexican-born radical then living in Moscow remembered the news arriving in the Hotel Lux. The Lux, he wrote, 'seethed from roof to basement' as residents emerged from their rooms to discuss the shocking event. He recalled a sense of perplexity creeping in as he thought over the assassination. After all, nobody could arrive in the Lux and visit him, a relatively obscure activist, without undergoing the bureaucracy of phoning up his room, having their *propusk* checked and indicating when they intended to leave.[18] How then could an assassin corner someone as important as Kirov alone in a government building?

The circumstances of the murder, and the possibility of Stalin's own involvement in Kirov's death, continues to divide historians. The posthumous martyrology of Kirov that Stalin sanctioned is, however, incontestable. The state-promoted veneration of Kirov demanded vigilance of internal enemies and offered a useful motive for clearing out the parts of Soviet society that Stalin felt needed 'cleaning'. The resulting terror would target social elements perceived by Stalin as responsible for Kirov's death and imagining other acts like it. The political emigrants, suspect by merit of their foreign birth, would prove key targets of the repressive measures being fine-tuned by the NKVD ahead of the 1936–8 waves of arrests. In these years, past political deviations, real or perceived, would turn from black marks on a personal record into grounds for arrest and even execution.

In a reference to Rose that becomes more chilling with the hindsight of the path her life would take in the coming years, Bennett noted in early 1935: 'There are rumours that the ex-Trotskiites are getting the equivalent of "the run around" these days – but the few I know – and the one you know, the blossoming rose, seems to have lost none of her eternal bloom and is as filled with assurance, etc., as ever.'[19] In pencil mark on this letter, Ruth Kennell wrote 'Rose Cohen' beside this paragraph. I was taken aback when I read this: in all my research, I never found evidence of Rose Cohen's sympathy with the left opposition. But then again, I thought, did the reality of her opinions really matter in determining her fate in Stalin's Moscow? Or did the perception of an individual's deviation in the minds of others matter as much, if not more, than the actual beliefs the person held?

The mental balancing act of living – and surviving – in Stalin's Moscow was a trying task, requiring both adaptability and the avoidance of complacency. But these patterns of living were not entirely new, even if the stakes became lethal under Stalinism. The terror of the late 1930s did not form its nightmares solely within Stalin's twisted imagination. It brought added severity and violence to existing elements of communist practice – in particular the commitment to exposing all forms of 'deviation'. This reliance on regularly purging harmful elements from the movement was an inheritance from Lenin's theories of how a revolutionary party should conduct itself when surrounded by enemies. This was how something like a great 'purge' of all the 'enemies of the people' became grimly intelligible to those compelled to live through it. It was simply another form of 'cleaning' experienced in workplaces or party cells but now directed against Soviet society writ large. Yet because this task was so enormous, so too were the penalties: no longer would a purge result in punishments as minor as loss of party status or unemployment; it was now about the deprival of basic freedom and the loss of life.

The *Alpenpost*

1

If Emmy Leonhard desired a place of exile cloistered away from the tribulations of the wider world, then she could scarcely have chosen better than Montana, the Swiss municipality where she settled with her two daughters after escaping Germany. Far above Lake Geneva, up through winding roads, postcard-beautiful wooden chalets stood against the backdrop of the snow-capped Swiss Alps when my partner Ciara and I visited Montana early one winter. I did not know the precise address where Emmy, Elisa and Alida stayed, only that their residence was an old wash shed that they had converted into a 'charming' home. Here, the Leonhard family lived together for years with their cat, Tigre. Above the fray of a continent contorting itself below, Emmy remained alive to the ideas that could provide a brighter path through a dismal decade.

At the time of the Leonhards' arrival as refugees, Montana already had a reputation as a retreat. At the turn of the century, a Genevan doctor had converted a Montana hotel into a sanatorium and started the transformation of the town into a medical resort. In early 1935 a French-Jewish couple who knew about Montana's restorative properties decided to send their daughter to regain her strength in the Swiss town. Bernard and Selma Weil had watched with concern as their daughter Simone conducted a series of political experiments upon herself. Their intellectually brilliant daughter was a frequent source of worry, for she was unable to simply consider her ideas in the abstract. Being a socialist for Simone meant submerging herself in the conditions she sought to change, not merely arguing for their improvement.

In 1934 Simone decided that this meant swapping her university teaching role for long shifts in a Parisian automobile plant. Her family and friends tried to dissuade Simone, who suffered from severe headaches, from undertaking the intensive physical labour. In the end, it was not parents nor friends but an ear infection that forced Simone to stop working, albeit only temporarily. She returned to her parents' home, a flat on the Rue Auguste-Comte with a view of the Eiffel Tower, where Bernard and Selma convinced their daughter to rest further in Montana.

During this first act of her short but astonishingly productive life, Simone was a Marxist philosopher – though one guided by certain heresies. Her stance was never the party line. After visiting Germany in 1932, she wrote a political report critiquing the communists for their rejection of any path to anti-fascist unity and the social democrats for their passivity. In a diagnosis that was better able to guide anti-fascist resistance than Comintern orthodoxy, she argued that fascism mobilised a constituency that included intellectuals, farmers, the unemployed and the middle class.[1] In other words, it was a genuine mass movement rather than, as the Comintern narrowly argued, the 'open dictatorship of the most reactionary, most chauvinist and most imperialist elements of finance capital'.[2]

Her broader ideas brought her into a polemic with Leon Trotsky, a man who somehow always found time for an argument though constantly harassed by states who rejected him and Stalinists who wanted him dead. The Weil–Trotsky debate took place in the Weil family flat in late 1933. Waiting outside the private room Simone requested for the meeting, Natalia Sedova, Trotsky's wife, allegedly gave Bernard and Selma a compliment that few parents must have ever received. She observed, with evident surprise, that their daughter was 'holding her own with Trotsky!'[3]

The same year of her tête-à-tête with Trotsky, Simone published an essay that still compellingly conveys all her intellectual spark almost a century later. The subtitle of the essay was a question:

'Are we heading for the proletarian revolution?' In short, her answer was no, at least, not any time soon. But in its full breadth, the essay spoke eloquently to the idea that even activists facing a defeat that risks the destruction of 'everything which lends value to human life in our eyes' must continue to struggle and – just as importantly – to think clearly. Even if you cannot prevent the calamity that is coming, Weil suggested, there was still value in understanding it. 'And we are not really without hope,' she argued. In a clarion call to all those who, like her, found themselves dissidents against their old intellectual homes, she affirmed that the 'mere fact that we exist, that we conceive and want something different from what exists, constitutes for us a reason for hoping'.[4]

The journal that carried Weil's essay was a syndicalist review, *La Révolution prolétarienne*, which gave a platform to radical intellectuals who argued for a vision of communism distinct from Soviet-style communism. The journal had at least one regular reader based in Montana, Switzerland: Emmy Leonhard. When Emmy came across Simone Weil's writings for *La Révolution prolétarienne*, she found herself struck not only 'by the loftiness of its judgements' but also by the deep knowledge of the workers' movements that the writing revealed.[5] Emmy wrote to the editorial board requesting to be put in touch with the author of such incisive texts.

Emmy's letter to the editors made its way from Montana to Paris, only for it to be forwarded onwards from the Weil apartment on Rue Auguste-Comte to Simone's actual location at that moment: Montana. The woman with whom Emmy so eagerly wanted to talk over the world revolution was, in fact, likely little more than a walk away from her, recovering from overwork and an ear infection in the same town. When Emmy's letter reached her, Simone was 'delighted by the coincidence' and went to visit this German socialist who had contacted her.[6]

It must have been just as exciting – and equally astonishing – for Emmy to learn that this insightful writer happened to be nearby. When she met Simone, a further surprise awaited. Emmy expected to meet a fellow veteran trade unionist, someone who was, like herself, 'widely experienced' in the movement.[7] Yet Simone Weil, this philosopher who had already published prolifically, whose thinking already spoke in searing and timeless terms to the human condition and who had stood her ground in a one-to-one debate with Leon Trotsky himself, was far younger than Emmy anticipated. In the same month Simone Weil arrived in Montana, she had just celebrated her twenty-sixth birthday.

A friend of the Weils recalled how a 'great affection' developed not only between the two left-wing intellects, Simone and Emmy, but also tied together the wider Weil family with all the Leonhard women: Elisa, Alida and their mother Emmy.[8] Eventually, when it became time for the Leonhard castaways to sail on from Montana, they found shelter in a home owned by Bernard and Selma Weil south of Paris.

Any relief Alida and Elisa may have felt from gaining a family friend closer in age than their own parents would surely have been mitigated by the fact that this new family friend was arguably the most intense thinker of the twentieth century. Remembering her friendship with Simone decades later, Emmy recalled how 'when we were together, we were always talking of changing the world'.[9] Clearly, Simone's extraordinary 1933 essay had a lasting effect upon Emmy, for when I finally traced the remnants of Emmy's archive, I found an old German-language translation of the essay among other documents relating to Simone.

With the introduction of Simone Weil into their circle, the already illustrious list of supporting characters in the Leonhard childhood gained yet another major figure of their era. Around this time, Elisa and Alida also began caring for the first of many pets to accompany them in exile, a cat named Piet.

2

As his partner talked philosophy in the Swiss Alps and his daughters chased their new friend around their converted wash shed (their cat Piet, not Simone Weil), Edo Fimmen patrolled his organising routes, moving among anti-Nazi exiles and fellow trade unionists in Amsterdam, Paris and other cities in Western Europe and Scandinavia. Plotting out his movements on a map would show Edo orbiting, but not entering, the very country that focused most of his attention: Nazi Germany.

Soon after the Nazi takeover, Edo's union the ITF began rolling out publications that would combine reports from resistance cells and the movement in exile with their own analysis to try and convey to its members the dangers represented by Nazism. In 1933 the ITF distributed *Hakenkreuz über Deutschland* (Swastika over Germany). Its masthead carried an image of a black swastika crashing into a crowd of civilians. To one side of the image, an SA man baton-charged a woman. To the other, a destitute mother looked over the scene forlornly with her frightened children embracing her. The ITF evidently – and correctly – calculated that the time for holding punches was over.

Edo was shocked by the response of many former German comrades who acquiesced to Nazi rule. One German trade unionist, Fritz Scheffell, wrote to Edo demanding that he 'stop the witch hunt' against Nazi Germany, continuing that all the 'horror stories' and 'tales about the Jews' should be 'laid to rest'.[10] Edo confided that 'one wanted to hide out of shame' after reading some letters from Germany.[11]

But Edo found many counterpoints to turncoats like Fritz Scheffell who repulsed him through an acquiescence to Nazi rule. He befriended Willi Eichler, the Berlin-born son of a postal worker who was the chairman of the International Socialist Combat Group, known by its German initials: the ISK. Although mentioned earlier, the ISK demands further explanation, for this group's history marks one of the more unusual subplots in the annals of resistance. A small but determined movement of anti-Nazi socialists, the ISK first developed under the leadership of a Kantian philosopher named Leonard Nelson. ISK members viewed their political doctrines as inseparable from their commitment to *lebensreform*, a theory of personal conduct that advocated vegetarianism, language-training in Esperanto and abstinence from alcohol. The ISK argued *against* democracy and for a society ruled over by its own rigorously trained elect. The future leadership were cultivated under conditions that included training through Socratic dialogue and the severance of ties with family and friends beyond the movement. As the ISK watched the Nazi vote count rise, their leadership felt only more assured in their distrust of the masses.

Unpalatable as their anti-democratic politics and cult-like practices may seem to modern eyes, the ISK's development of a tightly networked, intensely committed and loyal membership found its moment when Hitler unleashed his crackdown on opponents. The conspiratorially honed and determined ISK membership remained remarkably effective at underground work.

In Paris, Edo's friend in the ISK leadership, Willi Eichler, and his comrades frequented the movement's exile outpost in France: a vegetarian restaurant that, like other ISK-run restaurants, offered both a meat-free diet and a gathering point for clandestine operatives and anti-Nazi materials. The vegetarian offerings were not simply a means of concealing subversive activity: the legumes and leaflets were part of an internally consistent theory of action.

The movement of people and materials was the part of the resistance equation where Edo's union proved essential for anti-Nazi groups like the ISK. According to historian Dieter Nelles, by the start of 1935 the ITF had ties with one hundred distinct groups of transport workers undertaking illegal anti-Nazi activities within Germany.[12] Central to this operation were Edo's own personal contacts moving within and beyond Germany, especially Hans Jahn, an organiser on German railways who was well prepared for the Nazi takeover. By 1932 Jahn had created a network of activists in Saxony who were ready to block all major rail routes 'within a few hours' in the event of a general strike against the Nazis being called.[13] The ITF paid Jahn a stipend to continue his organising work after the Nazi takeover. He travelled as a wine merchant representing an Amsterdam-based company, a cover that allowed him to move through Germany, trading wine, organising anti-fascists. From early 1936 Edo, Hans Jahn and another ITF comrade regularly met German resistance leaders in a town on the Dutch – German border, an action not without its own risks but which Edo decided upon through a commitment to personally meeting the activists excavating the underground routes.

The first phase of the transport workers' resistance organised by Edo and his comrades involved distributing anti-Nazi literature on the train carriages of Germany with the hope that it would be chanced upon by sympathetic readers. Before trains crossed from the Netherlands, ITF-loyal Dutch rail workers would also fill window rims with illegal publications. Coded postcards would be dispatched to German resistance co-ordinators, such as ISK members, indicating where to find the cache of materials progressing towards them on the rail routes. Shortly after Edo attended a 1935 conference in Denmark to assess the underground work, the Gestapo managed to break up ITF-backed resistance cells in Berlin, Hamburg and Stettin.[14] Yet the expansion of Edo's network continued despite the Gestapo's growing awareness of their determined opponents based in Amsterdam.

3

A few months after he received reports of cadre being rumbled by the Gestapo, Edo began receiving a different kind of report to his headquarters in Amsterdam. In early November 1935, the first issue of the *Alpenpost* was dispatched from its office in a converted wash shed in the Swiss canton of Valais and sent onward to the ITF headquarters. Edo's daughters Elisa and Alida had created a one-of-a-kind publication: what was almost certainly history's first ever fortnightly illustrated journal of anti-fascist exile written exclusively by two precocious girls. The issue, when I encountered it in the Leonhard family archive, astonished me in its creativity and its absolute commitment to maintaining all the formal conventions of an actual newspaper, including issue numbers, source accreditation, a humour column and a regular section for light fiction.

Reflecting the effortless multilingualism that became a family trait, the paper was written in a mix of German and French with occasional English and Dutch. Daring their readership (Edo and Emmy) to treat them as proper journalists and not just two kids, Elisa and Alida exclusively referred to themselves within reports as '*Die Redaktion*'.

26. Edo meeting with the *Alpenpost* editorial team, Montana, c. 1936.
Leonhard Fimmen Papers

The front page of the *Alpenpost*'s first issue set the tone for the publication's five years of existence. Issue one, written and coloured in by hand a month after Mussolini's invasion of Ethiopia – an invasion that the ITF forcefully condemned – opens with a description of ecological devastation wrought by the early years of Italian colonialism in North Africa. It is signed with an 'E' in a circle, indicating the authorship of the ten-year-old Elisa. Below this article, with an 'A' in its own bubble to mark it as a contribution by the three-years-younger Alida, is a light feuilleton about Honigo the Bear. Honigo, readers learn over several instalments, is a pet bear owned by two children named Ali and Toos, who, in this first chapter of his story, eats a pair of slippers belonging to Ali's mother.

Elsewhere in the issue, an advertising section suggests that the Leonhard family faced a rodent problem, with a notice allegedly submitted by the 'Mouse family' advertising a housewarming party in the pantry and specifying 'no cats'. There is even a death notice in the first ever *Alpenpost*: a paragraph contained within a black box requests sympathy for the bereaved family of 'our dear little tomcat Piet', who died suddenly at the age of four months.

Piet was barely cold in an Alpine grave when the arrival of his replacement, the more tenacious Tigre, was announced in the 'local news' column of the *Alpenpost*'s second number. The 'Humour Section' for this issue also contained a back-and-forth between Emmy and her two children, likely inspired by the measures their father and his union the ITF were advocating to counter fascist Italy's aggression against Ethiopia. 'What are sanctions?' the children asked. The reply: your mother 'sanctions all that you eat'. A small illustration in this issue, perhaps cut from the masthead of a letter, depicts a fist holding aloft a red banner emblazoned with 'ITF'. Around this time, resistance operatives in Leipzig were posting similar illustrations on public walls; red parchments of paper carrying the slogan 'Long live the ITF'.[15]

Readers sceptical that the *Alpenpost* was the genuine production of two children below the age of thirteen would share my own initial astonishment. Emmy surely provided 'editorial' support and we can assume the anti-imperialist analysis was not always wholly original but drew from the kind of journals their mother left lying around the house. Yet historians, like many other adults, often underestimate children, who rarely play a central role in the stories we tell about major movements and moments. In truth, Elisa and Alida's childhood provided exceptionally fertile conditions for independent intellectual development. Although their peripatetic refugee lives allowed little time for formal education, the yellowing pages of the *Alpenpost* reveal that both girls were intensively home-schooled by Emmy, even taking correspondence courses in Esperanto. There is every possibility that what we might regard as grown-up political analysis emerged from a ten-year-old's mind.

Elisa, as the final chapter of our journey through this history will show, was always regarded as astoundingly intelligent, meriting some comparison with the philosophical star who became one of the closest things she had to a consistent childhood friend: Simone Weil. From her first moments spent in the Hotel Lux, Elisa grew up in the company of radical intellectuals and with a mother confident enough to once write to Leon Trotsky to tell him how communism should be done. As the older sibling but also the Leonhard girl who became more intellectually inclined, Elisa was the guiding light of the *Alpenpost*'s editorial direction, in addition to being its lead illustrator.

Vanishingly few handwritten, biweekly 1930s newspapers recounting the lives and ideas of two girls raised by revolutionary parents have survived. Frankly, it is possible the *Alpenpost* is the only child-produced source of its kind that still exists today in such a complete form. Not only because of its remarkable survival, but also due to the astonishing – and often hilarious – details and illustrations it contains, the *Alpenpost* remains the most extraordinary historical document I have ever encountered.

27. The editorial team take a break, Montana, 1936.
Leonhard Fimmen Papers

Testimony

1

In a front-page cartoon for the 14 February 1937 edition of the *Alpenpost*, the thirty-fourth issue of Valais Canton's only hand-written journal of anti-fascism and children's fiction, Elisa Leonhard illustrated a stern Joseph Stalin holding up a list of names to a uniformed subordinate. 'Which Bolshevik from November 1917 have I not yet shot?' Stalin asks the member of his secret police standing in front of him. Pointing back at his boss, the officer replies, 'You, Comrade Stalin.' This cartoon, copied by Elisa from a Swiss weekly (with proper accreditation, as one would expect from a publication with integrity), used caustic wit to comment on a series of macabre spectacles that began in 1936.

A few months before Elisa Leonhard set out to sketch Joseph Stalin for the *Alpenpost*, the Soviet public prosecutor's office announced that a trial of major importance would take place in Moscow. The purpose of the trial was to reveal the nefarious workings of a 'Trotskyite-Zinovievite terrorist centre'. A group of defendants that included Grigory Zinoviev and Lev Kamenev, both participants in the October Revolution of 1917, were accused of plotting against the Soviet state and bearing responsibility for the murder of Leningrad Party leader Sergei Kirov. This show trial was a public component of a much larger process already under way by the time the defendants first made their confessions: the Stalinist terror, a repressive campaign that would reach into all corners of Soviet society.

The trial marked a particular threshold moment for the fate of foreign communists then resident in the USSR. Because some among

the accused were long-standing figures of prominence in the movement, few communists could honestly claim to be free of associations
with the defendants and their ideas. If former comrades of Lenin
himself could publicly confess to treason, then who could be
trusted? Certainly not those exposed to the corrupting influences
of life beyond the Soviet frontiers. The Comintern, with its international scope of operations, became perceived in the Stalinist
imagination as a bridging point for foreign spies intent on penet-
rating Stalin's red fortress.

Many who arrived in Moscow fleeing persecution from fascist
governments now found themselves under threat from the supposed
workers' state, their political pasts subject to harsh scrutiny. 'Any
suspicion of political opposition was cataclysmic in its consequences,'
writes historian Brigitte Studer: 'not only party and Comintern
authorities but ordinary party members were under an absolute
duty to follow up on every hint, no matter how small, and to report
the person concerned if need be'.[1] A spiralling cycle of accusation
kicked into gear.

In October 1936 the communist couple Willi Münzenberg and
Babette Gross, the close friends of Edo and Emmy from their time
in Berlin, travelled to Moscow. They stayed in a newly built hotel,
the Moskva. Nobody dared to visit them, Babette remembered, for
fear the couple 'might be among the damned'. 'People were
bewildered,' she recalled, and they 'wracked their brains to remember
any deviations from the party line of which they might have been
guilty and of which they could now be accused in the "Great Purge"'.[2]

Despite Münzenberg's extraordinary service to Comintern
propaganda efforts, he had reason to be cautious. Even though by
1935 the Comintern had realised the error of its ways and called
for a 'Popular Front' of all anti-fascist forces, this came after years
of catastrophically short-sighted political guidance that delayed the
mobilisation of a united anti-fascist front. Münzenberg was on the
record for having called this as he saw it, in addition to other errors,
like consorting with that social democrat lapdog of the bourgeoisie,
Edo Fimmen.

Towards the end of their short and unsettling time in Moscow, Willi and Babette met with Babette's brother-in-law Heinz Neumann, a once-prominent leader in the German communist party brought low by reprimands from Comintern disciplinary bodies. In the 1920s, Heinz Neumann had thrived in the Lux's social world and had met Joseph Freeman at parties he attended alongside Joseph's girlfriend Luise and his friend Sabo. A decade later, now deprived of political roles, Neumann was working as a translator in a publishing office. He was married to Babette's sister Margaret and the couple lived together in the Lux.

The hotel was a much more sober place than it had been in the 1920s. The residents lived under a pall of mutual suspicion. The oppressive atmosphere could even, it seems, seep into the furnishings. Ervin Sinko, a Yugoslavian writer who kept a diary of his life in the Lux from 1935 to 1937 – itself a dangerous activity – chillingly described the paranoia in the hotel. Once, when the independent-minded Sinko was criticising the quasi-religious adulation for Stalin at a private gathering, another Lux resident 'suddenly and nervously' drew Sinko away from the radiator and sat him in another chair.[3] Not only did you need to watch for coldly calculating comrades, you also needed to fear concealed listening devices.

Heinz Neumann ill-advisedly visited his sister-in-law and her husband to say goodbye before they left for their place of exile in Paris. 'He broke down when we took our farewell,' Babette remembered, 'we knew that we would never see each other again.'[4] Not long after returning from Moscow, deeply disturbed by an experience that catalysed his growing doubts into renunciations of his past allegiances, Willi Münzenberg resigned from the German communist party. Now out of the fold, rather than receiving Comintern backing, he was supported through personal, political and financial assistance from his friend Edo Fimmen, along with other anti-fascists disenchanted with international communism. Edo told a comrade in the ISK that he was pleased with Münzenberg's departure from the communist party, even if he also considered his friend complicit in the mistakes made by the communists.[5] Now able to associate more freely with 'renegades' like Emmy and Edo, Babette and Willi would occasionally feature in Elisa and Alida's newspaper.

2

The terrified Heinz Neumann whom Willi and Babette met in Moscow in October 1936 contrasted starkly with a different version of Heinz Neumann, whom readers in the US and Britain encountered in a work published that same month: Joseph Freeman's autobiography *An American Testament*. The book brought readers into the Hotel Lux, providing vivid descriptions of people and events that I would rely on when I set out to delve into this world many decades later. In a darkly ironic confluence of events, a book that portrayed a world open and alive with revolutionary discussions was released precisely as the same building where so much of its action took place was riven by a ruthlessly enforced conformity. The rooms that once hosted freewheeling parties were now essentially holding cells for activists with diminishing prospects of surviving the decade.

The wave of arrests crashed over the Lux with such force that the 'NEP wing' of the building, where Joseph once roomed with the doctrinaire British intellectual Hugo Rathbone, was reserved as quarters for the families of the incarcerated.[6] It was a nightmarish reality that could have scarcely been imagined in the days when Joseph traversed the Lux's corridors, joining literary evenings in May's room, composing poems on his typewriter in Sabo's company and thinking over his own place in the grand historic struggle.

An American Testament portrayed its author as someone passionately committed to the people and ideas that brought him into the movement. Any moments that described crises of faith were followed by passages that dissolved the contradictions encountered by the protagonist in the substance of Marxist thought and practice. Written over the course of two years, Joseph initially conceived the book as a thousand-plus page 'Proustian' work considering the relation of 'the individual to contemporary society' from 'every possible aspect'.[7] He settled for a manuscript roughly half the initially planned size and less all-encompassing than his initially planned Proust for the proletariat.

Joseph's autobiography was published *after* the adoption of the Comintern's 'Popular Front' policy, a change in the political line that saw the international communist movement opening itself to political and cultural collaborations. This new-found openness to considering liberals and others beyond the far right as possible allies in the fight against fascism rather than complicit 'social fascists' facilitated the atmosphere where the book could find a wide audience. It landed a respectable publisher rather than rolling off the party press into the hands of a more select readership. An advert for the book in the *New York Times* heralded Joseph's work as a 'story of the found generation'.[8]

Implicitly rejecting the notion that communists were Stalin's automatons, Joseph quoted the dissenting opinions of his comrades and even the occasional compliment to Trotsky in his Moscow sections. In Joseph's account, communists – even those in Moscow – could fall in and out of love and moan about their bosses, just like anyone else. Comrades better known for the severity of their opinions were humanised and heroes of the movement recognised for their flaws. 'Kurt', a character who was really Heinz Neumann, was described just as Joseph remembered him: a lively young man causing a ruckus at Lux parties, delivering scathing, booze-fuelled impressions of the Bolshevik elite. Stalin supporters and those now cast out as renegades, who once shared meeting halls and even bedrooms, duly shared pages in the book. Joseph could even find comic moments amid his recollections of intense debates, such as when one opposition-minded comrade 'Hans', really the German communist Heinrich Kurella, childishly stormed out of a Lux room when he realised that his Central Committee-supporting older brother Alfred was inside it.[9] All of these pen portraits fitted the book's chosen subtitle – 'a narrative of rebels and romantics' – but jarred with the reality of what it actually meant to be perceived as a rebel, or even a romantic, in late-1930s Moscow.

Joseph found the early reactions to his narrative 'far better' than he 'hoped to dream'.[10] Praise reached him from across the spectrum of progressive opinion, from the likes of comrades and sympathisers such as Ernst Toller, Langston Hughes and John Strachey, to an old mentor from Joseph's student days, the philosopher Irwin Edman.[11] Boosted by the initial reception, Joseph tried to find the book an audience beyond the US. Immediately after release, plans were under way for a British edition to be distributed by the Left Book Club, a formidable agenda-setter in the 1930s world of progressive publishing.

The Left Book Club required numerous edits to the book, in many cases due to England's tighter libel laws. A reader for the British publisher noted, for example, that it was 'defamatory to say of Liam O'Flaherty that he's "wild", "drunk as a lord" and "crazy for women"'.[12] The reader recommended removing this and other incidents where Joseph insinuated identifiable people were – to include only a few examples – 'half-mad', 'decadent', 'a protagonist of nudism' and, in one case, effectively guilty of murder.

As negotiations with the Left Book Club progressed, Joseph sought a Soviet audience and wrote to friends in Moscow for help. One of his letters asking about a USSR edition was sent to a literary-minded US party member, Sender Garlin, then resident in room 8 of the Hotel Lux. Joseph sent another letter about a Russian edition and a copy of his book to a friend from his own time in the Lux, the critic and editor Sergei Dinamov.

Sergei read the copy that he received at least twice, several months apart, each time writing to Joseph with a response. The letters strike discordant notes. When he first met Joseph in May's room in the Lux, Sergei was just beginning his rise in the world of Soviet publishing. Writing to Joseph from Moscow at the end of 1936, he used the stationery of the well-respected journal that he helped edit, *International Literature*, a review of radical writing that appeared in multiple languages. Although his English was now more polished, there was still some evidence of that eclectic syntax which had so charmed Ruth Kennell back in the 1920s. 'With great pleasure I have read the entire book as well as the pages where you write about our meetings,' Sergei wrote to Joseph after his first read-through, thanking him 'for good remembrance'. 'Living past combined with big ideas that is a very rare thing in books,' he continued.[13]

A few months later and after a second reading, Sergei's tone changed. Writing in April 1937, as arrests of ordinary Soviet citizens and foreign residents were ramping up, Sergei wanted to make clear that he thought the book contained 'political errors'. 'You gave too much unnecessary space to insignificant facts, gossip and philistine anecdotes,' he wrote. 'You are too kind to our enemies,' Sergei continued, placing the name of one such enemy after this sentence: 'Lida'.[14] This was a reference to Lydia Gasviany, the Georgian woman whom Joseph and May met through Sergei and who appears in Joseph's book as 'Tamara'.

Dangerously for Sergei, Joseph shared the fact that Sergei was the connecting link between himself and Gasviany in his now published autobiography. The arrests of the terror moved along such connecting links, with the numbers of incarcerated spiralling as interrogators forced victims to name other 'enemies' with whom they consorted. It is possible that Sergei would have known through literary contacts that in July 1936 Lydia Gasviany was arrested by Georgian members of Stalin's secret police, the NKVD. A few months after Sergei's April 1937 letter to Joseph, she was sentenced to death and executed.

Another disturbing event may have influenced Sergei Dinamov's more critical re-reading of the tale told by *An American Testament*, an event revealed in documents from the bulging Comintern file on Joseph Freeman that I found in the Moscow archives. These were the same documents that the orthodox communist researcher with whom I shared my coffee breaks called 'a find': in a series of typescript pages written in Russian and English, I discovered that between the two dates of Sergei Dinamov's letters to Joseph, *An American Testament* had been put on trial by the Comintern.

3

Joseph had every reason to hope that his literary comrade Sender Garlin would enjoy his book. Shortly after the manuscript was completed, Garlin wrote to Joseph from Moscow to say how 'pleased' he was to learn that the book was now done. 'Needless to say,' Garlin continued, 'all of us are looking forward to cutting the leaves of the freshly-published book.'[15] Once his own copy arrived at the Hotel Lux, Garlin read it in great detail. Later, when the British edition arrived, he read this too. He was on specific assignment to do so: the Comintern's disciplinary body wanted to know precisely where and how both editions of the book differed and whether 'political errors' introduced in the first US edition were repeated in the later Left Book Club print. In short, they wanted a summary of what they believed would be the extent of the damage done to the movement by Joseph's book.

In March 1937 Sender Garlin was among a list of several names invited to participate in a 'Special Commission' appointed by the International Control Commission, the disciplinary enforcement wing of the Comintern, to investigate and pass judgement on Joseph's *An American Testament*. Although Garlin missed the initial sitting of the Special Commission, he would later be burdened with the task of cataloguing a total of 163 differences between the US and British editions of the book.[16]

The minutes of the meeting reveal that the Special Commission took a particular interest in Joseph's description of communists who had also come under investigation by the Control Commission: Heinz Neumann and Hans Kurella, both of whom met Joseph in the Lux. Joseph did not know that the lives of at least two people featured in the book now hung in the balance in Stalin's Moscow, although he would later learn of their fates. The minutes of the Special Commission make clear that his published words could not have helped them in their perilous situation.

'The book not only gives a scandal-mongering picture of Heinz Neumann which reflects badly on the Comintern as a whole,' noted the Special Commission, 'but it also quotes some alleged confid-ential notes sent by Comrade Stalin to Neumann.'[17] Regarding Hans Kurella, who like Neumann was a German party member then resident in Moscow, the commission members were particularly perturbed by Joseph's suggestion that, in 1926, 'Kurella was so much a Trotskyite that he would not even be in the same room with his brother, Alfred.'[18] 'The author does not designate Kurella by his own name, but under a pseudonym, but the description is unmistakeable as referring to Comrade H. Kurella,' the minutes noted. Few of Joseph's pseudonyms escaped unravelling by the Special Commission, who also realised that 'Hedda' was Sabo, and described his depiction of her and her husband as 'undesirable'.

The overall perspective of the book was, the commission believed, damnable. The author dared to mention 'Comrade Stalin . . . and such heroes of the workers, in the same breath and in the same incidents with Trotskyite renegades' and even gave 'enthusi-astic approval' to Trotsky's thoughts on literature. Reflecting the graceless language of condemnation that featured prominently in the rolling show trials, the commission decried how the book's description of the 'inner-workings of the Comintern' and Joseph's part within them 'almost becomes vicious because his vulgar scandal-mongering has an air of authority' due to his work for the Comintern.[19]

The commission made several recommendations, including that the book be condemned as an 'anti-Party' work and the wider Comintern 'literature distribution apparatus' be telegraphed to stop all distribution of the work. The most chilling recommendation, however, was one that would have implicated Joseph Freeman as a component, albeit a largely unwitting one, in the mechanisms of the terror itself. The commission proposed that the Communist Party of the USA 'investigate Freeman's charges against Henry Kurella, and demand of Freeman a written statement on the ques-tion, in which he states all his facts in a responsible party manner, giving real names not only in the case of Henry Kurella, but in the case of all other who are involved in the incidents he writes about'.[20]

Although Joseph's book would be publicly condemned by the Comintern, it is not clear if Joseph was ever compelled to make a statement about his characterisations. If he did, then I did not find it where I would have expected to uncover it: in his Comintern file. In any case, such a statement would have made little practical difference. By the time the book was released, the damage was already done. Heinrich Kurella was already under suspicion for his associations with Heinz Neumann.[21] Whether or not Joseph's description of him played any role in his fate, the gears were already in motion.

I remember the sinking feeling as I turned to my laptop with the transcript of the Special Commission on Joseph's book open before me in the Comintern archive. I typed the name 'Kurella' into a database of terror victims. I found exactly what I expected to find: Heinrich Kurella, born 1905, arrested 19 October 1937, convicted of 'membership in a counter-revolutionary organisation'. Executed 28 October 1937. Place of death: Kommunarka. It was one of the most unsettling experiences I ever had in an archive. This book that first set me on my journey into all this research had once been investigated for reasons so jarringly distinct from the questions that first brought me to it. The sources I use to recreate lives could have been the same documents used to damn them.

4

Living with his wife Charmion in their apartment in Murray Hill and travelling each day to the offices of the *New Masses*, Joseph, it seems, was still unaware in early 1937 of the controversy raging over his book in Moscow. He does not appear to have realised that no less a personality than Georgi Dimitrov, general secretary of the Comintern, intervened to try and prevent the book's planned release in Britain. Dimitrov, a star of the international communist movement, gained world renown in 1933 for his courageous performance in a Leipzig court during the Reichstag fire trial. Although once able to argue his way out of a Nazi court, Dimitrov proved unable to convince Viktor Gollancz, the British publisher and director of the Left Book Club, that Joseph Freeman's *An American Testament* should not be published.

In a May 1937 meeting in Moscow that was also attended by high-ranking members of the British party, Dimitrov impressed upon Gollancz that the book contained a mass of incorrect positions and could be 'used by our enemies'.[22] Dimitrov argued that a book that criticises fascism from a liberal position 'may be admitted', but this was something different, this was a 'book of Trotskyism'. Gollancz stood his ground, arguing that the book was, in its essential elements, one that supported progressive forces and any 'incorrect' views could be argued out in publications and meetings. His venture was, after all, a book club. Shortly after his return from Moscow, the Left Book Club edition of *An American Testament* went into print.

Another person present at the Dmitrov–Gollancz meeting would have been intimately aware of the atmosphere in Moscow: the general secretary of the Communist Party of Great Britain, Harry Pollitt. By the time of this meeting, Pollitt already knew that Rose Cohen's husband, David Petrovsky, a comrade with whom he had worked closely during Petrovsky's period as a Comintern emissary in Britain, was under arrest.[23] Although no longer working for the Comintern at the time of his arrest, Petrovsky still held a prestigious role through his work within the People's Commissariat of Heavy Industry. On 11 March 1937 the NKVD arrested Petrovsky and charged him with membership of a 'counter-revolutionary' organisation.

The arrest was greeted with disbelief within British communism, where Petrovsky's political credentials were considered unimpeachable. Rose Cohen, too, had a particular place in Harry Pollitt's heart: he claimed to have unsuccessfully proposed to her fourteen times before she married Petrovsky.[24] Pollitt had known both Rose and Nellie since at least the post-war years, when all navigated the circles of the East London left. It is not clear whether Pollitt visited Rose in May 1937, but by the time of his next trip to Moscow later that year, such an encounter would have been impossible, for she too was under arrest.

The final impressions of Rose before her arrest come from another British woman who, though not sharing Rose's politics, shared her status as the wife of a prominent figure in the Soviet political elite. Towards the end of her life, sometime in the 1970s, Ivy Litvinov recorded her memories of Rose. The two first became friends when Rose was working on the *Moscow News*. Though she enjoyed her company, Ivy regarded Rose as possessing a 'smugness and complacency' that came from 'shutting your eyes' to the sinister sides of Soviet life, like overcrowding and arrests. At the time of Petrovsky's arrest, Ivy was away from Moscow. When Ivy returned, her husband Maxim implored her not to see Rose. 'Maxim, I must,' Ivy remembered answering, before Tanya, their daughter, offered to fetch Rose and bring her to Ivy. It was a less conspicuous arrangement than a commissar's wife travelling to a flat recently visited by the NKVD. According to Ivy, the two met on a bench. They spent the day together, Ivy remembered. Rose told her that not 'a single one' of her friends had been to see her. Ivy remembered Rose seeming 'utterly lonely and trembling'. 'That was the last time I saw Rose,' Ivy noted.[25] On 13 August 1937, Rose Cohen was arrested by the NKVD.

I was already familiar with Ivy Litvinov's memories of her final encounters with Rose Cohen before I came across the original typescript among Ivy's papers in an archive in California. The recollection was published as an appendix in a 1983 biography, John Carswell's *The Exile: A Life of Ivy Litvinov*. I know that Rose's niece Joyce, daughter of Nellie, who was in her fifties by the time this biography was published, read Ivy's account of her aunt because, when I finally traced Joyce's archive to an attic in the Cotswolds, I found the pages on which it was printed ripped out of the biography and folded around a letter. In a choice whose rationale I am unable to decipher, a choice almost certainly made by Joyce, the pages were folded around the final letter that Nellie sent to her younger sister, Rose. The reason that this letter was in an attic in Britain, not with the seized archive of its recipient, was almost certainly because of Nellie's unfortunate timing. The date of the letter reads 14 August 1937, a day *after* Rose was arrested in Moscow. Probably, it arrived at a flat where nobody was home and was returned to sender.

5

'For weeks I've had it on my mind to write to you but always something has prevented,' Nellie wrote to Rose while coming to the end of an August 1937 holiday in Cornwall. Soon, they would be leaving, off to visit some relatively recently acquired family members in Liverpool: Nellie's in-laws. A few weeks after writing this letter, Nellie could mark the second anniversary of her marriage to Hugo Rathbone, Joseph Freeman's old room-mate from the Lux, a man who had been in pursuit of one or the other Cohen since the early 1920s. The three of them were together in Cornwall: Nellie, Hugo and Joyce, who appears to have adapted easily to life with her stepfather.

Joyce was now eight years old, some months older than her cousin Alyosha in Moscow, who was just shy of turning eight himself. 'It must be about 4 weeks since I got your letter telling me about Alyosha's measles,' Nellie wrote. 'It must have been a nasty time for you alone with him but its good he's over it without any after effects,' she continued, the word 'alone' providing one of the only references in the letter to what Rose was facing. 'I wish you could be here with him,' wrote Nellie 'you'd love it.'

Nellie's own updates were largely unexciting. She was doing some bookkeeping work for the *Daily Worker* and considering helping with a local paper. There was, however, a change in her husband. Hugo, she wanted to tell Rose, was 'just staying at home doing intensive reading'. 'He doesn't talk about future plans and I'm not pressing him about them,' she continued. This change came as 'quite a shock' to Nellie, even though she otherwise found him 'well and cheerful.'

Approaching, but hardly confronting, the situation that haunted this letter, Nellie wrote: 'I've been thinking of you quite a lot lately even if I haven't written.' She then turned quickly to a more pleasant topic: Joyce. There was some dissatisfaction with her present music teacher, but Joyce was practising her piano and violin. The music teacher at her school found her 'promising'. Joyce was a voracious reader too: capable of finishing a book a day. Bringing her letter to a close, Nellie asked what kind of books Alyosha might like her to send from England. She signed off: 'With lots of love and hoping all will go well with you, Nellie.'

6

At twenty minutes past two on 28 November 1937, a closed session of the Military Collegium of the Supreme Court of the Soviet Union assembled to decide its verdict in the case of Rose Cohen. She was charged with espionage on behalf of British intelligence. The court granted her a final word: she pleaded not guilty to the charges. The session closed. It had lasted twenty minutes. Following deliberations, the court sentenced her to be shot.[26] Shortly after, Rose Cohen was executed.

Some months earlier, the same court had convicted her husband, David Petrovsky, with a charge of membership of a counter-revolutionary organisation. He was shot on 10 September 1937. According to the official data of the Soviet secret police, the number of convictions for political crimes from 1921 to 1941 was more than three million, with 1,817,496 people placed in prison or sent to the Gulag during this same period.[27] One historian's estimate for the number of executions carried out from 1937–8 alone puts the number at approximately one million.[28]

During the years of the Stalinist terror, Rose Cohen and David Petrovsky shared their fate with thousands of others in the community of foreign residents in the Soviet Union, and hundreds of thousands of ordinary Soviet citizens. Like many others, they would be posthumously cleared of charges and 'rehabilitated' after Stalin's death.

7

Who knew? What did they know? What did they do? What could they do? These questions are important, but answers can prove difficult to find. Rose Cohen's arrest became a matter of public knowledge in Britain by the summer of 1938. According to the author Francis Beckett, who has researched Rose's story along with the stories of other British victims of the Stalinist terror, the British embassy in Moscow told the British press about Rose's arrest in April 1938, hoping that this 'would increase pressure on the Soviets to release her'.[29] Of course, by this point she was already dead, though this was not yet known. For anyone learning about Rose's disappearance in Britain, it was still just that: a disappearance, not a murder.

Notably silent on the case of Rose, at least in public, were her former comrades in the Communist Party of Great Britain. Harry Pollitt asked about her case and that of Petrovsky in meetings with high-level Comintern officials, but to no avail. Pollitt's biographer notes that Pollitt apparently 'made such vigorous representations to the Comintern leadership' about Rose that the 'question of his replacement as Party leader' was raised.[30] Ultimately willing to defer to Soviet authority, Pollitt did not press the case further. He did not join a public call for her release that was attempted by Maurice Reckett, an old friend of Rose's from their guild socialist days. Beckett notes that Maurice Reckett 'found it hard to get significant left wingers to sign a very moderate letter to the *New Statesman* protesting at Rose's disappearance'.[31]

Nellie, Hugo and May did not join this attempt to raise awareness about Rose's case. Nor have I found any evidence that Rose's other siblings, some of whom were left-wing but none of whom were Communist Party members, joined it either. Perhaps they believed it was better left to communists like Pollitt working through their own channels to intervene. Reasons for not protesting may be as simple as not having been asked, but in other cases silence could result from a deference to communist discipline. However catastrophically misguided, they may well have hoped that Soviet due process would see its way to clearing Rose.

Some other fragmentary pieces of evidence are worth mentioning. In 1972, speaking to Lucia Jones, a historian working on Sylvia Pankhurst, an elderly Nellie talked about Rose's disappearance. The comments were prompted by a memory that Pankhurst wrote to Nellie about Rose around this time. 'I don't know if you know about the purge time,' Nellie said. 'My sister was Rose Cohen' who was 'purged and we never heard anything about her'. Harry Pollitt and the communist MP Willie Gallacher 'tried to find out about her but they were so suspicious of everyone', she noted, then 'the War came in 1939 and we couldn't do anything then'. According to the memory of octogenarian Nellie, Rose 'died in 1938'. Nellie claimed not to know how she died.[32] Elsewhere, I found evidence that Nellie once believed Rose died of pneumonia during the war. Although I cannot find the origin point of this erroneous belief, it was a more passive imagined ending than the brutal directness of her execution and perhaps a form of denial.

In the same 1972 interview, Nellie also suggested the arrest's impact upon her husband. Hugo unexpectedly resigned from the communist party in 1937. In the interview, Nellie described feeling that Hugo 'was very unhappy' about Rose when he 'suddenly' left the party. However, such a crisis of political faith was nothing compared to what Rose's seven-year-old son Alyosha now faced. Following the execution of his parents, he was placed in an orphanage for the children of 'enemies of the people'. Unlike the English Cohens, his father's family did what they could to help and adopted Alyosha out of the orphanage. The wider Petrovsky relatives were pivotal in ensuring Alyosha could live a fulfilling life despite the trauma of his early childhood.

Where, during all of this, was May? Behind the counter of a left-wing bookstore in London, working her final, pre-retirement job. Although she never referenced exactly which bookstore, a likely candidate is Collet's, which stood on the Charing Cross Road and was owned by her friend Eva Reckitt. Only one document written by May in 1937 survives. It is a letter to Ruth sent in the month of Rose's arrest but not mentioning it, suggesting she may not yet have known. Instead, the letter, written on the northern French coast, describes a holiday and references a couple of old friends. May mentions Emmy Leonhard 'who has been living in Switzerland these past few years'. Soon, she noted, Emmy and her family were 'moving to Paris'. May also mentioned Joseph, having seemingly just learned that she featured in his book. She was annoyed he had not sent her a copy. In her typically catty fashion, she also referenced a rumour she heard that he was now overweight. 'I can imagine a fat Joe & I don't like the idea,' she wrote.[33]

In all May's writing that I have found, there is only one direct reference to the disappearance of a friend in the terror. During her work in the bookshop, May encountered numerous radicals, including some following the still-active Comintern trail moving between Moscow, London and New York. In 1969 Ruth wrote to May about their old friend, Sergei Dinamov. 'You mention Sergei,' May wrote in response, 'I have a recollection that one of the comrades on his return from Moscow did not want to give me any information – a bad sign.'[34]

La Guinguette

1

'You will be surprised to hear from me', May wrote in the opening line of a June 1938 letter to Sergei Dinamov. It had been some time since they were last in touch. She hoped that Sergei and another friend from her Moscow days, Olga Tretyakova, would excuse her lack of correspondence. May was clearly unaware that Olga was, by this point, under arrest and her husband Sergei Tretyakov already executed. 'I am so busy as a bookseller that I've no energy left over,' May explained, though 'life in England is so dull!' She was writing to seek a 'personal favour'. 'A very old friend of mine – at present in Paris – wants to introduce an English book about India to the USSR,' she explained. 'My friend', she continued 'thinks it is the kind of book that you would like over there and very suitable at the present juncture.' May herself was 'sure she is right as she has very sound judgement'.[1]

Enclosing this letter was a message from the friend in question. Writing from a home in the town of Chevreuse, south of Paris, Emmy Leonhard told Sergei Dinamov all about the new book on India she wanted to introduce to Soviet audiences by Frieda Hauswirth, a Swiss-born writer who was married to an Indian nationalist. The author, Emmy emphasised, was 'an enthusiastic partaker of the social and political struggles for freedom of India's youth and women during the last years'.[2]

It took more than a month for May to receive a response. The reply did not come from Sergei. 'Dear Miss O'Calhgan,' the Soviet staff member replied, mangling May's Irish surname, 'We have received your letter to "International Literature" addressed to S. Dinamov.' Dinamov, once an editor of *International Literature*, had not worked at the journal for the past year, the staff member informed her.

During Dinamov's last months as editor, Russian translations of excerpts from *An American Testament* were printed in *International Literature*. These were published just as the Comintern Special Commission was deciding how to condemn the book. Even though the excerpts appeared in censored form – with mentions of politically 'undesirable' persons and behaviours excised – Sergei's ultimate responsibility for Joseph's soon-to-be-damned writings appearing in Russian may well have contributed to the loss of his editorial role.[3]

A couple of months after May learned that her friend was out of a job, on 26 September 1938, Sergei Dinamov was arrested by the NKVD and taken from his apartment on Moscow's Strastnoi Boulevard. A few months later, after appearing on a list of names of prisoners that came before Stalin to have their sentences sanctioned, he was shot.

We cannot know if May had any presentiment that her friend Sergei's loss of his editorial role might be a prelude to his eventual fate. The nature of her letter, less its friendly tone and more its purpose, suggests a kind of obliviousness to the nightmarish scenario her friends in Soviet Moscow were confronting. After I encountered these letters in the archives located in a Moscow suburb, my mind continued to dwell on the context that surrounded them on the metro ride back to my accommodation. On one level, it was a banal occurrence: a woman was attempting to put her friend in touch with another friend for professional reasons. But what May did not realise was that Sergei was at risk, facing a moment of danger that could only be made worse through direct contact with someone like Emmy; an activist once proudly involved with the Trotskyist opposition. It was a both an everyday occurrence – letters between friends – and evidence of the kind of dangerous intimacies that Soviet interrogators stretched into conspiratorial fantasies.

2

When Emmy Leonhard wrote to Sergei Dinamov with a benign attempt to find a wider audience for an anti-imperialist writer she respected, she was adapting to new surroundings in Chevreuse. The first line of her address on her letter to Sergei read: 'La Guinguette', meaning 'The Tavern' in French. This was the name of the summer home owned by the Weil family. Sometime in 1937, Bernard and Selma Weil offered Emmy, her two daughters and their pets the home as a residence. Based in a quaint town dotted with small bridges over waterways, the home's location was every bit as peaceful as the Alpine setting of the Leonhard family's first place of exile. The building itself did not shout 'luxury': it was a small, stone-walled residence that could have been mistaken for an animal shed. Still, it was a roof over their heads and young Elisa and Alida had already demonstrated their ability to settle into a new home. The Leonhard family remained in Chevreuse from late 1937 until the threatened Nazi invasion of France caused them to move once more.

The reasons for leaving Montana for Chevreuse were likely practical. Edo could see his family more regularly in France than in Switzerland. From 1936, Paris became a more regular stop on Edo's itinerary. It was an important location for both Italian and German anti-fascist exile communities and the base of several close collaborators within the ITF networks. In addition, the French border with Spain was now a frontier of major importance for anti-fascist activities. The Spanish Civil War, which broke out in the summer of 1936, saw a left-wing popular front government under threat from a right-wing coup. The rebels under Franco were backed by both Hitler and Mussolini, while the democratically elected government became increasingly reliant on the Soviet Union for support. Spain became a major rallying point of the anti-fascist cause, inspiring volunteers from all over the world to fight, notably through the Comintern-directed International Brigades. Edo immediately and unreservedly mobilised his network of anti-fascist transport workers in the service of the Spanish republican cause.[4]

The simple factor of space may also have been a consideration for the relocation. Elisa and Alida were growing girls, with Elisa on the verge of becoming a teenager by the time the family arrived in France. Perhaps they had outgrown their converted shed on the side of a Swiss mountain. Based outside Paris, they could rely on personal support networks. Willi Münzenberg and his wife, Babette Gross, were based in the French capital and became closer to Emmy and the two girls in these years. Then, of course, there was the Weil family and their brilliant daughter. Ceaselessly committed as ever, Simone volunteered with an anarchist unit in Spain in 1936, but suffered an injury with some boiling oil before facing action. As a visitor to Emmy and the children when they lived in her own family's home, Weil was setting out on her next philosophical incarnation: Simone Weil the Christian mystic.

Elisa and Alida, in this idyllic setting, continued documenting their strange childhood as the combined reporting, editing and illustration team of their personal newspaper. Naturally, the publication needed a new title now that it was no longer produced in the Alps. The two girls settled on the name of their new home: *La Guinguette*.

Continuing with the same style and frequency as the *Alpenpost*, *La Guinguette* maintained all the elements that its readership (both of them) would have recognised from earlier editions. Some recent innovations were carried over too, like the 'Ratings' column, in which Emmy – and sometimes Edo – were given ratings for things like cooking, housework and time spent with Elisa and Alida. Neither child was a harsh reviewer. Emmy and Edo regularly scored highly in all categories. The primary language of the journal also transitioned from German to French, with the two girls retaining their absolute commitment to only referring to themselves within copy as the editorial team, but now becoming '*Les Rédacteurs*' instead of '*Die Redaktion*'.

The first issue of *La Guinguette* appeared on 4 November 1937, with a cover depicting the route taken by the family as they travelled from Montana to Chevreuse. The masthead featured the new name, two Gallic roosters and the slogan *Liberté, Egalité, Fraternité.* The editorial direction of the paper remained consistent; anti-fascist, anti-Stalinist, comradely critical of household pets and fiercely supportive of the ITF. The first time that *La Guinguette* marked Edo's birthday from its new headquarters, the editors produced an elaborate cover illustration. A ship, a car, two globes and several workers surround a wreath, upon which is written the phrase: 'We are building the world commune with you.' In small writing between each part of the wreath the children listed different moments from Edo's activist life in the ITF; '1919, Boycott of Hungary', '1920, Boycott of Poland', 'English General Strike', 'League Against Imperialism', 'Spain, 36–38'. Several spaces were left blank: room to write in future struggles, including a major fight looming on the horizon.

3

La Guinguette was one of several publications that allowed Edo Fimmen to survey his world. Others included the pamphlets that his union produced with the intent that they be distributed clandestinely among German seafarers. As German rearmament continued and Europe drifted closer to war, Edo and the ITF continued building a globe-spanning network. While the fascist powers used the Spanish Civil War to rehearse the coming European war, the ITF networks honed their own anti-fascist tactics in the same fight. Almost all ships that were used to transport weapons and troops to Franco's forces were known to the ITF, and the ITF in turn informed the world through the press and its contacts in democratic governments.[5] It was an operation of enormous complexity, whose tasks ranged from information-gathering to distributing vials of mercury to ITF agents that could be poured into ship engines to demobilise them following the outbreak of war.[6]

War, Edo understood, was coming, and the ultimate collapse of the Spanish republic in early 1939 convinced him that a broader European conflict was only a matter of time. In a July 1939 editorial for the ITF journal *Fascism*, Edo took stock of where he and his comrades stood on the eve of another world war. Edo admitted that twenty-five years after the First World War began 'there threatens a catastrophe which, if it cannot be averted at the eleventh hour, will dwarf what the world experienced in 1914–18'.[7] For Edo, this moment of acute and existential crisis, which he believed was once within his power to avert, called for a reckoning with old faiths and tired maxims.

What was to be done? Firstly, Edo reminded his readers that though the beautiful future once sighted on the other side of the trenches appeared ever more distant, there was still an idea worth struggling for: an indivisible idea of peace. Lasting peace could not be won through 'unjustifiable concessions', he argued, but only through uniting like-minded forces through 'calm determination'. 'If nevertheless Hitler should unleash a war,' Edo wrote, 'we shall do our part in the defence of the Fascist attack and to overcome the aggressors.' As Edo's ominous words predicted, the workers, at the eleventh hour, could not avert the catastrophe.

4

Before war broke out, Edo made one decision of enormous import-ance for the safety of his family: he found Emmy a husband. Throughout the summer of 1939, Emmy carried out the legal form-alities required to marry Daniel de Jager, seemingly a Dutch comrade of Edo then resident in Paris. The marriage, of course, was not the legal recognition of a real relationship but a preventative measure, and a foresighted one. By marrying Daniel de Jager, Emmy attained Dutch citizenship. This was crucial: Edo and Emmy understood that in the event of a German war against France, Emmy, had she remained a German citizen, would likely be interned. The arrangement required

Edo to ask for a further subterfuge to fully secure his family. To similarly protect their daughters, Edo and Emmy required de Jager to swear before Dutch and French lawyers that Alida and Elisa were his natural-born daughters by Emmy.

In late August 1939, a special 'Marriage Number' of *La Guinguette* was produced to mark the occasion. The masthead featured the editorial team presenting flowers to Emmy and Daniel de Jager, dressed in their wedding finery. *La Guinguette* did not betray the ruse, depicting the marriage as the end of a 'truly long wait'. Reflecting the fact that this was not a fairy-tale romance, Emmy took the bus to her own wedding. After waiting for two other couples to get married, Emmy sounded a quiet 'Yes' to all the announced legal clauses as she stood with her groom.

'Unfortunately,' the report continued 'the editors have to take this account from the witness reports.' Elisa and Alida remained at home, cooking the wedding breakfast. In a further breach with convention, the couple, after marriage, immediately went their separate ways. Emmy returned home to Chevreuse, where the *Guinguette* editorial team had a meal ready. If the report is to be believed, these two absurdly precocious children had yet another talent: cooking. The feast included omelettes, a casserole, escalope and sugar melon.

La Guinguette remained committed to keeping its readers abreast of world news, even in this special edition. In a round-up of fortnightly events squeezed onto the back page of the wedding issue, there was a brief note of events that took place on 22 August: 'Letter from Papa. Stalin-Hitler pact.' Commonly referred to as the Molotov–Ribbentrop Pact, this August 1939 agreement between the Soviet Union and Nazi Germany committed both countries to a decade of 'non-aggression' between one another. A secret protocol in the agreement, finally acknowledged by Soviet authorities in 1989, provided for German and Soviet spheres of influence in Eastern Europe in the event of war, setting the stage for both countries to invade Poland a month later.[8] For many in the international communist movement who had held up the USSR as the final line of defence against Nazism, it was an announcement with a vertiginous effect. The Soviets, who had supported the republic in Spain, were now willing to cut a deal with Hitler. However, it would take some time for the true extent of Stalin's betrayal of the anti-fascist cause to become known.

Although they would only learn of it later, the Leonhard family had a personal link to someone in the Soviet Union whose life would be altered by the Nazi–Soviet co-operation inaugurated by the pact. Babette Gross and Willi Münzenberg appeared in several reports in *La Guinguette*. In one issue, Elisa and Alida described a bus trip with the couple to see some grand estates in the winter of 1938.[9] Later, in their Ford automobile, the couple took the girls on further excursions and, in one case, Babette brought them to a matinee at the state theatre, the Comédie-Française. The connection between the two families clearly extended beyond the comradely ties between Willi and Edo into real personal affection. One *Guinguette* account of a visit from the couple reported that while 'the editorial team' filled their stomachs, 'Mama did the same for her spirits', talking over chocolate pudding and 'a good bottle' with her fellow former workers in the world revolution.[10]

While Babette visited her friends in Chevreuse, her sister, Margaret Buber Neumann, was imprisoned in a Soviet labour camp in Karaganda.[11] A few months after her husband, Heinz Neumann, was executed in November 1937, Margaret was also taken from the Hotel Lux by the NKVD and imprisoned, later being sent from a Moscow prison to a camp in Kazakhstan. Her time in this Soviet labour camp would be relatively brief, but only because, in a gesture of almost unfathomable cynicism following the Nazi–Soviet pact, Stalin extradited imprisoned German communists, including Margaret, back into Nazi Germany.

Returned by railcar into the nation she once fled, Margaret was eventually placed in the Nazi concentration camp Ravensbrück, the largest camp for women prisoners. Here, inmates from over thirty nationalities were gathered under a number of categories, including Roma, Jews, common criminals and the 'politicals'. There was, Margaret Buber-Neumman learned after arrival, another former Comintern employee who arrived in the camp before her, though she was already dead by the time of Margaret's imprisonment: Elise 'Sabo' Saborowski. According to historian Ronald Friedmann, who has researched the life of Sabo and her husband, Arthur, extensively, Sabo was on board one of the first transports bringing women to the newly established Ravensbrück in the summer of 1939.[12] Before that, she was imprisoned in Lichtenburg concentration camp. It was from Lichtenburg that she wrote her final letter to Joseph Freeman.

The Avalanche

1

Between the Comintern's open condemnation of his book and the announcement of the Molotov–Ribbentrop Pact, Joseph Freeman experienced political and personal events that would haunt him for the rest of his life. He had, in public pronouncements, defended the Moscow show trials as legitimate even as his book was undergoing its own trials behind the scenes. However, he soon joined the generation of radicals whose gradual disillusionment was catalysed by 1937 and confirmed by the Molotov–Ribbentrop Pact. Although his party membership was not formally revoked until 1939, from 1937 he withdrew from political activity.[1]

In later life he would continually return to a moment from this period in reflections that he composed on his typewriter: his final contact with Sabo in 1938. Since their contact ceased in 1929, Sabo and her husband lived a life devoted to Comintern activity, first in China, then in Brazil. Because she stopped writing to Joseph, it is a period that I have been unable to research in her own words. But the sources that remain reveal that it was a period of living dangerously and one that ended tragically.

A 1934 report by British intelligence on Sabo records her as someone who, during her political work in Shanghai, was always 'dressed well' and inconspicuously. She lived an 'extremely quiet life', the report noted, and spoke English 'with a decidedly foreign accent'.[2] After their Comintern work in China, the couple were posted to Brazil, where they became involved in a communist attempt to organise a military rebellion against the Brazilian government. The attempted rebellion was routed by Brazilian authorities in November 1935 and both Arthur and Sabo were imprisoned. Both were subject to severe torture by Brazilian police. In Arthur's case, the assaults were so extreme that he lost his sanity.[3] Sabo, along with her comrade Olga Benario, today a celebrated figure in Brazilian radical history, was extradited to Nazi Germany. The ship carrying the two women from Brazil arrived in October 1936.[4]

The Gestapo held Sabo in Berlin until May 1938, when she was transferred to the Lichtenburg concentration camp under SS governance. Here, she once came face to face with SS leader Heinrich Himmler himself.[5] Ronald Friedmann notes that in correspondence she maintained with her sister-in-law Minna Ewert, she remained deeply concerned about her husband.[6]

Joseph followed the case of his old friends Sabo and Arthur, eventually finding an address he could use to write to Sabo in Lichtenburg concentration camp. In September 1938, he wrote to her: 'Sabo, darling, How are you dear? I have thought of you often, and of those wonderful days in 1926,' citing the year when both were together in Moscow. Joseph wanted to remind Sabo of something between them: 'I gave you that eternal pass to my heart.' 'That pass is still good,' he noted.[7]

A month later, a reply to Joseph from Sabo arrived. It was written in German on poor-quality paper:

Joe, my dear, old friend, your lines of September 16th came as a great and happy surprise to me and I would have liked to answer you in English, because I can only think English when I think of you and all the dear friends, with whom we had so many happy days. Now you must collect all the knowledge you have of German, in order to be able to read these few lines . . . Your kind lines awakened a lot of very happy memories in me – for days I did not lose the 'remembering smile' from my face. Many years have passed since then, years full of experiences of sad and terrible events. But perhaps one must have experienced that in order to appreciate how rich and manifold life can be. Joe, sometimes I think of the many and long talks, which we had with each other – we, the 'twins'. How happy would I be to continue them, but this desire I take it will remain unfulfilled.[8]

2

In the months after receiving his final letter from Sabo, old friends from the Lux were on Joseph's mind. This was prompted not only by the letter from Lichtenberg concentration camp, but through a reconnection with another old friend from the Lux: Jack Murphy, who was, back in 1926, a British representative to the Comintern. Murphy was already many years out of the party, but he remained a committed socialist. 'What changes have taken place since we were together in Moscow!' he wrote. 'One hardly dares to think of all whom we knew there and what has become of them.' 'However,' Murphy continued, 'they were great days.'[9]

Towards the end of the letter, Murphy told Joseph about an exciting encounter he had in a London bookstore: he ran into May O'Callaghan. 'I hadn't seen her since the Moscow days,' he noted. Murphy described how May 'was full of enthusiasm for the charms of the American people, talked to me of you and lots of the people whom we both know'. 'And so we forgot about selling and buying books,' he wrote, 'and an hour quickly slipped by in all kinds of reminiscences.'[10]

'Dear Jack,' Joseph replied, 'It was good to hear from you after all these years.'[11] He asked Jack to send him May's address. 'If you see her, salute her for me,' continuing with a reflection like Murphy's: 'Those days now seem terribly far off, and it is hard to think of them, but as you say, they were great days.' Joseph concluded on a note of optimism: 'I think greater days are still to come: I can't bring myself to believe that Hitler will have his own way forever.'[12]

3

On 26 July 1939 Sabo died in Ravensbrück concentration camp, while carrying out exhausting physical work as part of a 'punishment'. She was fifty-two years old.[13] When Margaret Buber-Neumann arrived in the concentration camp the next summer, she learned of a notorious 'Block Senior', a fellow prisoner who enforced camp rules and regulations with ferocity. This Senior, she recalled, 'already had the death of one prisoner on her conscience, the Political Sabo, whom she had reported and who had then been sent to the Bunkers, where she died'.[14]

4

When Hitler invaded Poland in September 1939, the situation of the Leonhard family in France, along with their close friends Willi and Babette, suddenly became even more precarious.

When France and Britain declared war on Nazi Germany on 3 September, the advance of German troops towards the French capital became a matter of when, not if. The political pasts of people like Emmy, Willi and Babette placed them in danger. Of course, the Jewish Weil family also had much to fear from a Nazi takeover. But in the months before the Germans swept across the Netherlands, Belgium and Luxembourg towards France in May 1940, there was a window of opportunity to reach some place safer. From their friendship circle, the Leonhard family were the first to leave.

Anticipating the Nazi invasion of the Netherlands, the ITF leadership decided to move their headquarters from Amsterdam to England in early 1939. This would be the destination towards which Emmy, Elisa and Alida began planning. Edo himself was still on the move on the eve of the war and had been in Paris that April, meeting with Münzenberg and attending a meeting to co-ordinate support for refugees fleeing the collapse of the Spanish republic. As his union moved its people and papers from Amsterdam, he found time to ensure the safe evacuation of a bundle of documents of great personal importance: his copies of the *Alpenpost* and *La Guinguette*. Decades of ceaseless activity, as well as some unhealthy habits, now took their toll on Edo. By the end of 1939 his health was deteriorating rapidly and he suffered a stroke. He found himself finally rooted in one place under medical care in Britain. A lieutenant, Jaap Oldenbroek, took over the duties of ITF general secretary.[15]

News of Edo's dire health worried his family in Chevreuse as they planned their departure. Life must have been hectic, as the editorial team of *La Guinguette* changed from their standard broadsheet format to a more manageable, tabloid-size edition. *La Petite Guinguette* went into production at the beginning of 1940. The first issue contained an apology to its readership, written beneath an illustration of '*de redactie*' working busily at their desk. 'The times are difficult,' the editors acknowledged, 'the censorship is severe.' Due to the wartime conditions, future *Guinguette* editions would be more meagre, the message announced. But this was a resourceful publication whose team had committed to a regular print schedule over four years of life as anti-Nazi exiles. Despite the difficult present, the editors declared: 'we keep our hope alive'.

28. *La Petite Guinguette* editors' note. Leonhard Fimmen Papers

The 15 January 1940 edition of *La Petite Guinguette* expressed its gratitude to its one and only subscriber for acknowledging receipt of the previous edition. The fact that this acknowledgement was handwritten by Edo was a good sign for his health, the editors noted. 'We were even happier', Elisa and Alida continued, 'with your letter of 10th January to Mama.' The letter arrived the day before with news that must have come as a relief: Edo believed he could soon arrange for his family's arrival in England. It was 'a great joy', concluded this front-page article in *La Petite Guinguette*.

The Leonhard family's relocation to England was emotional and frantic. The 24 March 1940 'special number' of *La Guinguette* consisted entirely of a comic strip illustrated by Elisa depicting her family's final days in Paris and their journey to safety across the English channel. Elisa's accomplished cartoons reveal how the eve of their departure was filled with goodbyes to both two-legged and four-legged friends. With Babette's help, the girls brought their pet dog and cats to a refuge in Paris. The family chickens were adopted by a nearby farm. After rising early on their final day in Chevreuse, the girls watched as Emmy's personal archive was interred in the garden. Letters to Emmy from a partner absorbed by underground activity now found a suitably subterranean home. Shortly after, Babette fetched the Leonhard women and brought them to Paris by car, where Emmy, Elisa and Alida bid a moving farewell to Selma Weil.

There was no time to stop: a train from Paris Saint-Lazarre would soon depart for the Normandy coast. Here, from the port of Dieppe, the *Newhaven* set sail at four in the morning, carrying British servicemen and women, civilians and this small refugee family. On board the *Newhaven*, the Leonhard girls drank tea and met some 'tommies' in person. In a notable artistic choice, fourteen-year-old Elisa wrote a caption describing the dazzling 'grace and beauty' of the British women in uniform who joined them on the crossing. After several hours of sailing, the first sight of British land revealed that a much-anticipated meeting was finally near. In the last panel of her comic strip, Elisa touchingly depicted the reunion: Emmy, Alida and herself rushing into the open arms of their father, Edo. 'And then hurra, hurra,' the caption read, 'at last we found Papa!'

Et puis hurra, hurra
Enfin on trouve papa!

29. The final panel of *La Guinguette de Londres* comic, March 1940.
Leonhard Fimmen Papers

Some months later, Babette, worried for the family, wrote an anxious letter from Paris to London seeking an update from Emmy and the girls. There was not much to report on her end, Babette noted. She and her husband were busy with *Die Zukunft*, the anti-Nazi and anti-Stalinist paper edited by Münzenberg. They felt tired, sometimes questioning what they were doing. 'But on the other hand,' Babette wrote, recalling a conversation with Emmy, 'I often remember what we talked about in our little café, we have to try to survive the avalanche.'[16] Babette noted she had planted some flowers and held onto the cards describing the plants. She did this, she wrote, so that 'when you return' Elisa and Alida would be able to learn about them. Surely Babette realised such a return was unlikely anytime soon. Only days after Babette wrote this letter in early May 1940, the avalanche crashed over France. The Wehrmacht rapidly moved through the low countries and pushed into French territory.

The family friends in Paris who bid farewell to the Leonhards each had difficult roads ahead of them. Bernard, Selma and Simone Weil eventually made their way to Marseilles, where many hoping to leave France were gathering.[17] Eventually, in 1942, after being reunited with Simone's mathematician brother André, the Weil family sailed from Marseilles, bound for New York.

The journey taken by Willi Münzenberg and Babette Gross, both German nationals at the time of the invasion, was particularly fraught. Edo's illness was now severe, but his friends remained on his mind. He directed a contact with live networks in Paris to 'do something for Babette Gross'.[18] There was little that could be done, it seems. Willi and Babette were interned by the French government in May 1940 and sent to separate camps. Their fate proved Edo's prescience in removing his own family's German citizenship through the marriage to Daniel de Jager. As the German army advanced, Babette and other internee women whose political pasts placed them in danger were permitted to leave their camp. Babette tried in vain to contact her husband before crossing into neutral Portugal. In October 1940 her husband's corpse was found in a forest outside Montaigne. The exact circumstances of his death – whether it was suicide or perhaps murder by Nazi or Stalinist agents – remain a mystery.

5

As part of its preparations for an invasion of Britain, the Gestapo compiled its *Sonderfahndungsliste G.B.*, the 'Special Search List Great Britain'. After the German victory over France in June 1940, twenty thousand copies of the list were produced, only a couple of which survive today. Printed as a pocketbook labelled solely with the word '*Geheim!*' in red lettering, meaning 'Secret!', the list would be carried by SS soldiers accompanying the invasion force. The list marked out more than two thousand people for arrest, all selected due to their likelihood of becoming a thorn in the side of a Nazi occupation in Britain. The names included Jewish refugees, exiled anti-fascists, cultural figures and politicians. Turning to page sixty of their pocketbooks, members of the Gestapo would have found this entry close to the top of the page: 'Fimmen, Edo (Edu), 18.6.81 Amsterdam, Generlsekr d. ITF, London.'[19] Abbreviations following each entry singled out which Nazi security force would take charge of the captive. Edo was marked out for the Gestapo.

As the Gestapo in Berlin singled out Edo for arrest, his health was reliant on him taking an extended rest. After initially joining Edo in Cornwall, the family settled in Wilden, Bedfordshire, a short drive from Crossland Fosse, the red brick lodge that the ITF used as its wartime office. Their home was the Rose Cottage, a quaint house with a thatched roof and garden. For the first time in their childhoods, Elisa and Alida were able to spend extended time with their father. A final incarnation of their paper appeared: the *Gazette de Wilden*. It included a tender image of the family all together: Elisa, Alida and their mother, pushing Edo in his wheelchair, above the caption 'In memory of a lovely little walk'.

30. Illustration by Elisa Leonhard, 1940. Leonhard Fimmen Papers

Another full-page comic strip recounted each of the border crossings undertaken by the Leonhards, from the first covert crossing over the German–Dutch border in 1933 to the family sailing across the English Channel to reunite with Edo in 1940. It also contained an article on the inhabitants of the ITF wartime office, where Emmy assisted and the children sometimes visited.

By the time the *Gazette de Wilden* ceased publication, Elisa and Alida had achieved five years of a regular print schedule. They did not stop because of a lack of energy, but because their newspaper was always created in the hope that it would lose its rationale for existing. When it ceased production, the editorial team and the readership were together at last.

The early months of the war were trying for the ITF's resistance networks still operating in Nazi-controlled territory. Take the ordeal faced by two of Edo's resistance collaborators, brothers Kurt and Werner Lehmann. As Germans, they were interned in France after the outbreak of the war. Edo secured their release, but eventually they ended up captives of the Vichy government, which handed them over to the Gestapo. Werner Lehmann died as a prisoner in the Gestapo's infamous Berlin headquarters. In 1945 his brother Kurt was eventually found close to death by American soldiers after being marched out of Dachau concentration camp.[20]

As the ITF's lines of communication with the underground went dark and reports brought news of the terrifying successes of the German Army in the war's early phase, Edo began to despair, further imperilling his own health. Emmy was caring for a partner who was both physically and psychologically shattered. An early 1941 report an English doctor sent to Emmy makes this clear. Edo, the doctor recommended, should carry out 'movements of the fingers and toes' several times a day, revealing just how incapacitated this once border-hopping activist had become. 'Furthermore,' the doctor continued, 'I think he ought to occupy his mind with superficial interests' like card games and 'trashy detective novels'. He needed to 'get away from the big issues of life,' the doctor advised while acknowledging that this will 'be very hard for him, because of that ingrained sense of power around which his whole life has been built'.[21] With the British able to repel Germany's attempted invasion, Britain remained secure and the Gestapo were unable to cross Edo off their list. However, by the end of 1941, Edo was facing into an English winter under wartime conditions of rationing.

The family decided to move Edo to Mexico, where he could find a warmer climate and more plentiful supplies while retaining a support network of European leftists in exile. In a letter to a German resistance leader, Emmy wrote of how Edo insisted 'despite the advice of his doctors, to make a last visit to the ITF offices to say good-bye to his former collaborators'.[22] In November 1941, travelling on board the SS *Port Fairy*, Edo, Emmy, Elisa and Alida sailed from England to Mexico, stopping off at the US along the way. It was the first and only time in so many border crossings that the family relocated together.

6

As Edo, Emmy and the two children prepared to leave England for Mexico, Nellie, her husband Hugo, twelve-year-old Joyce and May were living together in the neighbouring county of Hertfordshire. Here, they would be safer from the threat of Luftwaffe bombing raids. It is from this period in Joyce's life that we find the first documents which allow this daughter of Nellie Cohen and Liam O'Flaherty to address the historical record in her own voice.

Writing to Ruth Kennell around August 1941, Joyce talked about life as an evacuee away from London with her family. She told Ruth about making model airplanes in school. She also recited some sporting achievements, like her ability to beat her stepfather Hugo in a game of ping-pong and lift stones from the bottom of a pool. The letter featured some drawings of a stick figure with a dog.[23] While having their own charm, the drawings were nothing on what that other child who May helped bring into the world, Elisa Leonhard, was capable of at the same age.

The reason Ruth received a letter from a twelve-year-old she had only ever met once was that, after a hiatus, May began writing again to her old friend from the Lux. 'The best way to celebrate Christmas' of 1941, May wrote in one letter, was to write to Ruth. Earlier that month, the US entered the war following the Japanese attack on Pearl Harbour. May wanted to know how this had had an impact Ruth and family. 'Anyhow,' she continued, 'we are all in a lovely mess thanks to the ravings of a couple of madmen': Hitler and Mussolini.

In an earlier letter, Ruth had shared news of old friends who were in the US. 'I was sorry to hear about Joe,' May responded, likely referring to Joseph's fall from grace within the communist party. 'Still, I have always a warm corner for him,' she noted, before revealing just how much her politics had mellowed. May advised Ruth not to let differences of opinion separate her from friends. 'Everyone has a right to think for himself,' May wrote, 'if we all thought the same how dull it would be!!' To May's surprise, Ruth also shared the news that Liam O'Flaherty was in the US. 'Your news that Liam was over there was a surprise,' she replied:

> The last I had heard was that he had gone to his old home. He is a strange lad full of good intentions and always doing things he is sorry for after. It is a strain of cussedness which many of us share. J[oyce] knows nothing about him: but has inherited a good bit of his brain and fractiousness – very musical and good at ALL subjects. No one believes she is not quite 13, her size and mentality make you think she is well in her teens. She still refuses to wear dresses!!!

May also referred to the other major development in the conflict that took place earlier that year. In June Hitler launched Operation Barbarossa, his invasion of the Soviet Union. Stalin's pact with Hitler betrayed, the USSR mobilised to defeat Nazism, inaugurating a heroic period that would see millions from the many Soviet nationalities make enormous sacrifices. The Soviet contribution proved pivotal in the ultimate liberation of Europe.

Before Hitler moved east, however, the international communist movement, still led by the purged husk of the Comintern, was compelled to describe the war between fascism and democracy as an inter-imperialist conflict. Suddenly on 22 June 1941, and to the relief of many sincere anti-fascists within the communist movement, the Allied fight against the Axis became a people's war. In the now pro-Soviet atmosphere of the wartime alliance, May told Ruth that she expected there may be a sales revival in some children's stories set in the USSR that Ruth had written, including one about a young boy in Moscow, *Vanya of the Streets*.[24]

Elsewhere in the letter, May updated Ruth on her friend Emmy, revealing that, although Emmy was based nearby until recently, care for Edo had meant the two friends could not visit one another:

You remember Leonhard of M[oscow] days. Well she was here for over a year and as Edo F came from Holland with the Bureau she got tucked away in the country where I could see nothing of her – he was in a very bad state and only sun and rest were said to be the cure – a few months ago they all went to Mexico and got there quite safely – I had a cable with greetings. I rather envy her the new country as I should love to see Mexico – all the writers and poets I have met have been so enthusiastic about it. But this eternal nursing seems to be wearing poor L out. The two girls are very nice. I lent them your *Vanya* to read, which I believe they liked.

Bringing the letter to a conclusion, May could not resist one of her jibes. 'You ask how things are with the family,' May wrote, 'well, Nellie does not look as though she were on short rations!!!' Tying up, she sent her best wishes for 1942 to Ruth 'and old friends'.[25]

For May, Nellie, Joyce and Hugo, their experience of the war would be typical of any other middle-class British family residing in a rural village. The only real distinction was that, as leftists, they attended events promoting the wartime alliance with the USSR and paid particularly keen attention to the progress of the Red Army.

Referencing plans to play her part in the war effort, May told Ruth how she would 'love to knit' something for the soldiers but did not want to make the Red Army 'suffer' from her 'incapacity'.[26] Joyce's few letters to Ruth depict a precocious teenager who was already achieving musically and was clued in to her parents' political discussions. In one letter from 1945, Joyce told Ruth that her mother found their Hertfordshire village 'so backward politically' that Nellie wanted to leave. 'But I consider that as somebody has got to begin livening the place up some day, why shouldn't it be us?' Joyce wrote.[27]

May also updated Ruth on Joyce's progress, describing her as a 'music mad' and tenacious young woman in her letters. Alongside keeping the channels of communication with Ruth in the US open, May remained in contact with Emmy in Mexico throughout the war, learning of her continued care for Edo and the lives of their two daughters.

7

Upon arriving in Mexico, Emmy, Edo and the two children settled in the city of Cuernavaca, already home to leftist refugees, many of them veterans of the Spanish Civil War. Life remained hectic for Emmy, who nursed Edo and continued political work. She wrote regular reports to ITF headquarters in England on Edo's health and sent requests for financial assistance. In Mexico, Emmy befriended Matilde de la Torre, a once-prominent figure in the Spanish Republican courts, and reconnected with old comrades from the struggle in Europe, including Babette Gross, who had made it safely to Mexico from Portugal, and the Russo-French revolutionary Victor Serge.

In early 1942 Edo's condition was worsening. Not only was he no longer able to work, but he was apathetic about life and requested to spend his days in a darkened room. Emmy found him 'continually obsessed by hallucinations' and sometimes in a 'frenzy of despair', requesting Emmy to take his life and occasionally attempting to do so himself. Emmy also sensed a tie between her partner's condition and the state of the front. Writing to an ITF comrade, Emmy noted how every time there was an improvement in his health, 'all efforts are spoiled again' by world events.[28] Watching their mother care for their desperate and debilitated father surely impacted young Elisa and Alida.

31. Alida, Elisa and Edo with pets and a member of household staff (name unknown), Cuernavaca, 1942. Leonhard Fimmen Papers

However, Edo began to improve just as the tide turned in the war throughout the year. Two battles in El Alamein resulted in a German defeat at the hands of the British, setting the course of the North African campaign towards an Allied victory. In November, the Soviet counter-offensive at the Battle of Stalingrad began, ultimately resulting in an encirclement of the enemy that inaugurated the start of the Red Army's westward push back against Axis forces.

Emmy observed that Edo learned to laugh again. He even began to dictate messages on topics of interest and returned to corresponding with comrades. However, he clearly sensed he was nearing his end. Amid caring for Edo, Emmy also took control of some of the political work he was too unwell to carry out alone. Writing back to the ITF headquarters in Britain, Emmy noted she was actively helping with Edo's rescue work.[29] This involved securing onward travel to Mexico for anti-fascists trapped in Europe and North Africa. She was also attempting to learn news of Edo's son from his marriage, Edo Steffan, a pilot with Allied forces flying missions against the Japanese in Indonesia. In September 1942 she received bad news. 'I am really at a loss, how to tell Fimmen of this,' she wrote to one of Edo's comrades. Edo 'loved his son', she continued. She worried how the news of his son's death in combat would impact her partner, given his own perilous condition.[30]

Some sources from Edo's final months find him in a reflective mood. In August he dictated a kind of testament surmising the course of his activist life. He entrusted the task of taking it down to his youngest daughter, Alida. Edo wanted to acknowledge to his comrades that he made many mistakes. These mistakes, he felt 'load me with a heavy responsibility for the defeat of European trade unions'. Above all, Edo felt, he had hesitated: 'Where I dealt criticism, I ought to have dealt blows, and where I spoke, I ought to have shouted.' Still, there was a reason for optimism. 'I am certain', he continued, 'that the catastrophe through which we are passing will mould better men than we were, a generation, feeling with Danton that the one thing necessary to lead men into the promised land is courage, courage, and courage again.'[31]

Edo's assessment reflected a grandiose belief that the future of Europe once lay on his shoulders. But could one person really have held such a responsibility? To consider the lives he helped save would have been a more reasonable measure of heroism. In this respect, Edo could count many people: from underground resisters like the ISK activist Otto Pfister to the unknowable number of lives spared by ITF sabotage operations against Nazi German war machinery.[32] Among the rescued, Edo could also count the fourteen-year-old girl to whom he dictated his note of both self-criticism and hope. Edo did not save European trade unionism. But he helped save Emmy and their two girls.

On 14 December 1942, despite prior improvements in his condition, Edo suffered a fatal stroke. He was sixty-two years old. Edo's death was international news but, of course, for Emmy, Elisa and Alida it was a personal tragedy first and foremost. In a letter to Sonia Doniach, the Russian-born wife of a prominent figure from Edo's resistance network, Emmy wrote that Edo 'passed without any pain or suffering, peacefully and quite unexpected for himself and everybody'. She continued: 'Keep smiling, we shall all meet again in better times, and keep the flag flying, as Edo should have wished us to.'[33] 'We embrace you heartily, all three of us,' Emmy signed off.

Tributes and letters of condolences arrived, sent by trade unionists and resistance fighters from their places of exile. Hans Jahn, one of Edo's most courageous operatives in the German resistance – the activist who once arranged rail sabotage under the cover of wine sales – wrote one of the few letters to specifically thank Emmy for caring for Edo. Jahn declared that 'the father' of the resisters 'has closed his eyes for ever'. 'Thank you for what you did for Edo,' he noted. 'You gave it for us too.' 'We suffer with you, but we are also proud that we were allowed to work and fight with Edo in a time that will go down in history as a heroic time,' Jahn wrote.[34] Unable to attend Edo's grand funeral in Mexico, comrades in England arranged a memorial service in a Dutch church on Bourdon Street, London. A tenor sang a Dutch socialist song, accompanied by an organ. Some Polish sailors joined together in a choir to sing anthems of their own struggle.

8

Before the war ended, the three Leonhard women experienced another tragedy, one that particularly upset Elisa. In August 1943, Simone Weil died in London after suffering cardiac failure. In a fatal meeting of ideals and physical reality, Simone worsened an existing illness by insisting her own food intake match the constrained rations of those in occupied France.[35] A year earlier she had crossed from New York to London, where she worked with the French resistance committees in exile and composed one of her most influential essays, *The Need for Roots*. When she died, she was thirty-four years old. Many years later, Elisa recalled weeping 'desperately' upon learning the news. She asked herself why 'had Simone allowed herself to die in that way?' Elisa, who was eighteen when Simone died, remembered crying 'above all in sorrow that I could not hold further conversations with her'.[36]

Emmy, despite all she experienced and the loss of so many comrades, remained resilient. It was a striking enough characteristic of hers that Victor Serge, her fellow revolutionary exile in Mexico, recorded it in his notebooks. In an entry for February 1943, a couple of months after Edo's death, Serge described encountering Emmy 'face peaceful beneath white hair, the gaze and speech of an old, enthusiastic militant thinking ceaselessly of her return to a Europe in revolution'.[37]

The Axis forces never reversed the turning point of 1942. The next year witnessed the Red Army gradually moving across Europe on the offensive, while a second European front was opened in the summer of 1944 with the D-Day landings. In late January 1945, on the date now marked as Holocaust Memorial Day, Soviet soldiers liberated Auschwitz concentration camp. Just over three months later, Adolf Hitler took his own life as the Red Army closed in on Berlin. Shortly after Hitler's suicide, Germany surrendered unconditionally.

Europe, much of it lying in ruins, with entire communities massacred and survivors emerging from camps, was about to begin its reconstruction. The continent was finally on the other side of an unprecedented period of mass violence. Some exiles could finally return.

In late October 1945 Emmy, Elisa and Alida crossed the Mexican border into the US. After around a fortnight in the US, they sailed from Philadelphia to Southampton. After some months in England, the trio travelled to Switzerland. In May 1946 the ITF held its first post-war conference in Zurich. Representing Mexico, Emmy was the only female delegate.[38] Around this time, the family moved into a home in Tannay, a town outside Geneva.

Since leaving Berlin for Moscow in 1926, Emmy had been on the move, compelled by personal and political transformations to change location every few years. Upon the family's arrival in Switzerland, Emmy was fifty-five years old. Her children needed to find their own careers, Elisa being twenty-one and Alida eighteen. Europe was finally entering a period of sustained peace. It was time to settle in one place. But Emmy did not believe it was time to stop dreaming of a revolution. Nor did she want to let friendships from her interwar journey deteriorate, especially her intimate connection with May.

A Jeter

1

A cursory online search for the name Joyce Rathbone told me two things: she died in December 2010 and she was a beloved music teacher. It was November 2016, the beginning of my journey into the life of May O'Callaghan, when I first began searching for information on Joyce. I was sitting at my desk in Oxford, only a few months into my doctoral studies. My assumption – which proved to be correct – was that Joyce would have inherited her mother's papers and anything that remained from May's archive.

I opened some tabs and read different memories from Joyce's piano students. One of her old pupils could perhaps help me trace what became of her archive, I figured. I found the personal website of Armand D'Angour, a classical scholar interested in ancient music. On his site, Armand noted 'I was taught the piano from the age of 5 by Joyce Rathbone.' I turned to the 'Contact Me' tab. *Are you serious*, I thought, as I read the contact details. Armand and I shared the same tail end of our email addresses. He was the dean of my college.

After introducing myself, I typed: 'I hope you don't mind me contacting you out of the blue but I wanted to ask you about the pianist Joyce Rathbone.' 'No doubt this enquiry seems oddly specific,' I noted, before explaining that I was researching Irish radicalism. 'You may know that Joyce's father was the Irish writer Liam O'Flaherty,' I explained.

Armand soon replied, bemused and astounded. A couple of days later, I made my way to his office, a two-minute walk from my room. I shared all I knew about Joyce's life; how her parents met through an Irish Comintern translator, details of her first years in New York and the tragic fate of her aunt Rose. Armand was interested to learn new details about a woman who was an important part of his early life. He did not know who had inherited Joyce's papers, but he suggested some people to follow up with.

Joyce had no direct descendants, I learned, but was close to her god-daughter Pippa Harris. In Joyce's will, Pippa was the sole heir. A prominent figure in the world of film and television, Pippa was easy to trace. Emailing her production company, I began to fear my request might seem strange. I wondered how I would feel if a stranger emailed me claiming they knew the precise details of a loved one's early life and wanted to root around my attic to learn more.

Fortunately, Pippa considered my request to get in touch earnest rather than unhinged. She replied that she was not sure if she could be of assistance, having never heard the name May O'Callaghan, but she was happy to chat over the phone. After talking, we planned to meet. In a further moment of good fortune, it turned out she was only a short bus ride away from Oxford.

Ciara and I met Pippa for a coffee in a Cotswolds village close to where she lived. Since we last talked over the phone, Pippa had done some initial searching among Joyce's papers. She handed me a letter: it was from the Irish playwright Sean O'Casey to May. *There must be more*, I thought.

Pippa graciously invited us to her house so that I could investigate further. Already, it seemed miraculous that *anything* had survived. People need space for themselves and cannot be expected to hold onto the debris of all the lives which came before them, especially when those lives have rarely featured in historical research.

We arrived at Pippa's beautiful Cotswold home. Apologising, Pippa told me that my time was limited because she needed to prepare for a party. She set out some boxes and left me to it. Over the course of an hour, I made some exciting finds, including communist party membership cards, Nellie and Hugo's wedding certificate and letters to Joyce. Turning to the bookshelf, I noticed a line of Liam O'Flaherty first editions, many of them signed and inscribed both to May and to Joyce.

But more fascinating to me were letters that revealed Joyce's intimate connection with another family whose history I was tracing. By this point, I already knew the broad contours of Emmy Leonhard's life and her long friendship with May. I was intrigued to find, among Pippa's material, postcards that Emmy sent to Joyce in the 1960s, Emmy's moving letter to Nellie, which she sent after May's death, and Elisa's list of eighteen 'house rules' for visitors to Tannay, the Swiss town where Emmy and her daughters lived after the war. I particularly enjoyed rule fourteen: 'Mama is usually a model of kindly interest and tolerance. Beware of jumping to conclusions about the sanity of her political views. Most of the time they prove to be right.'

I took as many photographs as I could, fascinated by the deep connection between the two families. However, Pippa's party was approaching, and she needed to drop me to the bus stop. I asked if there was further material, perhaps enough to merit a return visit? There was another box of letters, Pippa told me. She knew nothing about the woman who had sent them to Joyce but held onto the documents because she found them moving: they were love letters. The author of the letters, Pippa told me, was a woman called Elsa. *Wait*, I suddenly thought, before asking, 'Do you mean Elisa?' Pippa thought I was right. But it was now time to go. As we travelled to where I would catch my bus to Oxford, I told Pippa about my discoveries and asked if I could return to view the box of love letters.

Soon, I was back in Pippa's home, this time accompanied both by Ciara and my supervisor Senia Paseta, who was by now also wrapped up in May's story. The box of letters was awaiting me in the attic. As I headed upstairs, I tried to caution myself against disappointment. Perhaps these were letters from a woman called Elsa, whom I knew nothing about. It seemed too remarkable to be true: that Joyce and Elisa, two children of the revolution, both intimately connected with May, would one day meet and fall in love.

Searching the attic using my phone as a torch, I looked for the container with the letters from Elsa, Elisa, or perhaps someone else entirely. I found it and opened the lid with a satisfying pop, my heart now beginning to beat faster. There were several bulging blue folders stacked up in the box. *There must be at least a thousand letters in here*, I thought.

The light illuminated the white paper of one letter at the top of a bundle and I began to scan through it. Addressed to Joyce, it opened with declarations of love, continued with descriptions of everyday life, and then concluded with more declarations of love. I read the signature: 'Elisa de Jager'. It was her: Elisa Leonhard, born in the Kremlin hospital in 1925, who became Elisa de Jager in 1939 through her mother's marriage.

If, at that very moment, I descended from the attic and entered an MRI machine, perhaps a team of scientists could have viewed a neural explosion taking place inside my head. Imagery and ideas rapidly surged to the forefront of my mind as I attempted to process the staggering set of historical contingencies required to make this discovery – and this relationship – explainable. At the heart of everything was May O'Callaghan and her life in the Hotel Lux. It was May who paid for the taxi to bring Emmy from the Lux to the Kremlin to give birth to Elisa. It was May who remained close to Emmy in the decades that followed, even as their nominal communist allegiances diverged sharply. It was May who left behind her life in the Lux and brought Nellie to New York to help her navigate her pregnancy. In fact, it was May who was partly respons-ible for Nellie becoming pregnant in the first place, having introduced her to Liam.

Each of these personal encounters were produced by world-shaking events; the suffrage struggle, the Irish Revolution, the Russian Revolution. It must have been May, I thought, who intro-duced Elisa to Joyce on the other side of the Second World War. But what came next was something May surely did not predict. Not only did Joyce and Elisa meet, but they came to understand that they shared desires, both political and personal, that were of vital importance to their self-understanding. Bound together by this, they fell in love.

After descending from the attic with the box and regaining lucidity after processing a mental montage of the twentieth century,

I continued to read through the letters. There were far too many to get through in a single evening: Pippa, surely sensing my excitement, let me take the box home.

Back in Oxford, I made an important discovery. In one letter from 1970, Elisa wrote to Joyce about a new addition to her family: a nephew named Pierre. He was the son of her sister Alida and a Swedish doctor Alida met while working in Biafra. I did the math. He would be in his forties. In all likelihood, Pierre was still alive.

The possibility raised another prospect: maybe the other side of these love letters survived in Pierre's possession? That would be extraordinary. My journey into the life of an obscure Irish revolutionary would have led me towards uncovering what was possibly one of the best-documented romances between two women in mid-twentieth century European history. I *needed* to learn what became of the other side of the letters.

Only a few weeks passed between my email to Armand and my meeting with Pippa. I figured I could pull off something similar in my search for Pierre. Sure, I was more accustomed to Irish-Jewish family histories than Dutch-German-Swedish-Swiss genealogy, but how hard could it be?

Four years passed between the first time I learned about Pierre and our first meeting. By that time, I learned he was devoted to at least one family tradition: name changes.

2

As the months passed and trails went cold, a more sensible part of me insisted that I needed to focus more on my PhD than hunting out a man who may well have little interest in the reasons I was looking for him. My PhD topic was Irish radical women. Emmy's life was a tangent, albeit one I found increasingly fascinating.

Various methods of finding Pierre proved ineffective. My Facebook inbox was filled with people who shared his name, all of whom I cold-messaged with the exact same note: are you the grandson of Emmy Leonhard and Edo Fimmen? One Pierre sent me his own genealogy. Thanks, I replied, without mentioning that if he didn't descend from revolutionaries, then I wasn't interested. Most Pierres simply ignored me.

Another tactic I tried was a kind of family history lure. People often search for their ancestors online, I reasoned, so I typed up a short blog post about Pierre's family. I used all the various permutations of the family name to try and search-engine-optimise the post for any curious descendants.

Months later, meeting Senia in a café, my laptop open, showing her some sources I had found, I noticed an email come in with the subject line 'Information about Alida de Jager'. The email was sent by René, a man living near Frankfurt whose father knew both Emmy and her daughter Alida. René's father, Erwin Dumont, was a Comintern courier in the 1920s. Erwin looked up to Emmy as a 'political mother' and, like her, had sided with the opposition. At one point, Emmy gave Erwin a picture of her daughters torn in half. Emmy kept the other half. She told Erwin that they could use the torn photograph as 'a silent sign of danger' while carrying out political work.

32. Erwin Dumont's torn photograph of Alida (left) and Elisa (right).
Courtesy of René Dumont

Erwin survived the war, for a time coerced to serve in a German penal battalion and then held as a prisoner of war in the US. After returning to Europe, Emmy helped Erwin evade Soviet military police to reach a reception camp for anti-fascists in Switzerland. This camp was led by Alida, barely twenty years old but already committed to helping refugees. René sent me a picture of his father, his mother and Alida together in the camp. I replied to tell him how happy I was to hear from him and asked if he knew descendants of the family. Unfortunately, he did not know Pierre but he offered to help me with my search.

For two years, I kept searching, periodically updating René with discoveries about Emmy. But I never had anything to share about Pierre. Every approach was a dead end. After handing in my thesis, I figured I would try again. There were a few older investigative threads that I felt could be worth reviving. One involved a journalist, Isabella Fischli. She had written a biography of Ruth Dreifuss, the first woman president of Switzerland. In the acknowledgements, she thanked Pierre's mother, Alida, for information.

I had first reached out to Isabella around the time of my mass-bothering of the Facebook Pierres. My message to her went unread, likely filed away by the platform as junk mail. In late 2019 I revived the message thread, repeating my request for information. This time, she replied.

That December, Ciara and I were on holiday in Paris. One of the places I wanted to visit was the bookshop Shakespeare & Company, a regular hang-out for the literary left of the interwar period. As I browsed inside, I noticed a mirror covered in messages from visitors. On a Post-it note I wrote: 'Ivy Litvinov visited here after attending an orgy in 1920s Berlin' and stuck it on. I was emerging from the store, wondering to myself if my chronology were wrong and the orgy had occurred *before* the Paris visit, when I felt my phone vibrate. It was Isabella Fischli. She wanted to know more about my reasons for getting in touch. Quickly, I sent more details. Soon afterwards, she put me in touch with the first female president of Switzerland.

3

Ruth Dreifuss told me she had not spoken to Alida's son for some years, but the last time she had been in touch with him, he was living in Camariñas, a Galician fishing village. She did not have a contact for him, but she did share a detail that revealed why my previous searches never went anywhere. The man I thought was named Pierre was now known as Pedro. Armed with his actual name and a recent location, I felt as though I was getting closer. Around 5 pm on 18 January 2020, I posted on social media: 'I realise this is an absurdly specific research request, but do I know anyone on here with a connection to the Spanish town of Camariñas? The grandson of someone I research was recently resident there, so I am looking to make contact with someone local to help trace him.'

Within an hour, I began receiving offers of assistance – along with one message from a Galician nationalist pointing out that Camariñas was *not* a 'Spanish town'. Mario, a native of the area, contacted a local socialist politician on my behalf. I sent Mario some more information and waited anxiously. Four days later, I was sitting in a British Library reading room when I received a notification. It was a message from Mario: 'Found him!'

Using the contact information Mario had gathered, I sent Pedro a message. After that, I stood up and left the reading room. I was too excited to think of anything else. As I made my way home, an email from Pedro landed in my inbox. We arranged a call for that evening.

We said our initial hellos in the halting awkwardness common to video calls, but soon found a rhythm. I asked questions and Pedro did his best to recall the family history he imbibed from his mother. The first thing he asked was to describe how I traced him. 'This does come as a surprise,' he noted, stating that he had little interest in a digital presence. 'You were hard to find,' I agreed. I outlined it all; the mention of his name in Elisa's letters, the Facebook messages, the blog post, the assistance I received from a former Swiss president and the minor manhunt arranged on my behalf by members of the Galician left.

In our first call, we talked for two and a half hours. I was delighted to have finally met a member of the Kaemmerer/Leonhard/Fimmen/de Jager family and energised by an idea that our contact was the latest in a series of connections that began with an Irishwoman easing her heavily pregnant comrade into a Moscow cab. Pedro, who was six when Emmy died, remembered his grandmother. He sent me a photograph of a young boy with a mop of blond hair and an older lady looking affectionately towards him. It was Emmy and Pedro.

Pedro was particularly gratified that I was more interested in the life of his grandmother, who had barely bothered a footnote, than his much better-studied grandfather. There were plenty of documents, he told me, far too many to scan and send. He invited me to his home to look through everything. I threw out a date: how about April? Pedro said that would work. So it was decided: I would fly to Spain in April 2020.

4

Like many plans for 2020, this one fell through. More than a year later, with the pandemic easing but not over, I finally undertook my eagerly awaited trip to Galicia in August 2021. Pedro picked me up at the airport. In person, I could more clearly see the resemblance to a young Edo that I first noticed in our video calls. He dropped me off in Santiago, where I spent some time sight-seeing, and then drove me to Camariñas. We passed by a lighthouse, one of the local landmarks, and soon pulled up to his house. I took in the view: just in front of Pedro's home was a peaceful beach. On breaks, I would sometimes walk down to where the waves broke, take off my footwear and let my feet sink into the sand. *You wouldn't get this in a state archive*, I thought.

Upon my arrival I was greeted with a table of documents ready for me to look through. Soon, I learned that the garden shed I noticed as we first approached the house was also filled with documents. On the first night, we talked outside in the open air while sharing some local food and some whiskey I brought with me from Ireland. The lamp of the lighthouse illuminated the shape of the hillsides surrounding us and created silver steaks on the waves crashing nearby.

With increasing enthusiasm, I outlined the broad historical contours of the Comintern that first night. At one point I constructed a diagram connecting everyone that his grandmother knew in the Hotel Lux. Pedro broadly knew about his family's revolutionary past but had never researched it in detail. He was interested to learn more.

The next morning, I began to make my way through the documents. After years of lying mainly undisturbed, all the materials had acquired a distinctive stench and I began to feel unwell from all the dust I was inhaling. But the thrill of discovery kept me working.

The chaotic arrangement of the documents was humbling. One box contained handwritten letters from Simone Weil, some kind of charger and multiple photographs of a hog. Another contained political writings that were almost a century old and a manual for a Star Wars toy. The only items organised with any kind of coherence were the issues of the *Alpenpost* and *La Guinguette*.

As the days went by, Pedro began reading the documents too. At one point, I was standing at his kitchen table when he asked me a question about a letter that particularly struck him. It was a letter Edo drafted to his comrade Jawaharlal Nehru in 1940. Holding up the letter on the other side of the room, Pedro asked: 'Maurice, where has this idealism gone?' It was a good question.

In our conversations, I told Pedro that I was particularly determined to find out if the other half of Joyce and Elisa's love letters survived among the material in his house. But I did not want him to feel as though I would leave disappointed if I did not find them. This was true: the surviving issues of Elisa and Alida's newspaper alone vindicated my years of searching for Pedro. I told him that if the love letters did not survive, that was understandable. Elisa pre-deceased Alida by many years, so Alida inherited her older sister's material, including, I presumed, Elisa's letters from Joyce. It was not unknown for family members to destroy intimate documents after someone's death. When I mentioned this, I noticed Pedro was perturbed by this idea. He was proud of the spirit of tolerance his mother had modelled for him growing up. The image I conjured of Alida dumping her beloved sister's love letters was not the mother he knew.

As the date of my return flight approached, there was still no sign of the letters. On one of the final days, I asked Pedro to translate something. A lot of the documents I was photographing were bundled together in envelopes with the French phrase '*A jeter*' written across them by Alida. I asked: what does it mean? 'It means "to throw away",' he told me. More than a decade after his mother's death, he had never gotten around to it. *God bless rebellious sons*, I thought.

We rooted through increasingly fruitless bags of material; bin bags filled with decades of Christmas cards and postcards sent to Alida. To my shock and Pedro's laughter, I discovered a mouse in one bag from the shed. You wouldn't get this in a state archive, I conceded. By now I was content with what we discovered – rodents excluded – and was ready to declare the search period over.

I needed to leave aside a couple of days to photograph everything I thought worthwhile documenting. On my first day of photographing, the mist was catching on the hills surrounding Pedro's home, dulling the late-August sun. I was inside with my phone hovering over some letters written by Edo when Pedro came into the kitchen with a bulging black bin bag in his hand. 'Maurice, I found Joyce's letters to Elisa,' he said, pulling out a thick folder and placing it on the table. I opened it and read the sign-off from a letter: 'love, Joyce.' He had found them. I let out an involuntary 'Oh my God!' Pedro smiled and looked at me, vindicated. 'I knew my mother would never have thrown these away,' he said. I, too, was delighted to be proven wrong.

Leaving Galicia, I realised how so much of the story that I wanted to tell – the book you are now reading – relied on sources whose survival was determined by bonds of affection. The newspaper, the love letters and all the other documents I found in the Cotswolds and Galicia only survived because people cared enough to hold onto them. I thought again of how Pippa told me she kept Elisa's letters because they moved her and how Pedro was determined to find Joyce's letters to prove his mother's acceptance of her sister. Unlike all the sources I encountered in Moscow or the US, these documents did not make it through the decades under the care of professional archivists. They were preserved by the intimate relationships connecting one generation with those who came after.

PART IV

The Living Commune

1940s–1970s

The Lobby

33. Joseph Freeman with his second wife, Charmion von Wiegand, late 1930s. Hoover Institution Library and Archive, Joseph Freeman Papers, Envelope K

1

It seems as if Joseph Freeman's life completed a new narrative arc every decade. After leaving the communist party in 1939, he found purpose in supporting the US war effort against Nazi Germany. He also reconnected with an important figure from his past. After the Soviets joined the Allies, Maxim Litvinov was appointed ambassador to the US. Ivy travelled to America with her husband and spent time with Joseph and his wife, Charmion, in New York. It was Ivy, in fact, who, in 1931, first told Charmion about 'Joe', her handsome writer friend in New York, when Charmion was then a journalist based in Moscow.[1]

No longer a politician, Joseph returned to the path he left behind after Moscow: he wrote poetry. Still living in the same Murray Hill apartment and writing in a room with a window overlooking the East River, he continued to redraft his life story and compose reams of verse. In his memoirs, poems and fiction, he reflected continually on the world revolution and his part within it. In 1948 he finally received one of those moments of deep catharsis he craved. In March that year, Luise 'Lou' Geissler, the woman who left Joseph in Moscow for M. N. Roy, the same woman who was the connecting link between him and Sabo, unexpectedly reached out to him on a visit to the city. They agreed to meet in his apartment.

When Joseph met Luise in New York, their first meeting since Moscow, he felt that 'the world stopped' and he became, for a moment, caught in an 'immense hiatus of time'. They talked with one another about the world they now lived in and how radically different it was from world where they met. They talked about all the victims of Stalinism and Nazism they once knew intimately: Sergei Dinamov, Heinz Nuemann, Willi Münzenberg and many others. They talked at length about Sabo, of what a wonderful friend she was and about the tragic circumstances of her final days.

Joseph took the opportunity to apologise to Luise for his aggrieved portrayal of her in his book. In the diary-like typescript in which he recorded their encounter, he remembered telling Luise that his 'real education' only came in the wake of his break with the party. 'You remember how naive and stupid I was when you knew me,' he told her. According to Joseph, Luise 'nodded gravely' in response.[2]

Luise needed to leave for a meeting elsewhere. Joseph decided to walk with her. As they strolled together in the sunlight of a spring day, Joseph remembered Luise telling him how all that really counted was friendship. 'Holding her by the arm as I used to do twenty-one years ago, I felt glad she had said that,' Joseph recalled.

After Luise returned to Europe, Joseph wrote her a letter, describing how he found it 'hard to believe' their reconnection 'wasn't all a dream'. 'But it must have been real, for everything comes back vividly,' he continued, 'and I consider myself fortunate to have seen you again after so many years, and to have had an opportunity to understand a lot of things better.'[3]

2

The receptionist clearly knew his residents well because he could tell I was an outsider from the moment I stepped through the door. I stumbled into the opening lines of the introduction I had rehearsed on my journey down from Central Park. I was in New York, on my way to a research trip in Washington DC, and I had decided to scratch off another location on the list of addresses from my research. 'I'm writing a book that features someone who lived in this building, could I have a look around the lobby?' I said, attempting to convey a friendly tone.

My request sounded more reasonable inside my head than when I uttered it to the silent, confused man standing at the reception desk. I introduced myself: 'I am an Irish historian, my name is Maurice Casey.' If anything, my lines only baffled him more. He remained silent. I held onto the business card I was holding in my right coat pocket, sensing he was uninterested.

In my mind, I imagined the scenario playing out differently: a jovial New York doorman, fascinated by this Irish historian with an interest in the life of someone who once lived in the building, would welcome me in and listen to my tale about the charismatic Ukrainian Jewish communist who lived out his last decades in an apartment above our heads. I let myself daydream about a personal tour of the building.

But the doorman's facial expression revealed he was more interested in closing doors on the uninvited than opening them. His job, I realised, was not to entertain over-eager academics. After another moment of silent contemplation, he nodded towards the lobby. I understood: he was letting me in to see it. 'Thanks,' I said as I walked by. He returned to his task of sorting through the residents' mail.

Standing in the lobby, I took in the mid-century decor and maroon-painted walls. It was here, on the fifteenth floor of this building in Manhattan, that the final act of Joseph Freeman's life played out. Somewhere in an apartment above me, he sat at his typewriter and, over decades, composed reflections on the people and experiences he encountered during the eight months he spent in Moscow from 1926 to 1927. It was to this address that letters and memories of his old friends from Moscow arrived. And it must have been precisely here, in this lobby, that Joseph greeted Luise, the great love of his time in the Hotel Lux, after years of separation. *Maybe these postboxes or the elevator doors provided a backdrop to that moment*, I thought to myself. But the doorman was now looking towards me, willing me to leave. I thanked him and stepped back out into the balmy air of a warm autumnal day in Manhattan.

During the time I spent amid the debris of his life, I came to think of Joseph, for all his compromised politics and self-seriousness, with some affection. Historians are often reluctant to admit this for fear of it disrupting our 'objectivity', but it is a simple fact that the people we research almost become our companions. I visited Joseph's building because I felt I owed him something. His book had, after all, first led me to May, triggering the journey that trans-formed my work as a historian.

As I walked away from his building, I realised that I could, at least, give Joseph an ending with a satisfying emotional arc. As someone obsessed with the shape of his own life, I thought Joseph would have preferred an end that tied threads together rather than the grimly familiar tale of illness that marked his final days in 1965. I imagined him walking this same street, holding the arm of a woman he once loved, talking about the revolution that shaped their lives. *That was a suitable end for Joseph Freeman*, I thought.

Secret Speech

1

In late February 1956, with the Twentieth Congress of the Soviet Communist Party officially over, a gathering of party leaders assembled at the Central Committee building in Moscow to hear Nikita Khrushchev, Stalin's successor as general secretary, make a landmark speech. John Rettie, a British journalist posted in Moscow, recalled how the windows of the Central Committee building were 'ablaze with light, with the great black limousines of the Party elite parked all round it'.[1]

Although known as the 'secret speech', it did not remain a secret for long. In this speech delivered three years after Stalin's death, Khrushchev denounced Stalin's regime, setting in motion a process of 'de-Stalinization'. Almost one million people 'repressed' during Stalin's reign were declared innocent and rehabilitated.

2

In the period following the secret speech, someone, likely an archivist working in the archives of the Communist Party of the Soviet Union, retrieved Rose Cohen's Comintern personnel file. By then, nothing had been added to the folder for many years. Another set of documents was placed inside, including one dated 8 August 1956 and titled 'Decision of the High Military Court of the USSR, led by Justice Semika'. It noted that the court 'has established that Rose Cohen was sentenced as a member of an anti-Soviet organisation existing within the ECCI, and connected with intelligence.' The court decision was to cancel the case against her due to lack of evidence pointing to criminality,' the document stated.[2] Both Rose Cohen and David Petrovsky were posthumously rehabilitated.

3

Later in her life, Ivy Litvinov met a man she last encountered when he had been a young boy. During her final decades in Moscow, sometime around the early 1960s, Ivy received a phone call. 'Do you remember Rose Cohen?' the voice on the other end asked. 'Of course I do,' she answered. It was Alyosha, son of Rose and David Petrovsky. She recalled him telling her how 'now that my mother's and father's memory is more or less rehabilitated' he would like to come see Ivy, to learn something about his mother and perhaps to see some photographs. 'And so this pathetic, extraordinary, wonderful young man came to see me,' she remembered. He told her a story of his difficult life following his parents' execution, noting that he met 'some noble people who were very kind to me'. He was now a geologist with a wife and child. 'A scientist, imagine!' Ivy recalled. 'And such a mature man. I simply adored him.'[3]

The Famous Kiss

While her cousin Alyosha grew up as an orphan in the Soviet Union, Joyce was raised in comfortable surroundings in North London. Her stepfather's inherited wealth paid for a good education and a family home near Hampstead Heath. Eventually, Joyce moved into her own home on Chepstow Place, a central London street in Notting Hill that intersects with Moscow Road.

May periodically updated Ruth on Joyce's development. In 1951, writing from North London's Belsize Park where she spent her final decades, May wrote that Joyce was a 'charming young lady' who was 'completely wrapped up in music in all its aspects'. The Rathbone family were a walk across the Heath from May and she saw them regularly. 'Nellie continues to expand (she would hate to know I told you),' May wrote, while Hugo 'varies'. 'He is essentially kind, but it is almost impossible to discuss anything political UNLESS you agree with him,' she continued, before noting 'And of course I have my own ideas.'[1]

In the same letter, May shared news about two of her worlds connecting. 'When I was in Switzerland I met my old friend Leonhard again with her two daughters,' she noted of a recent trip. She told Ruth about Joyce's 1949 trip to Switzerland to study at the Conservatoire de Lausanne, not far from Tannay where Emmy, Elisa and Alida settled. On her visit, Joyce 'met them all' and 'they all got on famously', May wrote. Reporting back to May on her old friend from the Lux days, Joyce had told her that Emmy 'would be in bed one day' with heart trouble and then 'the next would find her rushing around with big buckets of water or fuel for the furnace – just mad'.[2]

Later, Joyce and Elisa marked this 1949 visit – the first time they met – as an important anniversary. Although their relationship did not become romantic until a further visit Joyce made in the early 1960s, both women recalled their first encounter fondly. 'And do I remember you from 13 years ago,' Elisa wrote a couple of months into their relationship in 1962, 'I remember how you looked, very young and very, very lovely and very, very serious. I remember how you sat by mama's bed, and how you said at the Grand Théatre that London had nothing to be compared to the local rendering of *Mireille*.' Elisa wrote, 'the expression on your face and the tone of your voice were so earnest and sweet that it was the nicest compliment one can imagine'. 'I remember your talking about acquiring a scooter and taking me on a tour,' she continued, before noting, 'I've been waiting for that ever since.'[3]

34. Elisa de Jager, c. 1961. Leonhard Fimmen Papers

Sometime following their arrival in Switzerland after the war, Jewish identity became an important part of Elisa and Alida's lives. Emmy believed there may have been a Jewish connection on her mother's side, the Meyer family, but the adoption of this faith appears to have been a process of conversion. In any case, by the time Elisa began writing her letters to Joyce, she was deeply attached to her Jewish faith. For Elisa, Joyce's own Jewish heritage became another part of the bond between them.

From 1949 until the fateful return visit when Elisa and Joyce's relationship began, both Elisa and Alida continued their careers in international organisations: Elisa in the UN and Alida in the International Rescue Committee. They also became active in the Geneva Jewish community.

Meanwhile, their mother, Emmy, moved towards and beyond retirement age still politically active. In 1951 she was influential in the establishment of the Council of European Municipalities and Regions, a still-extant organisation that promotes local government and citizen participation. It was an echo of the de-centralised vision of politics she first advocated in the 1920s. She also began writing a manifesto of sorts, a political play called *The Living Commune* that she eventually self-published using the reparations payment she received from the German government.

Both daughters were struck by the resilience of their mother's revolutionary convictions and largely supported Emmy's belief that a revolutionary should never retire. Elisa, who inherited her mother's philosophising tendencies, was particularly encouraging. May, too, found Emmy's energy striking, if slightly concerning. Writing to Ruth in 1954, when May was in her early seventies and Emmy in her early sixties, she wrote that Emmy was 'madder than ever' and 'works like a lunatic on an idea'. May claimed that she had a stern talking with Emmy for fear that she was squandering her daughter's money on her political projects.[4] More than a decade later, May was still reporting to Ruth that Emmy remained 'indefatigable in her energy to create a new world!'[5]

2

35. Joyce Rathbone, c. 1960s. Leonhard Fimmen Papers

For Joyce, the decades after the war were a time of advancing recognition in the world of music. She played regular concerts and became a dearly remembered tutor to a generation of pianists. For years, however, there remained an unresolved mystery in her life: the identity of her father. According to family memory, the clue that led her to Liam O'Flaherty was her mother's untidiness. Nellie, so the story goes, kept a cluttered household, with the books on the shelves covered in dust. Joyce, however, noticed that Nellie continually tidied one set of books: the works of Liam O'Flaherty. Turning to an author photo, she would have found a resemblance. Perhaps she also heard May or Nellie refer to him as a figure from their past. In any case, by the mid-1950s, Nellie confirmed to Joyce the identity of her father and Joyce set out to contact him.

Around 1957 Joyce began drafting letters to Liam. 'Dear Liam O'Flaherty,' opened one, 'I have been wanting to get in touch with you for a very long time, but I have never been able to decide how to do so.' 'I have begun and torn up several letters because what I want to say sounds absurdly dramatic no matter how I word it,' she wrote, before stating that the 'only way seems to be a bald statement of fact – that you are my father, that I was born in February 1929 and that my mother's name when you knew her was Nellie Cohen'. Joyce described holding a 'strong hope that you have some curiosity to see me'.[6] I found this letter unsent among Joyce's papers. Another draft from January 1960 revealed her attempt was met with silence. 'I cannot know whether or not my letter reached you,' Joyce wrote, 'if it did, you clearly do not wish to meet me & I cannot hope to change your mind.'[7]

After spending much of the war in the US, Liam returned to Ireland with his partner Kitty Tailor, whom he had met after his separation from his wife. The couple lived together in Dublin, where Liam continued to write, though with less success. According to O'Flaherty family lore, Kitty first noticed the letters coming in from a woman claiming to be his daughter, which Liam was ignoring. Kitty implored him to reply.

Joyce and Liam first met in 1960. Despite his absence from her life and his delayed decision to contact her, Joyce developed an immediate affection for Liam. It soon became mutual. 'You were really wonderful to me,' she wrote in a letter after an early visit.[8]

Through connecting with her father, Joyce discovered her half-sister Pegeen, who also lived in London. They became close. The story goes that Pegeen, raised an only child, learned of Joyce unceremoniously. On the way out the door from a meeting with her father, Liam said something to the effect of, 'By the way, you have a sister.' A year into Joyce's connection with her Irish family, May told Ruth that Joyce likes Liam 'very much & he proudly introduces her as "my daughter"'. 'But the nicest thing,' May continued, 'is she has found her half-sister, who lives quite near – she is seemingly a Russian linguist.'[9] By the time she learned of her half-sister with family roots in the Russian Empire, Pegeen was already fluent in Russian and a Russian Orthodox convert.

In the space of a couple of years at the beginning of the 1960s, Joyce met her father, her half-sister and, on a visit to Switzerland, began her own love story.

3

In October 1961 Emmy wrote to Joyce about how much she appreciated Joyce's recent trip to their home in Tannay. Although it was years since they last met, Emmy noted that it felt as though only hours had passed.[10] Elisa planned a journey to Joyce in London for the next summer. Visiting Emmy and her daughters in Switzerland ahead of Elisa's return visit to London, May talked with Elisa about Joyce. It was almost as though May was scoping out a family member's suitor.

Upon her return to London after her stay in Emmy's 'nest on the banks of the lake', as May called the Tannay home, May relayed all the news of Switzerland to Joyce. Fortunately for the historical record, Joyce provided a transcript of one of their back-and-forths in a letter to Elisa. Joyce used the nickname by which everyone knew May, O'C:

O'C: I had a talk with Elisa about you. I told her that you regarded her as a friend (!) and I wanted to find out how she thought of you – as a friend or as a young whipper-snapper.

Joyce: But for heaven's sake – I'm not that much younger than Elisa (this in some embarrassment.)

O'C: Oh! But it is not a question of *years* but of mind! Elisa, you know, is *very* intelligent.

Beneath this transcript, Joyce wrote four further exclamation marks and noted that this was 'only slightly funnier than most of O'C's efforts'. Joyce also related this encounter to Pegeen. 'Well, Joyce,'

Pegeen said, 'I always thought your I.Q. well above average, but clearly your O.C.Q. is below par.'[11] Joyce's confidantes were sharing well-intentioned put-downs as she encouraged Elisa towards a recognition that she desired her not just as a friend, but as a 'friend (!)'.

While Joyce was willing to place knowing exclamation marks, Elisa remained more guarded. After her London visit, Elisa wrote that London was 'absolutely wonderful'; 'London streets, Richmond Park, dinner at the Italian restaurant, plus waitress, your films, your sister, your family, smoked cheese, excellent coffee and raspberries, and dear company.' 'I feel rather deeply honoured to have you as a friend,' Elisa told Joyce.[12]

Any coyness was understandable. So many women searching for an articulation of their own desires in these years would have struggled to find the right vocabulary. In this pre-LGBTQ activist era, the bulk of writing on queer sexuality that attempted to move beyond judgement was clinical in tone; the work of psychologists or the dated writings of early-twentieth-century sexologists. While the US had a lesbian publication, *The Ladder*, from the mid-1950s, the first UK lesbian magazine, *Arena Three*, would not appear until 1964. Meanwhile, consensual sexual acts between men remained illegal in Britain until 1967. Sex between women was not similarly criminalised. This inconsistency resulted from societal ignorance of women's sexuality, not from tolerance.

How could women who desired each other even signal this fact? Joyce and Elisa stumbled upon an answer. The moment where all became clear was, it seems, a kiss Joyce planted on Elisa's forehead. Elisa initially felt as though such a small kiss meant that Joyce's intentions were chaste. In a letter remembering the moment, she wrote: 'Thank you, my dear, sweet love, for proving me wrong.'[13]

In one of her first letters to Joyce after 'that famous kiss' – as Elisa called it – she described the moment of revelation when she realised she could begin loving Joyce. 'My darling, darling Joyce,' the letter began, 'This longing for you should get more bearable with time – four and a half days since you left and they seem four weeks at least.' Towards the end of the letter, Elisa told Joyce how she wanted to dream 'that you are here and I'd feel your arms around me'. Continuing, Elisa noted, 'If my memory is right it was on Saturday night, one week ago exactly, that you managed to break down the last barrier by saying "Thank you for letting (!!!) me love you" and slow-witted Elisa finally realised that restraint was not only not necessary but actually quite inappropriate.'[14] 'God bless you, my dear, and, as you would say to mama, look after yourself,' Elisa signed off.

The emotional floodgates opened and Elisa and Joyce began years of sending effusive letters back and forth between Chepstow Place, London, and Tannay, Switzerland. They never lived together: Joyce remained in London, close to her students, Elisa at home, close to her mother. Distance, of course, created longing and a paper trail, but it also required its own subterfuge. How could Elisa explain to her mother, Emmy, the velocity of letters arriving from London and the even more frequent letters going in the other direction? At first, Elisa relied on a PO box.

Two months into their relationship, Elisa described how the post office clerk was 'taking a kindly interest in my obvious passion' and 'beamed' while presenting her with two letters 'as if they had been for him'.[15] This also meant that Elisa could speak more directly about her desires than Joyce, for Joyce's letters to Elisa risked being picked up by the older revolutionary housemate who Elisa described as her 'innocently inquisitive mama'.[16]

It was also the case that Elisa was a more exuberant writer than Joyce and more interested in love's philosophical underpinnings. In another letter sent soon after they first told one another 'I love you', Elisa described how fortunate it was that she and Joyce were not 'one of those principle-ridden people' who believed 'that love between persons of the same sex is not part of the preordained scheme of things'. 'We would be sunk if we were, wouldn't we, my darling love?' she wrote.[17] Gesturing towards the extraordinary circumstances that brought them together in a letter sent a mere day later, Elisa claimed: 'all my previous life seems but a preparation for loving you'.[18]

'And I'm very much tempted to write my memories in relation to you', Elisa confessed in another letter, 'starting on a day in February 1929 when Elisa struggled with *la difficulté d'etre*, unaware of very important happenings in New York which 33 years later would overwhelm her with happiness.'[19]

On one occasion, the ruse was almost blown. A year or so into the relationship, they seemingly dropped the post office precaution. This resulted in Emmy reading a letter Joyce intended for Elisa, thinking it was for her, and being startled to find herself addressed as 'Dearest little piggie-wig.'[20] In truth, it is difficult to believe that the older generation were entirely oblivious to what was going on.

Certainly, Elisa believed, May had some sense of things. Although May referred to Joyce and Elisa as 'bosom friends' when writing to Ruth, Elisa believed May understood her passion for Joyce.[21] May, in her brutal honesty, would sometimes tell Elisa that she was 'complacent'. But after their relationship began, Elisa wrote to Joyce that May's 'mind became obfuscated by the realisation that you had chosen to love me and everything about me became just wonderful, in the humility of her old heart'.[22]

36. Elisa and Joyce on O'Connell Bridge, Dublin, c. 1963. Leonhard Fimmen Papers

While Elisa's letters were percolated with philosophical digressions – like her disagreement with Erich Fromm's Marxist analyses of love – and occasional illustrations that mirrored her earlier work for the *Alpenpost*, Joyce's replies were more typical love letters. 'I love you, I love you, love you,' went one characteristic 1963 letter, 'Oh Elisa, my sweet darling, my dearest love. You have no idea what a person you are, my darling.'[23] It was straightforward stuff, but Elisa still thought Joyce's letters – and everything about her – was wonderful.

Elisa spoke of her tireless mother's political plans and the various people from Emmy's activist life who would drop into their house, like Babette Gross or the pacifist and founding member of the Women's International League for Peace and Freedom, Gertrude Baer. There were occasional visits to Selma Weil in Paris too.

Elisa was every bit her mother's daughter, while Alida, certainly in her approach to her career, was closer to her father. The daughters inherited the dynamic of their parents: Elisa, taking after Emmy, was interested in ideas; Alida, following Edo, was a person of action. Throughout her life, Alida was a dynamic organiser of refugee work, active in both Europe and Africa. She appeared frequently in Elisa's letters, but she was almost always on the move between places like Biafra and the Congo.

Joyce grew close to her effective mother-in-law, Emmy, with the ageing radical considering Joyce, in turn, almost like a daughter. Even though she suffered constantly with heart troubles, Emmy's revolutionary commitment remained. This was reflected in her final project, her revolutionary play. Joyce, Emmy hoped, would write the English translation.

For Emmy, faith in world transformation was something she could sense in others. As her dear friend May entered her eighties, she felt that May was losing that spark they once shared. In a 1963 letter to Joyce, Emmy described that, although May was the greatest translator she knew, Joyce was the person she wanted to handle her play. Emmy claimed she could 'never' ask May to do it, 'because she is not living any more in our day, because she does no more enjoy life, events, the world and therefore cannot transmit that joy anymore to others'. 'Please *do* destroy this card after having read it and never let her know a word,' Emmy stated.[24]

Emmy's play was eventually released in two French editions. In the first, published in 1963 under the title *Demain* (*Tomorrow*), Emmy used the revolutionary name she chose for herself after leaving home in 1915: Leonhard. The subtitle betrayed her ceaseless optimism: 'everyday life in 1970'. Black lettering on the cover posed the question: will municipalities replace the state? It tells a story set in a world of equality that arises after a revolution that overthrows the state and all its bureaucratic arms. It was not a programme for achieving this world, rather a testament to Emmy's belief that it was important simply to imagine it.

The second edition was published in 1974 under the title *La Commune Vivante* (*The Living Commune*). For her author name, Emmy allowed herself to use a surname that, legally speaking, was never hers, but which she felt that she could finally claim: Fimmen. The play contained a further nod to her own life: a reference to the story of Robinson Crusoe, the same tale her daughters read during their childhood as castaways on the refugee routes of the 1930s.

4

At the end of her long and eventful life, May lived alone in her garden flat before she moved to a nursing home. In her final decade, May's closest friends were all living legacies of her Moscow days – with the exception of Nellie, whose bond with May stretched further back into the suffrage struggle. It must have given her some contentment to know that she was a crucial part in bringing together Joyce and Elisa. After all, Joyce's very existence attested to the fact that she had played the role of matchmaker before.

After her death in 1973, May's funeral was a small one. Only close family attended: Nellie and Joyce.[25] Meanwhile, the love letters continued to pass between Chepstow Place and Tannay. In a birthday letter sent to Elisa shortly after May's death, Joyce gave thanks to all who brought Elisa into the world: to God, to her mother Emmy, to her father Edo and, of course, 'to O'C'.[26] Elisa's letters, meanwhile, carried news of her family's recent addition: a little boy named Pierre.

Sympathy

1

A letter from Emmy Leonhard to Nellie Rathbone (née Cohen), 21 May 1973. Discovered within a plastic storage container in a Cotswolds home during the summer of 2017.

My dear Nellie,

Though expected, the death of O.C. hurt me very much. It is a happy and great time of my life which ends with her. Of course, I have not seen her very often during these latter years. I have been sometimes in Locarno when she visited her sister and she also came here from time to time. The last time I saw her was in your house at Christmas. But just because I have not seen her very often latterly, she remains present in my mind as young, as happy and as successful as she was in Moscow.

She had a very awe-inspiring job then at the Komintern as Director of the French, English and Spanish translation services. I still remember our first lunch together at the Lux and I remember how horrified she was by bortsch – though she became accustomed to it later.

We had lots of fun together, with Tom Mann and Harry Pollitt, who, as you know, became President of the British C.P. I think in his pure and well-behaved soul he was at times sorely shocked by what we did.

Sometimes the soldiers fetched us in the evenings to go with them to the big army camp near Moscow. O.C., a girl called Lisa Ulrich (who later fell as a victim of the great purge) and I, used to have a good gallop in the camp. Trotsky was then the Napoleon of the army and I still hear the soldiers at night singing 'Trotskyia, Boukharina'. O. C., although Irish, did not want to go on horseback and sat all the time in the officers' mess. I believe it was there that she first made the acquaintance of the girl who later became a general in the Red Army and was her lasting friend.

Of course, in 1925 and 1926 it was still the great time with Trotsky, Boukharine and Radek and Tschicheran and many people around them were still the greatest group of men who I have ever met. Stalin also was among them but was so uninteresting and unimportant that nobody ever thought that he was going to destroy all the others.

I suppose you know the story of how O. C. helped Elisa to be born. She found the cab which brought me to the Kremlin hospital and she paid the fee for the doctor and midwife, which I had not got.

I believe it was at your house at Christmas that O. C. showed me a book written by Ruth Kennell (I do not remember her married name) about her trip to Moscow later on with some well-known American authors. There is a wonderful picture of O. C. in this book, exactly as she was then, and she promised to give it to me, but I suppose she forgot. If you still have the book, please let Joyce bring it the next time, so that I may photocopy it and send it back to you. I can't find it here.

I cannot tell you how thankful I am that you cared for her during her last days and how happy I am that we know each other and that the next generation, Joyce and Elisa, have become such good friends so that O. C. will ever be for us, as long as we live, a living presence.

Very affectionately yours.

2

In December 1975 *La Révolution Prolétarienne*, the long-standing radical journal where Emmy first encountered the words of Simone

Weil, published the last of Emmy's writings to ever appear in print. It was a letter objecting to the journal's analysis of the American defeat in the Vietnam War. 'The Vietnamese victory will be one of the causes of the American revolution, just as the victory of the Americans over the English in their time was one of the causes of the Revolution of 1789, and just as the defeat of the great Russian war fleet off Port Arthur was one of the causes of the Russian Revolution of 1905,' Emmy predicted. 'Nevertheless,' she wrote, 'I shall remain faithful, as shall my daughter,' to *La Révolution Prolétarienne*.[1] In 1976, in her mid-eighties and still dreaming of revolution, Emmy Leonhard died.

37. (L) Elisa, Nellie and cat. (R) Joyce, Nellie and cat, mid-1970s. Leonhard Fimmen Papers

Epilogue: Impossible Desires

1

On 24 May 1993 the *Cork Examiner*, an Irish newspaper, carried an article titled: 'Whatever happened to May O'Callaghan?' Roger Howe, the article's author, was a Cork-based journalist who, in 1991, received an enquiry from a specialist in German literature. A team at the Austrian Academy of Science in Vienna were editing the diaries of the Austrian playwright Arthur Schnitzler. They wanted to discover further details on one of Schnitzler's correspondents, a woman named May O'Callaghan.

Researching in the era before digitisation, Roger Howe reflected on how he was only able to trace the 'merest outline of a life'.[1] Even so, he succeeded in finding a source that had thus far eluded me: living people who remembered May. He found them in Ballinesker, the village where she was raised.

Ballinesker residents Christine and Jack Harding, mother and son, told Roger Howe their memories of May and her wider family. 'I remember Miss May O'Callaghan when we were coming home from school,' the elderly Christine Harding told the journalist. 'God she was lovely,' Christine told him. May's accent, she remembered, was grand and bore the marks of her life in England.[2]

On a crisp and cloudy New Year's Eve in 2017, Ciara and I made our way to Ballinesker. The village looks over a long and dramatic stretch of beach that was once used by Stephen Spielberg to shoot the D-Day landing scenes for *Saving Private Ryan*. In the car park beside the beach, I noticed a woman in a high-visibility jacket picking up rubbish. I approached her and explained I was researching a woman who grew up here in the late nineteenth century. Taking out my phone, I showed her a screenshot of the 1993 article, which featured a photograph of the Harding family. To my surprise, she smiled and said, 'That's my uncle, Jack Harding.' He was still around, she told me. In fact, he lived just up the hill.

Jack Harding and his son welcomed us into their home. At the kitchen table, we were offered biscuits and a hearty mug of tea. Jack was born in the early 1930s and spent part of his childhood inside the O'Callaghans' household. May's family, it turned out, employed his mother for a time. He began talking about May's father, Patrick O'Callaghan, who was a local policeman. I showed him a picture of May. Yes, he remembered her. He began reciting a memory of May visiting home on what must have been a late 1930s trip. The image that came back to him was of a woman sitting beneath a chestnut tree for several hours, reading a book. He remembered collecting acorns around the tree while she read. There was something suggestive about this recollection and I think about it still. I imagine May, perhaps in a moment of contemplation, back in the place where her journey began.

I asked him some further questions. Did you know she was left-wing? 'People in those days would have kept such knowledge to themselves,' he replied. Which house belonged to her family? He described it. From his description, I recognised it as one we passed on our way down to the beach. Other families had lived there since, but it was nonetheless in a state of disrepair. I thanked him for his time. We headed out towards the house where May spent her childhood.

Here, before a derelict house, its walls covered in ivy, I thought over the broad arc of May's life. In leaving Ireland, May took part in the age-old historical process of Irish emigration. In this, at least, she was unexceptional. Generations before and since have left behind these husks of homes: decaying walls abandoned by the disenchanted and disenfranchised. May moved away and eventually found another home among the exiles of her era.

38. The O'Callaghan family home, Ballinesker Lodge, 2017.
Author photograph

2

Locating the axis around which a single life turned makes the historian's task easier. Although her village in Wexford surely provided the backdrop to important moments in her life, May rarely reflected on them. For May and many others whose stories have been told across these pages, Moscow's Hotel Lux in the mid-1920s was the place and moment through which their entire lives flowed. So many of their relationships, ideas, sacrifices and compromises were determined by those years.

In tracing these revolutionary lives that first collided in the Hotel Lux, I never lost my capacity to be astonished by how clearly these voices resonated out from the historical record. I was struck, also, by the astounding interconnectivity of this world and the durability of friendships and relationships which, in pure doctrinal terms, seemed unlikely. Following a desire trail through this past, I came upon living descendants who revealed to me that the very thing I was trying to research – affectionate bonds – also ensured the survival of the documents needed to tell this story.

All this time living amid the archival rubble of twentieth-century socialism has not dimmed my belief that we can, and should, commit ourselves to building a more just world. My career as a historian of revolutionary movements has convinced me that dreaming of something better, and mobilising towards that dream, is not only necessary but an irrepressible human trait.

Some suggest that the record of twentieth-century socialism reveals how greed will always triumph over desires for equality. But things look different from the perspective of the ordinary yet tenacious people who encountered that experiment in its many forms. In so many of their lives, we see a less considered through line: the recurring dream of a freer and more equal world and the conviction that ordinary people acting together can bring it into existence. If self-interest remains a theme of the human story, then so too does its counterpoint: solidarity.

Because this desire for something better arises again and again, the question for the future is how we harness that desire to imagine new ways of transcending the injustices of our time. If past movements provided an easily replicable template for social transformation, then we would not face the crises that now surround us.

Yet the stories of those who wanted to change the world in the past remain vitally important. Through these lives we can become aware of the routes towards tragedy and trauma we should not follow, while also reminding ourselves that joy, resilience and even love can be found in commitment to a cause. Such histories reveal that others thought like us before and that their lives had value and meaning. Like us, they were caught up in relationships that made them alternately hopeful, disappointed, vulnerable, determined, spiteful and caring.

Our political ancestors were never simply leaves blown about by the storm of history. At key moments, they were agents of their own destinies. The choices they made reveal that the prevailing winds of a society can always be turned. Each generation has the responsibility to determine that direction. We are not heading inexorably towards something better. The obstacles we face are terrific. But it would be a fatal misreading to interpret the histories of those who struggled before as a series of reasons to stop trying. Because we live in the shadow of their failures, we inherit the task of achieving what they could not.

So many past desires look impossible, unlikely, and even naive when we study them in retrospect. Considering the story through its outcomes, we risk losing sight of hopeful beginnings and the many endings that, by historical contingency, remained unrealised. Joseph Freeman dwelt on this idea in his final published work. It discussed, almost inevitably, his time in the Hotel Lux. Writing shortly before his death in 1965, he acknowledged that the era of high ideals and violence between the wars 'looks to many unreal or absurd'. However, he counselled, it is 'only when we encounter it in its own terms as the living experience of a generation that it regains its meaning'.[3]

To place myself in that encounter, I often recall an experience from the start of my research. When I first read through the folder of correspondence between May and Ruth held in the University of Oregon, I found myself moved deeply by a filing mistake. In a single evening, I read more than a hundred pages of correspondence arranged in near-perfect chronological order. A fragmentary version of the history charted on these pages can be traced through these letters. The correspondence begins in 1924 and ends in 1970. One letter, however, had slipped out of place. At the end of the folder, one of Ruth's earlier letters from Moscow emerged from behind May's final message to Ruth.

'Look here,' Ruth noted in this September 1927 letter to May, 'you have to get down to serious work.'[4] Throughout the letter, Ruth evoked the particularities of life in a revolutionary society, with its delegations, political meetings and intrigue. She described a suitor and recounted a conversation with Rose about a holiday in the Caucuses. Because an archivist or a previous researcher had shuffled the documents, I was suddenly flung back into the lives of these women as they stood on the precipice of what still seemed like a radiant future.

What was everyone who had once passed through the corridors of the Hotel Lux doing as Ruth typed this letter? Joseph was in New York, absorbed in his work. Elsewhere in the same city, Sabo was steeling herself against disenchantment. In Berlin, Emmy was making plans for the revolution while little Elisa, who had spent her earliest days in the Lux, was learning that the world was full of both risk and wonder. May was on her way to Ireland, excited to return home and to spend time with her new friend Liam. Ruth, the last one of them left in the Lux, tied up her letter: 'Goodnight, dear, give my best to Nellie.' So much was yet to come. Everything was still possible.

39. Final illustration from *La Guinguette de Londres*, 1940, featuring (L–R) Emmy, Alida and Elisa. Leonhard Fimmen Papers

Notes

A note on Transliteration, Names and Sources

To balance readability and accuracy, I use two Russian transliteration systems. In the text, I follow common English usage (e.g. Trotsky and Mayakovsky instead of Trotskii and Maiakovskii) and omit soft signs. In the notes, I have used the Library of Congress transliteration system.

In the case of the many-named Emmy Leonhard, I have adopted a system to retain clarity of narrative. Because, legally speaking, Emmy, Elisa and young Alida all shared the first name Alida, the family developed their own naming convention: their mother was known as Emmy, the oldest daughter known by her middle name Elisa and the youngest as Alida. Meanwhile, most of Emmy's comrades knew her as Alida Leonhard or – following her 1939 marriage – as Alida de Jager. May O'Callaghan called her Leonhard, sometimes Alida, but never Emmy.

To prevent confusion in the main text, I chose to refer to her as Emmy Leonhard, a combination of her familiar name and revolutionary name that also distinguishes her from her youngest daughter. However, in the endnotes, I use the name she used in each source cited so that researchers can find these sources with greater ease. For example, writing to Trotsky in 1931, she used the name Alida Leonhard but many years later when speaking with Simone Weil researchers she used the name Alida de Jager. I hope that readers, having been spared a carousel of Alidas, will forgive this intentional discrepancy.

Due to the large number of archival collections cited, I have adopted an abbreviation system in the endnotes wherein each collection is listed in full when first cited and thereafter abbreviated. Frequently cited correspondents (such as May O'Callaghan and Joseph Freeman) are also referred to by their initials after their first mention.

Every effort has been made to trace the copyright of materials used herein. Should any oversight have occurred, I encourage copyright owners to come forward for proper attribution.

Acknowledgements

My first note of thanks must go to those who granted me access to private family archives containing documents belonging to their loved ones. I particularly want to thank Pedro Ewald, Pippa Harris, Angus Melville, Greg Conway and the Petrovsky family for their generosity in sharing materials. All illustrations labelled Leonhard Fimmen Papers and Joyce Rathbone Papers are courtesy of Pedro Ewald and Pippa Harris respectively.

The work of many archivists based in several countries was crucial to this book. Thank you to all whose work preserves the past and enables us to share these stories. My gratitude goes to Dan Healey for helping me organise my archival trip in Moscow in 2018. In Moscow, James Ryan proved an invaluable guide to the archive. Over several years of video calls, my Russian teacher Andrei Belyobora prepared me to understand what I found there.

Much of this book rests on a foundation of research created during my DPhil studies at Jesus College, Oxford. Thank you to my supervisors David Priestland and Senia Paseta for their guidance and support throughout those years. Rob Quinlan deserves special mention for ensuring that the slog of graduate study was always counter-balanced by friendship, laughter and the Pogues (on repeat).

My DPhil project was funded by the Globalising and Localising the Great War Scholarship. An additional Fulbright award for 2018–19 enabled me to carry out research in California and Oregon, much of which I was able to harness for this book.

Thank you to Áine Tyrell, Tania Shew and Ryan Cropp for searching out archival material on my behalf. For assistance with translation from the Leonhard–Trotsky correspondence, thank you to Alex Hartley. Fellow time travellers to the past described here have always been generous with their notes and time. In this respect, I particularly want to shout out Brigid O'Keeffe, Josh Meyers and Julia Mickenberg.

The late Mairead Breslin-Kelly was the first living connection to this world that I met in person. Graceful and generous, her dedication to her parents' memory always moved me. In sharing his father Erwin's story with me, René Dumont also helped me understand why this was a story worth telling.

Because this is my first book, I should mention two people who played important roles in guiding my career. The late Nora Bartlett of St Andrews met the cloudy-headed and somewhat self-obsessed nineteen-year-old me, saw something in me and then encouraged me to follow my passions. Greg Jenner has proved generous and supportive over the years in my quest to be both an academic and public historian.

Thank you to colleagues and all the attendees at my talks who have heard versions of this story over the years and provided feedback and encouragement.

Thank you to my agent Donald Winchester who believed in this book and provided guidance that transformed the proposal. I am delighted we found the book a wonderful home in Footnote Press. Thank you to the Footnote team who 'got' the book and what I was trying to say from the very beginning. I was fortunate to have in Rose Green an editor who provided incisive editorial advice while also sharing my enthusiasm for the messy lives of these past revolutionaries.

Over the years, I have gathered around me a group of friends so loyal and like-minded that I could, if necessary, form my own impenetrable clandestine network. I will thank my friends collectively rather than list you by name (just in case we ever need to go underground).

My dad, Mossie, has always unconditionally supported me and my career. Thank you to Josephine, my mum, for shaping my interests and for always encouraging me to reach my potential. My sister Annmarie and brother-in-law Phily have provided encouragement and more lifts than I can count. Major parts of this book were imagined and written while living with my supportive Athlumney family: Monica, Denis and Ruth. The two most recent additions to my family, Luke and Arthur, already share my love of stories and keep my hope for the future alive.

Ciara has enthusiastically joined me for this adventure, patiently accepting an ever-expanding string of deceased revolutionaries into our relationship. In dedicating this book to you, I wanted to emphasise your importance in shaping this story. You gave me the confidence I needed to write this history. You helped me understand the love stories traced within it.

Index

About the Author

Maurice J. Casey is an Irish historian originally from Cahir, Co. Tipperary, and currently a Research Fellow in the School of History, Anthropology, Philosophy and Politics, Queen's University Belfast. His work focuses on the history of modern Ireland, queer history and the history of international communism in the interwar world. He holds degrees from Trinity College Dublin, the University of Cambridge and the University of Oxford, where he completed his DPhil in History in 2020. He was a Fulbright Scholar at Stanford University from 2018 to 2019. His writing has appeared in a variety of publications including *History Today*, the *Irish Times* and *Tribune* magazine. He writes a regular newsletter about his research titled *Archive Rats*. *Hotel Lux* is his first book.

List of Illustrations

Endnotes

O'C

[1] Theodore Draper, The Roots of American Communism (New York, 1957), p. 129.

[1] Joseph Freeman, *An American Testament: A Narrative of Rebels and Romantics* (New York, 1936), p. 508.

[2] Karl Schlögel, *In Space We Read Time: On the History of Civilization and Geopolitics*, trans. Gerrit Jackson (New York, 2015), p. 264.

Part I

The Dreadnought

[1] Victor Serge, *Memoirs of a Revolutionary*, trans. Peter Sedgwick and George Paizis (New York, 2012), p. 4.

[2] 'Thoughts_Mind Flashes', May O'Callaghan (Hereafter MO'C), 12 March 1927, Hoover Institution Library and Archives (Hereafter HILA), Joseph Freeman Papers (Hereafter JFP), Box 32, Folder 9.

[3] 'Unidentified Confession', undated, University of Oregon Special Collections (Hereafter UOSC), Ruth Epperson Kennell Papers (Hereafter REKP), Box 8, Folder 1.

[4] Sylvia Pankhurst, *The Home Front: A Mirror to Life in England during the World War* (Plymouth, 1932), p. 235.

[5] *Freeman's Journal*, 3 November 1913. See also: Katherine Connelly, *Sylvia Pankhurst: Suffragette, Socialist and Scourge of Empire* (London, 2013), p. 57.

[6] R. M. Fox, *Smoky Crusade* (London, 1937), p. 168.

[7] *Woman's Dreadnought* (Hereafter *WD*), 8 March 1914.

[8] Nellie Cressall interview, 5 April 1965, Museum of London, David Mitchell Papers, 73.83/21.

[9] These childhood memories are taken from recordings of a conversation between Nellie Cohen and her daughter Joyce, conducted around the mid-1970s and generously shared with me by Nellie's grand-nephew Greg Conway.

[10] Interview with Nellie Rathbone (*née* Cohen), conducted by Lucia Jones, 27 June 1972, Appendix A, Lucia Jones, *Sylvia Pankhurst and the Workers' Socialist Federation – the Red Twilight, 1918–1924* (MA thesis, University of Warwick, 1972). (Hereafter: Lucia Jones, Nellie Rathbone interview).

[11] Daisy Lansbury to 'Fred', c. January 1916, National Archives, Kew (Hereafter TNA), KV 2/1395.

[12] Report, Inspector Edward Park, 25 March 1916, TNA, KV 2/1395.

[13] Lucia Jones, Nellie Rathbone interview.

[14] *WD*, 18 March 1916.

[15] *WD*, 9 October 1915.

Rebel Ireland and the New Russia

[1] *WD*, 18 March 1916.

[2] *WD*, 6 May 1916.

[3] Ibid.

[4] Untitled Typescript, Patricia Lynch, National Library of Ireland (Hereafter NLI), Patricia Lynch and R. M. Fox Papers (Hereafter PLRMFP), MS 40,308/2; 'An Easter Monday', Typescript, Patricia Lynch, 24 April 1962, NLI, PLRMFP, MS 40,308/2.

[5] Adam Hochschild, *To End All Wars: A Story of Loyalty and Rebellion, 1914-1918* (New York, 2011), p. 185.

[6] Fox, *Smoky Crusade*, p. 216.

[7] *WD*, 8 September 1917.

[8] My recounting of the early days of the revolution is indebted to S. A. Smith, *Russia in Revolution: An Empire in Crisis, 1890-1928* (Oxford, 2017), esp. pp. 101, and N. N. Sukhanov, *The Russian Revolution 1917: A Personal Record*, trans. Joel Carmichael (Princeton, 1983), esp. p. 23.

[9] See *WD*, 3 February 1917 and *WD*, 3 March 1917.

[10] Faith Hillis, *Utopia's Discontents: Russian Émigrés and the Quest for Freedom, 1890s–1930s* (Oxford, 2021), p. 207.

[11] Ivy Litvinov, 'Litvinoff's Wife', unpublished memoir, c. 1960s, p. 29, HILA, Ivy Litvinov Papers (Hereafter ILP), Box 4, Folder 4.

[12] Ibid, p. 30.

[13] Ibid.

[14] *WD*, 31 March 1917.

[15] *WD*, 15 December 1917.

[16] *WD*, 17 November 1917.

[17] Report on Revolutionary Organisations in the UK (Hereafter RROUK), 2 December 1918, TNA, CAB/24/71/26.

[18] *New York Call*, 19 February 1918.

[19] *WD*, 17 November 1917.

[20] Lucia Jones, Nellie Rathbone interview.

[21] Conrad Noel, *Conrad Noel: An Autobiography* (London, 1945), p. 108.

[22] RROUK, 7 August 1919, TNA, CAB/24/86/35.

[23] Sylvia Pankhurst, *Red Twilight*, unpublished draft memoir, International Institute of Social History (Hereafter IISH), Estelle Sylvia Pankhurst Papers (Hereafter ESPP), Invent. No. 79, p. 19.

[24] Ibid, p. 22.

[25] Ibid, p. 23.

[26] Ibid, p. 18.

[27] Report of CPI, Oct. 1921–Oct. 1922, *Rossiskii Gosudarstvennii Arkhiv Sotsialno-Politicheskoi Istorii* (Hereafter RGASPI) 495/89/16/53.

[28] RROUK 24 June 1920, TNA, CAB24/103/37.

[29] Nellie Cohen referenced this meeting in her interview with Lucia Jones. Barbara Winslow also mentions this founding meeting: Barbara Winslow, *Sylvia Pankhurst: Sexual Politics and Political Activism* (London, 1996), p. 165.

[30] WSF membership card, c. 1919, RGASPI 495/198/822/1.

[31] Gavin Arthur, 'The Young Writers of Ireland', c. late 1920s, unpublished essay, 'Articles Written in the Heat of the Irish Revolution', Andrews Papers, in Private Possession. Thank you to Phil Longo for this reference.

[32] Kevin Kiely, *Francis Stuart: Artist and Outcast* (Dublin, 2007), p. 64.

[33] Ethel Mannin, *Young in the Twenties* (London, 1971), p. 107.

The Rotunda

[1] Jim Phelan, *The Name's Phelan* (London, 1948), p. 275.

[2] *Daily Herald*, 20 January 1922.

[3] Liam O'Flaherty, *Shame the Devil* (London, 1934), p. 17.

[4] Tom O'Flaherty, *Aranmen All* (Dublin, 1991), p.73.

[5] Autobiographical Note for P. H. Muir, c. July 1926, NLI MS 26,743.

[6] 'Reading & Other Arts', Pegeen O'Sullivan, c. 1990s, typescript reminiscences. Thank you to Angus Melville for sharing this source with me.

[7] Autobiographical Note for P. H. Muir, c. July 1926, NLI MS 26,743.

[8] Ibid.

[9] Ibid.

[10] Ibid.

[11] A. A. Kelly, ed., *The Letters of Liam O'Flaherty* (Dublin, 1996), p. 8.

[12] Ibid.

[13] Phelan, *The Name's Phelan*, p. 275.

[14] James O'Brien, *Liam O'Flaherty* (Lewisburg, 1973), pp. 22–3.

[15] *Ballymena Weekly Telegraph*, 28 January 1922.

[16] *Freeman's Journal*, 28 January 1922.

[17] *The Worker* (New York), 18 March 1922.

[18] *Derry Journal*, 23 January 1922.

[19] Report of CPI, Oct. 1922, RGASPI 495/89/16/53.

[20] *The Workers' Republic*, 13 January 1923.

[21] Constance Malleson, *After Ten Years* (London, 1931), p. 252.

[22] Liam O'Flaherty, *Two Years* (London, 1920), p. 75.

A Nest of Revolution

[1] Richard Dawson, *The Red Terror and the Green: The Sinn Féin-Bolshevist Conspiracy* (New York, 1920), pp. 249–50.

[2] RROUK, 7 May 1919, TNA, CAB/24/79/18.

[3] Anne Donlon, '"A Black Man Replies": Claude McKay's Challenge to the British Left', *Lateral*, 5:1 (Spring, 2016), https://csalateral.org/issue/5-1/claude-mckay-british-left-donlon/ (Accessed 5 May 2023).

[4] Ibid.

[5] Ibid.

[6] Lucia Jones, Nellie Rathbone interview.

[7] Claude McKay, 'How Black Sees Green and Red', in Cathy Bergin (ed.), *African American Anti-Colonial Thought 1917–1937* (Edinburgh, 2016), p. 69.

[8] Claude McKay to Joseph Freeman (hereafter JF), 19 March 1921, HILA, JFP, Box 29, Folder 5.

[9] Ibid.

[10] Lucia Jones, Nellie Rathbone interview.

[11] Rachel Holmes, *Sylvia Pankhurst: Natural Born Rebel* (London, 2020), p. 569.

[12] 'Pankhurst, Sylvia', Comintern personnel file, RGASPI 495/198/1843/1–4.

[13] 'Greetings to Comrade Sylvia Pankhurst from the Women Workers of Moscow', c. January 1921, RGASPI 507/3/11/2.

[14] Holmes, *Pankhurst*, p. 594.

[15] Pankhurst, *Home Front*, pp. 274–5.

[16] Maurice B. Reckitt, *As It Happened: An Autobiography* (London, 1941), p. 146.

[17] Ibid, p. 147.

[18] Ibid, p. 148.

[19] John Callaghan and Mark Phythian, 'State surveillance and communist lives: Rose Cohen and the Early British Communist Milieu', *Journal of Intelligence History* 12:2 (2013), p. 138.

[20] Credential note, 9 December 1920, RGASPI 495/198/831/2.

[21] Rose Cohen (hereafter RC) to Esmonde Higgins (hereafter EH), 15 July 1923, Mitchell Library, University of New South Wales (Hereafter ML), Esmonde Higgins Papers (EHP), ML MSS 740, Vol. 11.

A Tomb of Revolution

[1] Society for Cultural Relations with Foreign Countries (SCR), *Guide to the Soviet Union* (Moscow, 1925), p. 6.

[2] Karl Schlögel, *The Soviet Century: Archaeology of a Lost World* (Princeton, 2023), p. 31.

[3] SCR, *Guide*, p. 6.

[4] 'Attack on Memorial's office followed by Police Raid', *Amnesty, https://www. amnesty.org/ar/documents/eur46/4890/2021/en/* (Accessed 13 February 2024).

Part II

Checking In

[1] *Boston Daily Globe*, 27 November 1922.

[2] Yuri Slezkine, *The House of Government: A Saga of the Russian Revolution* (Princeton, 2017), p. 318.

[3] Alexander Berkman, *The Bolshevik Myth* (London, 1925), p. 62.

[4] Hillis, *Utopia's Discontents*.

[5] Margaret Buber Neumann, *Under Two Dictators*, trans. Edward Fitzgerald (London, 1949), p. 6.

[6] Walter Benjamin, 'Moscow Diary', *October*, 32 (Winter, 1985), p. 132.

[7] *Anketa*, 21–22 May 1923, RGASPI 495/198/733/58.

[8] Serge, *Memoirs*, pp. 206–7.

[9] RC to EH, 9 August 1923, ML EHP MS 740 Vol 11.

[10] Ibid.

[11] RC to EH, 30 October 1923, ML EHP MS 740 Vol 11.

[12] RC to EH, 9 August 1923, ML EHP MS 740 Vol 11.

[13] RC to EH, 13 October 1923, ML EHP MS 740 Vol 11.

[14] RC to EH, 28 November 1923, ML EHP MS 740 Vol 11.

[15] Ibid.

[16] Ibid.

[17] Comradeship of Foreign Workers in the USSR Publisher, *Programme of the Communist International* (Moscow, 1932), pp. 78, 80.

[18] G. M. Adibekov, E. N. Shakhnazarova and K. P. Shirinia, *Organizatsionnaia Struktura Kominterna, 1919–1943* (Moscow: Rosspen, 1997), pp. 9–10.

[19] Harry Pollitt to EH, 21 July 1924, ML, EHP, 740/11/423. Thank you to Terry Irving for sharing this source with me.

[20] Clara Zetkin, Sen Katayama, Fritz Heckert et. al, *We Have Met Lenin* (Moscow, 1939), p. 74.

Sweeping Away the Old Order

[1] *Pravda*, 7 November 1924.

[2] Julia L. Mickenberg, *American Girls in Red Russia: Chasing the Soviet Dream* (Chicago, 2017), pp. 141–2.

[3] Ruth Epperson Kennel (Hereafter REK) to Ella Epperson Tosh (Hereafter EET), 4 November 1924, UOSC, REKP, Box 9, Folder 8.

[4] Mickenberg, *American Girls*, p. 157.

[5] REK to EET, 31 October 1924, UOSC, REKP, Box 9, Folder 8.

[6] Ibid.

[7] Ibid.

[8] Ibid.

[9] REK to Family, 10 October 1924, UOSC, REKP, Box 9, Folder 4.

[10] Diary of Nikolai Mikailovich Mendelson, 7 November 1924, *Dnevnik Mendelson, N. M.*, Prozhito: https://corpus.prozhito.org/person/158 (Accessed 26 March 2024).

[11] REK to EET, 7 November 1924, UOSC, REKP, Box 9, Folder 8. Further descriptions of the anniversary celebrations in the preceding paragraphs are adapted from Ruth's descriptions in this lengthy letter.

[12] John Riddell (ed.), *To the Masses: Proceedings of the Third Congress of the Communist International, 1921* (Leiden, 2014), p. 781.

[13] Elizabeth A. Wood, *The Baba and the Comrade: Gender and Politics in Revolutionary Russia* (Bloomington, 1997), p. 30.

[14] Kristen R. Ghodsee, *Red Valkyries: Feminist Lessons from Five Revolutionary Women* (London, 2022), p. 70.

[15] REK to Sam Shipman (Hereafter SS), 3 May 1925, UOSC, REKP, Box 9, Folder 5.

[16] REK to EET, 28 May 1926, UOSC, REKP, Box 9, Folder 6.

[17] REK to SS, 14 September 1925, UOSC, REKP, Box 9, Folder 5.

[18] REK to SS, 3 November 1925, UOSC, REKP, Box 9, Folder 5.

[19] Ibid.

[20] Pierre Broué, *The German Revolution*, trans. John Archer (Leiden, 2005), p. 142.

[21] For biographies of Fimmen, see: Willy Buschak, *Edo Fimmen: Der Schöne Traum von Europa und die Globalisierung* (Essen, 2002) and Hans Schoots, *Edo Fimmen: De Wereld als Werkterrein* (Amsterdam, 1997).

22 Brigitte Studer, *Travellers of the World Revolution: A Global History of the Communist International*, trans. Davydd Roberts (London, 2023), p. 98.

The Language of Revolution

1 *Patriot*, 1 March 1923.
2 Jacob A. Zumoff, *The Communist International and US Communism, 1919-1929* (Boston, 2014), p. 179.
3 Ibid, p. 173.
4 Charles Shipman, *It Had to be Revolution: Memoirs of an American Radical* (Ithaca, 1993), p. 148.
5 Whittaker Chambers, *Witness* (New York, 1952), p. 223.
6 Albert Glotzer to James Monaghan, 13 January 1995, HILA, Albert Glotzer Papers (Hereafter AGP), Box 44, Folder 17.
7 Ibid.
8 Chambers, *Witness*, p. 233.
9 REK to SS, 20 March 1926, UOSC, REKP, Box 9, Folder 5.
10 Ibid.
11 Ibid.
12 Alan M. Wald, *The New York Intellectuals: The Rise and Decline of the Anti-Stalinist Left from the 1930s to the 1980s*, (Chapel Hill, 2017 [1987]), p. 168.
13 Tom O'Flaherty to REK, 10 November 1926, UOSC, REKP, Box 6, Folder 7.
14 Brigid O'Keeffe, *Esperanto and the Languages of Internationalism* (London, 2021), p. 98.
15 Ibid, p. 95.
16 Studer, *Travellers*, p. 99.
17 Freeman, *American Testament*, p. 508.
18 For the Kremlin palace's interior and history, see: I. Yu. Yudakov, *Moskovskii Kreml', Krasnaia Ploshchad'* (Moscow, 2007), esp. pp. 109–15.
19 John S. Clarke, *Pen Pictures of Russia under the 'Red Terror'* (Glasgow, 1921), p. 178.
20 REK to EET, 27 March 1925, UOSC, REKP, Box 9, Folder 6.
21 Studer, *Travellers*, pp. 206–7.
22 *Daily Worker* (US), 19 June 1926, 3 July 1926.
23 *Labor Defender*, July 1928, pp. 153, 159.
24 CPUSA to ECCI, 14 April 1926, RGASPI 495/261/2295/36.
25 Freeman, *American Testament*, pp. 17, 19.
26 'A Horse of Another Color', 4 July 1948, p. 18, HILA, JFP, Box 88, Folder 2. This document forms part of an extensive diary with fictionalised elements usually called *The Forbidden Tree* (hereafter TFT) that Freeman composed

over several decades. Freeman described the work as a 'novel' and regularly used pseudonyms to describe his friends, family and even himself. Where possible, I have corroborated details from this diary with other evidence. The diary contains many descriptions with scholarly value for Freeman's life and the lives of his contemporaries. Indeed, there is precedent for the typescripts being used in historical research: see Elena S. Danielson, 'The Elusive Litvinov Memoirs', *Slavic Review*, 48:3 (1989), pp. 477–83.

[27] Ibid.

[28] Ibid, p. 19.

Mixing Poetry and Facts

[1] REK to EET, 14 January 1926, UOSC, REKP, Box 9, Folder 6.

[2] J. T. Murphy, *New Horizons* (London, 1941), p. 242.

[3] REK to EET, 16 April 1927, UOSC, REKP, Box 9, Folder 6.

[4] Freeman, *American Testament*, p. 387.

[5] Studer, *Travellers*, p. 165.

[6] Ibid.

[7] Freeman, *American Testament*, p. 392.

[8] REK to EET, 14 January 1926, UOSC, REKP, Box 9, Folder 6.

[9] Freeman, *American Testament*, p. 509.

[10] Ibid, p. 508.

[11] Ibid, p. 510.

[12] Ibid, p. 509.

[13] Ibid. For a discussion of Lux bathing facilities, see: REK, 'The New Innocents Abroad', *American Mercury*, 17 (1929).

[14] Molly Murphy, *Molly Murphy: Suffragette and Socialist* (Salford, 1998), p. 191.

[15] M. Murphy, *Molly Murphy*, p. 104.

[16] Alan M Wald, *Exiles from a Future Time: The Forging of the Mid-Twentieth-Century Literary Left* (Chapel Hill, 2002), p. 179.

[17] Alida Leonhard to Ruth Fischer, 1 September 1925, RGASPI 495/205/3519/3–4.

[18] Alida Leonhard to ECCI, 19 October 1925, RGASPI 495/205/3519/6.

[19] Luise Geissler to Joseph Freeman, c. 1926, HILA, JFP, Box 21, Folder 22. The reference to O'Callaghan here is found in the line: 'she doesn't want to compete with O'Kachel'. Although O'Kachel is not definitively a rendering of O'Callaghan, the context of their friendship in the Lux, in addition to the singularity of the Irish O-apostrophe naming convention strongly implies that this is a reference to May.

[20] M. Murphy, *Molly Murphy*, p. 104.

The Family

1 Typescript Autobiography, Ruth Kennell, UOSC, REKP, Box 2, Folder 13, p. 246.
2 M. Murphy, *Molly Murphy*, p. 103.
3 Pankhurst, *Home Front*, p. 235.
4 Typescript Autobiography, Ruth Kennell, UOSC, REKP, Box 2, Folder 13, p. 284.
5 Ibid.
6 Ibid, p. 270.
7 Mickenberg, *American Girls*, p. 160.
8 Typescript Autobiography, Ruth Kennell, UOSC, REKP, Box 2, Folder 13, p. 284.
9 REK to EET, 18 July 1926, UOSC, REKP, Box 9, Folder 6.
10 Typescript Autobiography, Ruth Kennell, UOSC, REKP, Box 2, Folder 14, p. 299.
11 Ibid, p. 284.
12 Ibid, p. 290.
13 See: SD to JF, undated, c. 1927, 27 March 1928, 11 October 1927, HILA, JFP, Box 20, Folder 2.
14 Sergei Dinamov to V. F. Calverton, undated, c. 1930, V. F. Calverton Papers, New York Public Library, Series I, Box 4, Dinamov Folder.
15 REK to EET, 16 April 1927, UOSC, REKP, Box 9, Folder 6.
16 Ibid.
17 Freeman, *American Testament*, p. 511.
18 These pen portraits are adapted from Freeman, *An American Testament*, pp. 510–11.
19 *TFT*, 11 April 1949, HILA, JFP, Box 89, Folder 6.
20 Freeman, *American Testament*, p. 519.
21 Gregory Carleton, 'Writing-Reading the Sexual Revolution in the Early Soviet Union', *Journal of the History of Sexuality*, 8:2 (October, 1997), p. 231.
22 Ibid.
23 Gregory Carleton, *Sexual Revolution in Bolshevik Russia* (Pittsburgh, 2005), pp. 113–38.
24 Ibid, p. 124.
25 MO'C to JF, 20 March 1927, HILA, JFP, Box 32, Folder 9.
26 Ibid.
27 Ibid.
28 SD to JF, 27 October 1927, HILA, JFP, Box 20, Folder 2.
29 SD to JF, 6 September 1927, HILA, JFP, Box 20, Folder 2.
30 Ibid.
31 SD to JF, 11 October 1927, HILA, JFP, Box 20, Folder 2.
32 Sabo to JF, undated, HILA, JFP, Box 21, Folder 22.
33 'Ivy', typescript, c. 1934, Joseph Freeman, HILA, JFP, Box 78, Folder 3.

34 Ibid.

35 Ivy Litvinov (Hereafter IL) to Catherine Carswell, 4 December 1927, HILA, ILP, Box 1, 1927 Correspondence Folder.

36 'Prelude to Autobiography', Ivy Litvinov, 15 April 1943, HILA, JFP, Box 174, Folder 6.

37 John Carswell, *The Exile: A Life of Ivy Litvinov* (London, 1983), p. 110.

38 IL to Catherine Carswell, 1 February 1927, HILA, ILP, Box 1, 1927 Folder.

39 'Ivy', typescript, c. 1934, HILA, JFP, Box 78, Folder 3.

40 JF to George Fischer, 12 December 1958, Houghton Library (Hereafter HL), Daniel Aaron Papers (Hereafter DAP), Box 16, Folder 170.

41 Ibid.

42 Sabo to JF, 5 January 1927, HILA, JFP, Box 21, Folder 22.

43 Sabo to JF, 4 January 1927, HILA, JFP, Box 21, Folder 22.

44 Sabo to JF, 8 March 1928, HILA, JFP Box 21, Folder 22.

These Russian Boys Think Being Irish so Wonderful

1 JF to Daniel Aaron, 6 June 1958, HL, DAP, Box 15, Folder 166.

2 Freeman, *American Testament*, p. 563.

3 Ibid.

4 Ibid.

5 Olga Khoroshilova, 'Sea change: How a Company of Female Sailors Sparked a Gender Revolution in 1917', https://www.new-east-archive.org/features/show/8302/revisiting-revolution-sea-change-female-sailors-gender-1917 (Accessed 13 February 2024).

6 Freeman, *American Testament*, p. 564.

7 Alida de Jager to Nellie Cohen, 21 May 1973, Joyce Rathbone Papers (Hereafter JRP), in private possession.

8 Olga Khoroshilova, *Voina i Moda ot Petra I do Putina* (Moscow, 2018), p. 425.

9 Typescript Autobiography, Ruth Kennell, UOSC, REKP, Box 2, Folder 14, p. 300.

10 'Neskol'ko Stranits iz Moei Zhisni' *Rabotnitsa*, 32 (1927).

11 Khoroshilova, *Voina*, p. 425.

12 Freeman, *American Testament*, p. 566.

13 Khoroshilova, *Voina*, pp. 423–4.

14 Freeman, *American Testament*, p. 567.

15 'A Woman General', article typescript, c. 1929, UOSC, REKP, Box 6, Folder 23, p. 2.

16 Freeman, *American Testament*, p. 567.

17 Ibid.

18 Ibid.

19 MO'C to JF, 31 March 1927, HILA, JFP, Box 32, Folder 9.

20 For Joseph's account of this night, see: *TFT*, 11 April 1949, HILA, JFP, Box 89, Folder 6.

21 Sabo to JF, 8 March 1928, HILA, JFP, Box 21, Folder 22.

22 Sabo to JF, 7 April 1927, HILA, JFP, Box 21 Folder 22.

23 Lauren Kaminsky, '"No Rituals and Formalities!" Free Love, Unregistered Marriage and Alimony in Early Soviet Law and Family Life', *Gender & History* (November 2017), p. 719.

24 MO'C to REK, 7 August 1928, UOSC, REKP, Box 7, Folder 14.

25 MO'C to REK, 7 September 1928, UOSC, REKP, Box 7, Folder 14.

26 Insert placed between p. 133 and 134., UOSC, REKP, Box 2, Folder 14.

27 Theodore Dreiser, *A Gallery of Women* (London, 1930), p. 237.

28 MO'C to REK, 9 November 1928, UOSC, REKP, Box 7, Folder 4.

29 MO'C to JF, 20 March 1927, HILA, JFP, Box 32, Folder 9.

30 MO'C to JF, 31 March 1927, HILA, JFP, Box 32, Folder 9.

The New Stars and the Smaller Lights

1 Lucia Jones, Nellie Rathbone Interview.

2 Circular letter, 27 February 1925, John Johnson Collection, Pollard Box 1, Bodleian Library.

3 Minutes of the St Pancras Branch of the Communist Party, 28 January 1926, John Johnson Collection, Pollard Box 1, Bodleian Library, University of Oxford.

4 INO OGPU Report, 4 June 1926, RGASPI 495/198/733/49–50.

5 Ibid (l. 49).

6 Joshua Meyers, 'A Portrait of Transition: From the Bund to Bolshevism in the Russian Revolution', *Jewish Social Studies*, 24:3 (Winter, 2019), p. 121–2.

7 MO'C to JF, 23 April 1927, HILA, JFP, Box 32, Folder 9.

8 Ibid.

9 Meyers, 'Portrait', p. 125. For Rose in Lux in 1927, see M. Murphy, *Molly Murphy*, p. 103.

10 John Jagger, 'Rambling Remarks re: Russia', 6 December 1927, A Ron Harding Papers, CPGB Papers, People's History Museum, CP/IND/MISC/19/4.

11 MO'C to JF, 25 March 1927, HILA, JFP, Box 32, Folder 9.

12 Elizabeth Maguire, 'Sino-Soviet Romance: An Emotional History of Revolutionary Geopolitics', *Journal of Contemporary History*, 52:4 (October, 2017), p. 859.

13 REK to MO'C, 24 August 1927, UOSC, REKP, Box 7, Folder 14.

14 MO'C to JF, 2 June 1927, HILA, JFP, Box 32, Folder 9.

[15] MO'C to JF, 26 June 1927, HILA, JFP, Box 32, Folder 9.

[16] MO'C to JF, 15 July 1927, HILA, JFP, Box 32, Folder 9.

[17] SD to JF, 27 March 1927, HILA, JFP Box 20 Folder 2.

[18] MO'C to JF, 2 June 1927, HILA, JFP, Box 32, Folder 9.

[19] MO'C to JF, 26 July 1927. For further detail on MO'C and Baldwin's visit see: REK to EET, 18 July 1927, UOSC, REKP, Box 9, Folder 6.

[20] MO'C to JF, 2 June 1927, HILA, JFP, Box 32, Folder 9.

[21] MO'C to JF, 20 April 1927, HILA, JFP, Box 32, Folder 9.

[22] MO'C to JF, 25 March 1927, HILA, JFP, Box 32, Folder 9.

[23] MO'C to JF, 18 August 1927, HILA, JFP, Box 32, Folder 9.

[24] MO'C to REK, 18 August 1927, UOSC, REKP, Box 7, Folder 14.

[25] MO'C to JF, 18 August 1927, HILA, JFP, Box 32, Folder 9.

[26] MO'C to Vladimir Maiakovskii, 18 August 1927, *Rossiskii Gosudarstvennii Arkhiv Literaturii I Isskustva* (Hereafter RGALI), 336/5/111/1.

[27] Kasper Braskén, 'Making Anti-Fascism Transnational: The Origins of Communist and Socialist Articulations of Resistance in Europe, 1923-1924', *Contemporary European History*, 25:4 (2016), pp. 573–4.

[28] MO'C to JF, 18 August 1927, HILA, JFP, Box 32, Folder 9.

[29] Quoted in R. F. Foster, *Vivid Faces: The Irish Revolutionary Generation* (London, 2015), p. 25.

[30] MO'C to JF, 5 September 1927, HILA, JFP, Box 32, Folder 9.

[31] MO'C to JF, 28 September 1927, HILA, JFP, Box 32, Folder 9.

[32] MO'C to JF, 5 September 1927, HILA, JFP, Box 32, Folder 9.

[33] Ibid.

[34] MO'C to JF, 15 September 1927, HILA, JFP, Box 32, Folder 9.

[35] Ibid.

[36] Malleson, *Ten Years*, p. 252.

[37] Ibid.

[38] Ibid.

[39] LO'F to Royal Literary Fund, 22 January 1925, Registered Case No. 3231, Royal Literary Fund Papers (Hereafter RLFP), British Library (Hereafter BL).

[40] Dr N. S. Bett to Royal Literary Fund, c. January 1925, RLFP, BL.

[41] MO'C to JF, 28 September 1927, HILA, JFP, Box 32, Folder 9.

[42] Ibid.

The Eternal Propusk

[1] MO'C to JF, 18 August 1927, HILA, JFP, Box 32, Folder 9.

[2] Elise Ewert (Hereafter Sabo) to JF, 11 June 1927, HILA, JFP, Box 21, Folder 22.

[3] Ibid.

4 JF to Sabo, 31 August 1927, HILA, JFP, Box 21, Folder 22.

5 Sabo to JF, 4 July 1927, HILA, JFP, Box 21, Folder 22.

6 MO'C to JF, 5 September 1927, HILA, JFP, Box 32, Folder 9.

7 Sabo to JF, 24 November 1927, HILA, JFP, Box 21, Folder 22.

8 JF to Sabo, 31 August 1927, HILA, JFP, Box 21, Folder 22.

9 Sabo to JF, undated letter, c. September 1927, HILA, JFP, Box 21, Folder 22.

10 Ibid.

11 Sabo to JF, 7 September 1927, HILA, JFP, Box 21, Folder 22.

12 Ibid.

13 Ibid.

14 American Embassy London to Cpt. Liddell, 27 February 1936, TNA, KV 2/2336.

15 Sabo to JF, 24 November 1927, HILA, JFP, Box 21, Folder 22.

16 Ibid.

17 Sabo to JF, 25 November 1927, HILA, JFP, Box 21, Folder 22.

18 Sabo to JF, 24 November 1927, HILA, JFP, Box 21, Folder 22.

19 MO'C to JF, 24 December 1927, HILA, JFP, Box 32, Folder 9.

20 Ibid.

21 Ibid.

22 LO'F to MO'C, 8 November 1927, JRP.

23 MO'C to JF, 24 December 1927, HILA, JFP, Box 32, Folder 9.

24 Thomas P. Riggio, James L. W. West III (eds.), Theodore Dreiser, *Dreiser's Russian Diary* (Philadelphia, 1996), p. 35

25 Jere Abbott, 'Russian Diary, 1927–28', *October*, 7 (Winter, 1978), p. 128.

26 Alfred H. Barr, 'Russian Diary, 1927–28', *October*, 7 (Winter, 1978), p. 27.

27 Abbott, 'Russian Diary', p. 176.

On with the Dance

1 'Confession', undated, likely late 1920s, UOSC, REKP, Box 8, Folder 11.

2 MO'C to JF, 1 March 1928, HILA, JFP, Box 32, Folder 9.

3 Ibid.

4 SD to JF, 1 January 1928, HILA, JFP, Box 20, Folder 1.

5 MO'C to JF, 2 July 1927, HILA, JFP, Box 32, Folder 9.

6 Alida de Jager to Mr Schoots, 18 May 1997, Leonhard Fimmen Papers (Hereafter LFP), in private possession.

7 Leon Trotskii to Alida Leonhard, 12 April 1931, HL, Leon Trotsky in Exile Papers (Hereafter LTP), Box 34, Folder 8857.

8 Sabo to JF, 24 March 1928, HILA, JFP, Box 21, Folder 22.

9 Ibid.

10 Sabo to JF, 31 August 1928, HILA, JFP, Box 21, Folder 22.
11 Ibid.
12 JF to Sabo, 11 September 1928, HILA, JFP, Box 21, Folder 22.
13 LO'F to MO'C, 3 April 1928, JRP.
14 LO'F to MO'C, 27 April, 1928, JRP.
15 MO'C to JF, 1 March 1928, HILA, JFP, Box 32, Folder 9.
16 Huw Osborne, 'Counter-Space in Charles Lahr's Progressive Bookshop', in Osborne, ed., *The Rise of the Modernist Bookshop: Books and the Commerce of Culture in the Twentieth Century* (Surrey, 2015), p. 133.
17 MO'C to REK, 7 August 1928, UOSC, REKP, Box 7, Folder 14.
18 Ibid.

Archives at the End of the World

1 Catherine Hall, 'Thinking Reflexively: Opening Blind Eyes', *Past & Present*, 234 (January 2017), p. 262.
2 JF to Daniel Aaron, 19 July 1958, HL, DAP, Box 16, Folder 170.

Part III

The Time of Bad Roads

1 Holmes, *Sylvia Pankhurst*, p. 607.
2 Ibid, p. 629.
3 Ibid, p. 632.
4 Ibid, p. 630, 632.
5 Alexandra Smith, 'Reconfiguring the Utopian Vision: Tret'iakov's Play *I Want a Baby!* (1926) as a Response to the Revolutionary Restructuring of Everyday Life', *ASEES*, 25:1–2 (2011), p. 109.
6 MO'C to JF, 1 March 1928, HILA, JFP, Box 32, Folder 9.
7 Kaminsky, '"No Rituals and Formalities!"', p. 717.
8 Maria Zavialova, 'Red Venus: Alexandra Kollontai's *Red Love* and Women in Soviet art', in Ruth Barraclough, Heather Bowen-Struyk and Paula Rabinowitz (eds), *Red Love Across the Pacific: Political and Sexual Revolutions of the Twentieth Century* (New York, 2015), p. 229.
9 MO'C to REK, 7 August 1928, UOSC, REKP, Box 7, Folder 14.
10 MO'C to REK, 30 August 1928, UOSC, REKP, Box 7, Folder 14.
11 MO'C to REK, 18 September 1928, UOSC, REKP, Box 7, Folder 14.
12 MO'C to JF, 18 September 1928, HILA, JFP, Box 32, Folder 9.
13 Ibid.

14 MO'C to REK, 7 August 1928, UOSC, REKP, Box 7, Folder 14.

15 MO'C to REK, 30 August 1928, UOSC, REKP, Box 7, Folder 14.

16 Brigitte Studer, 'Communism as Existential Choice', in Silvio Pons and Stephen A. Smith (eds), *The Cambridge History of Communism*, Vol. 1 (Cambridge, 2017), p. 514.

17 Chambers, *Witness*, p. 223.

18 MO'C to REK, 29 October 1928, UOSC, REKP, Box 7, Folder 14.

19 JF to REK, 9 October 1928, UOSC, REKP, Box 6, Folder 34.

20 MO'C to REK, 20 October 1928, UOSC, REKP, Box 7, Folder 14.

21 Junius Woods (Hereafter JW) to REK, 26 October 1928, UOSC, REKP, Box 7, Folder 36.

22 Ibid.

23 JW to REK, 1 November 1928, UOSC, REKP, Box 7, Folder 36.

24 Ibid.

25 MOC to REK, 9 November 1928, UOSC, REKP, Box 7, Folder 14.

26 JW to REK, 2 November 1928, UOSC, REKP, Box 7, Folder 36.

27 Ibid.

28 Ibid.

29 Ibid.

30 JW to REK, 3 August 1930, UOSC, REKP, Box 7, Folder 36.

31 MO'C to REK, 9 November 1928, UOSC, REKP, Box 7, Folder 14.

32 MO'C to REK, 7 September 1928, UOSC, REKP, Box 7, Folder 14.

33 MO'C to REK, 10 February 1929, UOSC, REKP, Box 7, Folder 14.

Proust for Breakfast

1 Ione Robinson, *A Wall to Paint On* (New York, 1946), p. 59.

2 Ibid, p. 71.

3 Desmond Fitzgerald to Ernest Blythe, 8 July 1931, Desmond Fitzgerald Papers, UCD Archives, P80/507 (4).

4 Robinson, *Wall*, p. 71.

5 'Father as Father', typescript, Pegeen O'Sullivan, c. 1990s. Thank you to Angus Melville for sharing this source with me.

6 Robinson, *Wall*, p. 98.

7 *Zum 7 Octoker 1926*, poem, c. October 1926, HILA, JFP, Box 21, Folder 22.

8 Robinson, *Wall*, p. 102.

9 'The Mexican Reaction', *New Masses*, September 1929, p. 13.

10 Stephanie J. Smith, 'The Painter and the Communist: Gender, Culture and the Fleeting Marriage of Ione Robinson and Joseph Freeman, 1929–1932', *Journal of Women's History*, 31:3 (Fall, 2019), p. 15.

[11] Robinson, *Wall*, p. 120.

[12] Ibid, p. 123.

[13] Ibid.

[14] Ibid.

[15] Ibid, p. 127.

[16] Ibid, p. 123.

[17] Ibid, p. 129.

[18] Smith, 'The Painter and the Communist', p. 15.

[19] Ibid, p. 22.

[20] MO'C to REK, 22 March 1930, UOSC, REKP, Box 7, Folder 14.

[21] JF to Ione Robinson, 8 July 1932, HILA, JFP, Box 34, Folder 20.

[22] MO'C to REK, 5 April 1929, UOSC, REKP, Box 7, Folder 14.

[23] MO'C to REK, 11 November 1929, UOSC, REKP, Box 7, Folder 14.

[24] Mablay to Dinah, 13 May 1929, TNA, KV 2/1396.

[25] Nellie Cohen to Eva Reckitt, 18 December 1929, TNA, KV 2/1396.

[26] *The Militant*, 15 December 1928.

[27] MO'C to REK, 5 April 1929, UOSC, REKP, Box 7, Folder 14.

[28] MO'C to REK, 22 March 1930, UOSC, REKP, Box 7, Folder 14.

[29] MO'C to REK, 20 July 1931, UOSC, REKP, Box 7, Folder 14.

[30] Kevin McDermott and Jeremy Agnew, *The Comintern: A History of International Communism from Lenin to Stalin* (London, 1996), p. 81.

[31] Ibid, p. 83.

[32] Sheila Fitzpatrick, *On Stalin's Team: The Years of Living Dangerously in Soviet Politics* (Oxford, 2015), p. 10.

[33] McDermott and Agnew, *The Comintern*, p. 84.

Leaving the Land of Sorrows

[1] IL to Catherine Carswell, 22 May 1930, HILA, ILP, Correspondence Box 1, Folder 25.

[2] 'Ivy', undated typescript, c. 1934–5, HILA, JFP, Box 78, Folder 3. For an example of antisemitism, see: Liam O'Flaherty, *I Went to Russia* (London, 2013 [1931]), p. 157.

[3] MO'C to JF, 28 October 1933, HILA, JFP, Box 32, Folder 9.

German Family Robinson

[1] Gabrielle Fiori, *Simone Weil: An Intellectual Biography*, trans. Joseph R. Berrigan (Athens, 1989), p. 367.

[2] 'April 1916', poem and letter, 5 July 1956, LFP.

3 Alida de Jager to Willy Buschak, 27 February 1998, LFP.

4 Ibid.

5 Jonathan Hyslop, 'German Seafarers, anti-fascism and the anti-Stalinist Left: the "Antwerp Group" and Edo Fimmen's International Transport Workers' Federation, 1933-40', *Global Networks*, 19:4 (2019), p. 503.

6 Leon Trotskii to Alida Leonhard, 12 April 1931, HL, LTP, Box 34, Item 8857.

7 Alida Leonhard to Leon Trotskii, 31 July 1931, HL, LTP, Box 12, Item 2730. All subsequent quotes of Emmy's response to Trotsky are taken from this letter.

8 Terence Renaud, *New Lefts: The Making of a Radical Tradition* (Princeton, 2021), p. 5.

9 MO'C to Theodore Dreiser, 15 February 1932, Theodore Dreiser Papers, Kislak Center for Special Collections, Box 85, Folder 4612.

10 Studer, *Travellers*, p. 105.

11 Babette Gross, *Willi Münzenberg: A Political Biography*, trans. Marian Jackson (Ann Arbor, 1974), p. 155.

12 Ibid.

13 Pedro Ewald, interviewed by the author, 23 August 2021.

14 Tom Pfister, Kathy Pfister and Peter Pfister, *Eva & Otto: Resistance, Refugees and Love in the Time of Hitler* (West Lafayette, 2019), p. 65.

Belmor

1 Mary A. Nicholas and Cynthia A. Ruder, 'In Search of the Collective Author: Fact and Fiction from the Soviet 1930s', *Book History*, Vol. 11 (2008), p. 226.

2 Ibid, p. 227.

3 Cynthia A. Ruder, *Making History for Stalin: The Story of the Belomor Canal* (Tallahasee, 1998), p. 10.

4 Maxim Gorkii (ed.), *The White Sea Canal: Being an Account of the Construction of the New Canal between the White Sea and the Baltic Sea* (London, 1935).

5 Lisa Kirschenbaum, *International Communism and the Spanish Civil War: Solidarity and Suspicion* (Cambridge, 2015), p. 12.

6 Ibid, p. 52.

7 Katja Hoyer, *Beyond the Wall: East Germany, 1949-1990* (London, 2023), p. 16.

8 For more on the Moscow Daily News, including a discussion of Millie Bennett, see: Kirschenbaum, *International Communism*, esp. pp. 55–66.

9 *Anketa*, 11 December 1935, RGASPI 495/198/733/25.

10 *Anketa*, 14 October 1930, RGASPI 495/198/733//34.

11 Millie Bennett (Hereafter MB) to REK, 3 November 1934, UOSC, REKP, Box 6, Folder 41.

[12] Dan Healey, *Homosexual Desire in Revolutionary Russia: The Regulation of Sexual and Gender Dissent* (Chicago, 2001), p. 188.

[13] Ibid.

[14] MB to REK, 17 July 1933, UOSC, REKP, Box 6, Folder 41. Bennett's use of dates in these letters is not reliable. Actual dates can be discerned from mentioned events.

[15] Kevin Morgan, Gidon Cohen, et al and Andrew Flinn, *Communists and British Society, 1920–1991* (Chicago, 2007), p. 127.

[16] MB to REK, 29 January [1934], UOSC, REKP, Box 6, Folder 41.

[17] Ibid.

[18] Eudocio Ravines, *The Yenan Way* (New York, 1951), p. 128.

[19] MB to REK, 23 February 1935, UOSC, REKP, Box 6, Folder 41.

The Alpenpost

[1] Fiori, *Weil*, pp. 77–9.

[2] Renauld, *New Lefts*, pp. 74–5.

[3] Palle Yourgrau, *Simone Weil* (London, 2011), p. 49.

[4] Simone Weil, *Oppression and Liberty*, trans. Arthur Will and John Petrie (London, 1972), pp. 22–23.

[5] Simone Pétrement, *Simone Weil: A Life*, trans. Raymond Rosenthal (New York, 1976), p. 233.

[6] Ibid.

[7] Ibid.

[8] Ibid.

[9] Fiori, *Weil*, p. 307.

[10] Quoted in Dieter Nelles, 'ITF Resistance Against Nazism and Fascism in Germany and Spain', in Bob Reinalda, ed., *The International Transport Workers Federation, 1914-1945: The Edo Fimmen Era* (Amsterdam, 1997), p. 175.

[11] Ibid.

[12] Ibid, p. 177.

[13] Ibid, p. 176.

[14] Ibid, p. 178.

[15] Ibid, p. 179.

Testimony

[1] Studer, *Travellers*, pp. 368–9.

[2] Gross, *Münzenberg*, p. 290.

[3] Ervin Sinko, *The Novel of a Novel*, trans. George Deák (Lanham, 2018), ebook, loc. 335.

4 Gross, *Münzenberg*, p. 291.

5 Dieter Nelles, 'Eine Neue Internationale—Edo Fimmen und Willi Münzenberg, 1939/40', https://www.muenzenbergforum.de/exponat/eine-neue-internationale-edo-fimmen-und-willi-muenzenberg-193940/ (Accessed 9 January 2024).

6 Buber-Neumann, *Dictators*, p. 7.

7 JF to John Strachey, 3 November 1936, HILA, JFP, Box 72, Folder 12.

8 *New York Times*, 16 November 1936, HILA, JFP, Box 78, Folder 8.

9 Freeman, *American Testament*, p. 444.

10 Undated letter by JF, possibly to publisher, c. 1937, HILA, JFP, Box 72, Folder 13.

11 Summary of letters received, 28 November 1936, HILA, JFP, Box 72, Folder 12.

12 Report by Ronald Rubinstein, 19 May 1937, HILA, JFP, Box 72, Folder 14.

13 SD to JF, 23 December 1936, HILA, JFP, Box 20, Folder 3.

14 SD to JF, 26 April 1937, HILA, JFP, Box 20, Folder 3.

15 Sender Garlin to JF, 24 January 1936, HILA, JFP, Box 23, Folder 7.

16 Report, Sender Garlin, 23 June 1938, RGASPI 495/261/2295/86-90.

17 ICC Special Commission, minutes, 22 March 1937, RGASPI 495/261/2295/112.

18 Ibid (l. 113).

19 Ibid.

20 Ibid (ll. 114/115).

21 Studer, *Travellers*, pp. 370–3.

22 Notes on Meeting with Victor Gollancz, 9 May 1937, RGASPI 495/261/2295/102.

23 Francis Beckett, *Stalin's British Victims* (Sutton, 2004), p. 54.

24 Kevin Morgan, *Harry Pollitt* (Manchester, 1993), p. 126.

25 Autobiographical Notes, Ivy Litvinov, c. 1970s, HILA, ILP, Box 5, Folder 1.

26 Court Protocol, 28 November 1937, Petrovsky Papers, in private possession.

27 Hiroaki Kuromiya, 'Communism, Violence and Terror', in Silvio Pons and Stephen A. Smith, eds., *Cambridge History of Communism*, Vol. 1 (Cambridge, 2017), p. 281.

28 Ibid, p. 281–2.

29 Beckett, *Victims*, p. 68.

30 MacDermott, *Pollitt*, p. 175.

31 Ibid.

32 Lucia Jones, Nellie Rathbone interview.

33 MO'C to REK, 28 August 1937, UOSC, REKP, Box 7, Folder 14.

34 MO'C to REK, 17 December 1969, UOSC, REKP, Box 7, Folder 14.

La Guinguette

1 MO'C to SD, 13 June 1938, RGALI 1397/1/680/1.

2 Alida Leonhard to SD, 17 June 1938, RGALI 1397/1/680/5.

[3] Samantha Sherry, *Discourses of Regulation and Resistance: Censoring Translation in the Stalin and Khrushchev Era Soviet Union* (Edinburgh, 2015), pp. 77–82.

[4] Nelles, 'ITF Resistance', p. 187.

[5] Ibid, p. 188.

[6] Ibid. p. 189.

[7] *Fascism*, 15:7, 22 July 1939.

[8] David Wedgwood Benn, 'Review: Russian Historians Defend the Molotov-Ribbentrop Pact', *International Affairs*, 87:3, p. 709.

[9] *La Guinguette*, 13 November 1938, LFP

[10] *La Petite Guinguette*, 1 January 1939, LFP.

[11] Buber-Neumann, *Dictators*, p. 85.

[12] Ronald Friedmann, *Arthur Ewert (1890-1959)*, (University of Potsdam, PhD Thesis, 2015), p. 417.

The Avalanche

[1] Kent Beck, 'The Odyssey of Joseph Freeman', *The Historian*, 38:1 (November, 1974), p. 112.

[2] Report, 18A, late 1934, TNA, KV 2/2336.

[3] Shawn Smallman, 'Military Terror and Silence in Brazil, 1910-1945', *Canadian Journal of Latin American and Caribbean Studies*, 24:46 (1999), p. 16.

[4] Friedmann, *Ewert*, p. 412.

[5] Ibid, p. 415.

[6] Ibid, p. 416.

[7] JF to Sabo, 16 September 1938, HILA, JFP, Box 21, Folder 22.

[8] Sabo to JF, 25 October 1938, translated version in folder, HILA, JFP, Box 21, Folder 22.

[9] Jack Murphy to JF, 12 January 1939, HILA, JFP, Box 31, Folder 1.

[10] Ibid.

[11] JF to Jack Murphy, 23 January 1939, HILA, JFP, Box 31, Folder 1.

[12] Ibid.

[13] Friedmann, *Ewert*, p. 419.

[14] Buber-Neumann, *Dictators*, p. 189.

[15] ITF, *Solidarity: The First 100 Years of the International Transport Workers' Federation* (London, 1996), p. 100.

[16] Babette Gross to Alida Leonhard, 6 May 1940, LFP.

[17] Pétrement, *Simone*, p. 385.

[18] Willy Buschak, 'Edo Fimmen and Willi Eichler – A Political Friendship', in Bob Reinalda, ed., *The International Transport Workers Federation, 1914–1945: The Edo Fimmen Era* (Amsterdam, 1997), p. 207.

19 *Sonderfahndungsliste G.B.*, 1940, p. 60, Hoover Institution Library Materials, https://digitalcollections.hoover.org/objects/55425/die-sonder-fahndungsliste-gb (Accessed 13 January 2024).
20 'Werner Lehmann', Merlyn Moos, http://community-languages.org.uk/?p=246 (Accessed 14 January 2024).
21 H. Miller to Alida de Jager, 8 February 1941, LFP.
22 Buschak, 'Fimmen and Eichler', pp. 207–8.
23 Joyce Rathbone (Hereafter JR) to REK, 11 August 1941, UOSC, REKP, Box 8, Folder 24.
24 MO'C to REK, c. December 1941, UOSC, REKP, Box 7, Folder 14.
25 Ibid.
26 MO'C to REK, 3 October 1943, UOSC, REKP, Box 7, Folder 14.
27 JR to REK, 31 July 1945, UOSC, REKP, Box 8, Folder 24.
28 Alida de Jager to J. Oldenbroek, 27 April 1942, University of Warwick Modern Records Centre (Hereafter MRC) ITF/6/35.
29 Alida de Jager to J. Oldenbroek, 18 May 1942, MRC, ITF/6/35.
30 Alida de Jager to J. Oldenbroek, 1 September 1942, MRC, ITF/6/35.
31 'Dictated by Edo in August 1942', LFP.
32 Tom, Kathy, and Peter Pfister, *Eva and Otto*, p. 223.
33 Alida de Jager to Sonia Doniach, 21 Dec 1942, LFP.
34 Hans Jahn to Alida de Jager, 16 December 1942, LFP.
35 'Simone Weil', *Stanford Encyclopaedia of Philosophy*, https://plato.stanford.edu/entries/simone-weil/ (Accessed 2 February 2024).
36 Fiori, *Weil*, p. 367.
37 Victor Serge, *Notebooks, 1936-1947*, trans. Mitchell Abidor and Richard Greeman (New York, 2019), p. 232.
38 Harold Lewis, *The International Transport Workers' Federation* (ITF), *1945–1965: An Organizational and Political Anatomy* (University of Warwick, PhD Thesis, 2003), p. 19.

Part IV

The Lobby

1 *TFT*, 1 June 1948, HILA, JFP, Box 88, Folder 2.
2 A description of this meeting – on which this account is based – can be found here: *TFT*, 22 March 1948, HILA, JFP, Box 87, Folder 6.
3 JF to Luise Geissler, 8 June 1948, HILA, JFP, Box 24, Folder 10.

Secret Speech

1 John Rettie, 'How Khrushchev Leaked his Secret Speech to the World', *History Workshop Journal*, 62 (2006), p. 187.

[2] 'Decision of the High Military Court of the USSR', 8 August 1956, RGASPI 495/198/733/3.

[3] Autobiographical Notes, Ivy Litvinov, c. 1970s, HILA, ILP, Box 5, Folder 1.

The Famous Kiss

[1] MO'C to REK, 29 August 1951, UOSC, REKP, Box 7, Folder 14.

[2] Ibid.

[3] Elisa de Jager (Hereafter EdJ) to JR, 8 November 1962, JRP.

[4] MO'C to REK, c. January 1945, UOSC, REKP, Box 7, Folder 14.

[5] MO'C to REK, 26 August 1966, UOSC, REKP, Box 7, Folder 14.

[6] JR to LO'F, 25 September 1957, JRP

[7] JR to LO'F, 16 January 1960, JRP.

[8] JR to LO'F, 30 August 1960, JRP.

[9] MO'C to REK, 27 February 1961, UOSC, REKP, Box 7, Folder 14.

[10] Alida de Jager to JR, 15 October 1961, JRP.

[11] JR to EdJ, 24 June 1962, LFP.

[12] EdJ to JR, 13 July 1962, JRP.

[13] EdJ to JR, 5 October 1972, JRP.

[14] EdJ to JR, 22 September 1962, JRP.

[15] EdJ to JR, 6 November 1962, JRP.

[16] EdJ to JR, 20 September 1962, JRP.

[17] EdJ to JR, 9 November 1962, JRP.

[18] EdJ to JR, 10 November 1962, JRP.

[19] EdJ to JR, 4 October 1963, JRP.

[20] EdJ to JR, 9 May 1964, JRP.

[21] MO'C to REK, 26 August 1966, UOSC, REKP, Box 7, Folder 14.

[22] EdJ to JR, 16 November 1962, JRP.

[23] JR to EdJ, 25 May 1963, LFP.

[24] Alida de Jager to JR, 20 October 1963, JRP.

[25] NR to REK, 18 May 1973, UOSC, REKP, Box 8, Folder 24.

[26] JR to EdJ, 28 May 1973, LFP.

Sympathy

[1] 'Parmi nos Letters', *La Révolution Prolétarienne*, 618 (December, 1975), p. 13.

Impossible Desires

[1] *Cork Examiner*, 24 May 1993.

[2] Ibid.

[3] Joseph Freeman, 'A Year of Grace', *New Politics* (Winter, 1965), p. 119.

[4] REK to MO'C, c. early September 1927, UOSC, REKP, Box 7, Folder 14.